U. S. CENSUS of 1860
for
BARBOUR COUNTY, ALABAMA

Compiled by:
Helen S. Foley

Southern Historical Press, Inc.
Greenville, South Carolina

This volume was reproduced
from a personal copy located in
the Publishers private library

Please direct all correspondence and book orders to:
SOUTHERN HISTORICAL PRESS, Inc.
PO Box 1267
Greenville, SC 29602-1267

ISBN #978-1-63914-309-2
Printed in the United States of America

Foreword

Barbour County, Alabama, was formed in 1832 from the Creek Cession of 1812 and parts of Henry and Pike Counties. It was named for James Barbour of Virginia.

This census was copied from a microfilm and parts of it were very dim and almost illegible. The heads of the households arranged alphabetically, the value of their property (first number is the amount of real estate and the second one is personal estate) age, sex and birth place are given. Any member of a group with a different surname will be found in the household and also in the alphabetical listing.

Abbreviations of foreign countries:

Can. -	Canada	Ire. -	Ireland
Den. -	Denmark	Pol. -	Poland
Eng. -	England	Pru. -	Prussia
Fr. -	France	Rus. -	Russia
Ger. -	Germany	Scot.-	Scotland
Hol. -	Holland	Switz.	Switzerland

Communities in Barbour County:

Bkb -	Bucksbranch	Luvl -	Louisville
Bfd -	Buford	Mt. A. -	Mt. Andrew
Clay -	Clayton	Mdwy -	Midway
Euf -	Eufaula	Nwto -	New Topia
Flk -	Faulk's	Txv -	Texasville

Mdwy # 1013 (500-1500)
ABBET, Sarah 38 f Eng
SCOTT, Rosa 12 f Ala
Susan 9 f "

Euf # 506 Farmer (2800-15000)
ABBERCRUMBIE, Thos. A. 23 m Ala
Neary 20 f Ga
James 9/12 m "

Euf # 462 Farmer (15000-20000)
ABERCROMBIE, J. L. 28 m Ala
America 24 f "
Clarence 3 m "
Ella 6/12 f "

Euf # 78 Farmer (8000-15000)
ABNEY, William 57 m SC
Elizabeth 53 f "
Roxanna 23 f "
Sarah 13 f Ala
John C. C. 6 m "

Euf # 1351 Laundress (--- 300)
ADAMS, Ailsey 39 f Ala
William H. 12 m "
Charles 10 m "
James 8 m "
Mary 4 f "
Harris 3 m "

Mdwy # 1017 Farmer (--- 1000)
ADAMS, Alex 46 m Ga
Ann 40 f SC
Frances 19 f Ga
Emily 17 f "
David A. 16 m "
James M. 15 m "
Lawrence 13 m "
Jeptha M. 8 m Ala
A. E. J. 3 f "
Ann 1 f "
Benjamin 14 m Ga
Margary 76 f NC

Euf # 347 Farmer (--- 4000)
ADAMS, Allen 69 m NC
Mary 68 f "
Margaret 47 f "
Julia 25 f Ga

Euf # 348 Farmer (--- 200)
ADAMS, Allen, Jr. 27 m Ga
Wineford 25 f Fla
Laura A. 7 f Ala
James 6 m "
(Cont.)

(Euf # 348 cont.)
Octavia 4 f Ala
Asa 2 m "

Euf # 110 Teamster (--- 1500)
ADAMS, Elvin B. 41 m NC
Elizabeth 18 f Ga
Alfred 16 m "
Ellifair 10 f "
Georgian (?) 10 f Ala
Columbus 8 m "
Joseph 7 m "
Samuel 5 m "
Robert 3 m "
Jesse 1 m "

Euf # 1350 Farmer & Merchant (21,000-35,000)
ADAMS, H. P. 39 m RI
Elizabeth 35 f Ga
Harry 7 m Ala
LIGHTNER, Mrs. 60 f Ga
(--- 5000)

Mt. A. # 805 Farmer (--- 200)
ADAMS, Jackson 41 m SC
Sarah J. 26 f Ga
M. A. 6 f Ala
Thomas W. 17 m "

Euf # 158 Bookkeeper (500-1000)
ADAMS, L. P. 23 m RI

Euf # 346 Farmer (--- 400)
ADAMS, Lewis N. 45 m NC
Alley J. 38 f Ga
Mary E. 17 f "
Fabian 15 m "
John 13 m "
Margarite 11 f "
Caroline 9 f Ala
Thomas 7 m "
Preston 5 m "
Arthur 3 m "
Reed 1 m "

Mdwy # 943 Overseer (--- 500)
ADAMS, Monroe 37 m Ga
Frances 36 f SC
William A. 14 m Ala
John Q. 12 m "
James B. 10 m "
Josephine P. 5 f "
Benjamin F. 3 m "
Rebecca A. 2 f "
Joel V. 4/12 m "

Mdwy # 928 Planter (18,000-28,000)
ADAMS, Thompson T. 48 m Ga
Frances 42 f "
Thos. D. (Farmer) 21 m "
Wm. S. " 19 m "
James M. " 18 m "
Ann E. 16 f "
Alex A. 11 m Ala
John H. 10 m "
Martha F. 8 f "
Thompson T., Jr. 7 m "
Robert P. 3 m "
Samuel (Farmer) 76 m Va
Martha 62 f Ky

Euf # 460 Farm Overseer
ADAWAY, William 22 m Ga
Mary J. 19 f Ala
(Married within the year).

Clay # 44 In jail
ADCOCK, William 26 m Ga

Nwto # 589 Blacksmith (100-150)
AKINS, Barton L. 37 m Ga
M. F. 20 f Ala
James M. 12 m "

Flk # 466
ALDERMAN, Mary 38 f Ga
Isaac 10 m Ala
Marshall 5 m "
Amaria 2 f "
BUCHANNON, Mary 65 f SC

Euf # 567 Farmer (12, 000-32,500)
ALEXANDER, Ezekiel 57 m Ga
Sarah 55 f "
David (idiot) 35 m Ala
Moses (Farmer) 24 m Ga
TUCKER, Louisa 24 f "

Mt. A. # 832
ALEXANDER, Sarah 63 f SC
(See Daniel Kinnard).

Euf # 578 Overseer (--- 500)
ALFORD, William 34 m Ga
Jane 22 f Ala
Louisa 3 f "
Benj. F. 7/12 m "

Euf # 449 Laborer (--- ---)
ALLBRIGHT, Isaac 43 m NC
(Cont.)

(Euf # 449 cont.)
Audry 18 f Ga
Margaret 22 f NC
JOHNS, Pharos 2 m Ala

Euf # 456 Laborer (--- ---)
ALLBRIGHT, William 24 m NC
Elizabeth 40 f "

Clay # 68
ALLBRITTON, William 23 m Ga
(See M. M. Hinson).

Mdwy # 984
ALLEN, A. A. 24 f Ga
W. B. 2 m Ala
(See W. T. Colemon).

Euf # 299 Farmer (1,000-600)
ALLEN, Albert 49 m Va
Mary 45 f Ga
Isaac (Laborer) 18 m "
Henry " 16 m "
Savannah 12 f "
Laura F. 8 f "
William 5 m "

Luvl # 271 Clerk (--- ---)
ALLEN, Asa 24 m Ala
(See John M. Lampley).

Euf # 154 Merchant (2000-5000)
ALLEN, George L. 50 m Scot
Janet 48 f "
Catherine 16 f Ala
Mary 13 f "
George 10 m "
Mary 76 f Scot

Euf # 341 Laborer (--- ---)
ALLEN, James M. 34 m Ga
Elizabeth 31 f "
James H. 9 m "
Dolly A. 7 f "
Sarah J.(?) 5 f "
Mary M. 2 f Ala
BROWN, Jos. (Farmer) 17 m Ga

Euf # 89 Teacher (--- ---)
ALLEN, John F. 40 m Mass
Eliza 30 f Va
(See Colin Gardener).

Euf # 1139 Farmer (--- 100)
ALLEN, William B. 38 m Ga
Penelope C. 26 f "
Susan C. 9 f Ala
Josephine 7 f "
Henry P. 5 m "
George 9/12 m "

Euf # 1142
ALLEN, Wm. C. 9 m Ala
(See John Clark).

Bkb # 776 Farmer (3200-3500)
ALLEY, John 41 m Pa
Rebecca 36 f Ala
VERDON, Morgan 22 m SC
(Farm laborer).
BROADENAX, Martha 27 f Ala

Luvl # 546 Farmer (400-500)
ALLUMS, Briggs 60 m Ga
Martha 55 f "
Sarah 30 f "
Leroy 22 m "
Wheeling 17 m "
Polly 12 f Ala
Mandy 10 f "
Casttes (?) 6 m "

Nwto # 588 Blacksmith (300-200)
ALLUMS, L. A. 30 m Ga
Sarah E. 22 f NC
James H. B. 8 m Ala
George W. C. 7 m "
Mary M. A. E. 5 f "

Euf # 1043 Overseer
ALMAN, Thomas 23 m Ga
(See Leroy Upshaw).

Mdwy # 935 Overseer (400-1150)
AMAN, Andrew J. 28 m NC
Virginia T. 20 f Ala

Euf # 1344 Overseer (--- ---)
AMEN, Jack 25 m Ga
Elizabeth 23 f "
James 2 m Ala

Euf # 677
AMOS, William 5 m Ala
(See Wm. C. Payne).

Clay # 14 (500 ---)
ANDERSON, Alice 48 f SC
T. J. (printer apprentice) 13 m Ala
C. S. 11 m "

Euf # 250
ANDERSON, Chas. 10 m Wash. D.C.
(See Samuel Sandiford)

Euf # 596 Farmer (6000-5000)
ANDERSON, M. H. 53 m NC
Caroline E. 35 f SC
Howell H. 14 m Ala
Joseph D. 11 m "
Thomas L. 8 m "
Preston 4 m "
William 4/12 m "

Euf # 1365 (--- ---)
ANDERSON, Sarah 48 f SC

Flk # 440 Farmer (--- ---)
ANDERSON, Stephen 20 m Ala
Zachurs (Farmer) 17 m "
(See A. C. McNab).

Euf # 771 (?) Farmer (45000-45000)
ANDREWS, C. J. M. 39 m Ga
Catharine P. J. 27 f Ala
Louisa A. 16 f "
Leonora V. 11 f "
Mary A. 8 f "
SLACK, Jesse (Insane) 35 m Ga
(Miller (2000-20000)

Flk # 473 Farmer (--- 300)
ANDREWS, Gregory 30 m SC
Louisa 30 f Ala
Margaret E. 6 f "
Isabella 4 f "
Wm. T. 2 m "
Rhoda 8/12 f "

Luvl # 569 Mechanic (600-200)
ANDREWS, J. T. 20 m NC
Jane 18 f Ala

Nwto # 583 Farmer (600-400)
ANDREWS, R. P. 47 m NC
Mary 50 f "
Martha 24 f "
Mary 22 f "
Judy 18 f "
SHEHANE, Wm. M. C. 21 m Ga
(Farmer).

Flk # 438 Farmer (--- 2000)
Andrews, Robert 29 m Ala
Sarah A. 23 f "
Mary A. 5 f "
Artesia 3 f "
William W. 1 m "

Euf # 1223 M.E.Minister (10,000-10,000)
ANDREWS, U.(?) S. 38 m NC
S. M. 7 f Ala

Euf # 874 Farmer (6400-2400)
ANDREWS, W. A. 41 m Ga
Laura E. 22 f SC
R.E.M. 13 f Ala
Wm. D. 5 m "

Flk # 456 Farmer (100 ---)
ANDREWS, William 31 m Ala
Nancy 28 f "
Elouise 10 f "
Thos. E. 4 m "

Flk # 482 Grocery (120-400)
ANDREWS, Winston 23 m Ala
Florida 20 f Ga
Harmon 4 m Ala
Martha J. 7/12 f "
ADAMS, Thos. 22 m Ga
(Farmer, 120-5000)

Nwto # 586 Asst. Postmaster (150-300)
ANDREWS, Winston 24 m Ala
Florida 19 f Ga
Harmon 2 m Ala
M. J. 3/12 f "

Clay # 656
ANGLIN, Iomae 16 f Ga
Lucinda S. 4 f Ala
Pat 2 m "
Columbus 8/12 m "
(See Sinthia McKinney).

Luvl # 380 (2000-1200)
ANGLIN, Iomae 17 f Ga
Pat 3 m Ala
Columbus 1 m "

Luvl # 357 Farmer (960-4,000)
ANGLIN, Thos. 22 m Ala
E. C. 17 f "
Cornelia 6/12 f "
Andrew J. 20 m "
(Farmer, 960-3000)
Joseph 12 m "
(960-4000)
Victoria 6 f "

Luvl # 259
ANGLING, Victoria 5 f Ala
(See J. F. Harrison).

Clay # 664 Farmer (200-550)
ANGLIN, William 72 m Ga
Lavina 60 f "
(Cont.)

(Clay # 664 cont.)
Roxanna 18 f Ala
MADDOCK, Matilda 50 f Ga

Clay # 138
APPLETON, S. E. 21 f Ala
(See R. T. Tate).

Nwto # 626 Laborer (--- ---)
APPLING, J. 19 m Ala
Louisa M. 21 f "
M. E. 1 f "

Euf # 654
ARGRAN(?), Jane 56 f SC
(See Robert Carroll).

Bkb # 787 Laborer (--- 150)
ARINGTON, Amos 28 m Ga
Sarah C. 28 f "
Nancy 10 f Ala
John 6 m "
Mary J. 3 f "
Thomas 1 m "

Bkb # 752 Farmer (2000-2000)
ARINGTON, Elisha 46 m Ga
Mary J. 40 f "
Martha 18 f Ala
Eliza 14 f "
James 12 m "
Mary F. 10 f "
Victoria 5 f "
Georgia A. 4/12 f "

Luvl # 339
ARRINGTON, Sarah 30 f NC
Mary 14 f Ala
James M. 11 m "
Mary J. 10 f "
Margaret 20 f NC
(See John R. McRae).

Bkb # 753 Farmer (--- 500)
ARINGTON, William J. 24 m Ga
Missouri 22 f Ala
Sophrona 3 f "
Elisha 1 m "

Euf # 495 Farm hand
ARMSTRONG, John 17 m Ga
(See John C. Craig).

Luvl # 319 Farmer (--- ---)
ARMSTRONG, Wiley S. 58 m Ga
Cinthia 47 f "
Orrin G. 28 m "
(Cont.)

(Luvl # 319 cont.)
F. M. 26 m Ga
Martha R. 25 f Ala
Jesse B.(Farmer) 23 m "
Jas. W. " 19 m "
Isaac B. " 17 m "
Helen M. 15 f "
Virginia 13 f "
John 11 m "
Henry C. 8 m "

Euf # 1122
ARNOLD, Sallie 17 f Ga
(See Jno. P. Roquemore)

Mt. A. # 848
ARPE, Martha 19 f Ga
M. D. 4 f Ala
(See A. P. Padget)

Euf 698 Farmer (100-225)
ATKISON, Daniel G. 31 m Ala
Clarky 32 f SC
John J. 13 m Ala
Mary 12 f "
Thos. W. 9 m "
Marshall F. 7 m "
Clarky A. M. 4 f "
Rosa L. E. 1 f "
Nancy A. M., 1/12 f "

Euf # 699 Farmer (500-400)
ATKISON, Wm. J. 29 m Ala
Sarah A. 29 f SC
Mitty 10 f "
Henry E. 8 m "
Daniel L. 6 m "
Sarah A. M. 4 f "
Angeline 1 f "

Euf # 705 Farmer (4000-700)
ATKINSON, Wm. N 54 m NC
Rebecca 51 f Ga
LUDLAM, Sarah H. 6 f Ala
Savid(?) A. 8 f "
KIRKLAND, Jas. 18 m "
(Laborer)

Clay # 171 Mechanic (--- ---)
ATWELL, George W. 33 m Ga
Sarah 29 f SC
Malcom J. 9 m Ala
Wm. R. 7 m "
(Cont.)

(Clay # 171 cont.)
Eliza J. 5 f Ala
Jefferson L. 1 m "

Euf # 150 Seamstress
AUSTIN, Liza J. 20 f NY
(See Jas. G. L. Martin).

Bkb # 684 Farmer (--- ---)
AVANT, Andrew 21 m Ga
(See Geo. W. Fryer).

Bkb # 701 Farmer (--- ---)
AVANT, Asbury 22 m SC
(See John Gilmore).

Txv # 1158
AVANT, Elizabeth 50 f SC
(See James Day).

Txv # 1157
AVANT, Mary 23 f Ala
Wm. G. 3 m "
Eli S. 1 m "
(See Rodin Day)

Euf # 465 Overseer (--- 500)
AVERETT, A. J. 35 m Ga
Mary 37 f "
Henry 4 m Ala
Ambrose 2 m "
Frances 1/12 f "

Euf # 366 Farmer (--- 200)
AVERETT, John 52 m NC
Elizabeth 17 f Ga
(M. within the year).

Euf # 789 Overseer (--- 300)
AVERETT, John 27 m Ga
Nancy 22 f Ala
Rasbery 8/12 m "

Euf # 977 Overseer (--- 100)
AVERETT, Newton 25 m Ga
Mary 18 f "

Euf # 483 Farmer (15,000-60,000)
AVERETT, William 55 m Ga
Susan 47 f "
Jasper 18 m Ala

Euf # 912 Farmer (800-2,500)
BAILEY, B. B. 27 m Ga
Rebecca 22 f Ala

Euf # 910 Farmer (4000-10,000)
BAILEY, Hosea 52 m Ga
(Cont.)

(Euf # 910 cont.)
Mary A. 38 f Ga
Virginia 3 f Ala
GALLOWAY, Wm. 14 m "

Euf # 1378 Farmer (200-175)
BAILEY, J. W. 27 m Ala
Elizabeth 24 f "
Nancy 8 f "
John 6 m "
Thos. 4 m "
Sally 2 f "
Eliza 1 f "

Euf # 1377 Farmer (800-350)
BAILEY, James 65 m SC
Mary 47 f "
Daniel 14 m Ala
Elizabeth 12 f "

Euf # 173 Carpenter (1500-500)
Planter's Hotel
BAILEY, John 58 m Ga
Martha 46 f NC
POWELL, Nancy 52 f Ga
WHITCOME, Mahala 30 f Fla
PENTERCOSTER, D. H. 60 m Pa
(Carpenter)
KEYHOE, John 24 m Ire
(Brick Mason)
JACKSON, Wm. 27 m "
(Brick Mason)
FLINN, J. E. 30 m Ala
(Brick Mason)
BARRON, JOHN 22 m Ire
(Laborer)
McCLOUSKEY, James 24 m "
(Laborer)
GILLISPY, Richard 28 m "
(Laborer)
RILEY, John 32 m "
(Brick Mason)
FLANNAGIN, Wm. 25 m "
(Brick Mason)
BROCK, Wm. 19 m Ala
(Laborer)
WECLOH, Mathew 28 m Ire
(Laborer)
BROOKS, S. P. 51 m Me
(Book Keeper)
RODREGUS, Geo. 43 m Va
(Carriage Painter)

Mdwy # 1059 (1200-4000)
BAILEY, Martha 60 f NC

Euf # 1267 Farmer (--- 150)
BAILEY, Thos. 38 m Ga
Jane 35 f "
Geo. W. 19 m "
Sarah A. 18 f "
William 16 m "
James 11 m "
Jackson 9 m Ala
Mahala 7 f "
Munroe 5 m "
Mary A. 1 f "
BULLOCK, Wm. 19 m Ga
(Hireling)

Euf # 1379 Farmer (250-300)
BAILEY, Thos. H. 25 m Ala
Catherine 24 f "
James 6 m "
Susan 4 f "
Emily 2 f "
John 4/12 m "

Euf # 911 Farmer (--- 1000)
BAILEY, Wm. 25 m Ga
Elizabeth 17 f "
(Married within the year).

Euf # 382 Lawyer (10,000-43,000)
BAKER, Alpheus 34 m SC
Louisa 25 f SC
Courtney 7 m Ala
Alpheus 3 m "

Euf # 59 Clerk (--- ---)
BAKER, Chas. C. 17 m Ala
(See Jas. M. Brown).

Luvl # 567 Farmer (--- 200)
BAKER, Edward 34 m Eng
Sarah 30 f Ala
Annie 1 f "

Euf # 383 (12,000-2,500)
BAKER, Eliza H. 60 f Ire
FLOURNOY, Ellen M. 28 f SC
(--- 10,000)

Clay # 105 Farmer (2,500-6,000)
BAKER, Ellison 35 m SC
BARKER, Mary 32 f Ala
Americus 10 m "
Henry 8 m "
Coly 5 m "
Reese 3 m "

Mt. A. # 818 Farmer (1400-4500)
BAKER, Frank 38 m Ala

(Mt. A. # 818 cont.)
Elizabeth A. 38 f Ga
Selina 18 f "
Susan F. 16 f "
Oliver P. 12 m Ala
Thomas 9 m "
Frank 7 m "
Elizabeth 5 f "
PEACOCK, John J. 16 m "
BAKER, James 3 m "
George 1 m "

Euf # 100 Clerk (1500-4000)
BAKER, Henry W. 40 m Mass
Eliza 39 f SC
Martha 16 f Ala
Mary 12 f "
Emma 9 f "
Ella 2 f "
BEALS, Chas. 22 m NY
(Telegraph Opp. (-- 500)

Euf # 1214 Farmer (700-7000)
BAKER, James C. 42 m SC
Nancy 29 f Ga
John T. 8 m Ala
Theresa J. 3 f "

Txv # 1166 Farm Laborer
BAKER, James M. 25 m SC
Alexander 21 m Ala
(See Jas. Thos. Warr).

Euf # 1213 Farmer (600-2000)
BAKER, Jarret 39 m SC
Savannah 20 f Ala
James M. 2 m "
Mary J. 4/12 f "

Txv # 1148 Farmer (800-350)
BAKER, Larkin 50 m SC
Ellen 49 f "
Nathan (Idiotic) 27 m "
Mary A. 22 f Ala
Sarah A. 18 f "
Warren (Farmer) 16 m "
Pickens 12 m "
Lucinda 9 f "
Georgianna 6 f "

Flk # 439 Farmer (700-700)
BAKER, Larkin 53 m SC
Ellen 47 f "
Nathan (Farmer) 24 m "
Jas. (Farmer) 23 m Ala
Sarah A. 17 f "
(Cont.)

(Flk # 439 cont.)
Mary A. 19 f Ala
Alex. (Farmer) 20 m "
Pickens 11 m "
Lucinda 7 f "
Georgia A. 5 f "

Euf # 1174 (1000-300)
BAKER, Lydia 63 f SC
Margaret 23 f Ala
(1000-300)
Minney 21 f "
James (In school) 17 m "

Nwto # 595 Blacksmith (250-200)
BAKER, N. M. 42 m SC
S. D. 34 f "
L. C. 15 f Ga
James D. 9 m "
H. A. 6 f "
Mary E. 3 f Ala

Euf # 53 Physician (2500-15000)
BAKER, Paul DeLacy 30 m SC
Elizabeth 22 f "
Infant 1 f Ala

Luvl # 282
BAKER, Sarah 80 f SC
(See Wm. King).

Euf # 1177 Farmer (1000-200)
BAKER, Wm. 27 m SC
Molsey 22 f Ala
Joseph M. 6/12 m "

Txv # 1149 Farmer (--- 300)
BAKER, William 24 m SC
Elizabeth 21 f Ga
James 1 m Ala

Bkb # 706
BALL, Sarah 84 f Va
(See Benj. H. Emmerson).

Euf # 140 City Marshal (6000-6000)
BALLARD, Wm. L. 47 m Ga
Sarah A. 40 f "
Wm. L. (Apt. Machinist) 15 m "
Joseph W. 13 m "
Julian C 11 m "
Amelia C. 8 f "
Eugene M. 6 m Ala
Edgar E. 4 m "
Gertrude 1 f "

Txv # 1170 Farmer & Mechanic
(--- 200)
BARBEREE, John 50 m Ga
Sarah 40 f SC
TROY, Elizabeth 18 f Ala
Lurinda 16 f Ga
Zora 14 f "
John 12 m "
Andrew 9 m "

Euf # 146 (--- 800)
BARFIELD, Wineford 36 f Ga
John A. J. 22 m Ala
George W. (Printer) 17 m "
Charity 15 f "
Catherine 13 f "
Mary L. 11 f "
James M. 10 m "

Euf # 1060
BARHAM, Rebecca 38 f NC
Romulus 8 m Ala
David 2 m "
(See Wm. Kennedy).

Euf # 1009 Farmer (10000-30000)
BARK, (BAARK?) Joel G. 53 m NC
Frances 36 f Ga
Thos. J. (Student) 17 m Ala
HUTCHINSON, Mark 22 m Ga
(Overseer)

Clay # 1280 M.E. Minister
(3500-6500)
BARKER, Geo. W. 46 m NC
Tempe E. 47 f Va
Geo. T. (Farmer) 19 m Ala
Sarah E. 16 f "
R. C. 14 m "
Martha A. 12 f "
Thomas 8 m "

Clay # 1282 Farmer (--- ---)
BARKER, John H. 22 m Ga
Lurena 17 f Ala
George 4/12 m "

Euf # 498 Farmer (--- 500)
BARKER, Joseph 49 m NC
Areena 47 f "
Rebecca 24 f Ga
Wm. (Farm Hand) 21 m "
Samuel 18 m "
Sarah 17 f Ala
George 15 m "
Emma 13 f "
Robert 11 m "
Edward 10 m "

Clay # 105
BARKER, Mary 32 f Ala
Americus 10 m "
Henry 8 m "
Coly 5 m "
Reese 3 m "
(See Ellison Baker).

Euf # 1054 Wagon Maker (250-300)
BARKER, Robert 31 m Ga
Mary J. 22 f "
Sarah 8 f Ala
Nancy 4 f "

Euf # 831 Farmer (4000-15000)
BARKSDALE, B. R. 45 m Ga
Emily 42 f "
Beverly (Student) 19 m Ala
Frank " 17 m "
Mary J. 15 f "
John 13 m "
Thomas 11 m "
Ann 9 f "
Arch'd. 7 m "
Louisa 5 f "
Sarah 2 f "

Luvl # 651 Teacher
BARKSDALE, G. W. 23 m Ga
(See James S. Baxter).

Clay # 19 Student at Law
BARKSDALE, H. M. 21 m Ala
(Living in hotel).

Euf # 135 Grocer (7500-4000)
BARNARD, E. S. 36 m Ala
Olive 28 f "
Frances 10 f "
Martin J. 7 m "
Angus N. 5 m "
Mary J. 3 f "
Jesse 45 m NC

Euf # 605
BARNARD, Granbery 10 m Ala
(See David F. Harrell).

Euf # 378 (--- ---)
BARNES, Adaline 30 f Ga
Charles 2 m Ala
James B. 5/12 m "
BISHOP, Sarah 9 f "

Euf # 1328 Laborer (--- ---)
BARNES, James D. 27 m Ga
(Cont.)

(Euf # 1328 cont.)
Sarah 26 f Ga
William J. 6 m Ala
Candace 4 f "
Sarah 2 f "
James 1/12 m "

Euf # 1400 Laborer (--- ---)
BARNES, John 26 m Ire
(See William Jackson).

Euf # 218 Laborer (---450)
BARNES, William 46 m Ga
Ava 52 f "
CLEGHORN, Abigail 18 f Ala
(Laboring)
Henry 17 m "
Elizabeth 12 f "
Anna 10 f "

Euf # 1110 Marchant (3000-9000)
BARNETT, A. W. 33 m Ga
C. J. 27 f SC
William A. 8 m Ala
Samuel 6 m "
Emma 4 f "
Carrie 3 f "
TREUTLEN, C. 18 f "
Julia G. 16 f "

Euf # 176 Boarding House (3000-500)
BARNETT, Mary A. 40 f Ga
Julius C. (Clerk) 17 m Ala
Mary O. 13 f "
Sarah V. 10 f "
CORBITT, D. (Clerk) 23 m SC

Euf # 1052 Merchant (-- --)
BARNETT, P. E. 24 m Ga
Ellen 18 f SC
(See H. E. Jones).

Clay # 38
BARNETT, S. V. 12 f Ala
(See A. C. Wise).

Euf # 966 Physician (--1000)
BARR, J. M. 24 m Va

Flk # 468 Farmer (200-200)
BARR, J. P. 35 m NC
Martha J. 28 f "
Mary E. 10 f Ala
William A. 7 m "
Mandy A. 5 f "
John W. 2 m "

Mt. A. # 917 Overseer (---350)
BARR, John G. 36 m Ga
Elender 22 f "
Georgia A. D. 6/12 f Ala
James T. 6 m "

Clay # 84 Mechanic (--- ---)
BARR, Robert W. 28 m Ga
Harriett 21 f SC
Henry 4 m Ala
Eugenia 2 f "

Mdwy # 981
BARR, Sarah F. 11 f Ala
(See G. J. Turman).

Euf # 1117
BARR, Susan W. 52 f SC
(See Thos. J. Burk).

Euf # 125 Carriage Maker (--2000)
BARR, William 33 m Ga
Martha 27 f "
John T. 3 m "
Elexene 6/12 f Ala
DICKSON, J. T. 25 m Ga
(Teacher).

Clay # 47 Merchant (---1000)
BARRON, B. A. 40 m Ga
Mary A. E. 34 f Ala
(----8000).
Ann E. 14 f "
L. W. 12 m "
A. A. 1 f "

Clay # 36
BARRON, Helen 16 f Ga
(See J. S. Wellborn).

Clay # 730 Laborer
BARRON, James 24 m Ga
(See Elisha Finney).

Euf # 820 Farmer (---100)
BARRON, James H. 30 m Ga
Sarah A. 30 f "
Milton M. 5 m Ala
Sarah S. 3 f "
Nancy A. P. 2 f "

Euf # 173 Laborer
BARRON, John 22 m Ire
(See John Bailey).

Clay # 54 Mechanic (--- ---)
(Cont.)

(Clay # 54 cont.)
BARRON, Ridley 38 m Ga
Jane 30 f "
John 13 m "
Mary (Idiotic) 12 f "
Wm. B. 11 m "
Effie L. 6 f Ala
Edward P. 4 m "
E. S. 2 f "
LASSETTER, Henrietta 14 f Ga

Clay # 34 (150 ---)
BARRON, Samuel 80 m Md
Eliza 55 f Ga
BELL, Ann E. 15 f "
Ophelia 12 f Ala
Fletcher 8 m "

Euf # 363 Farmer (800-500)
BARROW, H. W. 42 m Ga
Sarah 30 f "
James (Farmer) 19 m Ala
Bolsora 18 f "
Harriet 16 f "
Sarah J. 11 f "
Mary 8 f "
Infant 7/12 f "
MITCHELL, Elizabeth 20 f Ga

Euf # 1186 Hireling (-- --)
BARRY, Wm. 38 m NC
Martha 27 f SC
Elizabeth J. 4 f Ala
Mary A. 2 f "

Euf # 43
BART, Sarah B. 28 f Ga
John W. 10 m Ala
(See Aaron Thomas).

Clay # 19 Harness Maker
BARTLETT, D. D. 24 m SC
(Living in hotel).

Euf # 681
BARTLETT, Mary A. 46 f Ga
BENEFIELD, Rufus 17 m "
(Laborer).

Euf # 241
BARTLETT, T. B. S. 11 m Ga
(See Eliza M. Hinsey).

Euf # 869 (--- 100)
BARTON, John 82 m SC
Lucretia 78 f "

Euf # 870 Bricklayer (--- 200)
BARTON, Nathaniel 35 m Ga
Jefferson P. 9 m Ala
Lucintha 7 f "
Victoria 5 f "

Euf # 975 Farmer (--- 4000)
BARTON, W. M. 33 m Ga
Mary S. 32 f "
Ann E. 13 f Ala
Wm. H. 10 m "

Mdwy # 1050 (6000-15000)
BASS, A. E. 54 f Ga
Thos. J. 19 m "
Emily 20 f "
SEAY, John 22 or 27 m Ala
(Overseer on farm)

Txv # 1156 Farmer (--- 200)
BASS, Allen J. 24 m Ala
Nancy C. 21 f "
FLOYD, D. M. 26 f "
Mary M. 4 f "
Joel C. 2 m "
THOMAS, Elijah W. 22 m Ga
(Farm Laborer).

Euf # 643 Farmer (200-50)
BASS, Andrew 30 m Ga
Ellen 21 f Ala
Henry W. 1 m "
Thos. B. 3 m "

Txv # 1173 Farmer (--- 210)
BASS, Daniel 20 m Ala
Jane 21 f "
Caroline 3 f "
Wm. Everett 1 m "
KIRKLAND, Aaron, 11 m "

Euf # 652
BASS, Edna 30 f Ga
(See John D. Collins).

Clay # 9 Clerk in store (3500 --)
BASS, James A. 29 m Ga
Ann D. 18 f Ala
(--- 3,600)
J. M. 4 m "
R. J. 2 f "

Txv # 1147 Farmer (--- 200)
BASS, John 24 m Ala
Abagail 21 f Ga
TEW, John (Laborer) 20 m Ala
HUTSON, Irvin 13 m "
(Cont. next page).

(Txv # 1147 cont.)
HUTSON, Robert 9 m Ala
(John & Abagail Bass married within the year).

Bkb # 766 Farmer (100-155)
BASS, John 70 m NC
Isabella 65 f "
GATES, Missouri 23 f "

Clay # 164 Owner of farm (1300-15000)
BASS, Nancy 41 f Ga
GAMMON, Benj. 20 m Ala
(Farmer ---6000)
BASS, Fletcher H. 15 m "
(Farmer, ---6000)
Laura F. 12 f "
(----3000)
Lucy C. (or E.) 8 f "
Joseph W. 6 m "
(Last two:-----$3000 each).

Clay # 178 In Poorhouse
BASS, Rebecca 84 f Va

Euf # 455 (Blind)
BASS, Samuel 53 m Ga
E. J. 50 f "
(See Washington Toney).

Txv # 1145 Farmer (--- 200)
BASS, Uriah 29 m NC
Rachael 28 f "
Henry W. 9 m Ala
Victoria A. 8 f "
James M. 6 m "
Calvin C. 4 m "
Sarah J. 7/12 f "

Txv # 1159 Farmer (500-300)
BASS, Willis, Jr. 24 m Ga
Drusilla 17 f Ala

Txv # 1155 Farmer (500-300)
BASS, Willis, Sr. 50 m NC
Jane 49 f "
Louisa 21 f Ala
Wm. J. (Farmer) 19 m "
Lucinda 17 f "
Willis 15 m "
Wiley N. 10 m "
James C. 8 m "
Milbry J. 5 f "

Euf # 507 Farmer (--- 300)
BASSET, Francis 74 m SC
(Cont.)

Elizabeth 64 f SC
Elizabeth 21 f "
Francis (Farmer) 18 m Ga

Bfd # 1254
BATEMAN, Mary L. 19 f Ala
(See D. C. Campbell).

Euf # 392 Farmer (7500-25000)
BATES, George M. 54 m SC
Roseanna M. 47 f "

Bkb # 711 Farmer (--- 200)
BATES, James 26 m Ga
Jane 24 f Ala
William 8 m "
Eliza 6 f "
Mary 4 f "
John 2 m "
James 1/12 m "
COX, Eliza 62 f Ga
John G. (Farmer) 23 m Ala

Mdwy # 1092 Overseer (--- 500)
BATES, John H. 28 m Ga
Louisa 18 f Ala
George 4/12 m "

Euf # 863 Farmer (22000-131,000)
BATES, Wilson M. 44 m SC
Milledge 20 m Ala
Andrew (At school) 16 m "
Mary 14 f "
Walter 6 m "

Euf # 1220
BATTLE, Elizabeth 9 f Ga
(See Wm. Clements, Sr.)

Euf # 1216 Farmer (500-200)
BATTLE, Ellington 36 m Ga
Susan 24 f Ala
Matilda 13 f Ga
Eliza 11 f "
William 7 m "
John T. 5 m "
Monroe 1 m Ala
Georgia A. 1 f "

Euf # 445
BATTLE, Junius K. 21 m Ala
Sarah 18 f "
(Married within the year).
McKLROY, Sarah 10 f "

Txv # 1177 Farmer (3000-11000)
BATY, Henry 59 m Ga
(Cont.)

(Txv # 1177 cont.)
Martha 47 f Ga
Wm. H. (or A.) 13 m "
Robt. (Farmer) 20 m "
Mary J. 9 f "
BLANCHET, John 18 m Ala
(Farm Laborer).

Txv # 1132 Farmer (7000-500)
Baxley, James 64 m SC
Rebecca 35 f "
Catherine 9 f Ala
James 7 m "
Benjamin 5 m "
MITCHELL, Hiram 13 m "

Txv # 1133 Farmer (1000-800)
BAXLEY, William 40 m SC
C. L. 38 f NC
L. M. 17 f Ala
Elliot 15 m "
Harriet 13 f "
Hethy 6 f "
C. L. 4 f "
Nancy 1 f "

Luvl # 651 Farmer (5000-10000)
BAXTER, James S. 38 m SC
Margaret 27 f NC
James 14 m Ala
Daniel 12 m "
John 8 m "
Hugh 5 m "
Isabella 3 f "
Ida 6/12 f "
CAMPBELL, Norman 75 m Scot
(Farmer)
BAXTER, Sarah P. 65 f SC
BARKSDALE, G. W. 23 m Ga
(Teacher)

Luvl # 334 Farmer (3400-12000)
BAXTER, Thomas F. 33 m Ala
Mary 32 f "
Margaret M. 12 f "
Pleasant W. 11 m "
David P. 6 m "
John M. 5 m "
Mary M. 3 f "
James T. 1 m "
Sarah P. 60 f SC
McCALL, Flora 7 f Ala
Kate (Black) 110 f SC

Mdwy # 1042
(Cont.)

(Mdwy # 1042 cont.)
BEALL, Alice 16 f Ga
Thomas 14 m "
Mittie 13 f "
(See Joseph Pou).

Euf # 100 Telegraph Operator
BEALS, Charles 22 m NY
(See Henry W. Baker).

Euf # 441 Tailor
BEALLS, Mr. 21 m Ger

Mdwy # 976 Farmer (2000-1000)
BEARD, Travis 49 m NC
Neomi 44 f Ga
Mary 18 f "
Joseph (Farmer) 17 m "
Eliza 14 f "
John 14 m "

Luvl # 378 Farmer (--- 3500)
BEASLEY, Asa F. 34 m Ala
Sarah 27 f "
Thomas 5 m "
Martha 3 f "
Zenobia 1 f "
HATCHER, Sophronia 19 f Ga
Mary (?) 4 f Ala

Luvl # 349 Farmer (--- ---)
BEASLEY, Daniel 27 m Ala
Malinda 25 f Ga
Catherine 5 f Ala
Ella 3 f "
James 6/12 m "

Clay # 9 Grocer (---400)
BEASLEY, Daniel T. 35 m Ala
Jane C. 26 f NC
Lousianna 8 f Ala
Mary A. 6 f "
Eugenia T. 5 f "
Louis P. 1 m "
HERRING, Ann 14 f "
Mary 11 f "

Luvl # 653
BEASLEY, J. C. 28 m Ala
(See E. W. Harrison).

Mdwy # 1080 Farmer (1820-800)
BEASLEY, James C. 25 m Ala
Susan 49 f Ga
Thomas (Farmer) 23 m Ala

Clay # 248 Farmer (--- 1860)
BEASLEY, James T. 39 m Ala
Rebecca L.(?) 32 f "
(--- 1200)
Narcissa 13 f "
Florence 5 f "
James 2 m "

Luvl # 283 Clerk (--- 600)
BEASLEY, John C. 35 m Ala
(See E. W. Harrison).

Luvl # 364 Farmer (4000-6000)
BEASLEY, John G. 67 m NC
Martha 51 f Ga
McKINNEY, Caroline 17 f SC
WOODWARD, Thomas 23 m Ga

Clay # 192 (--- ---)
BEASLEY, Martha A. 45 f Ga
Mary 17 f Ala
Wyley 15 m "
David 12 m "
Elizabeth 7 f "

Mdwy # 1003 (14000-1000)
BEASLEY, Nancy 50 f Ga
James 25 m "
Thomas 23 m "

Euf # 1074 Overseer (--- ---)
BEASLEY, T. J. 30 m NC
Ann 24 f "
Tince 6 f Ala
A. E. 4 f "
J. S. 1 f "

Clay # 88 Waggoner (--- ---)
BEASLEY, Wm. 21 or 27 m Ala
(See Robert Dill).

Clay # 657 Farmer (1200-5500)
BEASLEY, Wm., Sr. 55 m NC
Elizabeth 46 f Ga
Aly F. (Farmer) 23 m Ala
John " 22 m "
William " 20 m "
James " 17 m "
Mary 15 f "
Sarah 12 f "
George 10 m "
Kansas 4 f "

Euf # 156 Merchant (1500-2000)
BEAUCHAMP, A. H. 33 m Ala
Margaret E. 23 f Scot
(Cont.)

(Euf # 156 cont.)
William H. 13 m Ala
George W. 4 m "
Florence M. 2 f "
Clara 1/12 f "

Euf # 908 Farmer (16200-46000)
BEAUCHAMP, Green 57 m Ga
Caroline H. 50 f "
A. P. Parmer 16 m Ala
(In school, ---7882)
Andrew J. 14 m "
James 14 m "
John F. 12 m "
Green B. 8 m "
William B. 8 m "
KENNON, Jane 74 f Ga

Euf 2-2
BEAUCHAMP, John 11 m Ala
(See Wm. H. Boswell).

Euf # 597
BECK, Millard 10 m Ala
(See John G. Searcy).

Euf # 527
BECK, Samuel 7 m Ala
(See Joshua Sawyers).

Euf # 7-7 Clerk (1000-500)
BECKHAM, Green 28 m SC
Eliza C. 22 f Ala
Lizzie E. 5/12 f "

Luvl # 535 Farmer (--- 7000)
BEECHOM, Henry W. 26 m Ala
Rebecca 21 f "
R. L. 4 m "
M. M. 2 f "

Euf # 284 Planter (7000-5500)
BEDSOLE, John 58 m NC
Catherine 51 f "
Mary T. 22 f Ga
Nancy 20 f "
Emiline 18 f "
Cherry Ann 16 f "
William S.(?) 15 m "
John W. 13 m "
Catharine 10 f "
MIDDLETON, John 27 m Ga
(Laborer).

Euf # 321 Farmer (4000-500)
BEDSOLE, Stephen 30 m NC
Narcissa 28 f Ala
Harriet 28 f NC
Debbry A. 5 f Ala
Methena 4 f "
Alexander 2 m "
Henry 4/12 m "
EVERETT, Mary 13 f Ga

Euf # 41 Accountant (-- --)
BEEMAN, Julius 48 m NC
Serena A. 48 f "

Euf # 1276 Farmer (1800-3000)
BELCHER, Abner 30 m Ga
Emaline 28 f Ala
Mary 7 f "
John 5 m "
Amanda 3 f "
Lydia 10/12 f "

Euf # 623 Farmer (1000-3000)
BELSER, John 21 m Ga
Hetty 20 f "
Thomas 2 m Ala
Nancy 6/12 f "

Euf # 1151 M.B. Minister (800-2000)
BELCHER, Phillip 60 m Ga
Annis 55 f "
Phillip G. 18 m "
(Farm Hand).

Euf # 622 Farmer (1000-1500)
BELSER, Sherod 27 m Ga
Hariet 23 f Ala
Mary J. 2 f "

Clay # 34
BELL, Ann E. 15 f Ga
Ophelia 12 f Ala
Fletcher 8 m "
(See Samuel Barron).

Euf 1194
BELL, Elizabeth 10 f Ga
(See Wm. J. Martin).

Euf 1135 Hireling (--- 100)
BELL, J. P. 24 m Ga
Georgia 20 f "
Florigelle 1 f Ala
BOYD, Mary 60 f Ga

Euf 1192
BELL, James 9 m Ga
(See Joseph Snead).

Euf 270 Teamster (2000-500)
BELL, James A. 30 m Ga
Caroline E. 29 f "
Harriett 7 f Ala
Jeremiah 5 m "
George 3 m "
Celestia A. 1 f Ga
SMITH, Wm. (Laborer) 22 m Ala
BROWN, Laura 16 f Ga

Luvl # 320 Farmer (4000-400)
BELL, John 53 m SC
Laney 53 f "
Mary 23 f Ala
William (Farmer) 21 m "
John " 19 m "
Arch'd. C. " 15 m "
Laney M. 12 f "
McCOLLUM, ----(Teacher) 26 m SC

Euf # 972 Hireling
BELL, Joseph 20 m Tenn
(See E. P. Head)

Nwto # 604
BELL, Louisa 31 f SC
William J. 1/12 m Ala
(See M. K. Kelly).

Bkb # 693 (--- 150)
BELL, Mary 60 f NC
C. E. 34 f "
Irena 32 f "
V. S. A. 30 f "
Catherine 27 f "
Ettie 24 f "
Miles 22 m "
Lavina 20 f "
Ocas (Laborer, 100---) 18 m "
HOWELL, Susan 1 f "

Euf 232 Butcher
BELL, Orestess 40 m NC
Elizabeth 37 f Va
Henry W. 10 m Ala
Calladonia D. 4 f "
Bascomb 6/12 m "
FOUCHE, George 20 m "
(Laborer).

Clay 81 Overseer (-- --)
BELVIN,John A. 33 m NC
Cornelia 21 f "
Edward 1 m Ala

Txv # 1178 Farmer (--- 250)
BENEFIELD, Arnold 40 m Ga
Annie 32 f SC
Martha A. 15 f Ala
James 13 m "
Mary 11 f "
Nancy 9 f "
William 7 m "
Susanna 3 f "
John 1/12 m "

Euf # 681 Laborer
BENEFIELD, Rufus 17 m Ga
(See Mary A. Barlett).

Txv # 1189 Farmer (--- 200)
BENEFIELD, Zachariah 27 m Ga
Eliza A. R. 25 f "
William W. 8 m Ala
John 7 m "
Isaac 5 m "
James 3 m "
Eliza A. R. 7/12 f "

Luvl # 393 Farmer (1600-5000)
BENNETT, B. C. 24 m NC
Amanda 24 f Ala
HUEY, M. A. K.(?) 10 f "
Ellen D. 6 f "
BENNETT, J. M. 10/12 m "

Clay # 208 Farmer (1200-1300)
BENNETT, George 29 m Ala
Susannah 25 f SC
Green J. 5 m Ala
Monroe 2 m "
Worthy 1/12 m "
Augustus (Farmer) 19 m "
Elvira 17 f "

Mdwy # 1044 Farmer (200-200)
BENNETT, John W. 34 m Ga
E. F. 34 f SC
GLENN, Green T. 5 m Ga

Clay # 185 Mechanic
BENNETT, Orrin 34 m Ala
(See Elisha Davis).

Clay # 131 Farmer (12500-30000)
BENNETT, Ryan 50 m NC
William L. 21 m Ala
(Farmer --- 1500)
Joel 11 m "
Nancy 8 f "
(Cont.)

(Clay # 131 cont.)
Lucinda 6 f Ala
Jesse 3 m "

Clay # 236
BENNETT, W. G. 23 m Ala
(See Ezekial Bradley).

Clay # 58 Farmer (1000-3000)
BENSON, Geo. W. 55 m NC
Susan 52 f SC
(Cake Baker).
Geo. J. 13 m Ala
GEORG, William 28 m Ire
(Dublin, Ire.-Shoemaker)

Clay # 171 In the poorhouse
BENSON, Rebecca 34 f Va
William 4 m Ala

Euf # 64
BENTLEY, Missouri 16 f Ga
(See Johnathan Hales).

Euf # 662
BENTLEY, Vicey A. 10 f Ala
(See Barbary Walker).

Txv 1144 Farmer (550-500)
BENTON, Isaac 43 m SC
Lettie 36 f Ga
Samuel (Farmer) 18 m Ala
Elizabeth 17 f "
Marion 15 m "
Susan J. 13 f "
Ira T. 10 m "
Isaac W. 4 m "
Levi 3 m "

Luvl # 306 Farmer (--- ---)
BENTON, Samuel 34 m Ala
Marina 43 f SC
Sarah A. 15 f Ala
Mary 12 f "
Nancy L. 10 f "
Wright 8 m "
Roxana 4 f "
Alexander 4 m "
John 1/12 m "

Euf # 709 Laborer
BENTON, Mat(?) 20 m Ga
Margaret A. 18 f Ala
(Married within the year).

Euf # 116 Merchant (2000-4500)
BERNSTEIN, H. 35 m Pol
(Rus. Poland).
Theresa 30 f Fr
Malinda 3 f Ga
Mariah 2 f Ala
Sarah 9/12 f "
Benj. (Clerk) 37 m Pol
CHAMANKY, David 39 m Pol
(Clerk, b. Rus. Pol.)
BERNSTEIN, Phillip 25 m "
(Pedler - Rus. Pol.)
Phillipe, Louis 25 m "
(Pedler, b. Rus. Pol.
---- $500)

Euf # 350 Farmer (1000-300)
BERRY, John W. 49 m Ga
Elizabeth 22 f "
Sarah 17 f Ala
John 15 m "
Lucy 8 f "
Margaret 6 f "
Ade 4 f "
Frances 2 f "

Clay # 117 Laborer
BERRYHILL, Henry 20 m Ga
(See Luvinca Spears).

Txv # 1233, 1213, 1214
(320-200)
BERRYHILL, Sarah 48 f Ga
Nancy 28 f "
Henry 21 m "
Thomas 17 m "
Levin C. 14 m "
Frances 13 f Ala
COVINGTON, Elizabeth 36 f Ga
(--- 50)
Emily 15 f "
Mary 13 f Ala
Jeremiah 12 m "
Angeline 3 f "
Arvnine 6/12 f "

Euf # 65 Bookkeeper (--- 200)
BESSON, J. A. B. 33 m Fr
A. M. 32 f NY
Elloise M. 9 f Ala

Euf # 98 Druggist (--- ---)
BESSON, William E. 24 m Ga

Euf # 1390 (2500-2000)
BETHUNE, Elizabeth S. 49 f Ga
Cornelia 18 f Ala
William J. 16 m "
Sarah Y. 14 f "
JOHNSTON, Young M. 18 m Ga
(Clerk)

Euf # 317 Carpenter (300-1500)
BETHUNE, John S. 28 m Ga
Nancy 32 f "
Frances P. 10 f Ala
William A. 7 m "
John 2 m "

Euf # 811 (--- 16000)
BETTS, Elisha 71 m Va
Mariah 60 f Ga

Mt. A. # 865 Farmer (--- 150)
BEVEL, Robert 24 m Ala
Eliza 20 f Ga
Franklin 3 m Ala
Sarah 1 f "

Mt. A. # 864 Farmer (2000-2600)
BEVEL, Thomas 66 m SC
Milly 60 f "
William (Farmer,--100) 22 m Ala
Alex " 18 m "
George 15 m "

Mt. A. # 919 Teacher
BEVERLY, Ann E. 18 f NC
(See Joseph C. Russell).

Euf # 234
BEVERLY, Christian N. 16 f NC
Mary J. 18 f "
(See John G. McClendon).

Luvl # 372 Mechanic (--- ---)
BEVERLY, Daniel G. 44 m NC
Nancy 21 or 27 f Ala
William 15 m "
Martha A. 10 f "
John 8 m "
Barbara E. 6 f "
Kate L. 4 f "
Callie M. 6/12 f "
HUNTER, Jas. 26 m SC
(Mechanic)

Euf # 308
BEVERLY, William 12 m Ala
(See Angus McLeod).

Euf 9-9 Farmer (5000-22000)
BIGHAM, James 60 m Ga
Isabelle 51 f "
PARSONS, Elizabeth 10 f Ala

Euf # 1389
BILLINGS, Harriet 52 f Ga
(See John Black).

Euf # 340 Tinner (1200-4500)
BILLINGS, John D. 30 m Ga
Rebecca 28 f SC
A. F. 7 f Ga
John W. 5 m "
Sallie M. 1 f Ala

Euf # 330
BIRDSONG, Josephine C. 14 f Ala
(See William McLeod).

Euf # 490
BIRDSONG, Martha 28 f Ga
Amos J. 8 m Ala

Clay # 175 Farm Laborer
BISHOP, Brantley 19 m NC
(See Penelope Jones).

Euf # 995 Hireling
BISHOP, Columbus T. 25 m Ga
(See John C. Griffin).

Euf # 856 Farmer (3000-1300)
BISHOP, D.(?) H. 27 m Ala
Caroline 23 f "
BOWEN, John 23 m "
(Overseer)

Euf # 103
BISHOP, Elizabeth 19 f Ala
Mary E. 1 f "
(See Priscilla Watson).

Euf # 872 Teacher
BISHOP, Elizabeth 18 f SC
(See E. G. Hodges).

Euf # 957 Farmer (10000-20000)
BISHOP, J. B. 45 m SC
Nancy 37 f NC
Martha A. 15 f Ala
Mary T.(J.?) 13 f "
Emma 11 f "
William 9 m "
Milton 7 m "
Cornelia 3 f "
Charles 2 m "

Euf # 1207
BISHOP, Nancy J. 11 f Ala
(See Arthur Crews).

Euf # 378
BISHOP, Sarah 9 f Ala
(See Adaline Barnes).

Clay # 150 Farmer (8000-58000)
BISHOP, Westley 40 m Ga
Nancy J. 11 f Ala
William A. 7 m "

Clay # 158 Farmer (7572-22000)
BISHOP, William 37 m Ala
Rebecca S. 23 f "
Susan J. 6 f "
WARREN, James E. 17 m "
NOBLES, S. F. 22 m "
(Overseer).

Nwto # 640 Planter (3000-12000)
BIVIN(?), James F. 21 m Ga
(See R. C. Redding).

Nwto # 555 Farmer (400-200)
BIZZELL, H. B. H. 27 m Ala
Sarah 30 f SC
Mark A. 7 m Ala
Mary F. 5 f "
James H. 3 m "
William C. 4/12 m "

Flk # 491 Merchant (--- 1000)
BIZZELL, J. C. 22 m Ala
(See Musgrove Lewis).

Flk # 394 Teacher
BLACK, H. W. 38 m SC
(See Anderson Simms).

Euf # 139 Printer (6000-1000)
BLACK, Hugh 40 m Scot

Clay # 677
BLACK, John 8 m Ga
Mary J. 6 f Ala
(See John Tamplin).

Euf # 1389 Printer & Publisher
(2000-5000)
BLACK, John 38 m Can
Mary J. 31 f Ga
Caroline H. 12 f Ala
Edward J. 9 m "
Crillens 2 f "
ROBERTS, Andrew J. 19 m Ga
(Apprentice printer).
BILLINGS, Harriet 52 f "

Euf # 1167
BLACK, Mary 22 f Ala
Joseph 8 m "
(See Jesse Cabiness).

Euf # 201
BLACK, Polly 18 f Ala
(See Emanuel Posten).

Luvl # 301
BLACKBORN, Franklin 11 m Ga
(See Stephen H. Bounds).

Euf # 803 Overseer (--- 1800)
BLACKBURN, E. D.(?) 35 m SC
Salina 30 f Ala

Euf # 196 Farmer (--- 300)
BLACKBURN, Isaac N. 32 m Ga
Lucinda 31 f "
Mary A. E. 7 f Ala
Caroline 5 f "
Emaline 3 f "
Sarah 90 f SC

Euf # 615 Farmer (300-150)
BLACKSHEAR, David 39 m Ga
Elizabeth 45 f NC
Wm. (Farm hand) 18 m Ga
John C. 7 m Ala
KING, Caroline 17 f "

Clay # 200 Farmer
BLACKSHUR, James 67 m NC
Catherine 49 f "
Louisa J. 18 f Ala
Jesse W. (Farmer) 16 m "
Margaret M. 11 f "
William T. 9 m "

Euf # 486 (1800-600)
BLACKSTOCK, Elizabeth 34 f Ga
Joseph 14 m Ala
Henry 12 m "
John 10 m "
Nancy 8 f "

Euf # 1144 Farmer (600-2000)
BLACKWELL, Daniel 40 m Ga
Louisa 31 f "
Robert 14 m Ala
Kemp 8 m "
Thomas 5 m "

Clay # 1237 Farmer (10000-16000)
BLAIR, M. W. 42 m SC
Martha A. 31 f Ala
(Cont.)

(Clay # 1237 cont.)
Henry W. 4 m Ala
J. W. 11/12 m "
HARGROVE, Elizabeth 52 f SC

Clay # 153 Farmer (10000-40000)
BLAIR, William 55 m SC
Elizabeth 48 f "
Thos. T. (Farmer) 24 m Ala
John W. " 22 m "
S. A. " 18 m "
Elizabeth 14 f "
John H. 13 m "
Derrill 10 m "
Dixon 9 m "
Emma R. 7 f "
KILPATRICK, Sarah 22 f "
(Seamstress).

Euf # 184 Foundry Mgr.
BLAIR, William 29 m Ga
(See Chas. P. Smith).

Clay # 6 Clerk
BLAIR, William L. 18 m Ala
(See Benj. Morrison).

Txv # 1190
BLAKEY, Asa 19 m Ga
(See E. S. Warr).

Clay # 97 Farmer (6000-15000)
BLAKEY, Asa 50 m Ga
M. C. 41 f "
S. A. 6 m Ala
McANDREW, A. 36 f Ga
S. B. 7 m Ala

Clay # 127 Farmer (100-50)
BLAKEY, Jackson 35 m Ga
Mary Ann 26 f NC
William J. 9 m Ala
N. A. E. 5 f "
Mary J. 4 f "
Martha 2 f "

Clay # 98 Farmer (1500-8000)
BLAKEY, S. W. 46 m Ga
S. S. 17 f Ala
M. L. 15 m "
L. 13 f "
John D. (Farmer) 40 m Ga
(250 ---)

Clay # 126 Farmer (400-100)
BLAKEY, William 66 m Ga
Nancy 54 f "
(Cont.)

(Clay # 126 cont.)
Elijah (Laborer) 22 m Ga
Asa " 20 m "
Washington " 16 m Ala
Nancy 13 f "
Eli 10 m "

Txv # 1131 Laborer (--- 200)
BLAKEY, William 26 m Ga
Martha A. 18 f Ala
Mary A. 4/12 f "

Mdwy # 986 Painter (--- 200)
BLAKY, Columbus 30 m Ga
(See Sarah Owens).

Mdwy # 999 Cabinetmaker (--450)
BLAKY, J. W. 28 m Ga
Caroline 22 f SC
Frances 2 f Ala
George 1 m "
Mary 45 f Ga

Txv # 1177 Farm Laborer
BLANCHET, John 18 m Ala
(See Henry Baty).

Mt. A. # 911 Workman (--- 300)
BLEDSOE, G. L. 30 m Ga
Lovey 31 f "
William 9 m Ala
Susan 7 f "
Mary A. 5 f "
Josephine 4 f "
John L. 2 m "

Mdwy # 949 Physician (---15000)
BLEDSOE, J. W. 39 m Ga
L. A. 25 f Ala
James M. 8 m "
John W. 6 m "
M. J. 4 f "
CALLOWAY, Daniel 20 m "
(Student of medicine).

Euf # 236 Planter (10000-33000)
BLUDWORTH, J. M. 51 m NC
Harriett E. 23 f Ala

Euf # 710 (400-50)
BLUDSWORTH, Mary 65 f Ga

Luvl # 283
BLUDWORTH, Patrick -- -- --
(See E. W. Harrison).

Clay # 178 Keeper of Poorhouse
BLUDWORTH, Thos. F. 58 m NC
Thirza 56 f SC
Timothy 34 m Ga
(Brick Mason).
Charlotte 33 f SC
Thomas 11 m Ala
Thirza M. 9 f "
John Deven 8 m "
Mary R. 6 f "
William M. 4 m "
James M. 2 m "
BASS, Rebecca(Pauper) 84 f Va
CARTER, Samuel " 78 m "
KIRKLAND, Matilde 42 f NC
(Pauper)
ELLIS, Stephen " 30 m Ga
TYLER, James " 48 m SC
(Blind)
BENSON, Rebecca " 34 f Va
, William 4 m Ala
LATON, Lusinda(Pauper)40 f Ga
WHITE, Eliz. (Insane) 28 f "
VAINWRIGHT, Charlotte 40 f "
(Insane)
WATSON, Claiborne 68 m "
(Pauper)
WATSON, Claiborne, Jr. 6 m Ala
(Pauper)
WATSON, Jane " 45 f Ga
Watson, Eliz. " 11 f Ala
Rachael " 4 f "
KIRKLAND, Lucretia 6 f "
RHODES, Frances 6 f "
Thomas 8 m "
WATLEY, Eliza 15 f "
Emma 11 f "
William 6 m "
NIXON, Elijah 23 m "
(Last 7 are paupers).

Mt. A. # 863 Brick mason (450-250
BLUDWORTH, William 33 m Ga
Mary 31 f SC
Sarah F. 10 f Ala
William J. 7 m "
John T. 6 m "
Charlotte 2 f "
HAMNER, Daniel 21 m Ga
(School Teacher, 300-125)

Clay # 115 Teacher
BLUE, Sophia 21 f Ala
(See Malcom McCraney).

Euf # 479 Overseer (--- 50)
BLUNT, Thomas 35 m Ga
Rhody 18 f "
Infant 1/12 f Ala

Euf # 112 Clerk (2000-6000)
BOATWRIGHT, Geo. T. 32 m Ga
Eliza R. 20 f Ala
Chas. W. 2 m "
George 1 m "

Euf # 909 (--- 200)
BOBBETT, Lucy(?) 24 f Ala
Sophrona 20 f "
William (Hireling) 18 m "
Nancy 16 f "
Amanda 14 f "
Thomas 12 m "
George 10 m "
Victoria 7 f "

Euf # 913
BOBBET, Mary 22 f Ala
(See Harrell Flowers).

Euf # 420 Laborer
BODEFEORD, James 16 m SC
(See James Daniels).

Euf # 841
BOGGS,Harriett E. 14 f Ga
Sarah A. E. 13 f "
(See C. R. Moore).

Euf # 185 Machinist (-- 200)
BOLAND, T. M. 29 m Ga
Martha M. 21 f "
Nancy E. 4 f Ala
Mary J. 2 f Ga
William (Laborer) 24 m "

Nwto # 624 Farmer (--- ---)
BOLTON, Eli 50 m Ga
Betsey 40 f "
Westley (Farmer) 18 m Ala
Fillmore 14 m "

Bkb # 744 Farmer (825- 500)
BOND, James 30 m Ga
Sarah 24 f "
A. J. 4 f Ala
S. A. 3 f "
George W. 1 m "

Mdwy 1062
BONDS, Stephen 21 m Ala
(See Henry Stone).

Euf # 216 Farmer (10000-25000)
BONNELLE, Arch. 57 m Ga
Ann E. 47 f SC
Eudorah 12 f Ga
Orry T. 10 f "
Mary 8 f Ala
Louisa 6 f "
Archy 4 m "
Willie 2 m "
FREEMAN, Tandy R. 18 m Ga
(Student)

Euf # 606 Farmer (800-250)
BONNER, Thos. 33 m Ga
Elizabeth 33 f SC
Anderson J. 12 m Ala
Narissa 10 f "
Mary A. 8 f "
William T.(?) 7 m "
Joseph 3 m "
Infant 6/12 m Ala
HUGHES,Thos. A. 15 m "

Euf # 1392
BOOTH, James 13 m Ala
(See Thos, McKenna).

Clay # 669 Farmer (4000-1500)
BOOTH, Milton S. 66 m Ga
Sarah 62 f "
Jane 29 f Ala
Amanda 22 f "

Euf # 281 Ambrotheist (-- 2000)
BOOTH, Uriah W. 31 m Va

Euf # 712 Farmer (200-500)
BOOTH, William 25 m Ala
Jane 21 f "
Elizabeth 3 f "
Martha 1 f "
Robert (Laborer ---100) 21 m "

Clay # 670 Farmer (--- 200)
BOOTH, William A. 35 m Ga
Sinthia 26 f "
James 9 m "
John 7 m "
Zachariah 4 m Ala
Louisianna 3 f "
Amanda S. 2/12 f "

Clay # 57 Planter (2500-15000)
BORDERS, Abner H.(?) 48 m Ga
Mary L. 47 f "
A. S. 17 m "
S. E. 21 f "
FOSTER, John A. 30 m Ala
(Lawyer,---1000)
M. M. 23 f Ga
(---1500)

Clay # 22 Physician (800-2000)
BORDERS, J. C. 26 m Ga
Susan M. 20 f Ala
May 2 f "

Euf # 1172 Farmer (800-2000)
BOSTICK, Eli M. 60 m SC
Margaret 43 f "
James S. 20 m "
William W. 17 m "
Samuel G. 14 m "
Ezra 12 m "
Margaret A. 10 f "
Caroline 8 f "
Cornelia 3 f Ala

Luvl # 269 Merchant (1000-15000)
BOSTICK, Wm. C. 31 m NC
Lilly A. 25 f "
Mary 2 f Ala
McRAE, Christian 23 f "
John L. 28 m NC
(Gentlemen, 1000-10000)
HERRING, Emanuel 18 m Ala
(Clerk)
LITTLE, G. W. -- -- --
McLENNON, J. D. -- -- --
OLIVER, A. W. D. -- -- --
HARE, Dozier (clerk) 21 m NC
HOLMES, J. C. 40 m SC
(Teacher)

Euf # 1020 Overseer (--- 100)
BOSWELL, John W. 40 m Ga
Susan 35 f "
Nancy E. 18 f "
Rhody 17 f "
Missouri 15 f "
Sophronia 13 f "
Elizabeth 10 f "
John 8 m "
William 6 m "
Ella 4 f "
Walker 1 m "
Wesley Winn 8/12 m "

Euf # 2-2 Planter (2000-10000)
BOSWELL, Wm. H. 46 m Ga
Elizabeth H. 32 f SC
LOWMAN, Laura B. 14 f Ala
BEAUCHAMP, John 11 m "

Mt. A. # 920 Farmer (--- 500)
BOTTOMS, Burrell 45 m SC
Sarah 42 f Ga
Marietta 21 f "
Wm. H. (Farmer) 18 m "
Ann M. 14 f "
C. C. 12 m "
Sarah P. 8 f Ala

Mdwy # 1094 Overseer (--- 1100)
BOTTOMS, John 33 m SC
(See Elvy Lewis).

Bkb # 721 Farmer (600-800)
BOUNDS, Jesse L. 53 m NC
Nancy 53 f SC
P. A. 21 f Ala
Wm. E. (Farmer) 20 m "
John P. " 16 m "
Marintha J. 15 f "

Luvl # 301 Farmer (--- 600)
BOUNDS, Stephen H. 27 m Ala
Narcissa 20 f "
Mary 3 f "
William A. 1 m "
BLACKBORN, Franklin 11 m Ga
DRIGGARS, Martha 19 f Ala

Luvl # 300 Farmer (800-500)
BOUNDS, William M. 55 m NC
Martha F. 46 f Ga
Julia A. 19 f Ala
Lucinda 17 f "
Rebecca 14 f "
Osborn J. 12 m "
Eliza 9 f "
Martha C. 7 f "
James (Insane) 51 m NC

Luvl # 302 Farmer (--- ---)
BOUNDS, William R. 24 m Ala
Lydia 18 f "
Nancy A. 2 f "

Clay # 118 (--- 100)
BOWDEN, Eliza W. 30 f NC
E. A. 12 f Ala
Julia J. 10 f "
Winnie 4 f "
V. F. 1 f "

Clay # 116 Farmer (800-400)
BOWDEN, James 57 m NC
Elizabeth 56 f "
Francis M. (Farmer) 24 m Ala
Callie 17 f "
(Last two married within year).

Clay # 128 Farmer (800-200)
BOWDEN, Jas. A. 30 m NC
Mary A. 26 f SC
James N. 3 m Ala
Jane A. E. 1 f "
-- A. 8/12 f "
MORRIS, Riley 19 m Ga
(Farm Laborer)

Clay # 113 Farmer (1000-200)
BOWDEN, Jesse B. 42 m NC
Ann 42 f Ga
Wm. B. (Laborer) 17 m Ala
Nicholas W. " 15 m "
N. A. 12 f "
H. B. 10 m "
Danl. A. 8 m "
Saml. L. 5 m "
L. A. 3 f "

Euf # 1243 Hireling (-- --)
BOWDEN, John C. 25 m NC
Mary J. 8 f Ala

Clay # 101
BOWDEN, Louisa 30 f NC
(See A. S. Kennedy).

Clay # 117
BOWDEN, Sarah E. 17 f Ala
(See Luvinca Spears).

Euf # 856 Overseer (--- ---)
BOWEN, John 23 m Ala

Mdwy # 930 Planter (16000-90000)
BOWEN, William B. 34 m Ga
Anna S. 5 f "

Euf # 573 Printer (300-700)
BOWERS, John E. 50 m Conn
Susan 40 f SC
Cally 11 f NC
Thomas 10 m "
John 7 m Ga
William 4 m "

Clay # 675 Farmer (550-500)
BOYD, Francis M. 37 m Ga
Mary 38 f NC
(Cont.)

(Clay # 675 cont.)
J. M. (Farmer) 15 m Ga
James M. 13 m Ala
E. M. 11 f "
John W. 8 m "
Jere S. 6 m "
S. A. 5 f "
A. L. 1 f "

Euf # 1135
BOYD, Mary 60 f Ga
(See J. P. Bell).

Euf # 746
BOYD, Nathan N. 14 m Ala
(See Geo. T. Loftis).

Euf # 884 Teacher
BOYER(?), Eugenia A. 22 f Ga
(See Henry Hooten).

Euf # 851 Teacher (--- 300)
BOYER, James B. 53 m Va
Mary 44 f Ga
Susan 15 f "
Mary 11 f "

Euf # 805 Farmer (1500-38000)
BOYKIN, Francis 35 m Ga
L. A. 28 f "
Sallie 8 f "

Luvl # 257 Carriage Maker (300-5000)
BOYKIN, James 22 m Ga
(See Henry Freeman).

Clay # 21 Prop. of hotel (5000-6000)
BOYLSTON, J. C. 60 m SC
E. C. 49 f "
E. T. 21 m Ala
(Clerk at hotel).
H. M. 16 m "
J. C. 14 m "
WOUTERS, John 35 m Hol
(Carriage trimmer, --- 3500)
PARKER, Wm. F. 34 m Ga
(Brick mason, 3500-300)
HOOFMAN, Rudolph 25 m Pru
(Coach painter).
EVANS, D. W. 22 m Ala
(Carriage maker).
EVANS, J. B. 20 m "
(Coach painter)
BREWER, L. B. 24 m SC
(Apprentice)

(Clay # 21 cont.)

TUCKER, John W. (Apprentice)	22	m	Va
BRADLEY, S.(Mechanic)	26	m	Ala
M. E. (Born Carolina?)	18	f	
HOOFMAN, F. G. (Mechanic, ----1500)	56	m	Pru
MILLS, U. W.(---500)	27	m	Ky

Clay # 102 Overseer

BRADDAM, R.	30	m	SC
Sarah	25	f	Ala
John	6	m	"
Narcissa	2	f	"
infant	1/12	m	"
infant	1/12	m	"

Euf # 1015 (1000-500)

BRADBERRY, Jane S.	42	f	SC
Sallie A.	20	f	Ala
Cornelia	15	f	"
Hariet C.	13	f	"
Virginia	11	f	"
John J.	9	m	"
Jasper A.	6	m	"
James W.	4	m	"

Euf # 1091 Overseer (--- ---)

BRADLEY, Daniel	37	m	Ga
Mary	32	f	"
Jas. P. (Student)	17	m	"
Elizabeth	15	f	"
Susan	13	f	"
John W.	11	m	"
Mary F.	9	f	"
George M.	3/12	m	Ala

Clay # 236 Mechanic (1000-2000)

BRADLEY, Ezekiel	30	m	Ala
Nancy A.	25	f	"
Robert A.	8/12	m	"
BENNETT, W. G.	23	m	"

Luvl # 257 Clerk (--- 1000)

BRADLEY, Henry	24	m	Ala

(See Henry Freeman).

Luvl # 264 Farmer (700-1000)

BRADLEY, Hobbs	31	m	Ala
Lucy A.	21	f	"
Ann E.	8/12	f	"

Clay # 179 Farmer (2100-3000)

BRADLEY, Robert	50	m	SC
Elizabeth	51	f	"

(Cont.)

(Clay # 179 cont.)

Geo. (Farmer)	21	m	Ala
John "	19	m	"
A. M. "	17	m	"
Jas. J. "	15	m	"
Martha Ann	12	f	"
TAYLOR, Robert T.	8	m	"

Clay # 21 Mechanic (--- ---)

BRADLEY, S.	26	m	Ala
M. E.	18	f	NC

(See J. C. Boylston).

Nwto # 577 Farmer (500-250)

BRADLEY, Salathiel	58	m	SC
Elizabeth	55	f	Ga
HOLMES, Jane	63	f	"
Lucy	18	f	"

Clay # 1239 Farmer (350-1500)

BRANCH, Charles J.	47	m	NC
Nancy	37	f	"
Winneford	16	f	Ala
Nancy	14	f	"
John W.	13	m	"
Hilliard	11	m	"
Christopher C.	9	m	"
Elmyra	5	f	"
Almyra	4	f	"

Clay # 62 Mechanic (--- ---)

BRANNON, John P.	45	m	Ga
Nancy G.	43	f	"
Jane	20	f	"
Sarah E.	18	f	"
Susan	16	f	"
Fannie	11	f	"
Wilmoth	7	f	"
James H.	5	m	"
Hattie	2	f	Ala

Euf # 145 Trader (3000-3500)

BRANNON, T. A.	46	m	SC
Julia M.	44	f	Ga
Thos. J. (Clerk)	23	m	"
Albert N.	16	m	"
Alex H.	14	m	Ala
Julia L.	12	f	"
James W.	10	m	"
B. W.	7	m	"
Lizzy C.	5	f	"
Louisa	30	f	"

Euf # 58 Clerk (--- ---)

BRANNON, W. J.	22	m	Ga

Euf # 149 Merchant (1500-2000)
BRANNON, Wm. B. 47 m SC
Mary A 35 f "
Mary W. 12 f "
Earnest 1 m Ala
Louisa 31 f SC
Wm. B. (Clerk) 18 m "

Mdwy # 983 Shoe Merchant (--- ---)
BRANTLEY, William 51 m Va
E. S. 36 f Ga
John 15 m "
Edward 14 m "
Tonsia (?) 12 m Ala
Henry C. 11 m "
Vigor 9 m "
Eugene 7 m "
Richard L. 4/12 m "

Euf # 214 Farmer (--- 100)
BRASSELL, Benj. 21 m Ga
Mary A. 23 f Ala
Sarah 3 f "
Missouri 1 f "
DUBOSE, Sarah 53 f SC
(200-100)

Euf # 545 Laborer (--- 100)
BRASWELL, Jesse 28 m Ga
Mary 28 f Ala
Robert 8 m "
Green 5 m "
Catherine 3 f "
Infant 4/12 m "

Nwto # 606 (900-300)
BRAY, Elizabeth 27 f Ga
John 5 m Ala
Mandy 3 f "
Henry 2 m "
Mitchell 8/12 m "

Euf # 155 Tin Dealer (-- 3000)
BRAY, John E. 33 m Conn
Sarah A 30 f "
John W. 8 m "
Frank H. 6 m "

Euf # 77 Merchant (4000-5000)
BRAY, Nathan M. 30 m Conn
Cathrine N. 22 f Ga

Euf # 76 Merchant (7500-30,000)
BRAY, William H. 39 m Conn
Mary B. 22 f Ga
Tade 4 f "
(Cont.)

(Euf # 76 cont.)
William H. 2/12 m Ala
Wells J. (Clerk) 26 m Conn
Martha 22 f "

Euf # 1387 Carpenter (--- ---)
BREWER, J. E. 28 m NY
Laura 24 f SC
James 4 m Ga
Louisa 2 f "

Clay # 214 Farmer (100-200)
BREWER, James 52 m Ga
Ann (---$1,800) 50 f "
S. S. (Farmer) 18 m "
Mary J. 13 f "
Johanna 11 f "
Josephine 6 f Ala
Isabella 18 f "

Euf # 678 Farmer (1000-350)
BREWER, John 23 m Ga
Melvina 22 f "
Noah F. 2 m Ala

Clay # 21 Apprentice (--- ---)
BREWER, L. B. 24 m SC
(Living in hotel)

Bfd # 1241
BRIDGER, Martha 10 f Ga
William 8 m "
George 4 m "
(See Frederick Newton)

Euf 859
BRIDGES, Eliz.(Idiotic) 38 f Ga
(See H. D. Cumbie).

Clay # 1238 Laborer
BRIDGES, John 15 m Ga
(See Crawford Newton).

Euf # 370 Laborer (--- 100)
BRIGHAM, Seth 40 m Ga
Mary R. 37 f Ala
Harriet J. 10 f "
Alexander A. 7 m "
Mary F. 5 f "
Martha L. 1 f "

Euf #1370 Stage Driver (---1700)
BRIGHT, James 48 m Va
Mary A. 35 f Ga
Richard H.(Farm hand) 17 m "
George W. " " 15 m "
Catharine A. E. 11 f "
Ellen 9 f "
(Cont.)

(Euf # 1370 cont.)
Mary A. 7 f Ga
James A. M. 6 m Ala
Martha 4 f Ga
Robert A. 1 m Ala
HUNTER, Elizabeth 87 f Ga

Flk # 395 Farmer (--- ---)
BRIGUS(?), John 35 m Ga
Mary 21 f "
Amanda 1 f "

Euf # 484 (---7,5000)
BRITT, Ann S. 46 f Ga
Edmund N. (Clerk) 20 m "
Eugenia V. 18 f "
James J. 15 m "
Francis A. 13 m Fla
William F. 11 m Ala
Martha E. 8 f "

Clay # 166 (200-9000)
BRITT, Elizabeth 36 f Ga
Mathew T.(2500,10000)17 m Ala
Sarah E. " " 13 f "
John T. " " 12 m "
Moses W. " " 9 m "
WHITE, Sarah 19 f "
MYERS, William 47 m SC
(Farmer).

Euf # 262 Carpenter (---200)
BRITT, Madison D. 24 m Ga
Frances 24 f Ala
Samuel 3 m "
Mary 1 f "

Luvl # 366
BROACH, Ann 28 f Ala
(See F. W. Eidson).

Luvl # 367 Farmer (1000-7000)
BROACH, William 35 m Ala
Nancy 33 f "
James 4 m "
Narcissa 3 f "
Levi 1 m "

Bkb # 776
BROADENAX, Martha 27 f Ala
(See John Alley).

Euf # 440 Laborer (-- --)
BROCK, Jacob 28 m Ala
(See McNamara's R.R. Gro.)

Luvl # 369 Farmer (600-250)
BROCK, James 37 m SC
(Cont.)

(Luvl # 369 cont.)
Martha J. 28 f SC
William 14 m "
Tempe 12 f Ala
Mary J. 10 f "
Lilly A. 8 f "
Benjamin 5 m "
Christian 1/12 f "

Luvl # 650 Farmer (600-250)
BROCK, James 37 m NC
Martha 33 f "
Wm. (Farmer) 15 m Ala
Pennie 13 f "
Mary 11 f "
Benjamin 8 m "
Elizabeth 5 f "

Euf # 173 Laborer
BROCK, William 19 m Ala
(See John Bailey).

Mt. A. # 893 Laborer (400-100)
BROOKS, Isaac 23 m Ga
Caroline 17 f "

Euf # 832 M.B. Minister (1600-1800)
BROOKS, R. B. 43 m SC
Martha 23 f Ga
Susan A. 19 f "
Nancy C. 17 f "
John H. (Farm hand) 16 m "
Solomon A. 14 m "
William H. 12 m "
BURNISS, M. C. 18 m "
(Farm hand).

Mt. A. # 892 Farmer (4000-3000)
BROOKS, Reese 45 m Ga
Eliza 42 f "
Eliza 16 f "
Benjamin H. 13 m "
Ruhama E. 12 f "
Emily L. 10 f "
Luella O. 8 f "
Reese D. 6 m "
William T. 5 m "
Brooks 3 m Ala
Brown 1 m "

Euf # 691
BROOKS, Richard 10 m Ga
(See John Forehand).

Euf # 173
BROOKS, S. P. 51 m Me
(See John Bailey).

Euf # 24
BROOKS, Susan 8 f Ga
(See Carlisle Terry)

Euf # 170 Civil Engineer
BROUGHTON, Ezekiel 39 m Eng
Sarah 30 f Ire
Jesse 2 m Ala

Euf # 147 Planter (50000-80000)
BROWDER, Isham C. 54 m NC
Mary A. 38 f Ala
Ann E. 16 f "
Hartwell H. 14 m "

Luvl # 290 Farmer
BROWN, Allen 23 m Ala
Malinda 22 f Ga
(See John Daniels).

Euf # 1052 Grocer
BROWN, C. H. 30 m NY
(See H. E. Jones).

Euf # 404 Overseer (--- 500)
BROWN, C. L. 34 m Ga
Mary M. 33 f SC
Mary E. 12 f Ala
John R. E. 3 m "
Cicero L. 1/12 m "

Flk # 448 Mechanic (500-200)
BROWN, F. R. 58 m SC
Mary 56 f "
Samantha C. 24 f Ala
Amanda 19 f "
Nancy 78 f SC
CLARK, Joseph 20 m Ala
(Farmer)

Euf # 1384 Bookkeeper (20,000)
BROWN, George H. 38 m NY
(No real estate, only personal property).

Euf # 1287 Farmer (--- 100)
BROWN, J. W. 32 m Ga
Louisa 20 f Ala

Euf # 59 Clerk (--- ---)
BROWN, James M. 22 m Ala
Baker, Chas. C. (Clk.) 17 m "

Bkb # 695 Farmer (1120-1000)
BROWN, Jesse 60 or 69(?) m Ga
Elizabeth 52 f Ga
Wenlock (Farmer) 20 m "
(Cont.)

(Bkb # 695 cont.)
James (Farmer) 18 m Ga
Elizabeth 14 f Ala
Nancy 9 f "

Euf # 335 Farmer (1000-400)
BROWN, John P. 50 m Ga
Julia 51 f "
Lydia 22 f Fla
Dorcas 24 f "
Jesse D. (Farmer) 18 m Ga
Henry " 16 m "
Sarah 12 f Ala

Euf # 1056 Farmer (14000-33000)
BROWN, John W. 61 m Ga
Martha 46 f "
James H. 22 m Ala
Louisa 16 f "
Martha C. 11 f "
DENNARD, Mary F. 13 f "

Euf # 1114 Carpenter (200-100)
BROWN, John W. 26 m NC
Fredericka 25 f Md
Julia 8 f Ala
Columbus 2 m "
infant 4/12 m "
BROWN, Wm. W. 21 m NC
(Wagoner)

Euf # 341 Farmer
BROWN, Joseph 17 m Ga
(See James M. Allen).

Euf # 93 Clerk (--- 2000)
BROWN, L. N.(?)(H.)? 30 m SC
Mary J. 24 f Ga
William H. 4 m Ala
Lovick 1 m "

Euf # 270
BROWN, Laura 16 f Ga
(See James A. Bell)

Euf # 772
BROWN, Nancy E. 18 f Ga
(See Wm. T. Pearson).

Euf # 520 Overseer (--- 3000)
BROWN, R. C. 32 m Ga
Delia 27 f "
Mary E. 14 f "
John L. 12 m Ala
Sarah J. 10 f Ga
James L. 8 m "
Frances L. 6 f "
Rosetta 2 f Ala
Robert 2/12 m "

Euf # 852 Mechanic (--- 1300)
BROWN, Reubin E. 33 m Ga
Hester C. 33 f "
Isham L. 6 m Ala
Julius F. 4 m "
Frances 2 f "
MARSHALL, Thomas 61 m SC
(Mechanic, 500-150)
Catharine O. 17 f Ga

Euf # 549 Laborer (--- ---)
BROWN, Thomas 17 m Ga
(See Wilson Deshazo).

Euf # 1131 Overseer (--- 250)
BROWN, Thomas J. 27 m Fla
Eliza 29 f SC
(Married within the year).

Txv # 1218 Farmer (--- 300)
BROWN, William L. 27 m Ga
Celie A. 30 f Ala
L. M. 13 m "
Thomas 9 m "
John W. 6 m "
Sarah A. 1 f "

Euf # 620 Farmer (300-250)
BROWNING, Archy 52 m SC
Sarah 51 f "

Txv # 1207 Farmer (--- 100)
BROWNING, Jesse 60 m SC
Jinsy 64 f "

Euf # 621 Farmer (400-100)
BROWNING, W. J. 39 m SC
Bethann 39 f Ala
Elizabeth 9 f "
Hariet J. 6 f "
John J. 4 m "
Margaret M. 2 f "
Lucy 1 f "

Euf # 997 Overseer (--- 35,000)
BRUNDRIDGE, Jesse M. 42 m Ga
Elizabeth M. 31 f "
Henry J. 10 m "

Euf # 1124 Farmer (21000-63000)
BRUNSON, Marion A. 52 m SC
Catharine 30 f "
Allice S. 10 f Ala
Mary E. 7 f "
James H. 4 m "
Ada 1 f "

Euf # 754 Occp. none (--- ---)
BRUTON(?), C. 25 m Ala
Elizabeth 20 f "
PARISH, M. 43 f "
CHAMPION, Ann E. 14 f NC

Euf # 793 Farmer (Insane)(1500-300)
BRYAN, Frederick 30 m Ga
Serintha 35 f "
Josephine 9 f Ala
Theophilus 7 m "
Margaret 5 f "
Henry 2 m "

Euf # 279
BRYAN, Marriah 22 f SC
(See John W. Johnston).

Euf # 792 Farmer (5000-25000)
BRYAN, Theophilus 61 m NC
Levina 40 f Ga
Joseph 11 m Ala
Sophronia 9 f "
Theophilus, Jr. 26 m Ga

Mt. A. # 811 Farmer (5000-200)
BRYAN, W. H. 37 m NC
J.T.(Farmer,400-4500) 35 m "
Margaret 35 f Ga

Euf # 819 Farmer (--- 500)
BRYAN, William 48 m Ga
Epsay 28 f "
Ann 13 f Ala
Frances 12 f "
Needham 7 m "
Epsay V. 5 f "
Josephine 4 f "
James 2 m "
HILL, Wm. (Laborer) 16 m "

Euf # 1356 Laborer (--- ---)
BRYANT, A. 50 m SC
Caroline 52 f "
Sarah 18 f "
Anna 16 f "
Catharine 14 f "
Mariah 20 f "

Txv # 1222
BRYANT, Alice 70 f Ga
(See William Holland).

Euf # 502 Farmer (1400-100)
BRYANT, Fred 30 m Ga
(Cont.)

(Euf # 502 cont.)
Lerintha 27 f Ala
Josephine 8 f "
Theophilus 6 m "
Margaret 4 f "
Henry 2 m "

Clay # 135 Farmer (--- 200)
BRYANT, J. G. 35 m NC
Annis 33 f SC
Lawson J. (Laborer) 15 m Ala
Celie 11 f "
G. A. 9 f "
Hinton G. 7 m "
John A. 4 m "
Benj. B. 1 m "
GANEY, Andrew 18 m Fla
(Farm Laborer).

Euf # 948 Farmer (3000-4000)
BRYANT, John C. 46 m Ga
Janett 42 f "
Jno. D. (Farmer) 20 m Ala
F. M. " 16 m "
David D. 14 m "
Mary J. 10 f "
Tabitha A. 3 f "

Clay # 659
BRYANT, Mary 22 f Ala
(See Gilbert McEachern).

Euf # 973 (--- ---)
BRYANT, Mary M. 36 f Ga
Amanda 15 f Ala
Eliza A. 13 f "
Benj. 9 m "
Neil 8 m "
James 6 m "

Bfd # 1253 Farmer (880-600)
BRYANT, Needham 44 m Ga
Elizabeth 43 f "
Wm. T. (Farmer) 15 m Ala
S. A. H. 13 f "
John C. 12 m "
Mary A. F. 11 f "

Clay # 125 Farmer (--- ---)
BRYANT, Thomas 60 m NC
Ruth 60 f "
Clark W. 23 m Ga
(Farmer, $150-$100)
Richard 19 m "
(Farmer, $150-$150)
Mary 21 f "
Marie 17 f "

Clay # 1123 Laborer (--- ---)
BRYANT, Thos. M. C. 26 m SC
(See James M. Hays).

Euf # 390 Overseer (--- ---)
BRYANT, William 25 m Ala
Obedience 23 f "
Ella 8/12 f "

Euf 947 Farmer (--- 2500)
BRYANT, William 44 m Ga
Epsay 35 f "
Mansfield(In school) 16 m Ala
Franklin " " 15 m "
Epsay 14 f "
Richard 13 m "
William 9 m "
Parker 8 m "
Mary 6 f "
Sarah 5 f "
Hellen 2 f "
George W. 4/12 m "

Flk # 466
BUCHANNON, Mary 65 f SC
(See Mary Alderman).

Euf # 867 (--- ---)
BUCKHALTER, D. 18 m SC
(See William H. Foy).

Txv # 1229 Farmer (1100-600)
BUCKLES, N. J. 45 m Ga
Mary 35 f SC
Mary F. 15 f Ga
James 14 m "
William Eli 11 m "
Alexander 5 m Ala
Nancy A. L. 7 f "
Joseph 3 m "
Sarah M. 1 f "

Euf 267 Lawyer (5000-5000)
BUFORD, James M. 31 m SC
Maldonetta C. 23 f Ala

Clay # 23 Lawyer (29000-30000)
BUFORD, Jefferson 49 m SC
E. H. (---4500) 28 f Pa
John R. 18 m Ala
Jefferson L. 17 m "
Mary A. 14 f "
Eliza Ann 12 f "

Euf # 659 (--- 1200)
BULGER, Creasy 50 f SC

Mt. A. # 803 (Continued).

(Mt. A. # 803 cont.).
BULLARD, Ann 60 f NC
(See Henry J. Channell).

Mt. A. # 798 Farmer (1500-2300)
BULLARD, Henry 40 m NC
Emily C. 42 f Ga
Jeremiah (Farmer) 17 m "
Martha M. 15 f "
Frances C. 10 f Ala
Thomas E. 8 m "
Georgia V. 6 f "
TURNER, Jas. (Farmer) 23 m Ga

Euf # 665 Laborer (--- 100)
BULLARD, James 40 m SC
Catharine 45 f NC
William 11 m Ala
Wilson 10 m "
Joseph 8 m "
Thomas 4 m "

Mt. A. # 799 Farmer (--- 250)
BULLARD, James F. 19 m Ga
Martha S. 19 f "
Mary F. 6/12 f Ala

Euf # 1396 (350-200)
BULLARD, Nancy 47 f Ga
HALES, Sarah 9 f Ala
William 7 m "

Mt. A. # 871
BULLARD, Nancy A. 60 f NC
(See Jefferson Channell).

Mt. A. # 894 (--- 220)
BULLARD, Newton L.C. 27 m Ga
Martha J. 27 f "
Priscilla A. E. 8 f Ala
James B. 7 m "
Samuel McP. 4 m "
Sarah M. 4/12 f "
TUCKER, Daniel T. 21 m Ga
(Farm Laborer).

Euf # 381 Lawyer (25000-50000)
BULLOCK, Edw. C. 36 m SC
Eliza 13 f Ala
Sally 8 f "
SNIPES, Marion 17 f "
(--- $18,000)

Euf # 1197 Farmer (--- 400)
BULLOCK, John 64 m Ga
Mary 40 f "
Ransom 14 m Ala
(Cont.)

(Euf # 1197 cont.)
Caroline 12 f Ala
John 8 m "
Lithy 5 f "
Georgia A. 1 f "
WILLIAMS, Thos. 17 m Ga
(Hireling).

Euf # 1267 Hireling
BULLOCK, William 19 m Ga
(See Thos. Bailey).

Bkb # 708
BUNTIN, Seaborn 7 m Ala
(See William M. James).

Euf # 1053 Carriage painter
BURCKLE, John 30 m Conn
(See John W. McAlister).

Euf # 617
BURIDINE, Ann 17 f Ala
James 13 m "
(See E. M. McGehee).

Euf # 74 Carriage painter
BURDINE, David M. 35 m NY
(See Chas. C. Thompkins).

Luvl # 568 (2500-15000)
BURKE, Jane J. 53 f Ga
Hardy (Farmer) 28 m Ala
Martha 23 f "
James 15 m "
Mary A. 13 f "
Georgia A. 13 f "
L. A. 11 f "

Euf # 115 Planter (500-200)
BURK, John R. 25 m Ga
Julia E. 25 f Ala
Laura L. 2 f "
Mary E. 7/12 f "

Euf # 1117 Physician (--- 400)
BURK, Thomas J. 41 m Va
Matilda F. 38 f "
John W. 14 m "
Ann M. 12 f "
Carey R. 9 m "
Virginia 7 f "
BURK, Wm. * (Doctor) 65 m "
BARR, Susan W. 52 f SC

Clay # 152 Farmer (800-1000)
(Cont.)

* $2,000 personal property.

(Clay # 152 cont.)
BURLISON, A. D. 46 m Ga
E. 44 f NC
N. A. 25 f Ala
Eliza J. 22 f "
L. G. (Farmer) 19 m "
James M. 11 m "
George C. 5 m "

Euf # 592
BURNHAM, Maron 14 m Ala
(See Wm. C. Espy).

Euf # 200 Farmer (5000-15000)
BURNLEY, J. B. 53 m SC

Euf # 832 Farm hand (--- ---)
BURNISS, M. C. 18 m Ga
(See R. B. Brooks).

Euf # 50 Grocer (1800-4000)
BURRUS, Charles 34 m Fr
HUBNER, Henry 22 m Ger.
(Clerk, from Hanover, Ger).

Euf # 334
BURTON, William A. 10 m Ala
(See Allen M. O'Hara).

Euf # 1236 Farmer (4000-15000)
BUSH, Council 43 m Ga
Rebecca 35 f Ala
Louis B. 17 m "
Ryan O. 13 m "
Dixon H. 11 m "
Rebecca R. 8 f "
William B. 15 m "
Emma 6 f "
John C. 2 m "
James E. 1 m "

Euf # 1233 Farmer (3500-6600)
BUSH, David 40 m Ga
Julia 38 f "
Epsey 15 f Ala
Americus 13 m "
Ann 9 f "
Seth 6 m "
Emma 4 f "
David A. 3/12 m "

Euf # 1234
BUSH, Francis M. 11 m Ala
(See Anthony Windham).

Euf # 1394 Overseer (--- 800)
BUSH, G. B. 38 m Ala
M. A. 34 f "
(Cont.)

(Euf # 1394 cont.)
Eliza 13 f Ala
James 11 m "
Sarah 8 f "
John E. 6 m "
Elizabeth 4 f "
Green 2 m "

Euf # 1195 Farmer (5000-13000)
BUSH, M. E. 28 m Ala
Elizabeth T. 28 f "
Mary J. 10 f "
Moses E. 3 m "
James A. 1 m "

Clay # 110
BUSH, Mary 5 f Tex
(See James Wall).

Euf # 1269 (1000-10,000)
BUSH, Nancy 46 f NC
Savannah 19 f Ala
Johnson 17 m "
Tyson 15 m "
Paulina 13 f "

Clay # 76
BUSH, Sarah A. 10 f Ala
(See James A. Vickers).

Euf # 1203 (1500-5000)
BUSH, Selina 28 f SC
Zack 10 m Ala
Frances 12 f "
Charles 8 m "

Euf # 320 Farmer (4000-15000)
Bush, W. M. J. 37 m Ga
Eliza A. 28 f "
James J. 14 m "
William V.(?) 12 m "
Isaac N. 10 m "
Thomas M. 8 m "
Woody F. 7 m Ala
Frances E. 1 f "

Euf # 524
BUSH, William M. 9 m Ala
(See Neil Morrison).

Euf # 23 Drayman (120-150)
BUSH, Zachariah 33 m Ala
Soprona M. 27 f NC(?)
Frances 6 f Tex
infant 6/12 m Ala

Bkb # 725
BUTLER, Elizabeth 60 f SC
(Cont.)

(Bkb # 725 cont.)
James F. Farmer 18 m Ala
Alifair 16 f "
Narcissa 14 f "
Saml. (Farmer,200-250) 70 m SC

Luvl # 281 Farmer (--- ---)
BUTLER, John 22 m Ala
Susan 19 f Ga
John W. 2 m Ala

Flk # 416 Farmer (80 ---)
BUTLER, Solomon 37 m NC
Frances 36 f "
William (Farmer) 16 m Ala
A. A. 9 m "
John 6 m "
Mary J. 3 f "
Martha A. 1 f "

Euf # 440 Stone Cutter
BUTLER, Thomas 21 m Ire
(See McNamara's R.R. Gro.)

Flk # 475
BUTLER, William 15 m Ala
(See O. C. Doster).

Bkb # 724 Farmer (--- 200)
BUTLER, William P. 25 m SC
Malinda 22 f Ala
William S. 4 m "
James D. 2 m "
George W. 3/12 m "

Luvl # 277 Physician (---1500)
BUTTER, G. W. 33 m Tenn
E. C. 22 f "
A. A. 3 f "
M. E. 2 f "
L. J. 6/12 f Fla

Euf # 55 Publisher (--- 2000)
BUTT, Joseph H. 34 m Ga

Euf 1096 (10,000-18,000)
BUTTS, Catharine 35 f Ga
Mortimer 14 m Ala
Estelle 9 f "
David 6 m "
Catharine 3 f "
Nelly 1 f "
HARRIS, Henry 62 m NC
(Overseer)

Txv # 1188 Farmer (1930-8500)
BUTTS, Charles 46 m Ga
Sarah A. 36 f Ala
(Cont.)

(Txv # 1188 cont.)
Amanda 17 f Ala
Phillip 14 m "
infant 1 m "

Txv # 1179 Farmer (200-200)
BUTTS, Solomon 53 m Ga
Sarah 38 f "
Ridonia 14 f Ala
Thomas 13 m "
Edward 12 m "
Henry J. 8 m "
James 6 m "
John 4 m "
STEWART, Ann P. 16 f "

Euf # 1164 Farmer (1900-3000)
BYNUM, James 47 m Ga
Nancy 38 f "
Wm. T. (In school) 16 m Ala
Mary E. 14 f "
Reubin 11 m "
James J. 8 m "
Nancy 7 f "
Sarah J. 6 f "
John W. 5 m "
Morgan 2 m "

Txv # 1232 Farmer (--- 250)
BYRD
BIRD, Allen 40 m NC
Sarah 20 f Ala
Margaret 17 f "
Alexr. (Farmer) 18 m "
Wm. J. " 20 m "
Richard 14 m "
Gracie 12 f "
Gilbert L. 10 m "
James B. 4 m "
Eli 1 m "

Euf # 618
BYRD
BIRD, Benj.F. (idiot) 21 m Ala
(See Young Wood).

Clay # 660 Farmer
Byrd,
Bird, Jackson 20 m Ala
(See Daniel McEachern).

Euf # 154 Occp. none
Byrd,
Bird, Jeremiah 62 m SC
SPURLOCK, Sarah 24 f Ga
John 8 m Ala
(Cont.)

(Euf # 154 cont.)
Nancy 4 f Ala
Columbus 2 m "

Euf # 1167 Farmer (--- 150)
CABINESS, Jesse 51 m Ga
Sarah 44 f "
Elizabeth 24 f "
George C. (Farmer) 20 m Ala
Georgia 10 f "
Claudia 6 f "
BLACK, Mary 22 f "
Joseph 8 m "

Euf # 837 Farmer (--- 5000)
CADE, Dozier 24 m Ga
Mary 24 f "
James 6 m Ala
George 1 m "
Dozier 17 m "
HALL, Emaline 34 f "

Euf # 836 Farmer (12000-45000)
CADE, James J. 44 m Ga
Susan 41 f "
James (Overseer) 22 m "
WITHERINGTON, Chas. M. 21 m "
(Farmer --- 100)
Ann A. 20 f "
Susan 1 f Ala

Luvl # 263 Mechanic (--- ---)
CAIN, Augustus W. 21 m Ga
Mary J. 17 f Ala

Euf # 1010 (--- 300)
CAIN, Mary 40 f Ga
Franklin (Farmer) 18 m "
Abijah " 16 m "
Mason 14 m "
Elizabeth 12 f "
William 10 m Ala
John 7 m "
Mary 5 f "
Thomas 2 m "
HENRY, Amey 79 f Ga

Euf # 1051 Overseer
CALHOUN, Munroe 22 m Ga

Mdwy # 949 Student of Medicine
CALLOWAY, Daniel 20 m Ala
(See J. W. Bledsoe).

Mdwy # 1008 Farmer (4000-12000)
CALLOWAY, Daniel 61 m Ga
(Cont.)

(Mdwy # 1008 cont.)
Elizabeth 60 f Ga
Lucinda 26 f "
Frances Jane 25 f "
Caroline 23 f "
Emeline 22 f Ala
Benjamin (Farmer) 21 m "
William " 18 m "

Euf # 409 Brick maker (5000-6000)
CALLOWAY, J. S. 35 m Ga
Malissa A. 30 f "
Mary E. 11 f Ala
Narcissa L. 10 f "
Mitty K. 8 f "
Julia S. 3 f "

Euf # 434 Coach Maker (--- ---)
CAMERON, Alexr. 52 m Scot
Nancy 30 f SC
Henrietta 13 f Ala
Gracey 11 f "
Isabella 6 f "
Mary A. 4 f "
Angenetta 2 f "
Lemuel 4/12 m "

Euf # 557 Laborer (--- ---)
CAMERON, James W. 31 m NC
Matilda 30 f Ala
Greenberry 9 m "
Catherine 5 f "
Florida 4 f "
Minerva 4/12 f "

Mdwy # 966 Farmer (4000-10000)
CAMERON, John F. 31 m NC
Rebecca 22 f Ala
Haywood 2 m "
Eliza 1/12 f "
Christian 70 f NC

Euf # 238 Occp. none (200-50)
CAMERON, John W. 36 m NC
Matilda 29 f Ga
John 12 m Ala
Nancy 10 f "
Allen 4 m "
Mary A. 2 f "
PHILLIPS, John 37 m Ire
(Blacksmith)
DALEY, William 35 m "
(Laborer)
SHORTER, Mary B. 63 f Ga
(Estate: $12,000-$30,000)

Mdwy # 1085 (2000-7000)
CAMERON, Nancy 63 f NC
Mary 72 f "

Euf # 144 Teamster (100- 1500)
CAMERON, Thos. M. 23 m SC
Ann 14 f Ga
HALL, Jno. (Laborer) 23 m SC
DENBY, Matilda 40 f NC
CAMERON, Elizabeth 17 f Ga

Luvl # 385 Farmer (4000-40000)
CAMPBELL, A. D. 42 m NC
M. L. 35 f "
Emily M. 11 f SC
Beecher 9 m "
Maria J. 6 f "
Elvira 4 f "
Sarah J. 2 f NC

Flk # 492
CAMPBELL, Alex 11 m Ala
(See Needham Sutton).

Flk # 433 (750 ---)
CAMPBELL, Cornelius 46 f Ga
Cici A. 17 f Ala
Nancy A. 15 f "
Cinthia 13 f "
Duncan 12 m "
Amelia A. 11 f "
Daniel 7 m "

Bfd # 1254 Physician & Farmer (5,000-14000)
CAMPBELL, D. G. 48 m NC
A. J. 29 f "
Mary S. 6 f Ala
C. C. 4 m "
Nancy J. 1 f "
BATEMAN, Mary L. 19 f "
WOOD, Josephine 19 f "
(Teacher)

Euf # 730
CAMPBELL, Daniel 7 m Ala
(See Christopher C. Teal)

Flk # 479 (500-3000)
CAMPBELL, Elizabeth 65 f SC
Joab (Farmer) 28 m Ala
(250 ---)

Nwto # 632 (280-200)
CAMPBELL, Elizabeth 46 f Ga
John J. (Farmer) 25 m "
Thomas 15 m Ala
Sarah 12 f "

Flk # 478 Farmer
CAMPBELL, Jacob 30 m Ala
Mary 28 f NC
William B. T. 8 m Ala
Daniel A. G. 6 m "
Christopher C. 5 m "
J. E. 4 m "

Nwto # 627 Farmer (--- 175)
CAMPBELL, Jacob 26 m SC
Martha 29 f Ala
Britton 14 m "
Jacob 12 m "
Susanna 8 f "
William 6 m "
Q. A. 3 f "
F. W. 1 m "
Susanna 64 f SC

Luvl # 651 Farmer
CAMPBELL, Norman 75 m Scot
(See James S. Baxter).

Flk # 467 Farmer (200-100)
CAMPBELL, Westley 45 m SC
Charlotte C. 22 f Ga
Elizabeth A. 10 f Ala
Arazibur 8 f "
John 6 m "
Erastus 4 m "
Java 2 m "

Txv # 1192 (1200-3500)
CANNON, P. N. 56 f Ga
TRAMMELL, Eliza J. 23 f "
John H. (Farmer) 20 m Ala
J.A.P.J. 17 f "
GARY, Sarah F. (-700) 30 f Fla
Henry D. 8 m Ala
Fannie 5 f "

Euf # 525 Merchant (2500-1000)
CANNON, Thos. J. 31 m SC

Luvl # 377 Farmer (2500-6000)
CAPEL, James 60 m NC
Mary 45 f "
Jackson (Farmer) 20 m Ala
Frances 21 f Ga
Catherine 14 f Ala
Alexander 13 m "
Margaret 12 f "
Christopher 10 m "
Charles 5 m "

Mdwy # 964 Farmer (--- 1400)
CARAWAY, James 33 m Ga
(Cont.)

(Mdwy # 964 cont.)
R. E. 26 f Ga
Susan 9 f "
Frances C. 7 f "
Mary J. 5 f "

Luvl # 354 Farmer (3600-10000)
CARD, Leonard 41 m Ga
Camilla S. 32 f "
Mary F. 8 f "
Ida 6 f "
Abram D. 5 m "
McGEE, Jerry (Farmer) 22 m "

Mdwy # 982
CARDIN, Phoebe C. 18 f Ga
Mary 1 f Ala
(See H. D. Tidwell).

Euf # 20-20 Cabt. maker(--200)
CARGIL, Austin C. 29 m Vt
Priscilla 25 f Ga
Orlando J. 4 m "
William A. 2 m "
Wiley 1 m Ala
Mary 1/12 f "

Euf # 260 Tanner (10000-10000)
CARGILE, Thomas 58 m Ga
Louisa A. 50 f "
Wm. (Appt. Machinist) 17 m Ala
Thomas A. 22 m "
Benj. F. 13 m "

Euf # 936 (2000-5000)
CARIKER, Mary M. 53 f Ga
Jas. H. (Farmer) 23 m "
Wm. (Student) 19 m "
John 14 m "
Fanny 12 f "

Euf # 466 Machinist (---5000)
CARLISLE, Seaborn 42 m Ga
Winney 37 f "
Louisa 17 f "
Mary 14 f Ala
Martha 12 f "
Sarah 10 f "
Frances 8 f "
Amanda 6 f "
James 3 m "
infant 4/12 f "

Clay # 78 Gun smith (--- ---)
CARMICHAEL, Hugh 47 m NC
Flora 46 f "
William H. 13 m Ala

Mdwy # 957 Physician
CARMICHAEL, John 27 m SC
(See William E. Smith).

Clay # 233
CARMICHAEL, Nancy J. 10 f Ala
(See Abraham Prim).

Flk # 428 Farmer (500-200)
CARPENTER, R. N. 46 m NC
Nancy 35 f "
Nelson (Farmer) 19 m "
William " 18 m "
Dwight 16 m "
Gillain 14 m "
Ellen 10 f "
Margaret 8 f Ala
Susan 1 f "

Clay # 1111 Farm Laborer
CARR, George 20 m Ala
(See Malcom McEachern).

Txv # 1151 Farm Laborer
CARR, Jackson 17 m Ala
(See Wiley Glover).

Clay # 159 Farmer (530-800)
CARR, James 50 m SC
Catherine 72 f "
E. E. 22 f Ga

Euf # 914 Hireling
CARR, James 16 m Ala
(See Sarah L. Roberts).

Clay # 1116 Farmer (450-400)
CARR, James S. 25 m Fla
Elizabeth 24 f Ala
Sarah C. 7 f "
Frances L. 4 f "
Michael W. 1 m "

Txv # 1161 (--- 100)
CARR, Lucretia 36 f SC
Geo. W. (Farm Laborer) 18 m "
Jos. M. " " 16 m Ala
Elizabeth J. 12 f "
Wm. H. A. 3 m "

Nwto # 602 Farmer (600-600)
CARR, Trion 42 m SC
L. A. 30 f Ga
John 12 m Ala
David 8 m "
(Cont.)

(Nwto # 602 cont.)
Thomas A. 6 m Ala
Mary 1 f "

Clay # 44 In jail
CARROLL, Edward 44 m Ire

Euf # 416 Farmer (500-250)
CARROLL, Isham 46 m NC
Eliza 33 f "
Frances 6 f Ga
Daniel 5 m "
Mary 4 f "
Eliza 2 f Ala
Susan 7/12 f "
PETERSON, Permelia 16 f Ga
John (Student) 28 m "

Txv # 1197 Farmer (1280-500)
CARROLL, John 46 m SC
Elizabeth 35 f "
William (Farmer) 23 m Ala
John " 19 m "
Mary C. 16 f "
Stephen 14 m "
Robert 12 m "
Elizabeth 10 f "
Nancy 8 f "
Charity 4 f "
LEE, Ann 15 f "

Euf # 654 Farmer (600-500)
CARROLL, Robert 41 m SC
Elizabeth 36 f "
Rufus R. 15 m Ala
Irvin 13 m "
Sarah A. 11 f "
Narcissa 9 f "
John 6 m "
Mary 3 f "
Willis 6/12 m "
ARGRAN(?), Jane 56 f SC
(--- 3,000)

Flk # 500 Farmer (900-200)
CARROLL, Thomas 61 m NC
Sarah 51 f "
Frederick D. 15 m Ala
Nancy 13 f "

Mt. A. # 841 Farmer (--- 100)
CARSON, John 36 m NC
Sarah 40 f "
Wiley 7 m "
Nancy 5 f "
Samuel 2 m Ala

Euf # 993 Overseer (--- ---)
CARSON, Thomas 30 m Ga
Sarah 25 f "
Wesley 3 m Ala
Mary 2 f "
Sarah 4/12 f "

Clay # 1112 (--- 180)
CARTER, Elizabeth 18 f Ga
Nicholas 23 m "
(Married within the year).
(See Missouri Dickens).

Euf # 10-10 Merchant (--- ---)
CARTER, John J. 28 m Ala
(See Geo. W. Porter).

Euf # 1256
CARTER, Mary 55 f SC
(See John Watson).

Clay # 178 Pauper in poorhouse
CARTER, Samuel 78 m Va

Clay # 1240 Farmer (--- 200)
CARTER, Thomas 49 m SC
Elizabeth 42 f "
Elizabeth 22 f Ga
Thomas (Farmer) 20 m "
Robert 18 m "
Julia 16 f "
M.A.M. 13 f "
Z.P. 10 m "
Jefferson J. 8 m "
Anna L. 6 f "
Buchanon 3 m "
Benj. L. F. 1 m Ala

Mdwy # 994 Mechanic (--- 1200)
CARTER, William 52 m Ga
Elizabeth 38 f "
Mary J. 17 f Ala
William J. 15 m "

Mdwy # 1104 Farmer (1350-9000)
CARTLEDGE, Edmund 25 m Ga
Rhoda 20 f "
Euphemia 6 f Ala
Edmund 4 m "
Green 1 m "

Mdwy # 1016
CARTLEDGE, Green T. 1 m Ala
(See Green T. Thornton).

Clay # 13 Farmer (2000-10000)
CARTHERS, James L. 56 m NC
Lurena (4000-15000) 60 f SC

Clay # 1
CARUTHERS, John W. 22 m Ga
(See H. D. Clayton).

Euf # 202
CARTHERS, Louisa M. 14 f Ga
(See C. J. Pope).

Euf # 1-1 Clerk (2000-200)
CARVER, A. J. 32 m Tenn
Jane 29 f Ga
William H. 7 m Ala
Mary A. C. 5 f "
Andrew J. 3 m "
Himmelia A. J. 10/12 f "

Euf # 128 Carriage Maker (7000-500)
CARY (CORY?), Amos 31 m NJ
Mary A. 25 f Ga
Mary 6 f "
Fanny L. 1 f "
CAULDWELL, F. M. 21 m "
(Carriage Trimmer)
FENWICK, Fletcher 26 m Va
(Carriage Maker)

Euf # 862 Boat Maker
CARY, G. B. 45 m NC
(See H. J. Irby).

Euf # 1367 Lawyer (--- 6000)
CARY, Joseph M. 26 m Ga
HUNTER, H. M. 47 m "
(Physician, --- 3000)

Luvl # 525 Farmer (200-100)
CASEY, Alfred 29 m NC
Mary 27 f Ala
Rosetta 8 f "
Elizabeth 2 f
(Born Kansas Territory).

Nwto # 557
CASEY, Annie 37 f Ala
Matilda 20 f "
Benj. F. (Farmer) 18 m "
Huey 4 m "
(See Lafayette Ketchum).

Mt. A. # 884 Farmer (600-300)
CASEY, Hampton 36 m NC
Hepsy 38 f "
Sarah A. 16 f Ala
Asbury 14 m "
James 12 m "
William 10 m "
(Cont.)

(Mt. A. # 884 cont.)
Mary 7 f Ala
Virginia 5 f "
Daniel 3 m "
Calvin 7/12 m "

Mt. A. # 885 Farmer (300-290)
CASEY, James 78 m NC
Nancy 51 f SC
DESHAZO, Mary 15 f Ala

Nwto # 622 Farmer (900-200)
CASEY, James, Jr. 33 m NC
Mary 32 f Ga
Nancy 13 f Ala
John W. 11 m "
Alex 9 m "
Boldin 2 m "

Euf # 1102 Merchant (1000-1000)
CASEY, John 35 m Ire
Mary A. 34 f "
Theresa 26 f "

Luvl # 524
CASEY, Mary 39 f NC
(See Nancy Tilman).

Euf # 1154 Overseer (--- 300)
CASON, James 56 m NC
Sarah 40 f Ga
James H. 21 m Ala
Sarah 11 f "

Mt. A. # 833
CATENHEAD, Elizabeth 11 f Ala
(See T. W. King).

Clay # 232 Farmer (500-150)
CATES, John 30 m SC
Amanda 35 f "
A. T. 14 m "
William J. 12 m "
John W. 10 m "
S. E. 8 f Ga
James S. 5 m Ala
Mary 1 f "

Euf # 577 Lawyer (39000-50000)
CATO, Lewis L. 38 m Ga
Martha 30 f "
William 8 m Ala
Susan 6 f "
Louisa 2 f "
Martha 75 f Va

Mdwy # 1052 Farmer (800-500)
CATO, William 28 m Ga
(Cont.)

(Mdwy # 1052 cont.)
Lucy 79 or 19 f NC
Mary 45 f Ga
Sallie 35 f "
Lucinda 26 f "

Mt. A. # 751 Farmer (--- 200)
CATTENHEAD, Ivey P. 40 m Ga
Sarah 42 f SC
Powell K. 14 m Ala
John F. M. 12 m "
W. W. 10 m "
Phoebe E. 8 f "
Sarah 5 f "
James J. 5 m "

Euf # 54 Steamboat clerk
CATTEVILLE, E. L. 23 m Fr
(See A. T. Locke).

Euf # 128 Carriage Trimmer
CAULDWELL, F. M. 21 m Ga
(See Amos Cary).

Euf # 847 (--- 4000)
CAWTHORN, C. G. 50 f Ga
Martha S. 15 f "
(--- 4000)
William W. 22 m "
(Clerk, --- 4000)

Euf # 393 Farmer(1500-2000)
CAUTHORN, J. A. J. 27 m Ala
Elizabeth 26 f Fla
Ann 9 f "
Butler M. 7 m "
Roseanna G. 6 f "
William W. 4 m "
Julia A. 2 f Ala

Clay # 235 Farmer (--- ---)
CAUTHORN, J. W. 25 m Ala
Nancy J.(----12,000) 28 f Fla
William J. 5 m Ala
Thomas M. 3 m "

Euf # 846 Ambrotypist (---3000)
CAWTHORN, S. J. S. 24 m Ala
E. L. 20 f "
E. W. 8/12 m "

Euf # 849
CAWTHORN, Sarah E. 12 f Ala
(See Seaborn Jones).

Euf # 116 Clerk (Rus. Poland)
CHAMANKY, David 39 m Pol
(See H. Bernstein).

Luvl # 387 Farmer (--- ---)
CHAMBERS, I. H. 48 m SC
Malinda 38 f "
Martha A. 24 f Ala
Jane 22 f "
Louisa 20 f "
Amanda 16 f "
William 14 m "
Werby 12 m "
Isaac 10 m "
Cinderella 8 f "
Mary 6 f "
Catherine 4 f "
Leuzer 2 f "

Euf # 74 Carriage Maker
CHAMBERS, James H. 23 m Ohio
(See Chas. C. Thompkins).

Luvl # 370
CHAMBERS, Joseph 26 m Ala
(See Wm. R. Pool).

Txv # 1141 Farmer (--- 400)
CHAMBERS, L. D. 53 m SC
Mary A. 30 f "
Patsy F. 12 f Ala
Irena E. 10 f "
William M. 5 m "
M. Frances 4 f "
L. D. 3 m "

Euf # 1065 Tailor (300-200)
CHAMBERS, R. A. 24 m Ga
Margaret 24 f Mass
James 3 m Ga
Robert 1 m Ala
Urias 5/12 m "

Euf # 165 Planter & Lawyer
(45,000-90,000)
CHAMBERS, William H. 33 m Ga
Ann 29 f "
T. H. 12 m "
W. L. 8 m "
P. F. 6 m Ala
M. J. 3 f "
R. A. 6/12 m "

Euf # 754
CHAMPION, Ann E. 14 f NC
(See C. Bruton).

Euf # 752 Farmer (1000-300)
CHAMPION, William 43 m Ga
Ann E. 38 f "
Uriah F. 12 m "

Euf # 256 (--- 100)
CHANDLER, Nelson 45 m SC
Permelia 35 f Ga
James (Laborer) 17 m Ala
John J. 14 m "
Benj. T. 12 m "
William N. 8 m "
Ava J. 4 f "
Virginia 1 f "

Mt. A. # 803 Farmer (1200-530)
CHANNELL, Henry J. 39 m SC
Martha 31 f NC
F.A.R. 13 f Ga
Eliza C. 11 f "
Sarah J. 9 f Ala
Martha E. 7 f "
James H. 5 m "
H.C. 1 f "
BULLARD, Ann 60 f NC

Mt. A. # 872 Farmer (1800-500)
CHANNELL, James 36 m SC
R.A. 30 f Ga
Sinthia 70 f SC
UPTON, Rebecca 46 f "
Louisia 14 f Ga
CULPEPPER, Elijah 18 m "
(Farm Laborer).

Mt. A. # 871 Farmer (1200-900)
CHANNELL, Jefferson 39 m SC
Martha 37 f Ga
P.A. 14 f "
Caroline 11 f "
Jane 9 f Ala
Martha E. 6 f "
James H. 4 m "
Cornelia 2 f "
BULLARD, Nancy A. 60 f NC

Mt. A. # 843
CHANNELL, Susan 25 f Ga
(See Zachariah Wilkie)

Euf # 1106 Clerk
CHAPMAN, Henry 17 m Ga
(See John F. Treutlen).

Mdwy # 971 Merchant (---1100)
CHAPMAN, Thos. 32 m NC
C.H. 17 f Ga

Euf # 408 Ditcher (200-260)
CHARAN(?),Michael 52 m Ire
Michael, Jr. 28 m Eng
(Ditcher).

Euf # 90 Clerk
CHERRY, Robert 25 m Ga
(See H. P. Pratt).

Euf # 1171 Farmer (500-300)
CHESTNUT, Mitchell 51 m NC
Sarah 41 f Ga
Kitty Ann 16 f Ala
James W. 14 m "
John N. 12 m "
Mitchell H. 10 m "
Sarah R. 7 f "
Elizabeth S. 5 f "
Elijah Z. 5 m "
Tucker 2 m "

Mt. A. # 794 Farmer (150-125)
CHILDERS, Abner G. 27 m Ga
Elizabeth 27 f "
William 7 m Ala
John 3 m "
Nancy 1 f "

Euf # 679 Farmer (600-200)
CHILDERS, Elijah 26 m Ala
(See John Potts).

Mt. A. # 793 Farmer (150-125)
CHILDERS, James F. 33 m Ga
Mary 24 f "
Sarah 7 f Ala
Margaret 5 f "
Ella A. 3 f "
Drury N. 4/12 m "

Luvl # 252 Farmer (2000-1200)
CHILDS, Elijah 45 m NC
Nancy 43 f "
Penelope 20 f "
Nancy 18 f "
Mary J. 16 f "
Lilly A. 14 f Ala
Lydia 12 f "
Elizabeth 10 f "
William E. 7 m "
John M. 4 m "
STOKES, John S. 19 m "
(Farmer)

Luvl # 352 Farmer (--- ---)
CHISHOLM, Walter C. 22 m Ga
(See Catherine Currie).

Mt. A. # 847 Farmer (1000-600)
CHITWOOD, James 51 m Ga
Frances E. 35 f "
(Cont.)

(Mt. A. # 847 cont.)

Louis L.	18 m Ga
Emma A.	10 f Ala
James T.	9 m "
Frances A.	6 f "

Mdwy # 986 Farmer (8700-25000)

CHRISTIAN, Lewis	35 m SC
Frances	30 f Ga
Elizabeth	12 f Ala
Octavia	10 f "
Alice	8 f "
Ridonia	6 f "
Medora	4 f "
Ila	1 f "

Euf # 850 Tiner(?) (--- 100)

CHRISTOPHER, F. M.	31 m Ga
Sarah	28 f "
Marion W.	10 m "
Amanda C.	4 f "

Euf # 996 Farmer (1200-1300)

CLARK, James	28 m Ga
Amanda	30 f "

Clay # 209 Farmer (8000-17000)

CLARK, James	68 m SC
Harriett	65 f "
Mary (--- 6000)	45 f "
DANFORTH, Mary	18 f Ga
Angilla	16 f "

Luvl # 289 Farmer (2000-650)

CLARK, James R.	49 m SC
Dorcas	26 f Ala
Margaret	5 f "
Benj. C.	2 m "
William F.	1 m "
GRUBBS, Elizabeth	26 f SC

Flk # 406 Farmer (--- ---)

CLARK, James S.	37 m SC
Sophia	33 f "
Asa A.	12 m "
Laughlin	11 m "
J. C. W.	10 m "
John L.	8 m "
David D.	6 m "
Nancy C.	4 f "
Harriett E.	1 f "

Euf # 1142 Farmer (2000-1000)

CLARK, John	56 m Ga
Elizabeth	48 f "
Elizabeth	20 f SC
Missouri	18 f Ala

(Cont.)

(Euf # 1142 cont.)

John W. (Farmer)	17 m Ala
Vincent G.	12 or 13 m "
Mary C.	10 f "
ALLEN, William C.	9 m "

Euf # 319 Farmer (800-300)

CLARK, John G.	49 m SC
Lucinda L.	44 f Ga
William T. (Farmer)	26 m "
Martha C.	16 f Ala
Jane L.	14 f "
Lucinda E.	12 f "
Evaline	2 f "

Euf # 21 Merchant (15000-37000)

CLARK, John W.	35 m SC
Mary E.	29 f Ala
James	9 m "
Hatty	6 f "
John	4 m "
Frank	2/12 m "
WARREN, Sarah E.	18 f "
LEAIRD, Andrew J.	12 m "

Euf # 115 Farmer (400-5,000)

CLARK, Jonah	43 m NC
Ann	42 f "
Harris N.	16 m "
Cornelia H.	14 f SC
Benj. W.	12 m "
Emma	11 f "
Lucinda	9 f "
Preston B.	3 m Ala

Flk # 448 Farmer

CLARK, Joseph	20 m Ala

(See F. R. Brown).

Luvl # 295

CLARK, Kate	7 f Ala
Sally	2 f "

(See Emanuel Cox).

Nwto # 581 Farmer (1200-300)

CLARK, Lewis B.	30 m Ga
Nancy	20 f "
Elizabeth	1 f "

Euf # 1346 Farmer (800-10,600)

CLARK, Marion S.	44 m Ga
Mary	18 f Ala
Beatrice	14 f "
Narcissa M.	11 f "
James M.	7 m "
Elizabeth M.	5 f "
Luler	1 f "

Euf # 1143 (--- ---)
CLARK, Warren 23 m Ala
Hariet 19 f "
Ulalia 7/12 f "

Clay # 37 Merchant (5000-50000)
CLARK, Whit 33 m SC

Txv # 1228 Farm Laborer (---150)
CLARK, William 29 m Ga
Harriett 26 f SC
James 11 m Ala
Elizabeth 9 f "
John 4/12 m "
Malissa 6 f "
Sallie 3 f "

Euf # 186
CLARK, William H. 20 m Ga
(Mechanic)
HAGAMAN, Stinson 40 m NJ
(Cabinet maker)
EVERETT, John 22 m Fla
(Moulder)

Flk # Farmer (1200-150)
CLAYTON, Isaac 63 m Ga
Susan 60 f SC
John (Farmer) 22 m "
Marshall " 19 m "
S. A. E. 16 f "
ALDERMAN, Mary 38 f Ga
(Note: Mary Alderman should be with household # 466).

Clay # 1 Lawyer - planter (12000-25000)
CLAYTON, H. D. 33 m Ga
V.V. 27 f SC
J.A. 5 m Ala
S.E.B. 7 f "
Thomas N. 1 m "
H.D., Jr. 3 m "
J.C. 36 m Ga
(Planter, 8000-20000)
CARUTHERS, John W. 22 m Ga
(--- 1,000)
PAULLIN, J. S. 23 m Ala
(M. Bapt. Minister)
WOOD, William D. 23 m "
(Lawyer - surveyor)

Euf # 218
CLEGHORN, Abigail 18 f Ala
Henry 17 m "
Elizabeth 12 f "
(Cont.)

(Euf # 218 cont.)
Anna 10 f Ala
(See William Barnes).

Clay # 59 Shoemaker (--- ---)
CLEM (?), J. T. 29 m Ga
Lucretia 21 f "

Euf # 1218 Farmer (--- 100)
CLEMENTS, James 22 m Ga
Sarah 25 f "
Jefferson 3 m Ala
Mary 1 f "

Euf # 1244 (850-200)
CLEMENTS, Martha 43 f Ga
Wm. (Hireling) 14 m "
Wesley " 19 m "
Joseph " 17 m "
Eliza 15 f "
Martha 13 f "
Elias 9 m "
Tabitha 7 f "
Isaac 5 m "
JESTER, Thomas 16 m "

Euf # 148 Merchant (5500-10000)
CLEMENTS, P. R. 53 m Ga
Martha A. 49 f "
William A. (Teacher) 24 m "
(5,500-10,000)
Matthew W. (Student) 17 m "
E. M. 12 f "

Euf # 344
CLEMENTS, Rachael 45 f Ga
Lucinda 17 f "
(See Charles Hall).

Euf # 203 Physician
CLEMENTS, Westley 30 m Ga
Tennie 24 f "
William P. 5 m "
Thomas 3 m "
Elizabeth 7/12 f "

Euf # 1219 Farmer (--- 50)
CLEMENTS, William 25 m Ga
Lucinda 23 f "
Eliza O. 11/12 f Ala

Euf # 1220 Farmer (2200-3000)
CLEMENTS, William, Sr. 58 m SC
Eliza 50 f "
Clement (Farmer) 19 m Ga
Thomas 17 m "
(Cont.)

(Euf # 1220 cont.)
Joseph 14 m Ga
Henry 11 m "
BATTLE, Elizabeth 9 f "

Euf # 1146 Hireling (--- 100)
CLEMONS, Jackson 22 m Ga
Elizabeth 19 f Ala
TATE, Sarah 53 f Ga

Euf # 1030 Farmer (--- 5000)
COBB, Franklin 33 m Ga
Nancy 25 f Ala
Josephine 6 f "
Georgian 2 f "
Mary E. 2/12 f "
FAISON, Nancy 78 f Ga

Euf # 1121 Planter (3500-8000)
COBB, Hariet W. 47 f Ga
Carey L. 14 m "
Harriet W. 10 f Ala
William H. C. 8 m "
McClain A. 7 f "

Euf # 635 Farmer (200-100)
COBB, J. G. 28 m Ga
Matilda 25 f "
James P. 5 m Ala
Mary A. 3 f "
Nancy J. 1 f "

Mdwy # 959 Planter (8000-17000)
COBB, Jacob 74 m Ga
Henrietta 83 f SC

Mdwy # 1025 Farmer (2000-15000)
COBB, James A. 44 m Ga
E. J. 27 f "
Winfield 11 m Ala
Rachael L. 8 f "
Julia E. 6 f "
James 8/12 m "

Euf # 1029 Farmer (5300-30000)
COBB, Joseph 60 m Ga
Elizabeth 50 f "
Jacob (Farmer,---200) 24 m Ala
Thos. J. " " 20 m "
Anna M. 14 f "
Henrietta 11 f "
COOK, Deverux(?) 40 f "

Euf # 1088 Overseer (--- 400)
COBB, Joshua 28 m Ga

Mdwy # 963 Farmer (1000-3000)
(Cont.)

(Mdwy # 963 cont.)
COBB, W. D. 38 m Ga
Mary 29 f SC
Jacob 11 m Ala
Alex 7 m "
Franklin 5 m "
Henrietta 4 f "
James 1 m "

Clay # 93 Planter (1900-3000)
COCHRAN, B. L. 29 m SC
Cornelia 22 f Ala
G. C. 11/12 m "
CRYMES, George P. 16 m "
HALL, David 10 m "

Euf # 1340 Ret. Lawyer & Planter
(45000-135,000)
COCHRAN, John 48 m Tenn
Alfred W. 11 m Ala
John M. 9 m "
Marion 6 m "

Euf # 970 Merchant (--- 15,000)
CODY, Michael 32 m Ga
Mary E. 5 f Ala
Martha A. 3 f "
Sarah F. 2 f "
Francis C. (Clerk) 22 m Ga
CODY, Benj. (hireling)22 m "
(--- 300)
Melmon (hireling) 19 m "

Euf # 969
CODY, Philvea 17 f Ga
(See J. C. Kendrick).

Mdwy # 934 Overseer (--- 100)
COFIELD, Nathan 33 m Ga
Martha 32 f "
Almeda 10 f "
Elizabeth 9 f "
Elijah 7 m "
Nelson 6 m "
Alice 2 f "

Euf # 1118 (--- 1000)
COHEN, Elizabeth 42 f Ala
Daniel 12 m "
Matilda 8 f "
Susan 7 f "
Henry 3 m "
Julia 15 f "

Clay # 186
COHEN, James 22 m Ala
(See Lewis D. Ward).

Euf # 1268 Farmer (--- 300)
COKER, Thos. G. 27 m Ala
Jane 21 f "
Sarah 1 f "

Euf # 1040 Overseer (--- 7500)
COKER, Thos, L. 41 m Ga
Mary H. 34 f "
Martha E. 15 f "
Joseph C. 14 m "
Henry H. 11 m "
Richard P. 8 m "
Kate 1 m "

Euf # 442 (11,000-27,000)
COLBY, Charlotte 42 f Ga
Mary 14 f "
Ann 12 f Ala
Susan 10 f Ga
John 8 m Ala
Allice 5 f "
Agnes 3 f "

Euf # 1343 Overseer (-- --)
COLE, James 42 m Ga
Rebecca 31 f "

Euf 137 Vender (--- ---)
COLE, James 44 m Ga
Rebecca A. 32 f "

Mt. A. # 746 Farmer (800-1000)
COLE, Josiah, Sr. 59 m NC
Nancy 54 f "
Zilphy 32 f "
Nancy A. 20 f Ala
Josiah, Jr. 16 m "
Martha A. 14 f "

Euf # 473 Farmer(2100-1000)
COLEMAN, Andrew 44 m Ga
Verlinda 32 f "
Martha 15 f Ala
William 14 m "
Mary 12 f "
Harris 9 m "
John 8 m "
George 6 m "
David 4 m "
Effie 1 f "
Thomas 74 m NC

Euf # 511 Overseer (-- --)
COLEMAN, David 28 m Ga
Elvira 19 f Ala
Lizzie 1/12 f "

Clay # 66 Clerk of Court
(2,000-30,000)
COLEMAN, Geo. W. 30 m Ga
Lucy J. 27 f "
Linda R. 10 f Ala
H. E. 8 f "
Ella E. 5 f "
John S. 3 m "
Anna 4/12 f "

Clay # 19 Druggist
COLEMAN, John L. 25 m Ga
(Living in hotel)

Euf # 1107 Clerk (-- --)
COLEMAN, Joseph T. 26 m Ga
D. C. 11 m Ala

Mdwy # 1009
COLEMAN, Mary E. 8 f Ala
(See N. C. Wm. Smith)

Clay # 1287 (1000-7000)
COLEMAN, Nancy 38 f Ga
Eugenia 15 f Ala
Albert(?) 13 m "
Ann 11 f "

Clay # 144 Farm Laborer
COLEMAN, R. B. 22 m Ga
(See W. B. Holley)

Euf # 1077 Farmer (10000-58000)
COLEMAN, Thos. R. 45 m Ga
Sallie W. 36 f NC
Richard R. (Student) 21 m Ala
Laura 15 f "
Thos. G. 8 m "
Stephen L. 5 m "

Mdwy # 984 Planter (15000-30000)
COLEMAN, W. T. 28 m Ga
K. (or R.) 60 f SC
B. F. 20 m Ala
ALLEN, A. A. 24 f Ga
PRUETT, Virginia 12 f Ala
ALLEN, W.B. 2 m "

Euf # 291 Farmer (2000-6000)
COLEMAN, Wm. T. 49 m Ga
Mary E. 33 f NC
Ariadne L. 15 f Ala
John T. (Laborer) 16 m "
William 12 m "
Victoria 9 f "
Joseph 7 m "
Daniel 5 m "
Frank 2 m "

Euf # 652 Farmer (300-300)
COLLINS, John D. 54 m Ga
Martha 50 f SC
John R. 16 m Ga
GRESHAM, John S. 12 m "
BASS, Edna 30 f "
TEW, Rebecca 42 f NC
John (Laborer) 19 m Ala

Clay # 87
COLLINS, Louisa 26 f Ala
James 5 m "
Minna 4 f "
Justus 2 m "
VENTRESS, Mollie E. 23 f "
COLLINS, Hart 31 m "
(Farmer)
VENTRESS, W. E. 21 m "
(Clerk)

Clay # 39 Retailing Liquor
COLLINS, M. 35 m Ala
M. A. 32 f Ga
Camilla 5 f Ala
RAILEY, A. C. 9/12 f "
Nancy 15 f "
RAILEY, Josephine 12 f "

Euf # 1401 Laborer
COLLINS, Thomas 29 m Ire
(See A. J. Ramsay).

Luvl # 309 Farmer (12000-30000)
COLLINS, Wilson 74 m NC
RAILEY, Hulda 17 f Ala
SMITH, Firtha 13 m "
Rebecca 9 f "
Louisianna 4 f "

Euf # 982 (23,000-65,000)
COMER, C. L. 36 f Ga
Hugh M. (At school) 18 m "
John W. 15 m Ala
Legare 14 m "
Bragg 12 m "
Fletcher 6 m "
Edward 4 m "

Nwto # 605 Farmer (800-600)
COMMANDER, John 60 m NC
Henry D (Farmer) 24 m Ga
(300 ---)
Martha 22 f "

Euf # 1248 Hireling
COMMANDER, Peter 21 m SC
(See Edw. Houston).

Euf # 853 Farmer (200-500)
COMMANDER, Thos. J. 25 m Ga
Amanda 21 f Ala
James F. 2 m "
infant 2/12 m "

Euf # 538 Laborer (--- 50)
COMPTON, James 48 m SC
Emily 39 f Ga
Harriet 19 f "
Henry (laborer) 16 m "
Emily A. 9 f "
James T. 1 m Ala
Mary 44 f Ga
Drewcilla 9 f "

Bfd # 1258 Farmer (--- 525)
CONDRY, Dennis 25 m Ala
Sarah 21 f "
THOMAS, Mahala N. 16 f "

Bfd # 1255 Farmer (5500-15000)
CONDRY, John 52 m SC
Elizabeth 53 f "
J.D. (Farmer,---100) 21 m Ala
George 11 m "
Hugh 8 m "

Txv # 1201 Farmer
CONDRY, John 30 m Ala
Jas. (Farmer,640-500) 46 m SC
Alsy 43 f Ga
Eliza 20 f Ala
Elizabeth 18 f "
Mary A. 15 f "
William 12 m "
George W. 10 m "

Euf # 763
CONDRY, Penelope 12 f Ala
(See Wm. S. Purswell).

Euf # 420 Laborer
CONN, Edward 21 m RI
(See James Daniels).

Clay # 162 Farmer (--- ---)
CONNELLY, E. Mc. 19 m SC
Sarah 17 f Ala
(Married within the year).

Clay # 163 Farmer (--- 200)
CONNELLY, Jas. C. S. 27 m SC
Elizabeth (--- 2500) 30 f Ga
Lucy 5 f Ala
C. 2 f "
Ida 1/12 f "
HARRIS, A. (Laborer) 17 m "

Clay # 161 M.E. Minister (9200-160000)
CONNELLY, Jas. Z. 52 or 57 m SC
Rachael 50 f "
Ann 25 f "
N. A. 23 f "
E. K. 21 f "
David D. (Farmer) 17 m "
A. C. 15 m "
C. P. 13 m Ala
Sarah J. 12 f "
R. C. 10 m "
H. C. 8 f "
L. F. 4 f "

Euf # 1049 Farmer (24000-65000)
CONNER, George D. 40 m SC
Mariah 30 f Ga
Sela 3 f Ala
Mollie 1 f "
UPSHAW, Eugenia 10 f "
(9,000-36,300)

Euf # 516 Laborer
CONNER, William 19 m Ala
Louisa 17 f "
Sophronia 14 f "
George 10 m "
(See E. T. Sherman).

Euf # 432 Laborer (--- ---)
CONGERS, Henry 20 m Ga
Mary 16 f Ala

Euf # 1029
COOK, Deverux 40 f Ga
(See Joseph Cobb).

Bkb # 785 (1600-2150)
COOK, Elizabeth 34 f Ga
A. M. 12 m Ala
John T. 11 m "

Bkb # 777 Student
COOK, Harrison 17 m Ala
(See Wm. E. Green).

Euf # 1295 Hireling
COOK(?), Hiram 38 m Ga
Sarah Ann 28 f "
Peter 14 m Ala
Mariah 11 f "
Rosanna 7 f "
Thomas 5 m "
George W. 2 m "

Bkb # 784 Farmer (--- 200)
COOK, Perry 30 m Ga
Dorcas 27 f "
William 12 m Ala
Sarah J. 8 f "
Charity 6 f "
Elizabeth J. 5 f "
George 3 m "
Eliza 10/12 f "

Bkb # 782 Farmer (150-200)
COOK, Thos., Jr. 23 m Ga
Mary 21 f Ala
Martha M. 1/12 f "

Nwto # 594 Farmer (--- ---)
COOK, William 23 m SC
Sarah 16 f Ga
LOGANS, Wm. (Student) 24 m "

Euf # 1357 (2000-3000)
COOPER, Elizabeth 58 f NC
Sarah 23 f Ala
Jason (Farmer) 19 m "
Franklin 16 m "

Clay # 666 Farmer (500-1000)
COOPER, G. W. 33 m Ga
Harriett 28 f Ala
Mary 11 f Ga
Andrew E. 9 m "
Margaret L. 6 f "
Mandy S. 4 f Ala
A. Jane 2 f "
SHEPPARD, Wm. Harriet 2 f "

Euf # 459 Farmer (400-1650)
COOPER, Thomas 54 m NC
Elizabeth A. 40 f SC
Sarah E. 7 f Ala
Missouri C. 15 f "
John T. 13 m "
James W. 6 m "
William A. 6 m "
Robert F. B. 2 m "

Mt. A. # 820 Farmer (--- 250)
COOPER, Thos. M. 24 m Ala
Rebecca 23 f Ga
Lurena E. 2 f Ala
Isiah 1 m "

Mt. A. # 844 Farmer (2080-500)
COOPER, Wm. D. 36 m Ala
Sinthia A. 34 f "
James 9 m "
John 7 m "
(Cont.)

(Mt. A. # 844 cont.)
Sinthia 5 f Ala
William 4 m "
Thomas J. 2 m "

Euf # 526 (27000-16000)
COPELAND, Caroline 48 f SC
Florida C. 17 f Ala
Preston 15 m "
John 11 m "
Henry 6 m "

Euf # 375 Farmer (4500-1100)
COPELAND, Isaac 63 m Mass
Elizabeth W. 50 f SC
Benj. (Farm hand) 18 m Ga
Joshua 15 m "
Williard 13 m "
David 10 m "
WHITTINGTON, John 67 m SC
(Farmer, 1500-6000)
Mary A. 60 f "
Aurelia (Farmer) 25 m Ga
Jeremiah 21 m "

Euf # 126 Clerk
CORBETT, D. 23 m SC
(See Mary A. Barnett)

Euf # 84 Livery Stable
(3000-8000)
CORBITT, Patrick 38 m SC
Rosena 32 f "
Furman 18 m "
James 17 m "
Louisa 14 f "
Ossian 12 m "
Caldwell 10 m "
Evan 8 m "
Edwin 6 m "
Marsha 5 f "

Flk # 403 Farmer (1600-3000)
CORDAMAN, F. M. 21 m Ga
Catherine J. 29 f "

Euf # 440 Stone Cutter
CORLEY, Owen 48 m Ire
(See McNamara's R.R. Gro.).

Mt. A. # 854
CORLEY, Sallie 96 f SC
(See Matilda Heard).

Mdwy # 1055 Overseer (---3000)
COSBY, J. W. 25 m Ga

Mdwy # 638 Farmer (--- ---)
COSTIN, James 80 m NC
Eliza 63 f "
Margaret 14 f Ala

Mt. A. # 882 Blacksmith (240-600)
COSTEN, Owen 52 m NC
Ellender 50 f "
Martha 20 f "
Joseph 18 m Ala
Effie J. 16 f "

Euf # 153 (3000-2500)
COURIC, Chas. M. 41 m Fr
Henrietta T. 55 f "
(12,000-2,000)
Lucian (Painter) 19 m Ala
Frances M. 15 f "
Alexis A. (Clerk) 17 m "
Alida 12 f "

Txv # 1233
COVINGTON, Eliza 36 f Ga
Emily 15 f "
Mary 13 f Ala
Jeremiah 12 m "
Angeline 3 f "
Arvine 6/12 f "
(See Sarah Berryhill).

Txv # 1185
COVINGTON, Emily 15 f Ga
(See Daniel McGilvery).

Euf # 268 (12,000-13,000)
COWAN, Ann S. 45 f Ga
Ellen 18 f Ala
Emily 14 f "
Rose 12 f "
Willie 10 f "
James G. 20 m "
(Student at West Point).

Luvl # 362 Farmer (500-000)
COWAN, E. B. 45 m Ala
Catherine 35 f NC
Daniel 10 m Ala
Attira 7 f "
John 3 m "
Fanny 2 f "

Luvl # 361 Farmer (3500-10000)
COWAN, William R. 48 m Ga
E. C. 27 f "
Mary L. 3 f Ala
(Cont.)

(Luvl # 361 cont.)

ROLLINS, John R. 16 m Ga
ROBERTS, Louisa 9 f Ala

Euf # 480 Merchant (1200-5000)
COWLES, Wm. T. 40 m Ga
Frances A. 20 f Ala
Francis A. (Clerk) 34 m Ga

Luvl # 534 Farmer (800-600)
COX, C. A. 25 m Ga
Mary 20 f "

Nwto # 603 (---125)
COX, Charlotte 30 f Ala
J.M. 14 f "
J.W. 13 m "
Mary E. 12 f "
E.J. 10 f "
William S. 11 m "
Martha L. 8 f "
S.J. 3 f "
PAUL, Lucinda 11 f "

Bkb # 711 Farmer
COX, Eliza 62 f Ga
John G. 23 m Ala
(See James Bates).

Luvl # 295 Farmer (14500-50000)
COX, Emanuel 66 m NC
Sarah 56 f "
John 29 m Ala
Ann 30 f "
Charles 24 m "
Columbus 16 m "
CLARK, Kate 7 f "
Sally 2 f "

Euf # 845 Laborer (300-50)
COX, George 29 m Ga
Sally 26 f "
Martha 7 f Ala
Mary 3 f "
Margaret 2 f "
COX, John 72 m "
Mariah 52 f "

Nwto # 623 Farmer
COX, Gordon 18 m Ala
(See Benj. Herring).

Euf # 179 Doctor (2000-800)
COX, Green S. 44 m Va
Ann 34 f SC
Georgiann 19 f Ala
(Cont.)

(Euf # 179 cont.)
William 18 m Ala
Mary 14 f "
James 13 m "
Cleopatra 11 f "
John R. 10 m "
Christian 7 f "
Lucy 4 f "
Augusta 6/12 f "

Luvl # 286 Farmer (3000-6000)
COX, Jempsey 49 m Ga
Rachael 50 f SC
Roxana 24 f Ala
Nancy 23 f "
Mary A.M. 21 f "
Sarah A. 17 f "
Rachael 13 f "
Julia 11 f "

Clay # 201 Farmer
COX, John 31 m Ga
Gelena 27 f Ala
Elijah 7 m "
James 5 m "
Margaret 2 f "
John 1/12 m "
Thomas 12 m "

Flk # 428 Farmer (100 ---)
COX, John 25 m Ala
Charity 21 f NC
Wm. 2 m Ala
Isaac 9/12 m "

Euf # 701 Laborer
COX, John 16 m Ala
(See Thomas Shepherd).

Euf # 804 Farmer (9300-5700)
COX, W. I. 41 m Ga
C.W. 21 m "
McKLEROY, James T. 35 m "
(--- 3,000)

Luvl # 383 Farmer
COX, William 35 m Ala
Birha(?) 27 f NC
Jane 7 f Ala
Margaret 6 f "
William 3 m "
Mary 3/12 f "

Nwto # 596 Farmer (1600-1000)
CRAFT, Jeremiah 53 m Ga
Edie 48 f NC
LEWIS, John L. 23 m Ala
(Cont.)

(Nwto # 596 cont.)
LEWIS, Harrison 18 m Ala
POWELL, Caroline 12 f "
R.A. 10 f "
LEWIS, Martha 4 f "

Euf # 495 Farmer (1200-700)
CRAIG, John C. 33 m Ga
Nancy 33 f "
Mary V. 6 f Ala
Clinton C. 2 m "
ARMSTRONG, John 17 m Ga
(Farm hand).

Clay # 44 Convict
CRAIG, Thos. J. 21 m Ala

Euf # 499 Laborer
CRAIG, W. M. 24 m Ga
Mary E. 19 f "
(Married within the year).

Mt. A. # 748 (200-200)
CRAPTREE, Elizabeth 38 f Ga
Mary 35 f "
Matilda 29 f "
Sarah 27 f "
STRICKLAND, Louisa 12 f Ala

Euf # 1385 (24000-45000)
CRAWFORD, C. A. 46 f Ga
Ella 19 f Ala
Virginia 17 f "
Alexander 15 m "
Virgil 10 m "

Clay # 737 Farmer (1000-800)
CREECH, Aaron 35 m NC
Charity 32 f Ala
David B. 11 m "
Mary J. 9 f "
William J. 7 m "
John 5 m "
Jeptha 2 m "

Mt. A. # 914
CREECH, John T. 7 m Ala
(See David Johnson).

Txv # 1209 Farmer (880-250)
CREEL, Daniel 30 m SC
Sarah 25 f Ala
John 6 m "
Mary 5 f "
Frances 3 f "
Daniel 1 m "

Euf # 703 Teacher (--- 1200)
CREEL, J. F. 25 m Ala
(See William Helms).

Txv # 1208 Farmer (10400-7500)
CREEL, Levi 55 m SC
Linai 60 f "
Preston (Farmer) 20 m Ala
Fauny 17 f Fla
Duncan 15 m Ala
Levi 17 m "
CUCHIN, Jane 10 f "
(Preston & Fauny married within the year.)

Txv # 1202 Farmer (400-400)
CREEL, Thomas 45 m SC
Louisa 43 f Ga
William 16 m Ala
Thomas 13 m "
Elizabeth 10 f "
Caroline J. 8 f "

Mt. A. 822 Farmer (1200-600)
CREW, Caroline 48 f Ga
Wm. M. (Farmer) 29 m "
John T. (Farmer, 400--) 17 m "
Judson L. 15 m "
Sarah J. 12 f "

Euf # 1207 Farmer (8000-55000)
CREWS, Arthur 68 m Ga
Mary 65 f SC
BISHOP, Nancy J. 11 f Ala

Bfd # 1250 Physician & Farmer (1,500-9,000)
CREWS, J. E. 41 m Ga
Margaret E. 29 f SC
W. N. 8 m Ala

Euf # 403 Laborer
CREWS, James 27 m Ga
Elizabeth 24 f "
Winny 8 f "
James 6 m "
Harriet 3 f "

Clay # 48
CREWS, Mary V. 16 f Ala
Nancy 10 f "
(See Mary Fenn).

Euf # 1209 Farmer (36000-23000)
CREWS, W. B. 43 m Ga
Catherine 37 f NC
Mary V. 16 f Ala
Nancy J. 10 f "

Euf # 569
CREYON, James 20 m Ala
(See Daniel Shehan).

Txv # 1225 Farmer (700-350)
CROCKER, Carey 54 m Va
Rebecca 53 f SC
Bethel (Farmer) 18 m Ala
Martha 16 f "
Wiley 13 m "
Annie A. 11 f "

Flk # 407 Farmer (1000-1500)
CROCKER, Monroe 46 m Va
Eliza 48 f NC
TURNER, Sarah J. 18 f Ala
John 23 m Ga
CROCKER, Nancy J. 15 f Ala
Ann C. 11 f "

Txv # 1226 Farmer (--- 100)
CROCKER, William 38 m Ala
Catherine 25 f Ga
James 12 m Ala
John C. 10 m "
Jane 8 f "
William M. 7 m "
George 5 m "
Francina 4 f "
Nancy A. 11/12 f "

Euf # 443 (1,200-15,000)
CRUMBLEY, Mary E. 38 f Ga
William W. 13 m Ala
John 9 m "

Euf # 833 Physician (--- 1200)
CRYMES, A. C. 21 m Ga

Clay # 93
CRYMES, George P. 16 m Ala
(See B. L. Cochran).

Txv # 1208
CUCHIN, Jane 10 f Ala
(See Levi Creel).

Txv # 1211 Farmer (--- 200)
CUCHIN, Martin 56 m Ger
Rhoda 28 f Ala
Mary 18 f "
Daniel 16 m "
Nancy 12 f "
Cain 7 m "
Ephram 2 m "
John 4 m "
Alex 2 m "

Bfd # 1245 Shoemaker (160-200)
CULBRETH, Duncan 48 m NC
Sarah 49 f "
Mary 22 f Ala
Barbara J. 4 f "

Euf # 593 Farmer (--- 100)
CULPEPPER, Benj. 40 m Ga
Anna 30 f NC
William J. 8 m Ga
Winney P. 6 f "
John 3 m Ala
Mary E. 1 f "
TAYLOR, Jesse 26 m Ga
(Farm laborer)

Clay # 734 Farmer (--- 550)
CULPEPPER, E. C. 47 m Ga
Lucy 24 f "
William 18 m "
James 16 m "
Elijah 14 m "
Elizabeth 12 f "
John 10 m "
Sophrona 6 f Ala
Amanda 4 f "
David 1 m "

Mt. A. # 872 Farm Laborer
CULPEPPER, Elijah 18 m Ga
(See James Channell).

Euf # 859 Wheelwright (---50)
CUMBIE, H. D. 30 m SC
Sarah 22 f Ga
BRIDGES, Elizabeth 38 f "
(Idiotic)

Euf # 94 Farmer (--- 200)
CUMMINGS, Nelson 30 m SC
Mary 23 f Fla
James W. 10 m Ga
Mary J. 9 f "
Caroline 2 f Ala
Adaline 2 f "

Luvl # 522 Teacher (700 ---)
CUMMINGS, S. J. 43 m Ga
Mary P. 33 f NC
John B. 11/12 m Ala

Luvl # 331 Farmer (850 ---)
CUMMINGS, Seaborn J. 40 m Ga
Mary 30 f NC
John B. G. 10/12 m Ala

Euf # 1329 Overseer
(Cont.)

(Euf # 1329 cont.)
CUNNINGHAM, Archy 23 m Ala
(See John D. Snipes).

Euf # 1300 Farmer (2000-12000)
CUNNINGHAM, Duncan 60 m NC

Euf # 1297
CUNNINGHAM, James K. 31 m Ala
Martha E. 25 f Ga
Henry C. 7 m Ala
Catherine E. 6 f "

Euf # 1310 Farmer (500-300)
CUNNINGHAM, John 29 m Ala
Christian 31 f "
Roderick M. 6 m "
Duncan 4 m "
Sarah J. 2 f "
Mary C. 6/12 f "

Euf # 1326 Overseer (300-100)
CUNNINGHAM, Peter 39 m Ala
Amanda 24 f "
Catherine A. 9 f "
John W. 4 m "
Nancy A. 1 f "

Euf # 456 Ditcher (--- 500)
CUNNINGHAM, Phillip 30 m Ire
McGILL, Patrick 40 m "
(Ditcher).

Euf # 1136
CUNNINGHAM, Phillip 24 m Ire
(See O. McMurray).

Euf # 1309 Overseer (--- 200)
CUNNINGHAM, Rankin 21 m Ala

Euf # 482 Farmer (--- 200)
CURENTON, Richard 55 m Ga
Hester 46 f "
Martha 14 f "

Euf # 485 Overseer (--- 400)
CURENTON, Thos. 40 m Ga
Marianna 29 f "
Mathew 12 m "
Thos. J. 7 m Ala
Avanna 3 f "
Ida 2 f "

Euf # 496 Farmer (400-1600)
CURENTON, Wilson 44 m Ga
Mary 35 f "
Eliza 14 f Ala
Ichabod A. 13 m "
Litey 12 f "
(Cont.)

(Euf # 496 cont.)
Edgar 4 m Ala
Montgomery 1 m "

Euf # 141 House Painter (200--)
CURRAN, Michael 45 m Ire
Sarah A. 34 f Ga
Amanda 17 f Ala
Martha 15 f "
Catherine 14 f "
Adna 11 f "
Emily 6 f "
Sarah 2 f "

Luvl # 352
CURRIE, Catherine 45 f SC
John 27 m "
(Farmer, 1500-600)
Gilbert L. (Farmer) 25 m "
Mary 15 f Ala
Philip 13 m "
Barbara 11 f "
CHISHOLM, Walter C. 22 m Ga
(Farmer)

Luvl # 318 Farmer (6000-18000)
CURRIE, Daniel 64 m NC
Isabella 50 f "
MCRAE, Margaret 14 f "
Philip D. (Student). 18 m "

Flk # 426
CURRIE, Matilda 33 f NC
(See John McInnis).

Euf # 1093 (14,500-33,500)
CURRY, Jane E. 43 f SC
IVEY, William 7 m "
VANN, Francis 7 m Ala

Mt. A. # 812 (--- 250)
CUTTS, Ann 40 f Ga
Daniel (Laborer) 22 m "
Elton " 19 m "
Hardy " 17 m "
Giles 12 m "

Clay # 28 Mechanic (400 ---)
CUTTS, Micajah 35 m Ga
Elizabeth 33 f NC
William 4 m Ala
James 3 m "

Euf # 238 Laborer
DALEY, William 35 m Ire
(See John W. Cameron)

Euf # 769 Farmer (10000-60000)
(Cont.)

(Euf # 769 cont.)
DALE, Robert O. 58 m Ga
Catherine 59 f "
Angeline P. 15 f "
Jane 84 f NC

Luvl # 508 Farmer (800 ---)
DANFORD, Daniel 35 m NC
Jane 40 f Ga
Mary A. 17 f Ala
Sarah A. 17 f "
J. J. 13 f "
Fanny 8 f "
James W. 7 m "
Eliza H. 4 f "
W. M. 2 m "
Eli H. 5/12 m "

Clay # 216 Grocery (--- 600)
DANFORD, E. M. 37 m NC

Flk 454 Farmer (1500-200)
DANFORD, Joseph 46 m NC
Jane 39 f "
James (Farmer) 18 m Ala
Abram J. " 17 m "
Mary 15 f "
John 13 m "
Alexander 11 m "
Margaret 9 f "
Catherine 9 f "
Sally 4 f "
Daniel 2 m "

Luvl # 512 Blacksmith & Farmer (600-8000)
DANFORD, Thomas 50 m NC
Louisa 40 f Ga
Alexander 21 m Ala
Thomas J. 17 m "
Elizabeth T. 15 f "
Zachariah T. 12 m "
E. J. 10 m "
James N. 8 m "
Martha J. 4 f "
Walter L. 2/12 m "

Nwto # 639 Working at mill (--- 200)
DANFORD, William 43 m NC
Mary 43 f "
Martha J. 20 f Ala
Mandy 18 f "
John M. 15 m "
James J. 12 m "
William H. 9 m "
Dossie 6 m "
Mary 3 f "

Euf # 199 Farmer (8000-10000)
DANFORTH, J. H. 42 m Ga
Sarah A. 34 f SC
R. M. 18 m Ala
William S. 16 m "
Westley D. 14 m "
Henry S. 11 m "
Edward C. B. 9 m "
Mary 7 f "
Martha 5 f "
Marion 1 f "

Clay # 209
Danforth, Mary 18 f Ga
Angella 16 f "
(See James Clark).

Flk # 469 Farmer (--- ---)
DANNA, Joseph 51 m Ga
Adelia 45 f Ala
Eliza 18 f "
Sally 11 f "

Mdwy # 944 Lawyer (--- 1000)
DANIEL, J. W. L. 28 m Ga

Euf # 420 Laborer (--- ---)
DANIELS, James 23 m Ala
Mary 24 f "
John 6 m "
WARD, Patrick(Laborer) 30 m Scot
McCLUSKY, Jas. " 30 m Ire
BODEFEORD, Jas. " 16 m SC
FIFE, Robt. " 34 m Scot
STERRIT, Clark " 24 m Tenn
ODOM, Jack " 29 m Ala
McCLENDON, Sam'l." 20 m Ga
CONN, Edward " 21 m RI

Euf # 1333 Master Carpenter (--- 11,000)
DANIEL, James L. 60 m NC
Matilda 41 f "
Emma J. 16 f Ala
Sarah A. 14 f "
Chas. P. 12 m "

Luvl # 547
DANIEL, Jane 18 f Ala
Jane E. 4/12 f "
Martha 15 f "
(See John Sasser).

Luvl # 290 Farmer (2000-500)
DANIELS, John 48 m NC
Flora 43 f Ga
John (Farmer) 19 m Ala
James " 18 m "
(Cont.)

(Luvl # 290 cont.)
Elizabeth 14 f Ala
Scott 11 m "
Angus 8 m "
Joseph 5 m "
Clara 1/12 f "
BROWN, Allen(Farmer) 23 m "
McDANIEL, Flora 13 f "
BROWN, Malinda 22 f Ga

Flk # 435 Mechanic (--- 100)
DANIEL, John 44 m NC
Rebecca 21 f Ala
Jane M. 18 f "
Lydia A. 16 f "
Martha M. 15 f "
Elizabeth S. 2 f "
Elizabeth 5/12 f "

1592 - 1704 (illegible)
DANIELS, John 57 or 52 m NC
Jane 25 f Ala
Elizabeth 14 f "

Luvl # 373
DANIEL, Martha C. 36 f Ga
Howard 9 m "
Seaborn F. 7 m Fla
(See Reubin King).

Euf # 585 Farmer (3500-18500)
DANIEL, Saml. C. 27 m Ga
Laura A. 18 f Ala
James L. 1 m "

Euf 212 Milliner
DANIEL, Susan F. 20 f Ga
(See Ransom Godwin)

Euf. # 1230 Hireling (--- ---)
DANIELS, William 38 m Ga
Evaline 35 f "
Dolly M. 4 f Ala

Euf # 1386 Master Carpenter (4000-6000)
DANIEL, Z. J. 49 m NC
Ann H. 48 f "
Zadok T. 12 m Ala

Nwto # 580 Farmer (--- 150)
DANNER, Joseph 50 m NC
Adna 35 f Ala
Elizabeth 18 f "
Eliza 15 f "
Sally 14 f "

Luvl # 570 Farmer (3000-1000)
DANNER, Thos. M. 51 m Ga
Mary A. 48 f SC
Elizabeth 23 f Ala
Thos. 21 m "
Jane 18 f "
John 17 m "
Sara 16 f "
Abraham (Idiotic) 19 m "
Margaret 15 f "
Martha 14 f "
William H. 12 m "
Jeremiah 10 m "
Catherine 6 f "

Flk # 470 Farmer (600-200)
DANSBY, Hiram 29 m Ala
Mary A. 22 f "
Sarah M. 6 f "
Rinza 5 f "
John 2 m "
Daniel W. 1 m "

Flk # 471 Farmer (3500-800)
DANSBY, John 56 m Ga
Sarah 36 f "
John (Farmer) 23 m Ala
George " 18 m "
Betsy 22 f "
Winziy 18 f "
Catherine 17 f "
Jane 16 f "
Mahala E. 14 f "
Isham B. 7 m "
Daniel (Student) 24 m "

Mt. A. # 842 Farmer
DASHER, Thomas 18 m Ga
(See Jas. A. Scarborough)

Euf # 1261 Farmer
DOUGHERTY, Z. 37 m SC
Frances 23 f "
Martha 15 f "
Soprona 12 f "
William 10 m Ala
John 4 m "
Irvin 1 m "

Euf # 1005 Overseer (--- 50)
DAVIDSON, James T. 27 m SC
Nancy 23 f Ga
Arilla A. 2 f "

Mt. A. # 918 Planter (5000-21000
DAVIE, Marshall C. 43 m Ga
(Cont.)

(Mt. A. # 918 cont.)
Jane E. 35 f Ga
William (Farmer) 18 m "
R. A. 16 f "
Marshall 14 m "
Mercy 12 m "
Judson 10 m "
Bunyan 8 m Ala
Jesse 5 m "
Ida 2 f "

Clay # 185 Farmer (1500-250)
DAVIS, Elisha 57 m Ga
Cenia 45 f "
Pleasant (Farmer) 19 m Ala
Elizabeth 17 f "
Vashti 14 f "
Orrin 12 m "
Ann 10 f "
Adeline 8 f "
MATHEWS, Harrison 20 m Ga
(Farm laborer)
BENNETT, Orrin 34 m Ala
(Mechanic)

Bkb # 779 (300-200)
DAVIS, Elizabeth 60 f Ga
Thomas 11 m "

Bkb # 771 Farmer (500-350)
DAVIS, F. F. 27 m Ga
Frances 24 f "
W. F. 4/12 m Ala

Euf # 798 Farmer (10000-65000)
DAVIS, Gardner H. 54 m Ala
Mary 45 f "
Hiram A. (Farmer) 24 m "
Epenetus M. (Teacher) 22 m "
Henry H. (Student) 19 m "
William B. 15 m "
Sallie H. 13 f "
Zachary T. 11 m "
John G. 8 m "
Mary J. 6 f Ga
Emma L. 4 f "

Bkb # 770 Farmer (1500-600)
DAVIS, Howell 37 m Ga
Catherine 38 f "
Mary A. 15 f "
Virginia 12 f "
Antoniette 2 f "
Thomas 4 m "
Frances 11/12 f "

Nwto # 562 Farmer (--- 6000)
DAVIS, James 25 m Ga
M. E. 26 f "
SHANKS, James T. 4 m Ala

Nwto # 575 Farmer (--- 200)
DAVIS, James E. 32 m NC
Caroline 25 f Ala
Henrietta 7 f "
R. H. 5 m "
Mary J. 2 f "

Euf # 1025 Farmer (3000-2000)
Davis, John 57 m NC
Mary 49 f Ga
John (Farmer) 25 m "
Martha 21 f "
Right L. " 19 m "
D. W. " 16 m Ala
Benj. F. 13 m "
James M. 10 m "
Robert J. 8 m "

Euf # 612 Farm Hand
DAVIS, John 21 m NC
Sarah 18 f Ala
Silona 1 f "

Txv # 1230 Farmer (500-300)
DAVIS, John A. 26 m Ga
Nancy 23 f Ala
LOTT, William H. 5 m "
DAVIS, Jasper L. 4 m "
Westley S. 1 m "

Clay # 106 Farmer (800-400)
DAVIS, Louis 48 m NC
Rebecca 38 f "
Josiah (Farmer) 20 m Ga
Mary 16 f "
Richard 7 m Ala
M. E. 4 f "
P. S. 1 f "

Flk # 427
DAVIS, Mary A. 23 f Ala
(See B. W. Grubbs)

Mt. A. # 921 Overseer
DAVIS, Mason 21 m Ala
(See A. G. Smith).

Nwto # 587 Physican (2000-1000)
DAVIS, R. H. 36 m NC
Mary A. 30 f Ga
H. W. 13 m Ala
S. M. 11 f "
(Cont.)

(Nwto # 587 cont.)
N. C. (or H.?) 9 m Ala
M. L. 8 f "
M. J. C. 7 f "
Frances B. 3 f "
L. L. 1 f "

Nwto # 576 Farmer (2000-300)
DAVIS, Robert H. 34 m NC
M. A. 25 f Ga
Henry 13 m Ala
Sarah 10 f "
Nathan 8 m "
Mary 7 f "
Martha 6 f "
Frances 4 f "
Leemac 2 f "

Euf # 447 Laborer
DAVIS, Starling 40 m Ga
Frances 28 f SC
Reubin 13 m Ala
Allen 10 m "
Eugenia 8 f "
Melvina 6 f "
Amanda 1 f "

Euf # 1026 Occp. - none
DAVIS, Thos. H. 28 m Ga
Louisa 18 f "
Mary E. 1 f Ala

Clay # 145 Farm Laborer
DAVIS, W. J. 26 m Ga
Susan 20 f "
Benj. F. 5/12 m Ala

Euf # 695 Occp. - none
DAVIS, Wellborn 25 m SC
Jane (600-1600) 52 f "

Flk # 463 Farmer (600-150)
DAVIS, William E. 67 m NC
Lydia 50 f "

Flk # 441 Farmer (--- 150)
DAWKINS, Alexander 27 m Ga
Nancy 23 f "
Mary A. 3 f Ala
Josephine 10/12 f "

Luvl # 353 Mechanic (--- ---)
DAWKINS, John 56 m Ga
Nancy 50 f "
Susan A. 26 f "
Margaret 17 f "
Frances 16 f "
(Cont.)

(Luvl # 353 Cont.)
Josephus 14 m Ga
John W. 11 m Ala
Lucinda 8 f "

Euf # 599 Farmer (5000-10000)
DAWKINS, Robert H. 32 m Ga
Mary M. 28 f Ala
Sarah E. 8 f "
Martha V. 5 f "
Mary E. 3 f "
William F. 4/12 m "
WARD, Lafayette 9 m Ala

Bkb # 738 Farmer (--- 300)
DAWSON, John 65 m SC
Kezia 49 f Ga
Sarah 25 f "
Martha G. 20 f "
Thomas 18 m Ala
Susanna 16 f "
John F. 14 m "
Louisa J. 12 f "
James M. 10 m "
Amanda 4 f "
Henry 3/12 m "

Bkb # 739 Farmer (--- 150)
DAWSON, Joseph M. 24 m Ga
Eliza A. 18 f "
William T. (or F.?) 5/12m Ala

Luvl # 342 Occp. - none
DAWSON, William C. 20 m Ga
(See John A. Morris).

Clay # 189 Farmer (200-225)
DAY, Amariah 53 m NC
Elizabeth 50 f "
WALLER, Eliz.(idiotic)50 f "

Luvl # 321
DAY, Emeline 12 f Ala
(See Eli Edge).

Luvl # 273 Farmer (--- 400)
DAY, Henry 23 m Ala
Ann F. 20 f "
infant 3/12 m "
(See John D. Seals).

Txv # 1158 Farmer (600-300)
DAY, James 30 m NC
Lavina 26 f SC
William K.(or R.?) 7 m Ala
George W. 5 m "
Mary C. 3 f "
(Cont.)

(Txv # 1158 cont.)
John G. S. 2 m Ala
James 4/12 m "
AVANT, Elizabeth 50 f SC

Txv # 1157 Farmer (1000-500)
DAY, Rodin 78 m Va
Jane 65 f NC
AVANT, Mary 23 f Ala
William G. 3 m "
Eli S. 1 m "

Luvl # 338
Day, Sarah F. 32 f SC
Virella 8 f Ala

Nwto # 572 Farmer (500-300)
DAY, William 21 m Ala
Mary 24 f "
John W. 7/12 m "

Euf # 739 Farmer (--- 250)
DEASE, Isham 40 m Ga
Anna 41 f "
Riley (Farm hand) 15 m "
Doctor 13 m Ala
Milton 10 m "
Sidney 8 m "
Emory 6 m "
Nicholas 4 m "
Malcom 2 m "

Euf # 971 Student
DEAS, Plumer 18 m SC
(See S. M. Streater).

Mt. A. # 873 Farmer (480-250)
DEBENPARTE, P. P. L. 29 m NC
Mary A. 20 f Ga
John W. 1 m Ala

Bkb # 714 Farmer (--- 150)
DEES, Riley 30 m SC
Debbie 33 f "
Jane 6 f "
female 2 f "
female 1/12 f Ala

Txv # 1160
DEES, Sophia 50 f NC
(See Adam Haigler).

Euf # 332 Wagon maker
DEFNEL, Saunders 26 m Ga
Elizabeth 22 f "
Mary 5 f "
Thomas 3 m "
Louisa 1 f "

Euf # 331 Wagon maker
DEFNEL, Thomas 28 m Ga
M. C. 25 f "
Saunders 7 m "
Sally 5 f "
Jane 3 f "

Mdwy # 1049 Farmer (2800-3500)
DeLAUNAY, F. L. 30 m Ga
Annie 25 f "
Minnie 2 f Ala
G. G. 20 m Ga
E. W. 18 m "
Cephalie 15 f "

Flk # 486 Farmer (250 ---)
DELOACH, John 27 m Ga
Susan 24 f NC
Nancy A. 6/12 f Ala

Flk # 487 Farmer (1500-200)
DELOACH, Sandiford 60 m NC
Keaty 55 f "
Caroline 25 f Ga
Rina 15 f "
Sarah 14 f "
Catherine 12 f "
Nancy 10 f "
Polly 6 f Ala
Rina 6/12 f "

Euf # 144
HENBY, Matilda 40 f NC
(See Thos. M. Cameron).

Euf # 414 Farmer (1500-2500)
DENARD, John E. 68 m Ga
America 55 f Va
ELLIS, Fielding 84 m "
FLOURNOY, Marvin 21 m Ga
(Laborer).

Euf # 1058
DENNARD, Mary F. 13 f Ala
(See John W. Brown).

Euf # 101 Clerk (1500-2000)
Denning, J. W. 33 m Ga
Cinthia 22 f "
John W. 5 m "
N. S. 4 m "
Lafayette 2/12 m "

Bkb # 757 Farmer (200-200)
DENNIS, Richard 43 m Ga
Mary J. 36 f SC
(Cont.)

(Bkb # 757 cont.)
Rosamond 4 f Ala
Chistopher 3 m "
Lorenzo 1 m "

Euf 1354 Farmer (15000-45000)
DENT, John H. 45 m NY
Fanny A. 32 f Conn
Harry (Student) 19 m SC
Elizabeth 18 f "
Herbert (Student) 15 m Ala
Charles 11 m "
Annie 12 f "
Sallie 8 f "
Kate 7 f "
Fanny 3 f "
George 1 m "

Euf # 1330 Lawyer (800-2500)
DENT, S. H. 26 m Md

Clay 141 Farmer (1000-1500)
DESHAZO, Frank 39 m SC
L. A. 35 f Ga
James L. T. 12 m Ala
E. J. 9 f "
C. A. 4 f "
Thos. J. (Farmer) 22 m "
A. E. " 18 m "
Gracie 65 f SC
McLEOD, Milly 45 f "
TENICH, Jefferson 19 m Ga
(Laborer)
GORDY, Noah 50 m "
(Teacher)

Luvl # 566 Farm Laborer
(--- 300)
DESHAZO, Hamilton 28 m SC
Sarah 24 f Ala
Alabama 8 f "
Monroe 6 m "
Calhoun 4 m "
Preston 2 m "
infant 3/12 m "

Mt. A. # 885
DESHAZO, Mary 15 f Ala
(See James Casey)

Euf 547 Farmer (500-400)
DESHAZO, Moses 25 m Ala
Amanda 20 f Ga
Theodosia 1 f Ala

Euf 548 Farmer (--- 150)
DESHAZO, Paul W. 28 m Ala
(Cont.)

(Euf 548 cont.)
Sarah 28 f NC
Alabama 7 f Ala
Munroe 5 m "
Calhoun 3 m "
Mary 2 f "

Euf # 549 Blacksmith (500-150)
DESHAZO, Wilson 53 m Ga
Delilah 50 f "
Annis 13 f Ala
BROWN, Thos. (Laborer) 17 m Ga

Euf # 97 Clerk (from Bavaria)
DESSON, A. 25 m Ger
(See Isaac Young)

Euf # 751 (-- --)
DICKENS, Frances 26 f Ga
Susan 3 f Ala

Clay 1112 (250-200)
DICKENS, Missouri 36 f Ga
CARTER, Elizabeth 18 f "
Nicholas (-- 180) 23 m "
(Last two m. within the year).
DICKENS, Benj. (Student) 16 m Ga
Thos. " 14 m "
Ann 13 f "
Virginia 9 f Ala
Rebecca 6 f "
Frances 4 f "

Euf # 181 Blacksmith (1700-400)
DICKERSON, Alfred H. 45 m Va
Louisa M. 33 f Ga
Arthur C. 19 m "
(Appt. carriage trimmer)
Alfred K. 14 m "
Margaret C. 10 f Ala
HOLDER, Drew (seamstress) 19 f Fla

Clay # 112 Farmer (--- 200)
DICKERT, James W. 32 m Ga
M.J. 24 f "
M.J. 6 f "
M.A. 4 f "
L.A. 2 f Ala
FUTCH, Asbury 8 m Ga

Luvl # 565 M.E.C.Minister (500 --)
DICKINSON, A. S. 51 m SC
Martha S. 38 f "

Mdwy # 967
DICKSON, Daniel 4 m Ala
Eugenia L. 3 f "
(See Clayton Dixon).

Euf # 125 Teacher
DICKSON, J. T. 25 m Ga
(See William Barr).

Mdwy # 968 Farmer (4500-25000)
DICKSON, James 46 m Ga
Luna 50 f SC

Mdwy # 1000 Farmer (3500-15000)
Dickson, John J. 57 m Ga
Lunna 53 f SC
Lunna A. 10 f Ala

Euf # 1127
DICKSON, Martha 23 f Ga
(See Thos. Hammock).

Clay # 88 Supt. of wagons (2600-6000)
Dill, Robert 54 m NH
E. P. (Milliner) 37 f Me
Wm. (2500-400) 21 m Ala
Andrew 13 m "
Hattie 3 f "
John W. 7/12 m "
BEASLEY, Wm. 21 or 27 m "
(Wagoner)

Euf # 513 Farmer (3000-16000)
DILLARD, Edmund 54 m SC
Mary 40 f Ga
W.M.E. 5 m Ala
ROAD, Nathaniel, Jr. 22 m NC
(Overseer)

Luvl # 365 Idiotic
DILLEHAY, Jeff 18 m Ga
(See John Flournoy).

Euf # 342
DILNO(?), Mary A. 14 f SC
Catharine 13 f Ga
Josephine A. 2 f "
(See William Harper).

Euf # 1073 Overseer (--- 2000)
DISMUKES, J. T. 32 m Ala
Emma 24 f "
E.M. 7 f "
John T. 4 m "
William A. 2 m "

Mdwy # 967 Farmer (--- 5000)
DIXON, Clayton 30 m Ga
Sarah 34 f "
James C. 8 m Ala
Luna(?) A. 12 f "
(Cont.)

(Mdwy # 967 cont.)
Daniel 4 m Ala
Eugenia L. 3 f "

Euf # 116 Teacher (9000-35000)
DOBBINS, John S. 46 m Ga
Evaline W. 46 f "
Roberta W. 18 f "
Moses 14 m Ala
John A. 12 m "
Robert W. 11 m "
Mary L. 9 f "
William A. 6 m "
Sarah E. 2 f "

Clay # 7
DOLY, Charles 12 m La
(See H. B. Hill).

Txv # 1139 Farmer (600-500)
DOMINY, William J. 39 m Ga
Susanna 26 f "
Sarah E. 15 f "
James G. 12 m "
Amanda 10 f "
William L. 8 m "
Jane 6 f "
Godfrey L. 4 m Ala
John J. 3 m "
Daniel 1/12 m "

Luvl # 330 Farmer (2000-2500)
DORMAN, William 60 m SC
Penelope 50 f Ga
Jerusha 22 f Ala
Thos. M. (Farmer) 20 m "
James " 18 m "
Alexander " 16 m "
Rebecca 13 f "
Amanda 10 f "
John 8 m "
HOLMES, Nathaniel 85 m SC
J. Z. (Farmer) 22 m Ala
Mollie F. 23 f "

Flk # 475 Farmer (3000-2000)
DOSTER, O. C. 47 m NC
Mary 24 f Ala
Obed C. 5 m "
Mary J. 7 f "
Emeline 3 f "
Joel T. 1/12 m "
BUTLER, William 15 m "

Euf # 398 Farmer (--- 500)
DOUGHTIE, Edward 44 m Ga
Unice 43 f "
(Cont.)

(Euf # 398 cont.)
William H. 18 m Ga
James E. 16 m "
John H. 13 m "
Thomas T. 11 m "

Euf # 1062 Teacher (500-1000)
DOUGLASS, D. S. T. 38 m NY
Frances H. 34 f Va
Charles 12 m Ala
Frank 10 m "
David W. 8 m "
John T. 6 m "
Eugenia P. 3 f "
DUGGER, W. M. 79 m Va
(Pub. officer).

Luvl # 265 Physician (350-3300)
DOUGLASS, John C. 32 m NC
Sarah J. 26 f Ga
Willie C. 7 m "
Maria 2 f Ala
Katy (--- 2400) 51 f NC
HENDERSON, Joseph 35 m Ala
(Farmer, 2500-350)
Margaret 37 f NC
William 10 m Ala

Euf # 388 Barber (Colored)
DOWDELL, Harris 26 m Ga
Joshua 13 m "

Clay # 30 M.E.C. Minister
(25000-55000)
DOWDELL, Lewis F. 30 m Ga
A. E. 28 f
R. M. 6 m Ala
J. C. 4 f "
J. L. 3 f "
James 7/12 m "

Euf # 915 Farmer (8500-2200)
DOWLING, Elias 73 m SC
Elizabeth 62 f "
Keziah D. 22 f "
Seneth Davis 24 f "
William 6 m Ala

Clay # 176 Farmer (385-400)
DOWLING, Elias G. 39 m SC
Lucilla A. 34 f NC
FLOURNOY, James C. 15 m Ala
Leander 13 f "
DOWLING, Josephine 10 f "
Leonora A. 6 f "
Noah C. 3 m "

Euf # 916 Farmer(3100-13000)
DOWLING, Hansford 43 m SC
Martha 34 f Ga
Walter 12 m Ala
Asbury 10 m "
Joseph B. 8 m "
Andrew T. 6 m "
George P. 4 m "
Susan 2 f Ga
WEAVER, Ellen 29 f SC

Euf # 1100
DOZIER(?), Sarah 20 f Ga
(See David Johnson).

Euf # 481 Teacher (--- 1500)
DRAKE, Nathan B. 30 m Ga
Elizabeth 24 f "
Mary 4 f "
Charles 1 m Ala

Mdwy # 950 Physician (--- 16000)
DRAKE, W. G. 25 m NC
V. A. 22 f Ga
T. L. 6/12 f Ala

Mt. A. # 856 Farmer (800-300)
DRAPER, Benjamin 38 m Ga
Mary 40 f NC
William T. 15 m Ga
Mary A. 14 f "
Milledge 12 m "
Peter 9 m "
Martha 7 f "
Alley 5 f "

Mt. A. # 857 Farmer (700-350)
DRAPER, John 48 m Ga
T. C. 51 f SC
John S. 19 m Ga
N. S. 14 m "
Elizabeth S. 13 f "
GREEN, Sophia 14 f "
Wm. (Farmer) 22 m "

Mt. A. # 860 Farmer (1600-300)
DRAPER, Peter 52 m Ga
Lavica 45 f SC
Lucinda R. 17 f Ga
Elizabeth 15 f "
Caroline 12 f "
John T. 10 m "
Benjamin F. 7 m "
Amanda 4 f Ala
Frances 2 f "
PICKETT, Mary A. 21 f Ga
(Cont.)

(Mt. A. # 860 cont.)
PICKETT, George H. 3 m Ala
GREEN, William 20 m Ga
(Carpenter)

Mt. A. # 862 (--- 75)
DRAPER, Thomas 75 m Va
Rebecca 74 f Ga
Claiborne (Farmer) 23 m Ala

Mt. A. # 861 Farmer (--- 150)
DRAPER, William 23 m Ga
Narcissa 20 f "
Elizabeth 3 f Ala
Plarena(?) 9/12 f "

Euf # 886 Farmer (--- 100)
DREW, Emanuel 40 m Ga
M. E. 35 f "
Frances 10 f "
Sarah 7 f Ala
John W. 4 m "

Euf # 921 Hireling (-- --)
DREW, William 45 m Ga
John (Hireling) 16 m "
Malissa 40 f "
Frances E. 14 f "
James K. 12 m "
Eugenia 10 f "
Josephine 8 f Ala
Thomas 6 m "
Charles 8/12 m "

Euf # 980 (7500-20000)
DREWRY, Elizabeth 64 f Ga
Corinne(---15000) 24 f "
James A. (Farmer) 23 m "
(5000-16000)
H. H. (Farmer) 21 m "
(5000-16000)

Euf # 976 Physician (10000-48000)
DRURY, John W. 32 m Ga
Elizabeth 30 f "
Elizabeth 6 f Ala
Ellen 5 f "
Charles 3 m "
John 3/12 m "

Mdwy # 985
DRURY, William D. 6 m Ala
John W. 4 m "
(See Elizabeth A. Owen).

Clay # 1115
DRIGGARS, Artemesia 21 f Ga
(Cont.)

(Clay # 1115 cont.)
Narcissa J. 4 f Ala
Louisianna A. 1 f "
(See Bidsey Lott).

Clay # 63 (--- ---)
DRIGGARS, Eliza 31 f SC
Elizabeth 15 f Ga
HILL, Lotty 42 f NC
DRIGGARS, C. A. 6 f Ala

Euf # 1132 Bricklayer (--- 50)
DRIGGERS, John 34 m SC
Eliza 32 f "
Mary A. 15 f Ga
HILL, Lotty 40 f "

Luvl # 301
DRIGGARS, Martha 19 f Ala
(See Stephen H. Bounds).

Euf # 493 Overseer (--- 1000)
DRIGGERS, Samuel 42 m SC
Elizabeth 42 f "
John 19 m Ala

Luvl # 507 Farmer (--- ---)
DRIGGARS, Stephen 65 m SC
Nancy 48 f NC
C. C. (Farmer) 20 m Ala
Emily A. 19 f "
Oliver R. 16 m "
T. A. 15 f "

Euf # 1381 (--- ---)
DRISKILL, Avagena 23 f Ala
Elizabeth 20 f "
Martha 21 f "
Catharine 12 f "

Euf # 1376 Farmer (800-400)
DRISKILL, Elgit 46 m SC
Sarah E. 38 f "
Moses (Farm hand) 17 m Ala
Sarah H. 13 f "
Sintha 15 f "
William N. 8 m "
Johanna 5 f "

Euf # 685 Farmer (2000-400)
DUBOSE, D. D.(?) 36 m SC
Milbry 32 f Ga
James F. 15 m Ala
Lucinda J. 14 f "
William H. 12 m "
Martha 9 f "
Catharine 7 f "
Mary F. 4 f "
infant 4/12 f "

Euf # 686 Farmer (--- 200)
DUBOSE, Isiah 29 m SC
Edny 28 f Ga
Ann M. 10 f Ala
Virginia S. 7 f "

Txv # 1130 Farmer (400-300)
DUBOSE, James 54 m SC
Mary 46 f "
Nancy A. 23 f Ala
Sallie 21 f "
Jane 19 f "
Jeptha 17 m "
Arabella 13 f "
Alsy A. 11 f "
Robin E. 9 m "
Martha A. 7 f "
William H. 5 m "
Dississo 3 m "

Euf # 1262 Farmer (--- 100)
DUBOSE, John P. 23 m SC
Sarah 18 f Ala
Leonora 1 f "
PARMER, Geo. W. 21 m "
(Student, --- 150)

Euf # 690 Farmer (1200-400)
DUBOSE, Robert 45 m SC
Ailsey 36 f NC
Sarah 17 f Ala
Jeptha (Laborer) 18 m "

Euf # 1286 (--- ---)
DUBOSE, Sarah 58 f SC
Josephine V. 15 f Ala

Euf # 1264 Farmer (5000-18000)
DUBOSE, Seaborn 57 m Ga
Julius A. 21 m SC
(Farm hand, --- 150)
George W. 15 m Ala
Lydia V. 13 f "
Mincidora(?) 11 f "
THOMAS, Drusilla A. 26 f SC
(--- 3000)
Jesse N. 5 m Ala

Euf # 316 Farmer (2000-6500)
DUDLEY, George W. 27 m SC
Emaline 27 f Ala
George A. 4 m "
Carrie M. 3 f "

Euf # 864 Overseer (--- 1500)
DUFFILL, John 50 m Ga
Mary 40 f "
(Cont.)

(Euf # 864 cont.)
James Ann 14 f Ga
Margaret 12 f "
Elizabeth 10 f Ala

Euf # 1062 Pub. officer
DUGGER, W. M. 79 m Va
(See D. S. T. Douglass).

Mdwy # 1076 Overseer (--- 100)
DUKE, W. W. 40 m Ga
(See W. J. Moore)

Euf # 778 Farmer (--- 300)
DUNAWAY, George 21 m Ga
Mary 19 f "
(Married within the year).

Euf # 531 Overseer (--- 100)
DUNAWAY, John 28 m Ga
Sarah 27 f "
Melvina 8 f "
Theophilus 2 m Ala

Euf # 396 (200-50)
DUNFORD, Penelope 60 f SC
Elizabeth A. 35 f "
Margaret 8 f "
CAM--ON, J.(overseer) 23 m "

Euf # 446 Farm hand (--- ---)
DUNFORD, William G. 27 m SC
Elizabeth R. 23 f Ga
Emma R. 2 f Ala
William G. W. 1 m "

Euf # 1322 Farmer (--- 4000)
Dunn, A. J. 24 m Ga
Sarah 24 f "
Eugenia 6/12 f Ala

Euf # 303 (2000-4500)
DUNN, Ann 47 f Ga
Mary L. 21 f Ala

Luvl # 254 Farmer (800-300)
DUNN, Levi 44 m Ga
Epsey 22 f SC
Lavinia A. 16 f Ga
Sophronia 14 f "
J.M.T. 12 m Ala

Clay # 177 (1600-7500)
DUNN, Mary 45 f Ga
Wm.(Farmer,--- 1000) 21 m "
M.C. 18 f "
Susan 16 f "
Elizabeth 13 f "
(Cont.)

(Clay # 177 cont.)
P.M. 11 f Ga
Joseph H. 9 m "

Flk # 420 Overseer (--- ---)
DURDEN, Beverly 25 m Ga
Lucretia 17 f "
Henry B. 8/12 m Ala

Flk # 404 (--- ---)
DURDEN, Marian 50 f Ga
Elisha (Farmer) 30 m "
Hepsey 24 f "
Amanda 6 f Ala
Jane 4 f "
Ella 4/12 f "
Jerry 20 m Ga
Nancy 18 f "
Mary 12 f "
Major 10 m "
Reuben 7 m "

Nwto # 549
DURDEN, Sallie 57 f SC
(See P. J. Strength).

Euf # 180 Engineer (1500-1500)
DURDAM, James H. 27 m Ga
Jane 28 f Fla
Mary E. 5 f Ala
Frances W. 4 f "
Alonzo 1 m "
MCDONALD, Eliza 32 f "

Luvl # 517 Miller (--- ---)
DUTTON, Mathias 28 m Eng

Flk # 502 Farmer (--- ---)
DYE, William A. 21 m Ga
Louisa 22 f "
George 8/12 m "

Euf 534 Laborer
DYER, Thomas A. 23 m Ga
(See Monroe Stanford)

Euf # 661 Farmer (--- 150)
DYKES, Isaac 27 m Ala
Lydia 24 f SC
Minerva 5 f "
Alonzo 3 m Ala
Zylphy 1 f "
JOHNSON, Joseph 11 m "

Euf # 666
DYKES, Nancy J. 12 f Ala
(See Samuel Wilkerson)

Bkb # 719 Farmer (1000-600)
DYKES, William 39 m SC
Nancy J. 30 f Ala
George W. (Farmer) 15 m "
Margaret 13 f "
Susan A. 11 f "
William 9 m "
Mary 6 f "
Easter 4 f "
John 1 m "

Euf # 983
EADEY, Josephine 16 f Ala
(See E. B. Mershon)

Nwto # 621 Farmer (400-200)
EASTERLING, Daniel B. 37 m SC
Margaret 33 f NC
Margaret 16 f Ala
Allen 14 m "
William 16 m "
Mary 13 f "
Enoc 12 m "
Sarah 10 f "
Andrew 8 m "
Elizabeth 8 f "
Daniel 2 m "
Miles 3/12 m "

Euf # 440 Stone cutter
EATON, Charles 26 m NY
(See McNamara's R.R. Gro.)

Euf # 786 Farmer (34000-47500)
EBERHART, Samuel 54 m Ga
Mary 60 f "
EBERHART, Samuel, Jr. 26 m "
(Farmer)
Irene O. 16 f "

Euf # 848 Farmer (1300-5500)
ECHOLS, S. C. 27 m Ga
M.E. 25 f "
George 7 m "(?)
Laura 5 f Ala
Albert 2 m "
MINTER, M. S. 55 f Ga
(--- 4700)

Mdwy # 1067 Overseer (860-1200)
EDGAR, John 45 m SC
Frances 30 f Ga
Emma 2 f Ala

Luvl # 348 (900---)
EDGE, Casa 70 f Ga
GREEN, Marion 25 m "
(Cont.)

(Luvl # 348 Cont.)
Jane 21 f Ala
LEWIS, Jane L. 4 f "

Luvl # 321 Farmer (--- ---)
Edge, Eli 25 m Ala
Elizabeth 25 f SC
Jesse 6/12 m Ala
DAY, Emeline 12 f "

Clay # 67 Farmer (---100)
EDGE, Levi 31 m Ala
Matilda 26 f "
William L. 7 m "
John W. 5 m "
E.L. 2 m "

Mdwy # 1078 Farmer (1365-1200)
EDMUNSON, Andrew 41 M SC
Mary 41 f Ga
Emma 20 f "
John 19 m "
Martha 17 f Ala
Caroline 15 f "
Jane 14 f "
Isabella 12 f "
Julia 11 f "
Andrew 19 m "
Eliza 7 f "
Victoria 3 f "
William 5 m "
Eugenia 1 f "

Luvl # 314 Farmer (--- ---)
EDWARDS, David D. 52 m NC
William (Farmer) 24 m Ga
Thos. L.J. " 22 m "
Jane 17 f NC
Martha D. 14 f Ala
John 13 m "

Luvl # 652 Merchant (8000-12000)
EFURD, G. C. 28 m Ala
Martha 24 f "
John 7 m "
----- 4 m "
HERRING, W.W.(clerk) 19 m "
GRUBBS, Green J. 24 m "
(---2,000)

Mt. A. # 834 (---8,500)
EFURD, Mary 55 f SC
Giles C. (Farmer) 23 m Ala
LEWIS, Mary 16 f "
Antionette 8 f "

Luvl # 359 Farmer (---2,000)
(Cont.)

(Luvl # 359 cont).
EFURD, Thomas C. 28 m Ala
Elizabeth 24 f "
Thomas W. 3 m "
Emanuel 2 m "
William C. 3/12 m "

Clay # 104 Farmer (1000-7900)
EFURD, Wm. T.J.C. 33 m Ala
Elizabeth 20 f "
Thos. R. 5 m "
Martha 4/12 f "
LONG, M. 45 f NC
Gilbert 14 m Ala
Newton (Farm laborer) 16 m "

Luvl # 366 Farmer (1000-4000)
EIDSON, F. W. 25 m Ala
Rhoda 68 f NC
BROACH, Ann 28 f Ala
RIGDON, John (Farmer) 18 m "

Luvl # 325 Farmer (--- ---)
EIDSON, James 70 m SC
Sally (Insane) 34 f Ga

Euf # 996 (896) Overseer
EIDSON, James J. 25 m Ga
(See Wm. H. Lowman)

Clay # 221
EIDSON, Mary J. 29 f NC
George 14 m Ala
James A. 10 m "
Ann 5 f "
Martha E. 1 f "
(See Polly Herring).

Luvl # 324 Farmer (25000-16000)
EIDSON, Wiley 37 m Ga
Martha A. 35 f Ala
John 10 m "
Harris 8 m "
James L. 6 m "
Mary 5 f "
Rhoda 3 f Ala
Jane 1/12 f "
George 13 m "
Janus 12 m "

Mt. A. 819
ELAM, Elizabeth 60 f Ga
(See John C. White).

Mdwy # 986 Tanner
ELDER, John -- --
(See Sarah Owens)

Clay # 19 Carriage maker
ELGEA, James A. 24 m NJ
(Living in hotel).

Clay # 203 Farmer (200-100)
ELLIOTT, James 55 m SC
Jane 42 f "
John W. (Farmer) 22 m Ala
James H. " 18 m "
Joseph F. " 16 m "
S. F. 12 m "
C. M. 10 m "
M. J. 6 f "
Alexander 3 m "

Clay # 202 Farmer (--- ---)
ELLIOTT, Thomas 21 m Ala
Celia A. 14 f "
(Married within the year).

Euf # 136 Clerk (-- 65)
ELLIS, E. C. 25 m Ga

Euf # 414
Ellis, Fielding 84 m Va
(See John E. Denard).

Clay # 178 Pauper in poorhouse
ELLIS, Stephen 30 m Ga

Mdwy # 1072 Farmer (4300-4000)
ELLIS, T. H. 31 m Ga
Mary E. 28 f "
Ida F. 3 f Ala

Mdwy # 1007 Farmer (---500)
ELY, William E. 27 m Ga
(See J. H. Smith).

Bkb # 706 Farmer (4000-2000)
EMMERSON, Benj. H. 45 m Ga
Narcissa 44 f "
Crawford (Farmer) 22 m Ala
Sinthia 17 f "
Wade 15 m "
John 14 m "
Green 13 m "
BALL, Sarah 84 f Va

Euf # 367 Laborer
ENDFINGER, William 21 m Ala
(See James A. Welch)

Euf # 1372 (3,000-12,000)
ENGRAM, Mariah L. 38 f Ga
Colquit C. (Farmer) 19 m Ala
A. N. 16 f "
(Cont.)

(Euf # 1372 cont.)
John E. 16 m Ala
Sanders D. 12 m "
E. Y. 10 f "
Louisa 5 f "
MASSEY, Mary J. 21 f Ga
(--- $4,000)

Euf # 418
ESPY, Caroline 33 f Ga
(See R. M. Hardwick).

Euf # 8-8 Clerk (--- ---)
ESPY, James M. 18 m Ala
RUSSELL, James H. H. 19 m "
(Clerk)

Euf # 591 Farmer (1500-2500)
ESPY, John S. 27 m Ga
Elizabeth J. 26 f "
John R. 3 m "
Louisa 1 f "
WILLIAMS, James R. 24 m "
(Laborer).

Euf # 592 Farmer (1600-2200)
ESPY, William C. 29 m Ga
Hariet 27 f Ala
Elizabeth 3 f "
Leonora 9/12 f "
BURNHAM, Maron 14 m "
GRIGGERS, Wm. F. 24 m SC
(Laborer)

Euf # 421
ETHRIDGE, James 23 m Ga
(See E. N. Fountain)

Euf # 214 Laborer (--- ---)
ETHRIDGE, John 35 m Ga
Alethe 40 f SC
John 4 m Ala
George 2 m "
Jane 1/12 f "

Euf # 1161 Farmer (1000-14000)
ETHRIDGE, Richard 60 m NC
Betsay G. 54 f SC
Meshach (Student) 21 m Ala
Abednego " 18 m "

Euf # 1158 Farmer (---200)
ETHRIDGE, Shade 27 m Ga
Lydia A. 19 f "
Esther M.M.M. 1 f Ala
Eli R. 2/12 m "

Euf # 765 Farmer (500-200)
ETHRIDGE, Stephen 35 m Ga
Malissa R. 22 f Ala
William D. 2 m "
Columbus A. 3/12 m "

Mdwy # 1040 (1700-2000)
EUBANKS, Nancy C. 60 f Ga
A.F.(Farmer, (--2000)30 m "
Nancy 20 f "

Clay # 21 Carriage maker
EVANS, D. W. 22 m Ala
J. B. 20 m "
(Carriage painter)

Bkb # 700 Farmer (2000-6000)
EVANS, J. L. C. 38 m Ga
Martha A. 43 f "
B. T. 2 m Ala

Euf # 1237 Farmer (800-400)
EVANS, James 60 m Ga
Jane 23 f Ala
Sarah 21 f "

Flk # 497 Farmer (--- ---)
Evans, John 46 m SC
Polly 38 f Ala
Jane 20 f "
Elizabeth 18 f "
Rhoda 13 f "
Charlton 11 m "
Salathiel 8 m "
Margaret 6 f "
Robert 4 m "
Jeremiah 2 m "

Euf # 1238 Farmer (--- 150)
EVANS, William 28 m Ala
Julia 20 f "
James 5 m "
Martha 2 f "
infant 1/12 f "

Euf # 1055 Dentist (2500-2000)
EVANS, William W. 39 m Ga
Mary S. 60 f NC
Levonia A. 20 f Ga
Lucinda D. 16 f "

Clay # 17 Carriage Trimmer
EVARTS, S. B. 33 m Conn
H. A. 23 f Ga
H. E. 1 f Ala

Euf # 441 Foundry man
EVERETT, John 22 m Ga
(See Mary H. Lowman).

Euf # 186 Moulder(?)
EVERETT, John 22 m Fla
(See Wm. H. Clark).

Euf # 321
EVERETT, Mary 13 f Ga
(See Stephen Bedsole)

Euf # 325
EVERETT, R. E. 10 f Ga
Jane E. 6 f Ala
(See James P. Scott).

Mdwy 985 (---4000)
FASON, Elizabeth 30 f Ga
Rebecca (---3000) 22 f "
Rosaline 6 f Ala

Euf # 1030
FAISON, Nancy 78 f Ga
(See Franklin Cobb).

Mdwy # 1022 Overseer (--- 100)
FASON, William D. 50 m Ga
Linny 45 f "
William W. 6 m Ala
James H. 3 m "

Euf # 152 Confectioner (--500)
FARLEY, John 25 m Ire
Margaret(Confectioner) 26 f "
Mary 1 f NY

Txv # 1203 Farmer (960-500)
FARMER, Benjamin 55 m SC
Eliza 32 f "
Wm. R. (Farmer) 23 m Ala
Sarah A. 18 f "
Catherine 16 f "
Matilda E. 11 f "
Henry K. 10 m "
Nancy J. 9 f "
TURNER, Caroline 22 f Ga

Txv # 1197-1198
FARMER, Molsey 50 f NC
Martha (160-150) 26 f Ala
Jane 19 f "
Amanda 15 f "
Sarah 12 f "
MORRIS, Abram(Laborer) 26 m "
(--- 100)
Mary 22 f "
George 1 m "

Bfd # 1252 Farmer (160-200)
FARMER, William 25 m Ala
Rachael 23 f "
Molsie 1 f "

Mt. A. # 817 Planter (10000-23000)
FARRIOR, Henry 36 m NC
Sarah A. 27 f Ga
Ann W. 8 f Ala
P.A. 6 f "
Claudia 5 f "
Alberta 3 f "
Frederick W. 3/12 m "
JACKSON, Wm. 23 m "
(Overseer)

Clay # 94 Planter (5000-10000)
FARRIOR, Wm., Sr. 52 m NC
Sarah 35 f Ga
Martha A. 16 f Ala
James 15 m Ga
Mary A. 14 f Ala
Francis M. 12 m "
William, Jr. 9 m "
Joseph 7 m "
Sarah 5 f "
Louisianna 2 f "
Thomas 4/12 m "

Flk # 493 Farmer (8000-30,000)
FAULK, A. W. 50 m Ga
Charlotte 48 f SC
Nancy A. 21 f Ala
C.F. 18 f "
Henry B. (Farmer) 17 m "
James K. " 15 m "
Mark W. 13 m "
Winston 11 m "
William 7 m "
Zenobia A. 5 f "
RUNNELS, John A. 23 m Ga
(Farmer)

Flk # 419 Farmer (6000 - 20,000)
FAULK, H. L. 45 m Ga
Sarah J. 36 f SC
W. W. 15 m Ala
Henry W. 13 m "
James H. 11 m "
Mary J. 9 f "
Leroy A. 7 m "
Nancy E. 5 f "
C.A.J. 2 f "

Nwto # 556 Farmer (1800-7500)
FAULK, Henry 62 m Ga
Sarah 59 f SC
William 36 m Ala
Emeline 30 f "
Martha 25 f "
Sarah A. 20 f "
James M. 20 m "

Flk # 418 Farmer (120-4000)
FAULK, J. W. 28 m Ala
Henry W. 10 m "
N. W. 9 m "
Sarah J. 6 f "
John C. 4 m "
Francis M. 2 m "

Flk # 412
FAULK, Lafayette 22 m Ala
(See Francis Johns).

Mdwy # 1015 Farmer (8000-16000)
FAULK, Lorenzo 48 m SC
Mary 42 f Ga
William B. 20 m Ala
R.J. 17 m "
James M. 15 m "
John F. 13 m "
Daniel H. 11 m "
Elizabeth L. 9 f "
Viola 6 f "
George H. 3 m "
SPENCE, Lewis 22 m "
STUCKEY, Mary J. 6 f "
FAULK, Sarah (idiot) 55 f SC
PATTERSON, Dougald 30 m NC
(Teacher, --- 1000)

Flk # 411
FAULK, Lucretia 11 f Ala
William 9 m "
Henry 7 m "
(See John B. Ivey)

Flk # 409 (1,000-11,000)
FAULK, Lurena 38 f NC
Nancy 14 f Ala
Rhoda 11 f "
Jefferson 13 m "

Mdwy # 948
FAULK, Mary A. 50 f Ga
(See W. B. Griffin)

Flk # 417 (800-2000)
FAULK, Nancy 60 f Ga
LOVELACE, E. L. 20 m Ala
(Student, 150-1000)
(Cont.)

(Flk # 417 cont.)
FAULK, M. W. 30 m Ala
(Farmer, 1000-1100)
Nancy 9 f "
Henry N. 7 m "
Cinthia J. 4 f "

Luvl # 288
FAULK, Sarah 18 f Ala
(See Leroy E. Stafford).

Luvl # 278 (1000 ---)
FAULK, Sarah 16 f Ala
Mary (--- 1500) 15 f "
James (--- 1500) 10 m "
Martha (--- 1500) 8 f "
(See John Sloan)

Euf # 225 Hewer
FAULK, Thomas 61 m NC
Penelope 40 f Ga
Emily M. 18 f "
Jeremiah (Laborer) 16 m "
Rachael 14 f "
James 12 m Ala
Elizabeth 9 f "
Eliza 8 f "
Thomas 3 m "
John 3/12 m "

Mt. A. # 825 Overseer (-- 200)
FAULKNER, Franklin 26 m Ga
Prudence 22 f "
Clara 6/12 f Ala

Euf # 1053 Carriage trimmer
FAULKNER, Peter 27 m Conn
(See John W. McAllister).

Euf # 177 Hat maker (-- --)
FAUGIEL(?), R. 44 m Fr
Denise 36 f "
Cheaphile(?) 9 m "

Mt. A. # 890 (300-150)
FAVOURS, Tabitha 44 f SC
John 10 m Ala
William T. 6 m "
Matilda 16 f Ga

Mt. A. # 807 (-- 50)
FAVOURS, Winneford 60 f SC

Mdwy # 947
FEAGIN, Ella 6/12 f Ala
(See J. M. Head).

Mdwy # 1001 (--- 5000)
FEAGIN, G. W. 37 m Ga
Dorothy 30 f "

Mdwy # 980 Merchant (--- 11000)
FEAGIN, Isaac B. 27 m Ga
Daniel 23 m Ala
(Merchant, --- 1500)
Mary 19 f "

Mdwy # 1002 Planter (1400-50000)
FEAGIN, James M., Sr. 46 m Ga
Elmira 38 f Ala
Samuel J. 19 m "
Noah B. 17 m "
Martha E. 14 f "
Wealthy M. 12 f "
Missouri A. 10 f "
James M., Jr. 7 m "
Elmira 5 f "
Louisa J. 2 f "

Mdwy # 946 Book keeper (--4300)
FEAGIN, Samuel 36 m Ga
Julia T. 34 f "
Georgia A. 10 f Ala
Josephine A. 8 f "
Frances A. 6 f "
Samuel 4 m "
Cornelia 2 f "

Euf # 813 Farmer (--- 300)
Fedrick, John S. 47 m Ga
Katura N. 27 f SC
Thomas 9 m Ga
Ellen 8 f "
Philletus 6 m "
Willie 4 m "
Josephine 2 f Ala

Clay # 102 Planter (---5000)
FENN, J. T. 25 m Ala
R. A. 22 f SC
Sallie M. 11/12 f Ala
BRADDAM, R. 30 m SC
Sarah 25 f Ala
John 6 m "
Narcissa 2 f "
infant 1/12 m "
infant 1/12 m "

Clay # 48 (6000-10000)
FENN, Mary 22 f Ga
C. W. (Calvin) 23 m Ala
(Clerk, --- 2000)
(Cont.)

(Clay # 48 cont.)
MCMILLAN, Laura 19 f Ga
(Teacher)
FENN, S. A. 14 f Ala
Ella 13 f "
Mary E. 10 f "
Susan 10 f "
MCMILLAN, A. 45 m NC
(A.S.P.Clergyman & teacher,
----- 3,000)
Eliza 38 f Ga
(Teacher in Female College -
A. & Eliza McMillan married
within the year).
CREWS, Mary V. 16 f Ala
Nancy 10 f "

Luvl # 531 Planter (14000-
32000)
FENN, Matthew 62 m Ga
Cordelia 24 f SC
Cullus (Farmer) 18 m Ala
Sallie V. 14 f "
Mary E. 10 f "
James 12 m "
Eugenia 7 f "
M. Z.(?) 6 f "
G. A. 2 f "
Anna R. 1 f "

Euf # 80 Carriage maker
(8,000-7,000)
FENN, William A. 40 m Conn
Jane 42 f "
Elizabeth 20 f Ga
Frances 18 f "
William 15 m Ala
Jane 12 f "
Willard 9 m "
Henrietta 3 f "

Euf # 128 Carriage maker
FENWICK, Fletcher 26 Va
(See Amos Cary).

Euf # 172 Brick mason
(75,000-20,000)
FERGURSON, Robert 48 m Ire.

Euf # 1393 Tailor (--- ---)
FERRELL, Peter 25 m Ire
MCENTE, Margaret 18 f "
FERRELL, Daniel 19 m "

Euf # 1366 (5,000-7,000)
FIELD, Sarah 29 f NC
Henry 7 m Ala

Euf # 233 Farmer (3,850-
6,200)
FIELDS, B. B. 44 m SC
Amanda B. 33 f Ga
Martha 17 f Ala
John W. 15 m "
Charles R. 14 m "
Mary T. 12 f "
Amanda E. 11 f "
Alexr. B. 9 m "
Sam 7 m "
Eva 4 f "
Ida 2 f "
Sallie M. 6/12 f "

Euf # 420 Laborer (--- ---)
FIFE, Robert 34 m Scot
(See James Daniels).

Euf # 1187 Farmer (--- 150)
FILLINGIM, J. 35 m Ala
Margaret 26 f "
Mary A. 10 f "
William 8 m "
Harriet L. 6 f "
John 2 m "

Euf # 1188
FILLINGIM, Mary 51 f Ga
Ann 18 f Ala
Malissa 16 f "

Euf # 760 Farmer (--- 200)
FILLINGIM, Robert 21 m Ala
Mary 20 f "
(Married within the year).

Euf # 796
FINCH, Charles 8 m Ala
(See W. B. Knight).

Euf # 799 Wheelwright (1000-
2000)
FINCH, William H. 44 m Ga
Mary 40 f "
John F. (Wheelwright) 22 m "
James M.(In school) 16 m "
Jesse S. 14 m "
George W. 12 m "
Mary 10 f Ala

Clay # 730 Farmer (120-375)
FINNEY, Elisha 52 m Ga
Sarah 37 f "
Sarah A. E. 20 f "
Lucinda 16 f "
Amanda N. 12 f Ala
(Cont.)

(Clay # 730 cont.)
James H. 10 m Ala
F.A.M. 8 f "
M.A.M. 5 f "
L.A.L. 11/12 f "
BARRON, James 24 m Ga
(Laborer)

Euf # 173 Brick mason
FLANNAGIN, William 25 m Ire
(See John Bailey)

Clay # 19 Merchant (--- ---)
FLERSHEIM, S. 26 m Ger
(Born Hessen, Germany)

Euf # 1047 Farmer (30,000-100,000)
FLEWELLEN, E. R. 50 m Ga
Susan W. 45 f "
Martha E. 19 f "
James R. 17 m "
Mary A. 15 f Ala
Georgia E. 12 f "
Susan Z. 10 f "

Euf # 173 Brick mason (-- --)
FLINN, J. E. 30 m Ala
(See John Bailey).

Luvl # 375 Farmer (2500-12000)
FLINN, R. J. 35 m Ga
Martha A. 22 f "
John 7 m Ala
William 5 m Ga
R. J. 9/12 m Ala

Luvl # 351 (3,000-12,000)
FLINN, S. J. 36 f NC
Julia 8 f Ga
Henrietta 7 f Ala
Charles 5 m "
Caroline 3 f "

Euf # 1023 Farmer (10,000-50,000)
FLORENCE, John 53 m Ga
Margaret L. 42 f "
Adam H. 22 m "
(Overseer, --- 2,500)
John F. 15 m "
Mary E. 17 f "
Cornelia M. 12 f "
Cora 11 f "
Allice 6 f "
Thos. J. (Student) 20 m "

Mdwy # 1020 Overseer on farm
FLORENCE, M. J. 24 m Ga

Euf # 1050 Farmer (14,000-45,000)
FLORENCE, Obediah 50 m Ga
Arramitta 38 f "
Charles 16 m Ala
Mary F. 14 f "
Martha V. 12 f "
Samuel 11 m "
Peter 7 m "
Lucy 5 f "
William 2 m "

Mdwy # 1037 Overseer on farm (--- 1,500)
FLORENCE, Thomas 27 m Ga

Euf # 1036 Farmer (6400-34000)
FLORENCE, Thomas J. 46 m Ga
Mary S. 42 f "
Mary J. 20 f "
Elizabeth 13 f Ala
Henry B. 11 m "
Ellen 6 f "
VAUGHN, Webster 17 m Ga
Hireling).

Euf # 383
FLOURNOY, Ellen M. 28 f SC
(See Eliza H. Baker)

Euf # 743 (800-150)
FLOURNOY, Feriby 30 f Ala
William F. 11 m "
Eliza J. 5 f "

Euf # 457 Ward of R.R.Howard
FLOURNOY, Frances 17 f Ala
(See Robert R. Howard).

Clay # 176
FLOURNOY, James C. 15 m Ala
Leander 13 f "
(See Elias G. Dowling).

Luvl # 365 Farmer (3500-3000)
FLOURNOY, John 33 m NC
Ailsey 64 f "
Ann 40 f "
Harriett 37 f "
ROBERTS, Wm. 14 m Ala
FLOYD, Stephen 24 m NC
(Farmer)
DILLEHAY, Jeff 18 m Ga
(Idiotic)

Euf # 166 Farmer (20000-35000)
FLOURNOY, Josiah 19 m Ga

Euf # 414 Laborer
FLOURNOY, Marvin 21 m Ga
(See John E. Denard).

Euf # 224 Farmer (8000-17000)
FLOURNOY, Robert 25 m Ga
Susan 20 f Ala
Walter D. 1 m "
Charles M. 2/12 m "
Osborn 16 m "
Thomas 14 m "

Euf # 170 Carriage driver
FLOURNOY, William M. 25 m Ga
Ocean 24 f "
(See Wm. D. Hailey)

Euf # 913 Farmer (3000-2000)
FLOWERS, Harrell 34 m Ga
Frances J. 12 f Ala
Cintha 10 f "
William 8 m "
Daught A. 7 f "
BOBBET, Mary 22 f "
FLOWERS, Nancy A. 5 f "
Josephine 2 f "
John W. 6 m "

Euf # 918
FLOWERS, Penelope 79 f SC
(See Wm. D. Horn)

Mt. A. # 907 Farmer (220-350)
FLOWERS, Wm. J. 27 m Ala
Rebecca 23 f "
John W. 8 m "
George 3 m "

Euf # 609 Farmer (4000-16000)
FLOWERS, Wright 40 m NC
Celia 40 f "
Thos. H. 14 m Ala
Berry L. 13 m "
Rebecca A. 11 f "
John A. 9 m "
Mary P. 7 f "
Warren G. 5 m "
Abner 2 m "
Levin M. 39 m NC
(Carpenter, 600-500)
Abner 26 m Ala
(Carpenter, 500-300)
(Cont.)

(Euf # 609 cont.)
SEARCY, King (Laborer) 20 m Ga
HENDLEY, Richard 20 m "
(Laborer)

Euf # 271 Overseer (1500-300)
FLOYED, James M. 42 m Tenn
Mary E. 30 f "
GOODING, Ebeneza 28 m NC
(Laborer, --- 25)

Txv # 1156
FLOYD, D. M. 26 f Ala
Mary 4 f "
Joel C. 2 m "

Euf # 544 (--- 50)
FLOYD, Fady 43 f SC
Sarah 16 f Ala
Robert 12 m "
John 8 m "

Euf # 1160 Farmer (1800-2500)
Floyd, James 25 m Ala
Martha 20 f "
William 2 m "
Peter 1 m "

Clay # 1113 Farmer (360-250)
Floyd, Josep H. 23 m Ala
Sarah A. 19 f "
William C. 2 m "
Thomas G. W. 5/12 m "

Euf # 488 Overseer (--- 1,500)
FLOYD, Joseph H. 25 m Ga

Euf # 1281
FLOYD, Mary A. 17 f Ga
Hardy 13 m "

Clay # 731 (--- 150)
FLOYD, Mary E. 48 f SC
Martha A. 20 f Ala
Frances 16 f "
Thomas S. 11 m "

Clay # 246 Farmer (--- ---)
FLOYD, Michael 69 m Va
Sally 47 f NC

Clay # 1282 Farmer (3500-8000)
FLOYD, Page 43 m NC
Elizabeth 39 f SC
Wm. P. (Farmer) 21 m Ala
John J. 17 m "
Molsey J. 15 f "
(Cont.)

(Clay # 1282 cont.)
Louisa 13 f Ala
Ann E. 11 f "
Colen 5 m "
Henry L. 3 m "
infant 1 m "

Luvl # 365 Farmer
FLOYD, Stephen 24 m NC
(See John Flournoy).

Luvl # 303 Farmer (--- ---)
FLOYD, Theophilus 28 m Ala
Elizabeth 28 f "
Benjamin N. 7 m "
Angelina 5 f "
William H. 2 m "
MCKINNEY, James 11 m "

Euf # 1204 Farmer (500-1200)
FLOYD, Wilson H. 21 m Ga
Mary A. 15 f Ala
FLOYD, Frederick 26 m Ga
(Farmer, 500-400)
Frances 19 f "
Leonora E. 1 f "
(Wilson H. & Mary A. married within the year).

Euf # 12-12 Shoemaker
FOLLMER, Phillip 29 m Ger

Euf # 302
FOLSOM, Elizabeth 39 f Ga
James M. (Tinner) 17 m "
Amanda 15 f "
Mary F. 13 f Ala
James T. 39 m Ga
(Tin Plu(?)500-300)
George W. 11 m Ala
Martha A.E. 9 f "
Richard E. 7 m "

Euf # 518 Carpenter (-- --)
FORD, Jonathan 28 m Ire
Catharine 28 f "
MCANTY(?), Margaret 18 f "

Euf # 440 Laborer (-- --)
FORD, Patrick 26 m Ire
(See McNamara's R.R. Gro.)

Mdwy # 1088 Farmer (5000-5500)
FORD, William C. 50 m SC
Mary A. 38 f Ga
Thos. J. H. 18 m Ala
(Cont.)

(Mdwy # 1088 cont.)
Sidney 16 m Ala
Oscar L. 14 m "
V. V. 12 f "

Euf # 1130 (250-150)
FOREHAND, Jane 30 f Ala
Stephen 2 m "
MYERS, Ellen 18 f "

Euf # 691 Farmer (700-100)
FOREHAND, John 23 m SC
Elizabeth 18 f Ga
Jane 1 f Ala
Jesse (Laborer) 21 m "
BROOKS, Richard 10 m Ga

Euf # 1391 Carpenter (--- 500)
FORT, Willis 28 m Ga

Euf # 151 Clerk (--- 1000)
FOSTER, Clark W. 20 m Ga
KALBFLEISCH, Herman 31 m Ger
(Baker, -- 500, born Hesse, Ger)

Clay # 57 Lawyer (-- --)
FOSTER, John A. 30 m Ala
M. M. 20 f Ga
(See Abner Borders).

Euf # 232 Laborer
FOUCHE, George 20 m Ala
(See Orestus Bell).

Euf # 431 (-- --)
FOUCHE, Lucy 40 f Ga
William (Laborer) 19 m Ala
George " 21 m "

Euf # 543 Wheelwright (-- --)
FOUCHE, William 50 m Ga

Euf # 421 Bricklayer (3000-3000)
FOUNTAIN, E. N(?) 26 m Ga
Martha E. 20 f "
ETHRIDGE, James 23 m "
(Occp., none- 3000-3000)

Euf # 867 Farmer (125,000-8,500)
Foy, William H. 47 m SC
Mary 29 f "
James E. 8 m Ala
John 5 m "
Simpson 3 m "
Levi 9/12 m "
HOWELL, P. A. 35 f SC
Randolph (Overseer) 20 m "
BUCKHALTER, D. 18 m "

Euf # 379 Farmer (1600-15000)
FRANKLIN, Edwin 50 m Ga
Sarah Y(?) 40 f "
Mary F. 20 f "
Elizabeth 18 f "
Sarah 16 f "
Martha 14 f Ala
Laura 12 f "
John 11 m "
Edwin 8 m "
Benjamin 5 m "
infant 4/12 f "

Mt. A. # 791 (--- 100)
FRAZIER, Ann 41 f SC
Louis (Farm Laborer) 16 m Ala
James T. 14 m "
Rebecca 10 f "
F. M. 6 f "
William M. 4 m "
Mary F. 1 f "

Mdwy # 927 Farmer (--- 200)
FRAZIER, James 30 m Ga
Sarah 25 f "
Missouri 2 f Ala

Bkb # 741 Farmer (--- 150)
FREE, Isiah K. 38 m SC
Nancy 33 f Ga
Greenberry 9 m Ala
Mary E. 8 f "
Elizabeth 4 f "
William A. 1/12 m "

Bkb # 740 Farmer (--- 200)
Free, Malaci 44 m SC
Winnie 40 f Ga
Martha 20 f SC
William 14 m Ga
Peter 7 m Ala
Joseph D. 3 m "

Luvl # 257 Merchant (1000-5000)
FREEMAN, Henry 35 m NC
Mary F. 31 f Ala
Davis 11 m "
Louisa 9 f "
Robert N. 7 m "
Charles 4 m "
Edward 2 m "
MCLENNON, Phillip 30 m NC
(Clerk, 1200-3000)
GRUBBS, G. G. 22 m Ala
(Merchant, 400-3500)
(Cont.)

(Luvl # 257 cont.)
BRADLEY, Henry 24 m Ala
(Clerk in store, -- 1000)
MORETON(?),W. W. 25 m Ga
(Physician, ---1000)
BOYKIN, James 22 m "
(carriagemaker, 300-5000)

Euf # 216 Student
FREEMAN, Tandy R. 18 m Ga
(See Arch. Bonnelle).

Bkb # 684 Farmer (4000-16000)
FRYAR, George W. 48 m SC
Matilda 49 f "
John H. (Farmer) 23 m "
Wm. R. " 16 m Ala
M. E. 13 f "
Sidney A. 11 m "
AVANT, Andrew 21 m Ga
(Farmer)

Clay # 53 Planter (17000-11000)
FRYER, R. H. 40 m SC
Lucinda 31 f Ala
C. M. 1 f "

Euf # 561 Farmer (1600-300)
FULLER, James S.(?)T. 27 m Ga
Sophia 31 f Ala
Emma J. 4 f "
Thos. P. 1 m "

Euf # 17 (---45,000)
FULMORE, Joseph R. 52 m Ala
Caroline S. 47 f "
Mary 13 f "
(See Wm. A. McTyre).

Mdwy # 1086 Overseer (1300-250)
FUQUAY, David 39 m Ga
Mary A. 27 f "
James 5 m Ala
John 4 m "

Euf 1229 Farmer 2600-1300
FUQUAY, John 38 m NC
Jency 35 f Ala
Calvin S. 13 m "
James A. 12 m "
Levin A. 11 m "
Nancy J. 7 f "
William M. 5 m "
Andrew J. 3 m "

Euf # 1141
FUQUAY, Mary A. 17 f SC
(See Lotty Landrum).

Txv # 1194 Farmer (220-275)
FUQUAY, Randolph 41 m Ga
Mary A. E. 30 f SC
Randolph 9 m Ala
Margaret E. 5 f "
George W. 3 m "
William 5/12 m "

Txv # 1220 Farmer (480-300)
FUQUAY, Sterling 40 m Ga
Maria 36 f "
Eliza 15 f Ala
Sterling 13 m "
Martha 10 f "
Mahala C. 9 f "
Jesse 7 m "
Mary J. 5 f "

Euf # 1140 Overseer (--- 50)
FUQUAY, William 30 m Ala
Lydia 22 f "

Euf # 749 (-- --)
FURMAN, Jeremiah F. 22 m Ga
Argain 30 f "
(Married within the year)

Clay # 112
FUTCH, Asbury 8 m Ga
(See Jas. W. Dickert).

Clay # 111
FUTCH, Elijah 13 m Ga
(See John S. Nix).

Euf # 500
FUTCH, Mary 14 f Ala
Catharine 12 f "
Stephen 10 m "
(See William Jones).

Euf # 439
FUTCH, Mary 12 f Ga
Catherine 8 f "
Stephen 6 m "
(See William Jones).

Mdwy # 1034 Farmer (---9500)
GACHET, C. B. 33 m Ga
Mary 21 f "
Chalmers 1 m Ala

Clay # 213 Farmer (--- ---)
GAINEY, Andrew 18 m Fla
(See James Hailey).

Euf # 910
GALLOWAY, William 14 m Ala
(See Hosea Bailey).

Clay # 164 Farmer
GAMMON, Benjamin 20 m Ala
(See Nancy A. Bass).

Clay # 164 Farmer (2800-7000)
GAMMON, D. M. 24 m Ala
Mary J. 24 f Ga
Jack 102 m Va

Clay # 135 Farm Laborer
GANEY, Andrew 18 m Fla

Clay # 206 Mill Wright (--350)
GANNON, William 52 m Mass
Sarah B. 42 f SC
Ivy(?) Ann 26 f Ala
Gaston 14 m "
Frances V. 7 f "
James 1/12 m "

Euf # 89 Banker (5000-40000)
GARDENER(?), Colin 48 m NY
Jane 47 f Ga
Ida L. 8 f Mass
ALLEN, John F. 40 m Mass
(Teacher, ---$2,000)
Eliza 30 f Va

Euf # 111
GARDENER, John 10 m --
Benjamin 7 m --
(See T. F. Segler).

Euf # 788 Farmer (40000-42000)
GARLAND, Edward 49 m Va
Mary 39 f Ga
Ailsey C. 13 f Ala
Mary 9 f "
John B. 7 m "
Fanny 5 f "
Sarah V. 3 f "

Euf # 829 Hireling
GARLAND, Jeff 22 m Ga
(See Sarah Massey).

Luvl # 571 Farmer (1000-1000)
GARNER, John 56 m NC
Vicey 44 f Ga
Dicey 23 f Ala
L. M. 21 f "
Sarah 19 f "
Martha 11 f "
John A. J. 16 m "
Henry 6 m "

Nwto # 578 Farmer (300-200)
GARNER, Simeon 40 m Ga
Mary 38 f "

Euf # 469 Joiner (-- 50)
GARRETT, James V. 42 m Ga
Sarah 28 f "
Ann E. 18 f "
Emma P. 11 f "
Sarah 8 f "

Flk # 455 Shoemaker &
Farmer, (800-150)
GARRING, John J. 50 m Ger
(Born in Baden, Ger.)
Elizabeth 42 f SC
Mary 18 f Ga
Martha 16 f "
John B. 14 m "
Sarah 12 f "
James 10 m "
Julia 8 f "
Nancy 5 f "
Amanda 1 f Ala

Euf 514 Overseer (-- --)
GARRINS, Moses 25 m Fla
Mary 22 f Ala

Luvl # 547
GARRIS, Elizabeth 35 f Ala
Brittain 17 m "
Elizabeth 11 f "
(See John Sasser).

Flk # 431
GARRIS, George W. 14 m Ala
(See John N. McRae).

Luvl # 649
GARRIS, S. A. 12 f Ala
(See William McRae).

Euf # 1016 Farmer (3000-6700)
GARY, Abner M. 43 m Ga
Elizabeth 42 f "
William P.(Farmer) 21 m "
Martha 19 f "
Nancy 18 f "
Tabitha 16 f "
James H. 13 m "
Mary A. E. 12 f "
Benjamin D. 10 m "
Rudolphus 8 m "
Margaret J. 2 f "

Euf # 1017 Farmer (--10000)
GARY, James 47 m Ga
Ellen 38 f Ga
Roderick (Farmer) 20 m "
(Cont.)

(Euf # 1017 cont.)
Mary E. 18 f Ga
William 17 m "
Harper 15 m Ala
Rebecca 13 f "
Virginia 11 f "
Ellen 9 f "
Laura 7 f "
James 4 m "
Sanders 2 m "

Txv # 1192 (--- 700)
GARY, Sarah F. 30 f Fla
Henry D. 8 m Ala
Fannie L. 5 f "
(See P. N. Cannon).

Euf # 440 Quarryman
GARY, Thomas 46 m Ire
(See McNamara's R.R. Gro.)

Euf # 159 Clerk (150-2800)
GASTON, A. L. 30 m Ga
Mary P. 26 f "
John Z. 6 m Ala
Addie L. 3 f "
SINQUEFIELD, Linney 57 f Ga
($2,000-$1,800)
Thenie W. (Teacher) 20 f "

Euf # 783 Clerk (--- ---)
GASTON, L. Q. C. 33 m Ga
Amanda T. 30 f Fla
(22,500-30,000)
JOHNSON, Marcian 10 m Ala
Isham D. 9 m "
John P. 7 m "
Richard M. 5 m "
(L.Q.C. & Amanda married
within the year).

Euf # 183 Clerk (-- --)
GASTON, William 19 m Ga

Bkb # 766
GATES, Missouri 23 f NC
(See John Bass).

Bkb # 773 Farmer (400-200)
GATES, Stephen 47 m SC
Sarah M. 46 f Ga
Benjamin F. 15 m Ala
William F. M. 12 m "
Sarah 10 f "
Epsey E. 7 f "

Euf # 477 Overseer (---1200)
GATEWOOD, Griffin 36 m NC
(Cont.)

(Euf # 477 cont.)
Mary 28 f Ga
Burwell 6 m Ala
Sarah L. 2 f "

Clay # 58 Shoemaker (-- --)
GEORG, William 28 m Ire
(Born Dublin. See Geo W. Benson).

Euf # 515 Laborer (-- --)
GIBBONS, John 53 m NC
Mary 47 f SC
Espey A. 19 f Ala
Stephen (Laborer) 18 m "
Mary A. 17 f "
Loisa 14 f "
John W. 12 m "
William T. 10 m "
SMITH, Quincy A. 23 f "
Mary 1 f "

Euf # 1277 Farmer (2000-10000)
GIBBONS, Steven 51 m NC
Eliza 52 f SC
John W. T. 16 m Ala

Euf # 536
GIBHART, Eliza 50 f SC
Camilla M. 48 f "
SHORTER, Harriet 52 f "
Caroline 20 f "
RAINES, Mary
Mary A. T.
Sally A.
Auroraborealis
(Last 4 colored house servants)
PREIST, Ebenezer 21 m Ga
(Cabinet maker)
OWENS, Henry M. 19 m Mass
(Laborer)

Euf # 208 Laborer (-- --)
GIBSON, James 19 m Ga
(See John C. McRae).

Clay # 55
GIBSON, Mary 65 f Ga
(See L. Hinson).

Clay # 77 Carpenter (500 ---)
GIBSON, William H. C. 35 m Ga
Sarah E. 20 f Ala
Ann V. 1 f "

Txv # 1137 Farmer (450-300)
GIBBERT, Calvin 44 m NC
(Cont.)

(Txv # 1137 cont.)
Lucy 36 f Ga
Milly S. 15 f "
M. J. 14 f "
John M. 12 m "
Matilda 10 f "
William C. 9 m "
Daniel G. 7 m "
Mary 5 f Ala
Raiford J. 1 m "

Euf # 1375 Farmer (500-300)
GILCHRIST, Daniel 37 m NC
Elizabeth 28 f Ala
Gilbert 10 m "
John 8 m "
Catharine 6 f "
Macom 4 m "
James 1 m "

Euf # 1249
GILCHRIST, Lowell 14 m NC
(See James Stinsell).

Euf # 1312
GILCHRIST, Lucy 40 f NC
Catharine 18 f Ga
Solomon 16 m "
Thulder 14 f Ala

Euf # 83 Blacksmith (-- --)
GILES, Isaac H. 35 m Md
Matilda 38 f Ga
Jane 16 f "
Louisa 13 f "
Ann 10 f "
John H. 8 m "

Euf # 1104 (-- --)
GILL, William, Jr. 21 m SC
Janett 18 f "
(Married within the year).

Euf # 1103 Boot & shoe maker (350-100)
GILL, William, Sr. 46 m Va
Mary 53 f SC
Thomas 22 m "
Augustus (Laborer) 18 m "
George 17 m Ala
Robert 13 m "
Frances 12 f "
Daniel 9 m "

Euf # 801 Wheelwright (--- 400)
GILLENWATER, John W. 26 m Va
Anna 23 f Ala
John 2 m "

Euf # 800 Blacksmith (1200-300)
GILLENWATER, Thomas 54 m Va
Nancy H. 48 f "
Nathan (Laborer) 21 m Ala
Virginia 17 f "
Mary 13 f "
Thomas 12 m "
Richard 8 m "
Jerome 4 m "

Euf # 802 Blacksmith (--- 100)
GILLENWATER, Wm. 24 m Va
Elizabeth 20 f Ala
William 8/12 m "

Clay # 133 Overseer (--- ---)
GILLIS, Charles 40 m NC
Nancy (--- $100) 35 f "

Euf # 759 Farmer (250-500)
GILLIS, John 56 m NC
Catharine 57 f "
Nancy 22 f SC
Sarah 21 f "
Malcom (Laborer) 19 m Ala
Effy 14 f "
McLEOD, Christian 72 f NC

Txv # 1195 Farmer (240-210)
GILLIS, John 25 m NC
Catherine 24 f "
Daniel A. 2 m Ala

Mdwy # 1066
GILLIS, Mary 50 f NC
(See Catherine McMillan).

Clay # 1166 Farmer (--- 530)
GILLIS, Neill 43 m NC
Nancy 25 f Ala
Alex 11 m "
Ichabob 9 m "
Malcom 8 m "
Mary A. 7 f "
Charity 4 f "
Virginia A. 2 f "
James D. 4/12 m "

Luvl # 360 Farmer (--- 500)
GILLIS, Neill 44 m SC
Nancy 26 f NC
Alex W. 11 m Ala
Ichabob 10 m "
M. C. 8 m "
Mary C. 5 f "
Charity 4 f "
Virginia A. 2 f "
William D. 4/12 m "

Clay # 124
GILLIS, Sarah 60 f Scot
(See Hugh McGilvery).

Euf 173 Laborer
GILLISPY, Richard 28 m Ire
(See John Bailey).

Euf 1292 Farmer (--- 200)
GILMORE, George 26 m Ga
Rebecca P. 25 f Ala
William J. 1 m "
James 25 m Ga
H. M. (Farmer) 22 m "

Clay # 672 Farmer (--- 290)
GILMORE, Jacob 24 m Ala
Elizabeth 20 f "
John 10/12 m "

Bkb # 701 Farmer (--- 3000)
GILMORE, John 56 m Ga
Margaret 56 f "
James L. 14 m Ala
AVANT, Asbury 22 m SC

Euf # 814 M. E. Minister (--- 4500)
GILMORE, Wiley 68 m Ga
Elizabeth 65 f NC
GRANTHAM, Eliza J. 35 f "

Clay # 671 Farmer (1400-1000)
GILMORE, William 53 m Ga
Elizabeth 46 f "
George (Farmer) 17 m Ala
Martha 22 f "
Rebecca A. 20 f "
Joseph G. 10 m "
A. W. 12 m "

Euf # 219
GINN, James 12 m Ga
Levina 10 f "
(See James Newberry).

Mt. A. # 845 (--- 200)
GIRLEY, Colen 40 f NC
David M. (Farmer) 20 m Ga
Hiram W. " 18 m "
Andrew J. B. " 17 m "
Henry J. 15 m "

Euf # 1147 Farmer (--- 100)
GLASS, L. D. 50 m Ga
Nancy 40 f "
John 17 m Ala
Nancy 14 f "

Euf # 1148 Farmer (--- 150)
GLASS, Thomas 23 m Ala
Mary E. 20 f "
Georgia A. 5 f "
John (Farm hand) 19 m "

Euf # 1149 Farm hand (---100)
GLASS, William 23 m Ala
Cinthia 20 f "
Matthew M. 10/12 m "

Euf # 1059 Yankee Hater (---17,000)
GLENN, A. S. 39 m SC
Lucy F. 34 f NC

Euf # 942 Farmer (2500-10000)
GLENN, A. T. 35 m SC
Martha 25 f "
John T. O. 7 m Ala
Alexis J. S. 6/12 m "

Euf # 1341
GLENN, D. V. 27 m SC
Rebecca 23 f "
(See T. H. B. Rivers).

Euf # 1345 (--- 13,400)
GLENN, Elizabeth 68 f SC
SCREWS, Henry O. (Farmer) 38 m NC
Angeline 30 f SC
Jesse 6 m Ala
Henry 1 m "

Mdwy # 1044
GLENN, Green T. 5 m Ga
(See John W. Bennett).

Euf # 782
GLENN, John S. 46 m SC
(See Thos. A. Roquemore).

Euf # 1108 Farmer (16000-55000)
GLENN, M. M. 43 m SC
B. W. 38 f "
E. H. 16 m Ala
S. E. 14 f "
H. C. 12 m "
A. F. 10 f "
Claudia 6 f "
E. M. 4 m "
J. B. 8 f "

Euf # 468 M.E. Minister
GLENN, Thornton S.(?) 87 m SC
Mary 76 f "

Euf # 1368 Farmer (750-2500)
GLENN, William E. 44 m Ga
Nathan (Farm hand) 19 m Ala
James " " 17 m "
John " " 15 m "
Louisa 10 f Ga
Zeph 8 m "
Samuel 5 m Ala

Euf # 311 Trader (--- 10,000)
GLENN, William W. 36 m Ga
Louisa E. 31 f SC
Simpson A. 12 m Ga
Mary B. 9 f "
Joseph 8 m Ala
Elizabeth 6 f "
Ella 3 f "
Aravilla R. 64 f Ga

Txv # 1152 Farmer (--- 300)
GLOVER, Augustus 24 m SC
Wineford 18 f Ga
Matilda 3 f Ala
L. C. 1 f "
PATTERSON, Seth 19 m "
(Farm Laborer).

Euf # 640 (--- 100)
GLOVER, Elizabeth 51 f Ga
Wm. J. (Farmer,200-50) 22 m "
Martha A. 19 f "
Mary A. 14 f "
Louisa C. 12 f "

Euf # 954 Farmer (5000-14000)
Glover, Hilliard G. 49 m NC
Sarah 49 f Ga
Martha E. 18 f "
Levinia 15 f Ala
Missouri 11 f "
Frances 9 f "
Josephine 5 f "

Euf # 630 Farmer (2000-7000)
GLOVER, John P. 76 m NC

Txv # 1193 Farmer (1350-500)
GLOVER, John R. 29 m Ga
E. A. 24 f "

Euf # 631
GLOVER, Malissa 8 f Ala
(See Wm. McBride).

Euf # 779 Blacksmith (---500)
GLOVER, Newton J. 30 m Ga
Ellen 57 f "
Ann E. 17 f "

Txv # 1206 Farmer (800-2650)
GLOVER, Samuel 29 m Ga
Narcissa 17 f "

Euf # 632 Farmer (800-300)
GLOVER, Sam'l. D. P 27 m Ga
Narcissa 18 f "

Euf # 129 Farmer (1000-1500)
GLOVER, Thos. J. 40 m Ga
Rachael 31 f "
Jane 12 f "
James M. 10 m Ala
Elizabeth 8 f "
Catherine A. T. 6 f "
Mary L. 3 f "
Thos. W. 64 m "

Txv # 1151 Farmer (--- 350)
GLOVER, Wiley 30 m SC
Dorinda 24 f Ala
Wylie 55 f SC
CARR, Jackson 17 m Ala
(Farm Laborer).
GLOVER, Matilda 26 f SC

Euf # 212 Trader (2000-300)
GODWIN, Ransom 50 m NC
Eliza A. 33 f "
(Milliner, ---6000)
John D. 12 m Ala
Sarah C. 10 f "
Ransom, Jr. 8 m "
Missouri 4 f "
William H. T. 2 m "
DANIEL, Susan F. 20 f Ga
(Milliner).

Txv # 1146 Laborer
GODWIN, Right H. 21 m Ga
(See Burrell Price).

Euf # 399 Carpenter (4000-2600)
GOFF, A. J. 39 m Ga
Martha 32 f "

Clay # 237 Printer
GOLSON, James E. 22 m Ala
(See James W. Mabry).

Euf # 1021 Overseer (--- ---)
GOODE, Joseph 37 m Ga
Maria M. 37 f "
Julius 15 m "
Dawson 14 m "
(Cont.)

(Euf # 1021 cont.)
Indiana 12 f Ga
Palestine 8 f "
Amanda 6 f "
Cicero 4 m "
MERIT, M. C. 27 m "
(Farmer, 2000-3800)

Euf # 271 Laborer
GOODING, Ebeneza 28 m NC
(See James M. Floyed).

Euf # 1294 Farmer (1500-6000)
GOODSON, N. H. 34 m Ga
E. J. L. 32 f SC
Antonett 13 f Ga
Penelope 10 f "
Nancy W. 8 f "
Laura 5 f "
Robert 3 m "
Carrie 1 f Ala
WOOD, James 18 m "

Clay # 141 Teacher
GORDY, Noah 50 m Ga
(See Frank Deshazo).

Euf # 415 Farmer (5000-12000)
GOW, John 36 m Ire
James (Farmer) 38 m "

Euf # 953 Overseer (--- 500)
GRANBERRY, H. W. 31 m Ga
Mary 25 f "
Oscar 5 m "
Ella J. 2 f Ala

Euf # 1007 Shoemaker (--- 100)
GRANGER, A. S. 31 m Ga
Eliza 27 f Ala
William M. 5 m "
Fanny W. 3 f "
John W. 1 m "
HATCHER, Thomas 20 m Ga
(Blacksmith apprentice)
Martha 15 f "
William 10 m Ala

Euf # 1105
GRANT, James 43 m --
(See Wm. A. McCarty).

Clay # 172 Farmer (1000-6000)
GRANT, John A. 36 m NC
Laura 20 f Ala
John F. 1 m "
(Cont.)

(Clay # 172 cont.)
Elizabeth (---6000) 65 f NC
Elizabeth 29 f "

Luvl # 648 Farmer (500-350)
GRANT, John W. 36 m SC
Serena 36 f Ga
Wm. Giles (Farmer) 15 m "
John T. 14 m Ala
James F. 13 m "
Sarah A. E. 12 f "
Mary A. V. 10 f "
Elizabeth A. P. 10 f "
Benjamin F. 5 m "
Jasper N. 3 m "
Ella J. 1 f "

Euf # 1202 Overseer (--- 250)
GRANTHAM, E. J. 20 m SC
Caroline 16 f Ala
John S. 5/12 m "

Euf # 814
GRANTHAM, Eliza J. 35 f NC
(See Wiley Gilmore).

Clay # 155
GRANTHAM, G. 16 f Ala
(See W. T. Hightower).

Euf # 1241
GRANTHAM, Mary T. 16 f SC
(See Mary Johnston).

Flk # 461 (500-5000)
GRAVES, Rhoda 65 f SC
THOMPSON, Robert 25 m Ala
(Farmer)

Euf 1349 Prof. Military Inst.
(800-2000)
GRAY, George 32 m Va
Elizabeth 26 f "
Sarah 4 f "
James 1 m Ala

Euf 143 Carpenter
GRAY, J. H. 25 m NY

Bkb # 743 Farmer (--- ---)
GREATHOUSE, Isaac H. 21 m Ga
Mary E. 21 f "
Martha C. 1/12 f Ala
Mary (150-100) 57 f Ga
Sarah M. 14 f "
RENFROE, John 18 m Ala
(Farm Laborer).

Bkb # 742 Farmer (--- 100)
GREATHOUSE, Wm. M. 30 m Ga
Mary E. 15 f Ala

Bkb # 696 Farmer (--- 250)
GREEN, A. P. 31 m Ga
Maria 23 f "
Martha J. 9 f Ala
Benjamin F. 8 m "
Missouri 6 f "
Ann 4 f "
Frances 2 f "

Bkb # 778 Farmer (--- 150)
GREEN, A. P. 32 m Ga
Maria 26 f "
Martha J. 10 f Ala
Benj. F. 8 m "
Missouri S. 6 f "
Susanna E. 4 f "
Frances 1 f "

Clay # 151
GREEN, G. A. 33 f Ga
John D. 8 m Ala
(See Thomas Varnodare).

Bkb # 687 Farmer (800-300)
GREEN, George 70 m NC
Elizabeth 65 f Ga

Mdwy # 1065 Farmer (--- 500)
GREEN, Irvin 30 m Ga
Catherine 20 f Ala
John D. 8/12 m "

Euf # 574
GREEN, Isabella 25 f Ala
Violetta 19 f "
Marion 16 f "
Ann 14 f "
(See James L. Pugh).

Clay 678 Farmer (100-200)
GREEN, Joseph 27 m Ga
Amanda 20 f "
George 4 m Ala
John 2 m "

Luvl # 348 Farmer
GREEN, Marion 25 m Ga
Jane 21 f Ala
(See Casa Edge).

Mt. A. # 857
GREEN, Sophia 24 f Ga
William (Farmer) 22 m "
(See John Draper).

Clay # 186 Farmer
GREEN, Thomas 21 m Ga.
(See Lewis D. Ward).

Euf # 424
GREEN, Thos. 30 m Ire
Laborer
PYNN, John 63 m NC
Teacher

Luvl # 392 Farmer (--- ---)
GREEN, Thomas 69 m NC
Robert 26 m Ga
Nancy Jane 20 f "
Thomas 19 m Ala
Elizabeth 16 f "
George 13 m "
John 11 m "
Martha S. 9 f "
Sarah A. 7 f "
Milly A. 2 f "

Luvl # 311 Farmer (---2000)
GREEN, Thomas C. 40 m SC(?)
Emeline 39 f "
William 17 m Ala
Amanda E. 12 f "
James 8 m "
John 6 m "
Ann 5 f "
Thomas J. 2 m "

Mt.A. # 860 Carpenter
GREEN, William 20 m Ga
(See Peter Draper)

Bkb # 777 Farmer (1600-500)
GREEN, William E. 30 m Ga
Mary 28 f "
Nathan C. 7 m Ala
A.A.S. 4 f "
William A. 2 m "
George D. 5/12 m "
COOK, Harrison 17 m "
(Student)

Mt. A. # 839 Teacher(415-225)
GREGORY, Thomas J. 49 m NC
Elizabeth 38 f SC
Laura A. 14 f La
William F. 11 m "
Harriett E. 11 f "
Susan 8 f "
H.M. 5 m Ala
Frances B. 3 f "

Euf # 990 Farmer (2500-1000)
GREGORY, Wilson 52 m SC
Mahala 45 f Ga
Littleton 24 m "
(Farmer, --- 150)
Jane 20 f "
Caroline 18 f "
Sarah 16 f "
Evaline 14 f "
Margyan 11 f Ala
Reubin 8 m "
Columbus 6 m "
Wilson 1 m "

Euf # 652
GRESHAM, John W. 12 m Ga
(See John D. Collins).

Euf # 211
GRICE, Elizabeth 21 f Ga

Euf # 210 Blacksmith (--- 500)
GRICE, John E. 42 m SC
Nancy A. 42 f "
Stephen (Farmer) 21 m "
William " 18 m "
John H. " 16 m "
Evan 14 m "
Arrilla 11 f "
Mary A. 7 f "

Euf # 397 Farm Hand (-- 50)
GRICE, Stephen G. 22 m SC
Elizabeth 26 f Ga

Mdwy # 963
GRIFFIN, J. E. 26 m --

Mdwy # 1071 Farmer (3000-10000)
GRIFFIN, James B. 25 m SC
Sarah 18 f Miss
Millard 1 m Ala
T.J. (Farmer, --300) 23 m SC

Mdwy # 969 Farmer (4000-24000)
GRIFFIN, John A. 50 m SC
Jefferson (Farmer) 22 m "

Euf # 995 Farmer (1000-1000)
GRIFFIN, John C. 50 m Ga
Delilah J. 50 f "
John H. (Farmer) 19 m "
Barikons(?) " 17 m "
Samuel E. 14 m "
Jeremiah 10 m "
Sarah 7 f "
Malissa 12 f "
BISHOP,Columbus T. 25 m "
(Hireling)

Mdwy # 986
GRIFFIN, Robert -- -- --
(See Sarah Owens).

Bfd # 1269 Farmer (--- 200)
GRIFFIN, Samuel F. 35 m Ga
Ruth 35 f "
Acy 1 m Ala

Mdwy # 956 Merchant (---2700)
GRIFFIN, Thomas 24 m Ga
(See W. J. Jordon).

Mdwy # 948 Merchant (1350-20000)
GRIFFIN, W. B. 27 m Ga
Sarah 19 f "
FAULK, Mary A. 50 f "
(1200 ---)
GRIFFIN, Elizabeth 22 f "
Martha 19 f "

Euf # 1081 Farmer (37000-98000)
GRIFFITH, Archer, 38 m Ga
Sarah K. 34 m "
Mary F. 17 f "
Crawford B. 15 m "
Martha A.M. 13 f "
William N. 11 m "

Euf # 28 Clerk
GRIFFITH, Moses 20 m Ala
(See Geo. W. McGinty).

Euf # 592
GRIGGERS, William F. 24 m SC
(See William C. Espy).

Euf # 474 Farmer (12000-50000)
GRIGGS, James 65 m Ga
Martha M. 48 f "
James O. 32 m "
(Teacher, 1000-13000)
George R. 21 m "
(Supt., ---500)
Mary 13 f "
John C. 12 m "
Lizzy M. 10 f "
(Deaf & dumb)
Emily 11 f "
Henry P. 10 m "

Euf # 809 Overseer (--- 1500)
GRIMES, John W. 31 m Ga
Nancy 31 f "
Eliza J. 6 f "
Mary E. 3 f "

Bkb # 1242 Farmer (1902-2800)
GRISSETT, Daniel M. 48 m NC
Matilda M. 41 f Ga
James G. 14 m Ala
Sabrina 11 f "
A. W. 9 m "
William W. 5 m "
John L. 3/12 m "

Euf # 1335 (1500-8500)
GROVES, Harriett E. 45 f SC
Caroline 19 f "
Martha L. 17 f "
Sarah J. 15 f "
Thomas 13 m Ala

Flk # 399 Farmer (10000-33000)
GRUBBS, Adam 54 m SC
Nancy 42 f Ga
Green 15 m Ala

Luvl # 513 Farmer (--- 150)
GRUBBS, B. A. 42 m SC
Maria 35 f "
R.A. 20 f Ala
Joseph 13 m "
Joshua 11 m "
F.L. 7 f "
Mary E. 5 f "
Emily 1 f "

Flk # 427 Farmer (--- 125)
GRUBBS, B. W. 42 m Ala
Jane 32 f "
DAVIS, Mary A. 23 f "
HARPE(?), Augustus 20 m SC
(Farmer)

Luvl # 289
GRUBBS, Elizabeth 26 f SC
(See James R. Clark).

Luvl # 256
GRUBBS, Elizabeth 78 f SC

Luvl # 542 Farmer (1150-10000)
GRUBBS, Friendly 43 m SC
E.J. 41 f Ga

Luvl # 257 Merchant (400-3500)
GRUBBS, G. G. 22 m Ala
(See Henry Freeman).

Luvl # 652 (---2000)
GRUBBS, Green J. 24 m Ala
(See G. C. Efurd).

Luvl # 276 Grocer (100-50)
GRUBBS, John T 36 m Ala
Lucitta 38 f "

Luvl # 511 (-- --)
GRUBBS, Margaret 68 f SC
Eliza 45 f "
Francis 26 m "

Nwto # 553
GRUBBS, Morgin 2 m Ala
(See A. C. Thompson).

Euf # 1198 Farmer (1600-3500)
GRUBBS, W. J. 23 m Ala
Sarah J. 23 f "
Mary M. 3 f "
Sarah J. 1 f "

Flk # 484 Farmer (500 ---)
GRUBBS, W. W. 20 m Ala
(See Hansford Lewis).

Euf # 1275 Farmer (11500-29000)
GRUBBS, William 57 m SC
Nancy 52 f Ga
Lydia 12 f Ala
John 10 m "

Luvl # 255 Farmer (5000-35000)
GRUBBS, Worthy J. 40 m SC
Mary A.S. 36 f Ga
William J.(Farmer) 15 m Ala
James F. 14 m "
Seth 12 m "
Samuel J. 8 m "
Susanna 6 f "
Worthy J. 4 m "
MCRAE, Daniel 35 m NC
(Farmer, --- 1500)

Mdwy # 989 Mechanic (---100)
GURRY, L. L. 23 m Ga
Theodosia 17 f "

Euf # 209 Carpenter (-- --)
GUERIN, John 47 m Fr
Amey 45 f Ga
Wm. (Laborer) 16 m "
John 11 m Ala
Randolph 8 m "
Mary 6 f "
Samantha 3 f "

Mt. A. # 824 Farmer (8500-11000)
GUISE, Thomas 58 m Ga
(Cont).

(Mt. A. # 824 cont.)
Lydia 39 f Ga
Jason (Farmer) 20 m "
Frances 8 f Ala
Bob 7 m "
Woody 6 m "
Louisa 3 f "
W. I.(or J.) 1 f "

Luvl # 642 (--- 200)
GULLEGE, Mary 75 f SC
WILKES, Caroline 38 f "
GULLEGE, Mary 6 f Ala

Nwto # 636 Engineer of Steam Mill (---150)
GULLEDGE, William 34 m SC
Martha A. 32 f "
W.J. 12 m "
Benj. N. 10 m Ga
L.C. 8 f Ala
M.J. 6 f "
J.T. 4 m "
T.E. 2 f "
infant 6/12 m "

Euf # 255 Wagoner (--- 300)
GUNNELS, Henry 28 m Ga
Sarah 23 f "
Julia E. 10/12 f Ala

Euf # 552 (-- --)
GUNTERSON, Martha 48 f Ala
Elizabeth 9 f SC
Sidney L. 14 m Ala

Euf # 186 Cabinet Maker
HAGAMAN, Stinson 40 m NJ
(See Wm. H. Clark)

Euf # 82 Wheelwright (-- --)
HAGAN(?), James 32 m NY

Euf 426 Laborer (-- --)
HAGAN, Thomas 28 m Ire
Jane 30 f "
Timothy 6 m SC
Bridget 4 f "
Thomas 2 m "
Mary J. 2/12 f Ala

Txv # 1160 Farmer (-- 150)
HAIGLER, Adam 25 m NC
Martha J. 20 f Ala
Margaret 5 f "
Catherine 3 f "
DEES, Sophia 50 f NC

Euf # 724 Farmer (900-800)
HAIGLER, Charles 45 m NC
Nancy 40 f "
Hiram (Farmer,--200) 21 m Ala
Martha 18 f "
Elizabeth 16 f "
Abijah (Laborer) 17 m "
Charles 12 m "
Henry 8 m "

Mt. A. # 843 Farm Laborer
HAIGLER, Henry 21 m Ala
Phillip (Laborer) 25 m "
(See Zachariah Wilkie).

Euf # 704 Occp. none
HAIGLER, Jacob 35 m NC
Catharine 35 f "
Jeremiah 22 m "
(Occp. none, ---$150)
Henry (Farmer) 21 m "
ROBINSON, Mary 3 f Ala

Mt. A. # 875 Laborer (-- --)
HAIGLER, John 25 m Ga
Emeline 30 f "
Adella 6 f Ala
Susan 4 f "
Ransom 2 m "
Margaret 17 f Ga

Nwto # 612 Farmer (500-250)
HAIGLER, Patterson 36 m Ga
Nancy 33 f "
Frances 5 f Ala
Malissa 4 f "
Milton 2 m "
E.J. 3/12 f "

Euf # 720 Farmer (2000-2000)
HAIGLER, Thomas 40 or 48 m NC
Mary 25 f Ala
Alex W. (Laborer) 22 m "
Josiah " 20 m "
James W. " 18 m "
Mary J. 13 f "
Frances 11 f "
Adam 8 m "
Josephine 3 f "
infant 1 m "

Euf 733 Farmer (1200-1000)
HAIGLER, Thos. J. 43 m NC
Mary 25 f Ala
W.A. (Laborer) 20 m "
Josiah " 18 m "
James " 17 m "
(Cont.)

(Euf # 733 cont.)
Mary 15 f Miss
Milton 12 m Ala
Fanny 10 f "
Adam 7 m "
Josephine 4 f "
George W. 1 m "

Mt. A. # 915
HAIGLER, Washington 33 m NC
(See Moses Shelby).

Clay # 29 Carpenter (-- --)
HAILEY, George W. 32 m NC
C.G. 25 f Fla
Hiram 30 m Ga
R.A. (Blind) 18 f "

Clay # 64 Clerk
HAILEY, J. C. 25 m Ala
(See Seth Mabry)

Clay # 213 Farmer (100---)
HAILEY, James 56 m NC
Elizabeth 56 or 36 f Ga
Richard 16 m Ala
Nancy 14 f "
Caroline 11 f "
Roxana 6 f "
Sarah J. 5 f "
GAINEY, Andrew(Farmer) 18 m Fla

Euf # 170 Chewalla Hotel
HAILEY, Wm. D.(Tinner) 40 m NC
Emily H. 32 f Ga
Ella 12 f Ala
Walker 7 m "
Will 4 m "
Emma P. 1 f "
HAILEY, John 37 m NC
Occupation - none.
KLEFFMILLER, Chas. 35 m Ger
Born Hesse, Ger. Prof. Music
Matilda(Fr. Teacher) 27 f "
FLOURNOY, Wm. M. 25 m Ga
(Carriage Dealer).
Oceon 24 f Ga
BROUGHTON, Ezekiel 39 m Eng
(Civil Engineer)
Sarah 30 f Ire
Jesse 2 m Ala
ROSS, John (Clerk) 20 m Ga
1. $7,000-3,000
8. ------ $2,000
10. ------ $13,000

Euf # 1168 (200-300)
HALE, Laurana 54 f Ga
Jackson 20 m "
Wm. (Farm hand) 17 m Ala

***
Euf # 64 Farmer (--- 300)
HALES, Johnathan 40 m NC
Rebecca 30 f Ga
William H. 12 m "
Arch M. 10 m "
Margaret 8 f "
Sion R. 6 m "
Mary 4 f "
George 1/12 m "
BENTLEY, Missouri 16 f Ga

Euf # 1396 (See Nancy Bullard)
HALES, Sarah 9 f Ala
William 7 m "

Euf # 1318 Farmer (350-150)
HALL, Chap. A. 28 m SC
Caroline 30 f Ga
Chappell 6 m Ala
Henry 4 m "
John 2 m "

Euf # 344 Occp. none (-- --)
HALL, Charles 56 m SC
Cintha J. 29 f Ga
CLEMENTS, Rachael 45 f "
Lucinda 17 f "

Euf # 167 Occp. none (-- --)
HALL, David 41 m SC
David, Jr. 9 m Ala
Mandana 11 f "
Thomas E. G. 7 m "

Clay # 93 (See B. L. Cochran)
Hall, David 10 m Ala

Euf # 1052 (See H. E. Jones)
HALL, E. A. 53 f SC

Euf # 837
HALL, Emaline 34 f Ala
(See Dozier Cade)

Euf # 380 Farmer (--- 200)
HALL, Hiram 55 m SC
Epsay 55 f "
William (Laborer) 17 m Ga
Harriet 15 f "
HALL, Malissa 8 f Ala

*** Euf # 556
HALES, Eliza 20 f Ga
(See Thos. B. Taylor).

Mdwy # 986 Physician (---800)
HALL, J. M. 26 m Ga
(See Sarah Owens).

Euf # 278 Laborer (--- ---)
HALL, John 22 m Ga
Amanda 16 f "

Euf # 144 Laborer (--- ---)
HALL, John 23 m SC
(See Thos. M. Cameron).

Euf # 881 Farmer (1800-12000)
HALL, John W. 48 m SC
Mary C. 49 f "
Wm. W. (Farm hand) 21 m Ala
Mary A. 24 f "
Jane (?) F. 19 f "
Almire 18 f "
Frances 16 f "
Irvin G. 15 m "
John W. 13 m "
Ella E. 12 f "
Linson H. 10 m "
JOHNSON, Alex 24 m SC
(Laborer)

Euf # 906 Laborer (--- 150)
HALL, M. 45 m SC
Martha 36 f Ga
Eliza J. 24 f Ala
Duncan (Laborer) 22 m "
Adolphus " 21 m "
Martha 14 f "
Thomas 10 m "
Franklin 2 m "
Frances V. 1 f "

Euf # 871
Hall, Mary 20 f SC
(See Colley Perdue)

Mdwy # 1098 Farmer (23000-30000)
HALL, Mathew 55 m Ga
Alpha 45 f "
John T. 18 m "
Frank 16 m Ala
Sarah E. 14 f "
Palestine 11 f "

Euf # 1231 (See Howard Tate)
HALL, Nancy 74 f SC

Mdwy # 1004 (1200-1500)
HALL, Rebecca H. 48 f SC
Wiley M. (Farmer) 24 m "
Caroline 22 f "
(Cont.)

(Mdwy # 1004 cont.)
William J. 14 m SC
Robert H. 13 m "
Mary E. 12 f Ala
Thomas J. 9 m "
Harriett 8 f "
Margaret 5 f "

Mdwy # 1097 Farmer (10800-25000)
HALL, Robert G. 40 m Ga
Sarah R. 38 f "
John R. 16 m "
Mathew W. 14 m "
Samuel T. 11 m Ala
Mary E. 9 f "
George R. 1 m "

Euf # 882 Occp. none (1400-400)
HALL, William 70 m SC
Effy 39 f "
Frances 37 f "
Wm. (Farm hand) 35 m "
Samuel " " 30 m "

Euf # 440 Laborer (-- --)
HALORAN, Martin 22 m Ire
(See McNamara's R.R. Gro.)

Euf # 440 Stone cutter
HALOHAND, Michael C. 31 m Wash. D.C.
(See McNamara's R.R. Gro.)

Euf 541 Farmer (--- 100)
HAM, Allen 26 m Ga
Bersheba 25 f "

Euf # 539 Farmer (150-100)
HAM, Smith 60 m SC
Sarah 40 f Ga
Eliza 25 f "
Jackson (Laborer) 20 m "
Elizabeth 18 f "
Benjamin 16 m "
Augustus 13 m "
Jacob 12 m Ala
Martha 9 f "
Mary A. 7 f "
Roxey 4 f "
Henry (Laborer) 22 m "

Euf # 326 Laborer (--- 100)
HAM, William 28 m Ga
Elizabeth 30 f "
Malissa 8 f Ala
Selema 5 f "

Euf # 949 Farmer (20,000-10,000)
Hameter, Joel 53 m SC
Elizabeth 52 f "
Carolina 14 f Ala
Elizabeth 12 f "
WILSON, Carolina 18 f "

Clay # 19 Painter
HAMILTON, J. S. 31 m Md
(Living in hotel)

Euf # 529 Farmer (2800-8000)
HAMILTON, James 56 m NY

Euf # 30 Clerk (--- 500)
HAMILTON, James W. 31 m Va
Mary E. 23 f Ala
Thomas O. 2 m Fla

Euf # 230 Occp. none (-- --)
HAMILTON, Richard P. 52 m Va
Elizabeth 51 f "

Euf # 52 Merchant (2000-5200)
HAMILTON, William N. 29 m Ga
Amillia 20 f SC
Carolle 1 f Ala
ODOM, Gabella 12 f SC

Mdwy # 991 Harness maker (--- 200)
HAMLET, G. A. 30 m NC
Elizabeth 21 f SC
Robert 4 m Ala
Rosa E. 3/12 f "
HANAGAN, Margaret 9 f SC

Euf # 290 Farmer (--- 1500)
HAMMOCK, Simon G. 48 m Ga
Jane C. 30 f "
Mary A. 14 f Ala
John L.(?) 10 m "
Sarah 9 f "

Euf # 1127 Farmer (4000-8000)
HAMMOCK, Thomas 64 m Ga
Mary 50 f NC
DICKSON, Martha 23 f Ga

Luvl # 285 Farmer (700-1000)
HAMMOND, T. L. 36 m NC
(See Isabella McNab).

Mt. A. # 863 Teacher (300-125)
HAMNER, Daniel 21 m Ga
(See Wm. Bludworth).

Mdwy # 991
HANAGAN, Margaret 9 f SC
(See G. A. Hamlet).

Mdwy # 1019 Farmer (--- 400)
HANCOCK, E. S. 42 m NC
Rebecca 35 f "
George 16 m Ala
John 13 m "
William 12 m "
(Not named) 6 m "
Melvina 3 f "

Mdwy # 975 Clerk (--- 3800)
HANCOCK, Isom 20 m Ala
(See Haywood Pipkin).

Mt. A. # 900 Overseer (3030-9000)
HANCOCK, James R. 24 m Ga

Euf # 1048 Overseer (--- 250)
Hansford, William 39 m Ga
Ellen 39 f "
George (Laborer) 17 m "
Sarah C. 14 f "
Thomas 11 m "

Euf # 124 Notary Pub.
HARDMAN, Jack 53 m Ga
Thos. Lamar 21 m Ala
(Telegraph operator)
Rosalie A.(Teacher) 19 f "
John J.(Student) 17 m "
William P.P. 14 m "
Arthur S. 11 m "
Emma L. 9 f "
Eugenia E. 6 f "
Franklin T. 3 m "
VAUGHN, Martha E. 29 f SC
(Montua(mantilla?) Maker)
Noel 10 m "
Henry B. 1/12 m Ala
(No. 1 - 7000-1500)

Euf 588 Farmer (600-250)
HARDWICK, James H. 22 m Ga
Elizabeth 19 f Ala
Stephen M. 8/12 m "

Euf # 418 Farmer (6500-9000)
Hardwick, R. M. 47 m Ga
Sarah 42 f "
Kiziah 18 f "
Robert 16 m Ala
Seaborn 14 m "
(Cont.)

(Euf # 418 cont.)
Caroline 10 f Ala
Charles 8 m "
Edmund 3 m "
ESPY, Caroline 23 f Ga

Euf # 638 Farmer (450-200)
HARDY, Allen 26 m Ga
Elizabeth 25 f "
Hugh 5 m Ala
Mary 2 f "
PHILLIPS, Emanuel 30 m Ga
(Farmer, 150-50)
Elizabeth 21 f Ala
J.W. 8/12 m "

Euf # 535 (--- 8000)
HARDY, Elizabeth 57 f Ga
NASH, Margaret 92 f NC
(Blind - 2500-200)

Euf # 192 Bank Cashier (2000-2500)
HARDY, John 43 m Eng
Delilah M. 24 f Ga
Sarah E. 5 f Ala
Fanny K. 1 f "

Mt. A. # 826 Farmer (2600-4500)
HARDY, Joseph E. 30 m Ga
Martha 20 f "
YOUNG, Augustus 22 m "
(Laborer, ---150)
Mary 22 f Ala

Luvl 269 Clerk
HARE, Dozier 21 m NC
(See Wm. C. Bostick).

Clay # 1237
HARGROVE, Elizabeth 52 f SC
(See M. W. Blair)

Clay # 2 Bookkeeper (1200-2000)
HARGROVES, Lem 29 m Ala
M.V. 25 f Ga
F.G. 2 m Ala
H.L. 5/12 f "

Flk # 427 Farmer
HARPE(?),Augustus 20 m SC
(See B. W. Grubbs).

Txv # 1154 (800-600)
HARPER, Catherine 44 f SC
Mary C. 21 f Ga
Robert P.(In school) 19 m "
(Cont.)

(Txv # 1154 cont.)
James B. (In school) 18 m Ga
Wade H. " " 16 m "
Wm. T. " " 14 m "
Jane B. " " 10 f "

Euf # 510(?) Overseer
HARPER, H. H. 22 m Ga
Vicey 18 f "
(See Jas. A Roquemore).

Euf # 825 Hireling (-- 50)
HARPER, John 48 m Ga
Mary 40 f SC
Nancy A. 18 f Ga
Milly J. 15 f "
Sarah 10 f "
Caroline E. 8 f "

Mt. A. # 850 (300-200)
HARPER, Mary 56 f NC
Mary A. 29 f "
Wm. J. (Farmer) 21 m Ala

Euf # 304
HARPER, Sally 16 f Ga
(See M. P. McDonald).

Mdwy # 977 Overseer (1000-600)
HARPER, W. E. 36 m NC
Elizabeth 30 f Ga
Harriett 8 f Ala
Susan 6 f "
Charles 5 m "
McNeill 3 m "
James 1 m "

Euf # 951 Farmer (3000-22000)
HARPER, William 65 m Ga
Catharine 50 f "
Lafayette(Overseer) 20 m Ala
Thadeus (Student) 18 m "
Eliza " 15 f "
Cincennatus 14 m "
Benj. F. 12 m "
Sarah 10 f "
Virginia 8 f "

Euf # 342 Laborer (-- --)
HARPER, William 42 m Ga
Nancy 31 f SC
(Married within the year)
DILNO(?), Mary A. 14 f SC
Catharine 13 f Ga
Josephine A. 2 f "

Euf # 605 Farmer (1700-600)
HARRELL, David F. 26 m Ga
Sarah F. 19 f "
John A. 3 m Ala
BARNARD, Granbery 10 m "

Euf # 103
HARRELL, Elijah 12 m Ala
Joshua C. (Farmer) 23 m Ga
Amanda 15 f "
(See Priscilla Watson).

Euf # 45 Tailor (--- 200)
HARRELL, Elijah S. 45 m NC
Mary A. 33 f Ga

Flk # 396 Farmer (--- ---)
HARRELL, G. W. 30 m Ga
Martha 18 f "
REYNOLDS, John A. 41 m NC
(Doctor & farmer, 15000-25000)
Sarah E. 36 f "
Robert D. 15 m Ala
Mary J. 13 f "
John B. 9 m "
Amanda 3 f "
James 11/12 m "

Euf # 336 Laborer
HARRELL, Henry 23 m Ga
(See Hamp Rachaels).

Euf # 102 Farmer (250-300)
HARRELL, Jesse J. 25 m Ga
Frances W. 30 f "
William 6 m Ala
Edwin 5 m "
Frances L. 3 f "
infant 1 f "

Clay # 75 Painter (-- --)
HARRELL, John 26 m Ga
E.J. 25 f SC
James R. 4 m Ga
John T. 3 m "
William H. 9/12 m "

Bkb # 722 Farmer (300-2500)
HARRELL, Mary A. 44 f Ga
Samantha 10 f Ala
Bird 3 m "
Ruth 2 f "

Euf # 1353 Farmer (--- 200)
HARRELL, William 36 m Ga
(Cont.)

(Euf # 1353 cont.)
Mary 26 f Va
George L. 11 m Ala
Marion T. 7 or 6 m "
John W. 2 m "

Euf # 780 Overseer (--- 450)
HARRELL, William H. 32 m Ga
Susan 23 f "

Clay # 163 Farm Laborer
HARRIS, A. 17 m Ala
(See Jas. C. S. Connelly)

Euf # 1096 Overseer
HARRIS, Henry 62 m NC
(See Catharine Butts).

Euf # 1078 Overseer (--- 500)
HARRIS, Napoleon B. 21 m NC

Euf # 1067 (500-100)
HARRISS, Eliza 48 f NC
John B. (Clerk) 20 m Ala

Clay # 40 Merchant (---4000)
HARRISON, A. L. 23 m Ala
M.J. 19 f "
William L. 9/12 m "

Euf # 741 Farmer (300-250)
HARRISON, Alfred 36 m SC
Catharine 42 f "
Sharp 14 m "
Jane 12 f "
Harriet 10 f "
Sarah E. 6 f "
Alfred R. 1 m "

Euf # 1339 Physician (--1000)
HARRISON, Benjamin J. 51 m Va
May E. 32 f SC
Cornelia 8 f "
Edward A. 6 m Ala
Mary J. 3 f "

Luvl # 653 Merchant (---2000)
HARRISON, E. W. 26 m Ga
Elizabeth 23 f Ala
Arabella 4 f "
William 2 m "
BEASLEY, J. C. 28 m "

Luvl # 283 Grocer & Shoemaker (1700-6000)
HARRISON, E. W. 26 m Ala
Elizabeth 24 f "
(Cont.)

(Luvl # 283 cont.)
Arabella 4 f Ala
Willis 2 m "
STEVENS, Mary 17 f "
BEASLEY, John C. 35 m "
Bludworth, Patrick -- m --
(John C. Clark ---600).

Txv # 1175 (1200-8000)
HARRISON, Elizabeth 57 f NC

Luvl # 292 Merchant (6000-10,000)
HARRISON, G. W. 28 m NC
M.A. 19 f Ga
(See Temperance McGuire)

Luvl # 259 Merchant (2700-10,000)
HARRISON, J. F. 30 m NC
Ann T. 16 f Ala
ANGLING, Victoria 5 f "
(J.F. & Ann T. married within the year).

Txv # 1153 Farmer (1920-500)
HARRISON, John 39 m Ga
Martha B. 38 f "
Martha F. 16 f "
William H. 13 m Ala
Charles E. 11 m "
John F. 9 m "
Thomas P.(or T.) 6 m "
Georgia T. 3 f "
Mary J. 1 f "

Euf # 131
HARRISON, John C. 3 m Ga
(See Alex Hyde).

Euf # 1224 Overseer (-- --)
HARROD, John 32 m Ga
Margaret 28 f "
Martha 4 f "
William 1 m Ala

Euf # 1302 (1200-300)
HARROD, Sarah 47 f NC
Elijah (Overseer) 26 m Miss
Margaret 24 f "
John (Farm hand) 21 m Ala
William A. 18 m "
Sarah E. 16 f "

Euf # 5-5 Warehouse (25,000-30,000)
HART, Henry C. 30 m RI
(Cont.)

(Euf 5-5 cont.)
Sarah 23 f Ga
Sally 3/12 f Ala

Euf # 22 Farmer (30,000-45,000)
HART, John 54 m NC (or NH?)
John B. (Clerk) 27 m RI
Charles B. " 25 m "
Elizabeth 23 f "
Sarah 21 f Ala
Harrison 18 m "
Frank 16 m "
Marriah 13 f "
William 10 m "

Euf # 54 Clerk (-- --)
HART, T. B. 30 m RI
(See A. T. Locke)

Euf # 584 Carpenter (--- 150)
HARTLEY, George 53 m Pa
Mary J. 34 f NC

Euf # 168 Shoemaker (1500-300)
HARTUNG, John 26 m Ger
(Born Bavaria)
Barbary 32 f "
(Born Wertembg)
Joseph 16 m "
(Born Bavaria)
Ferdinand 15 m "
(Born Bavaria, App. shoe-maker).

Txv # 1127 (160-185)
HARTZOG, Celie 49 f SC
Mary 16 f Ala
Hiram 14 m "
Julia 10 f "
Joseph 6 m "

Txv # 1216 Farmer (350-300)
HARTZOG, Daniel 30 m SC
Elizabeth 41 f "
Sarah E. 13 f Ala
George Wiley 11 m "
Mary A. 10 f "
Hepsy A. 9 f "
Daniel J. 6 m "

Txv # 1128 Farmer (--- 150)
HARTZOG, Francis 35 m SC
Rebecca 32 f "
Sallie 15 f Ala
(Cont.)

(Txv # 1128 cont.)
Jane 12 f Ala
Daniel 9 m "
Henry 5 m "
Molsie 3 f "
James 1/12 m "

Txv # 1129 Farmer (120-150)
HARTZOG, James W. 27 m SC
Martha A. 28 f NC
William S. 10 m Ala
George W. 2 m "

Clay # 1121
HARTZOG, Margaret 23 f Ga
(See John Warr)

Txv # 1198 Farmer (1000-1500)
HARTZOG, Wiley 42 m SC
Hepsey 36 f "
Daniel 17 m Ala
Timothy 15 m "
John 13 m "
James 10 m "
Henry 10 m "
Nicholas 7 m "
Mary 5 f "
Robert 1 m "

Txv # 1135 Farmer (--- 150)
HARTZOG, William 23 m Ala
Mary 20 f "
L.M. 1/12 f "

Euf # 1314 Farmer (3500-9000)
HARWELL, James H. 42 m Ga
Caroline 40 f SC
Mary 12 f Ala
Jackson 8 m "
Jane 10 f "
Wilbur 6 m "
Martha 6 f "
Ella 4 f "

Euf # 369 Farmer (2500-10000)
HARWELL, S. W. 32 m Ga
Martha C. 29 f "
Samuel 9 m Ala
Elizabeth 7 f "
John 6 m "
Henry 4 m "
Frances 2 f "

Euf # 624 Farmer (600-375)
HASP(?), Henry T. 32 m Ga
Lydia E. 39 f "
James 5 m "
(Cont.)

(Euf # 624 cont.)
Josephine L. 4 f Ga
William 3 m "
Lela 1 f "

Clay # 656
HATCHER, Sophronia 21 f Ga
Lutitiae 18 f "
(See Sinthia McKinney).

Luvl # 378
HATCHER, Sophronia 19 f Ga
Mary (?) 4 f Ala
(See Asa F. Beasley)

Luvl # 379
HATCHER, Sophronia 19 f Ga
Mary (?) 4 f Ala
MCK------ W. (torn) 65 f SC
Tisher 15 f Ga

Euf # 1007 Blacksmith Appt.
HATCHER, Thos. 20 m Ga
Martha 15 f "
William 10 m Ala
(See A. S. Granger)

Euf # 1060 Apprentice
HATCHER, Thos. 19 m Ga
(See Wm. Kennedy)

Euf # 532 Farmer (1200-500)
HATFIELD, John J. T. 55 m SC
Mary 40 f "
John (Farm hand) 16 m "
Mary S. 14 f "
James S. 11 m "
Samuel T. S. 9 m Ala
Nancy 7 f "
George W. 4 m "
Sarah E. 1 f "
REEDY, James 19 m SC
(Laborer)

Euf # 1260 Farmer (225-150)
HATFIELD, Robert A. 37 m SC
Sarah 35 f Ala
Roland 5 m "
Samuel 3 m "

Euf # 440 Quarryman
HAVERTY, Stephen 34 m Ire
(See McNamara's R.R. Gro.)

Euf # 371
HAWES, Emily 18 f Ga
(See Silas Jones).

Euf # 791 (-- --)
HAWS, Mary A. 40 f Ga
Jackson (Deaf & dumb) 20 m "
Levina 15 f "
Irwin (Farm hand) 16 m "

Mdwy 986 Shoemaker (--- 100)
HAWKINS, John 45 m NC
(See Sarah Owens).

Luvl # 645 Farmer (--- 200)
HAWKINS, Robert 33 m Ala
Martha 24 f NC
Mary J. 1 f Ala

Euf # 586 Laborer (-- --)
HAYS, D. H. 29 m SC
Henry 2 m Ala
Catharine 26 f SC
Sarah J. 4/12 f Ala

Mdwy # 1033 Farmer (300-200)
HAYS, James 26 m Ire
Bridget 24 f "
James 3 m Ga
Michael 1 m Ala
HAYS, John 28 m Ire
(Farmer, 300-200)
Margaret 27 f "
Stephen 4 m Ga
Mary A. 6/12 f Ala

Clay # 1123 Farmer (--- 250)
HAYS, James M. 48 m SC
Prudence 38 f NC
Ashbury 18 m Ga
Susanna 14 f Ala
Elvira 12 f "
James J. 9 m "
Missouri A. 6 f "
Catherine 4 f "
BRYANT, Thos. M.C. 26 m SC
(Farm Laborer)

Euf # 1191 Hireling (-- --)
HAYWOOD, John 30 m Va
Martha 33 f Ga
Nancy M. 7 f "
John 3 m Ala
Charles 1 m "

Euf 972 Farmer (11000-2750)
HEAD, E. P. 30 m Ga
SWINNING, Ned 20 m SC
(Hireling)
BELL, Joseph 20 m Tenn
(Hireling)

Mdwy # 947 Farmer (2000-6000)
HEAD, J. M. 37 m Ga
M.J. 30 f "
William M. 10 m Ala
M.A. 5 m "
FEAGIN, Ella 6/12 f "

Clay # 1292 (--- 150)
HEAD, Lurinda 38 f Ga
Belton 9 m Ala
Epsy E. 7 f "
W.B. 5 m Ala

Euf # 861 Overseer (-- --)
HEAD, Neal 22 m Ala
(See Levi R. Wilson)

Mt. A. # 853 Farmer (2000-1500)
HEAD, Richard E. 40 m Ga
Epsey 37 f Ala
Sarah E. 11 f "
George McD. 10 m "
S.C. 7 f "
L.E. 6 m "
Nancy A. E. 3 f "
Sarah E. 2 f "
WILLIS, Joel 75 m NC
Elizabeth 66 f Ga

Euf # 329 Overseer (-- --)
HEAD, Robert M. 25 m Ala

Mt. A. # 854 Teacher (175-150)
HEARD, Matilda 45 f SC
St. Helena 16 f Ala
Matilda P. 12 f "
Robert W. 10 m "
CORLEY, Sallie 96 f SC

Txv # 1180 Farmer (480-220)
HEITH, Miles 41 m Ga
Jannett 40 f NC
Sarah 16 f Ala
Isaac 15 m "
Edward 14 m "
John 13 m "
Willis 11 m "
Henry 9 m "
Jane 7 f "
Patsy 4 f "
Eli 2 m "

Euf # 43
HEITT(?), Sarah 61 f NC
(See Aaron Thomas)

Euf # 687 P.B.Minister (----7,5000)
HELMS, Aaron 44 m NC
Mary 25 f Fla
Frederick M. 18 m Ala
Judge H. 14 m "
Matilda 12 f "
John D. 10 m "
Mary 6 f "
Amanda E.V. 3 f "
Moses A. 9/12 m "

Euf # 715 Farmer (2000-500)
HELMS, Abraham 43 m NC
Nancy 42 f "
Emily 21 f Ala
Wm. (Laborer) 18 m "
Aaron 16 m "
Joel 14 m "
Allan 12 m "
Charles 9 m "
Thomas 6 m "
Neil S. 3 m "
Abraham C. 10/12 m "

Nwto # 613 Farmer (---200)
HELMS, Charlie 40 m Ga
R.V. 38 f "
William (Farmer) 26 m Ala
Denman " 22 m "
Marion " 17 m "
Luvina 8 f "

Luvl # 505 Farmer (1500-200)
HELMS, Henderson 50 m NC
Abigail 46 f "
J.L. 16 m "
S.N. 13 m "
John W. 12 m "
Frances H. 9 f "
Gilbert W. 10 m "
R.J. 7 f Ga
George D. 3 m "
John W. 1 m Ala

Luvl # 317 Farmer (1200-1000)
HELMS, Hilliard 43 m NC
Mahala 40 f "
Luvincia 23 f "
William T. 20 m "
Jesse 19 m "
Mary J. 17 f "
Elizabeth A. 15 f "
James R. 12 m "
(Cont.)

(Luvl # 317 cont.)
Lucinda 11 f NC
Rachael S. 8 f "
Henry 7 m "
John 6 m "
Margaret 4 f "
Hilliard 3 m "
Aaron C. 2 m "

Euf # 734 Farmer (4000-11000)
HELMS, John 49 m NC
Hally 42 f "
George N. (Farmer) 20 m Ala
Joel S. 17 m "
Milbry S. 13 f "
Aaron N. 12 m "
Jacob S. 9 m "
Leendy 7 f "
Joseph 5 m "
Hally E. 10 f "
Mary E. 3 f "
Hilliard 2 m "
Milbry (---200) 61 f NC
Rachael (idiot) 37 f "

Euf # 737 Farmer (--- 50)
HELMS, John J. 21 m Ala
Frances A. 18 f "
(Married within the year).

Nwto # 616
HELMS, L. E. 6 f Ala
Mary M. 5 f "
(See John Thomas).

Mt. A. # 869 Farmer (800-500)
HELMS, Sampson D. 33 m NC
Missouri C. 28 f Ga
Louisa C. 8 f "
Teresa E. 6 f "
Henrietta F. 4 f "
Cater A. 1 m Ala
JOHNSON, Wm. (Laborer) 20 m Ga

Nwto # 619 Farmer (--- ---)
HELMS, Silas 25 m Ga
Susan 30 f "
HUTSON, M. 14 f Ala

Clay # 245 Farmer (1000-10000)
HELMS, Thomas C. 28 m NC
Sally S. 40 f Ga
Kansas A. 3 f Ala
Mary 1 f "
(Cont.)

(Clay # 245 cont.)
WARREN, Thomas M. 19 m Ala
(Farmer, --- 2000)
Joel M. (---2000) 14 m "

Nwto # 628 Farmer (200-250)
HELMS, Uriah 38 m NC
Martha 30 f Ga
Alonzo D. 13 m Ala
Wade 10 m "
Malissa 9 f "
Emma 7 f "
George M. 5 m "
Sarah F. 3 f "
Robert C. 1 m "

Euf # 703 Grocer (600-500)
HELMS, William 21 m Ala
Martha 24 f "
CREEL, J. F. 25 m "
(Teacher, ---1200)
PITTS, John W. 16 m "
(Student, ---800)

Euf # 736 Farmer (700-125)
HELMS, William 24 m Ala

Flk # 427 Farmer (--- ---)
HENDERSON, David 28 m Ala
Lucinda 30 f "
Joseph 6 m "
Daniel 3 m "
Isaac 8/12 m "

Mdwy # 953 Physician (2000-5000)
HENDERSON, J. E. 34 m SC
Mary E. 28 f Ga
William F. 9 m "
Robert 8/12 m Ala
MOSS, Mary B. 68 f Conn
(--- 4,000)

Flk # 457 Farmer (150-150)
HENDERSON, James 40 m Ga
Sarah M. 35 f Ala
Henry E. (Farmer) 20 m "
Joseph J. 14 m "
Jimpsey 12 m "
William 10 m "
Daniel 9 m "
Harmon 5 m "
Thomas B. 1 m "

Clay # 265
HENDERSON, Joseph 35 m Ala
(Cont.)

(Clay # 265 cont.)
Margaret 37 f NC
William 10 m Ala
(See John C. Douglass.)

Luvl # 265 Farmer (2500-350)
HENDERSON, Joseph 35 m Ala
Margaret 37 f NC
William 10 m Ala
(See John C. Douglass).

Mdwy # 1012 (--$3500 each)
HENDERSON, W. I. 11 m Ala
John C. 7 m "
(See J. C. Ray).

Euf # 609 Laborer (-- --)
HENDLEY, Richard 20 m Ala
(See Wright Flowers).

Mdwy # 1073 Farmer (3500-12000)
HENDRICK, Franklin 37 m Ga
Sarah A. 25 f "
Thomas 2 m Ala
Mary E. 1 f "
Martha E. 3/12 f "

Euf # 448 Farmer (--- 2,500)
HENDRIX, Benjamin N. 28 m SC
Henrietta 24 f "
Mary L. 2/12 f Ala

Euf # 917 Farmer (300-200)
HENDRIX, Henry 55 m SC
Mary A. 36 f Ala
Margyan 14 f "
Hansford A. 8 m "
Thomas D. 2 m "
Mary A. 1 f "

Euf # 437 Carpenter (500-75)
HENDRIX, John 72 m NY
Lucinda 58 f SC
Mary J. 18 f Ala

Euf # 1079 Farmer (1700-200)
HENDRIX, Whit B. 32 m SC
Jane A. 26 f Ala
Munroe 8 m "
Cullen 6 m "
John 5 m "
Milly 4 f "
Edward H. 1 m "
Jesse 3/12 m "

Luvl # 308 (300 ---)
HENLEY, Adam 38 m Sc
Leta 37 f "
(Cont.)

(Luvl # 308 cont.)
Hezakiah 14 m Ala
George A. 19 m "
Martha 8 f "
Isaiah 5 m "
Adam, Jr. 2 m "

Mdwy # 995
HENLEY, Mourning 60 f Ga
(See O. S. Reynolds)

Euf #1185 Overseer (700-300)
HENLY, Adam 38 m SC
Letty 36 f "
Hezakiah 13 m Ala
Georgia A. 10 f "
Martha 8 m "
Isaiah 6 m "
Adam 2 m "

Euf # 1010
HENRY, Amey 79 f Ga
(See Mary Cain).

Euf # 1090 (---4,000)
HENRY, Benjamin R. 23 m Ga
Margaret 16 f SC

Euf # 1089 Physician (17,800-57,270)
HENRY, J. B. 39 m Ga
Catharine W. 30 f "
Benj. J. 12 m Ala
Mary L. 10 f "
John A. 6 m "
Sarah T. 4 f "
Elizabeth F. 1 f "
B. M. (Student) 20 m Ga

Bkb # 688 Physician & Farmer (300-500)
HENRY, William B. 36 m Ga
Mary E. 31 f SC
Calvin F.(or T.) 9 m Ga
Thomas C. 3 m "

Bkb # 689
Hermier(?), Eveline 21 f SC
Harriett 16 f "
(See Abner Johnson).

Clay # 136 Farmer (400-600)
HEROD, James 46 m Ga
Martha A. 35 f "
Nancy A. 17 f Ala
M.E. 15 f "
M.C. 14 f "
S.T. 11 f "
(Cont.)

(Clay # 136 cont.)
C.S. 9 f Ala
J.J. 7 m "
L.M. 5 f "
N.McN. 3 m "
Louisa 1 f "

Clay # 137 Farmer (600-500)
HEROD, Thomas 52 m Ga
M. 35 f "
Nancy 7 f Ala
William T. 5 m "
V.S. 1 f "

Luvl # 288 Physician & Farmer (8,000-40,000)
HERON, E. M. 49 m SC
Derrill J. 12 m Ala
Edward 11 m "

Bkb # 687 Farmer (-- --)
HERON, Richard 20 m Ala
(See Geo. R. Scroggins).

Clay # 9
HERRING, Ann 14 f Ala
Mary 11 f "
(See Daniel T. Beasley)

Nwto # 623 Farmer (360-200)
HERRING, Benjamin 50 m Ga
Patsey 42 f "
COX, Gordon (Farmer) 18 m Ala
HERRING, Thomas 13 m "
B.A. 10 f "
Ellen 8 f "
William 7 m "
David 4 m "

Luvl # 282
HERRING, Chloe 22 f Ala
(See William King).

Nwto # 611 Farmer (800-450)
HERRING, Duncan 35 m NC
Susan 22 f Ga
Sarah E. 4 f Ala
B.C. 2 f "
John 1 m "

Nwto # 610 Farmer (500-180)
HERRING, Eli L. 30 m NC
Eliza (--- 180) 18 f Ga
William 3 m Ala
Louisa E. 11/12 f "
Mary F. 1/12 f "

Luvl # 269 Clerk
HERRING, Emanuel 18 m Ala
(See Wm. C. Bostick)

Mt. A. # 881 Farmer (400-250)
HERRING, G. W. 23 m Ala
Elizabeth 23 f "
(Married within the year).

Luvl # 249
HERRING, H. J. 15 f Ala
G. W. 13 m "
(See John W. Railey)

Euf #13-13 Silversmith (50-500)
HERRING, Henry C. 37 m Ga

Nwto # 608 Farmer (650-380)
HERRING, James 50 m NC
H. 39 f Ga
Thos. (Farmer) 18 m Ala
John 15 m "
Lewis 13 m "
Joseph 11 m "
Mary 9 f "
George 6 m "
Martha 4 f "
Shorter 1 m "

Euf # 18-18 Clerk (2500-6500)
HERRING, James 50 m Ga
Mary 70 f "

Nwto # 607 Farmer (--- ---)
HERRING, John 82 m NC
Ann 72 f "
Elizabeth 27 f "
Margaret 22 f "
William 40 m "
Farmer, 600-500)

Luvl # 310 Farmer (1000-500)
HERRING, John W. 30 m NC
Catherine 30 f SC
James W. 10 m Ala
George 6 m "
William G. 4 m "
Eli S. 2 m "
Mary E. 4/12 f "
Ezekiel Alfred 15 m "

Luvl # 297 Farmer (1500-2000)
HERRING, Lewis G. 25 m Ala
Elizabeth 22 f "
Jane E. 4 f "

Clay # 1291 Farmer (--- 500)
HERRING, Louis G. 26 m Ala
Elizabeth 23 f "
Jane 3 f "

Clay # 221 (400-1640)
HERRING, Polly 58 f NC
EIDSON, Mary J. 29 f "
George 14 m Ala
James A. 10 m "
Ann 5 f "
Martha E. 1 f "
HOUGH, Sarah (black) 120 f NC

Nwto # 618 Farmer (800-600)
HERRING, Stephen S. 48 m NC
Mary A. 35 f SC
James 14 m Ga
Annie 11 f Ala
Susan 9 f "
George 7 m "
Samuel 6 m "
Benjamin F. 5 m "
Mary 11/12 f "
Ann K. 70 f NC

Luvl # 298 Farmer (1600-4000)
HERRING, Stephen 23 m Ala
Caroline 18 f "
John H. 8/12 m "

Luvl # 652 Clerk
HERRING, W. W. 19 m Ala
(See G. C. Efurd).

Clay # 1290 Farmer (8000-22,000)
HERRING, West 52 m NC
Charity 53 f "
Jackson (Farmer) 15 m Ala
Martha A. 12 f "

Nwto # 609 Farmer (--- 200)
HERRING, William 20 m Ala
Frances 16 f "
(Married within the year).

Mt. A. # 840
HERRINGTON, Mary 19 f Ala
(See Edmund Willis).

Euf # 407 Laborer (--- 100)
HICKEY, E. 45 m Ga
Roxanna 34 f "

Txv # 1205 Grocery Co.(--350)
HICKEY, Elijah 46 m Ga
Roxie A. 36 f Ala

Euf # 657 Laborer (--- 100)
HICKS, Henry 25 m Ga
Elizabeth 24 f "
M. J. 2 f Ala

Txv # 1172 Farmer (200-200)
HICKS, Henry 26 m Ga
Sarah 23 f "
Henrietta 7/12 f Ala

Euf # 757 Farmer (200-300)
HICKS, James 58 m SC
Sarah 56 f "
Caroline 19 f Ga
Elijah 13 m "

Euf # 735 Farmer (100-50)
HICKS, James M. 30 m Ga
Martha J. 23 f Ala
Elizabeth 1 f "
(Married within the year).

Euf # 758 (--- ---)
HICKS, Merrit 25 m Ga
Missouri 21 f "

Euf # 752 Farmer (--- 300)
HICKS, Manning 32 m Ga
Mary A. E. 25 f Ala
Mary L. 2 f "

Euf # 667 Farmer (--- 100)
HICKS, Noah 55 m SC
Molsey 52 f "
Elizabeth 16 f "
John 6 m Ala

Euf # 755 Farmer (250-150)
HICKS, Royal J. 34 m SC
Elizabeth E. 31 f Ga
Sarah A. 11 f "
James B. 8 m Ala
Ella A. 6 f "
Emeline 4 f "
William 2 m "
John 1/12 m "

Euf # 32 Waggoner (--- 400)
HIDRICK, Jacob 30 m SC
Sarah 32 f Ala

Euf # 34 (--- ---)
HIDRICK, Macon 21 m Ga
Susan 18 f "
(Married within the year).

Euf # 33 Wagoner (--- ---)
HIDRICK, Miles 23 m Ga
Jane 18 f "

Euf # 828
HIGDON, Mary 45 f SC
(See Thomas Pate).

Luvl # 358 Farmer (1300-400)
HIGHSMITH, Isaac 53 m NC
Eliza A. 50 f "
John J. (Farmer) 18 m Ga
W. F. " 16 m "
Lewis C. 14 m "
Mandy 7 f Ala

Bkb # 786 Farmer (4000-1000)
HIGHT, Felix 39 m Ga
Delila 35 f "
Robert (Farmer) 22 m "
Martha 20 f "
Frances 13 f Ala
Henry H. 10 m "
Thomas J. 7 m "
M. J. 5 f "
Felix F. 4 m "
Mary E. 3 f "
S. A. 2 f "
John A. 1 m "

Bkb # 768 Farmer (200-200)
HIGHT, James 42 m Ga
Mary J. 32 f SC
James H. T. 12 m Ga
John W. 11 m "
Eliza 9 f "

Mdwy # 937 Overseer (2400-2300)
HIGHTOWER, J. L. 28 m Ga
Sarah F. 26 f Ala
Frances J. 9 f "
George T. 7 m "
James T. 5 m "
William H. 3 m "

Euf # 894 Farmer (2300-5000)
HIGHTOWER, Leroy G. 45 m Ga
Sarah J. 40 f "
William D. 20 m Ala
Anne E. 18 f "
James R. 17 m "
Nancy S. 15 f "
Emma F. 13 f "
Joseph L. 10 m Ga
Thomas P. 8 m "
John R. 6 m "
(Cont.)

(Euf # 894 cont.)
Jesse C. 4 m Ga
Whit C. 1 m Ala
TOMLIN, T. J. 20 m Ga
(Hireling).

Clay # 1283 Farmer (240-500)
HIGHTOWER, Robert 48 m Ga
Angeline 26 f SC
Elizabeth A. 10 f Ala
William 8 m "
James D. 6 m "
Nancy J. 4 f "
Robert S. 2 m "
POYNER, John W. 55 m NC
(School Teacher,---50).

Clay # 154 Farmer (4800-4500)
HIGHTOWER, Thomas A. 55 m Ga
R. A. 55 f NC
Mary J. 13 f Ala
Pochahuntas 11 f "
Joseph M. 9 m "
C. T. 5 m "
McCALL, Nathaniel 21 m "
(Farm Laborer)
OLIVER, John 62 m NC
(M. E. Minister).
RUSSELL, Mary A. 70 f NC

Clay # 155 Farmer (--- 500)
HIGHTOWER, W. T. 25 m Ga
Julia 19 f "
Charles(?) 1 m Ala
GRANTHAM, G. 16 f "

Euf # 1132 Physician (55,000-105,000)
HILL, A. S. 52 m Ga or La(?)

Clay # 186 Farmer (--- ---)
HILL, Augustus 21 m Ala
(See Lewis D. Ward).

Mdwy # 974 Farmer (--- ---)
HILL, Egbert 25 m Ga

Euf # 337 Farmer (3000-500)
HILL, Francis W. 59 m Ga
Edney 57 f "
Edward F. 32 m "

Euf # 844 Teamster (200-300)
HILL, G. G. 35 m SC
Susan 26 f "
MOSIER, Mariah 25 f "
(Cont.)

(Euf # 844 cont.)
MOSIER, Anna 7 f Ala
William 3 m "

Clay # 7 Builder (1000-3500)
HILL, H. B. 49 m Vt
Jane 27 f Ga
DOLY, Charles 12 m La

Euf # 368 Farmer (--- ---)
HILL, J. R. 37 m Ga
Eliza A. 27 f "
Cornelia 9 f Ala
Alexander 6 m "
Eli 4 m "
James R. 3 m "
SMITH, Green 18 m Ga
HODGE, Eliza J. 12 f Ala

Clay # 80 Carpenter (1000-1200)
HILL, James E. 32 m SC
Louisa S. 31 f "
Thomas J. 8 m "
George W. 5 m "
S.B. 3 m "
Virginia C. 5/12 f "

Euf # 338 Wagoner (--- 300)
HILL, James R. 27 m Ga
Elizabeth F. 25 f "
Orrin M. 1 m Ala
Ellena 5/12 f "
PRICE, Mary T. 9 f "

Euf # 934 (--- 11000)
HILL, Lewis 83 m Va
Mary 78 f SC

Clay # 63
HILL, Lotty 42 f NC
(See Eliza Driggers).

Euf # 1132
HILL, Lotty 40 f Ga
(See John Driggers).

Euf # 1001 Farmer (2000-43000)
HILL, M. R. 39 m Ga
Eliza 21 f "
Margaret 4 f Ala
Laura C. 2 f "
WARREN, Thomas W. 40 m Ga
(Overseer - 4,200- ---)

Euf # 933 Farmer (300-1500)
(Cont.)

(Euf # 933 cont.)
HILL, W. H. 30 m Ala
Sarah 26 f "
Mary 5 f "

Euf 819 Laborer
HILL, William 16 m Ala
(See William Bryan).

Euf 1109 Overseer (--- ---)
HILL, William 60 m Ga
Elsey 60 f "
William 17 m "

Euf # 35 (--- ---)
HINRICK, Powell 66 m SC
Jemima (?) 52 f "

Euf # 241 (--- 300)
HINSEY, Eliza M. 31 f SC
BARTLETT, T. B. S. 11 m Ga

Euf # 997 Hireling
HINSON(?), Elijah 28 m Ala

Clay # 56 Shoemaker (-- 700)
HINSON, James 25 m Ala
M.D. 18 f "
(Married within the year).

Txv # 1224 Miller (--- 200)
HINSON, Jesse 75 m NC
Catherine 30 f Ga
M.E. 5 f Ala

Clay # 71 (--- ---)
HINSON, L. 62 f NC
Lucy 22 f "
Levi (Laborer) 20 m "

Clay # 55 Shoemaker (---1200)
HINSON, L. 34 m NC
Elizabeth 30 f Ga
Mary 1 f Ala
GIBSON, Mary(--85) 65 f Ga

Clay # 68 Shoemaker (-- --)
HINSON, M. M. 30 m NC
Mary 23 f Ala
Lucy J. 3 f Ga
N. H. 6/12 m Ala
ALLBRITTON, Wm. 23 m Ga

Euf # 971
HINSON, Nancy 85 f NC
(See S. M. Streater).

Clay # 69 Shoemaker (1000-1700)
(Cont.)

(Clay # 69 cont.)
HINSON, William 51 m NC
Maria 49 f "
Jesse (Shoemaker) 25 m Ala
A. S. (Wagoner) 20 m "
W. F. (Shoemaker) 15 m "
Albenia 12 f "
C. H. 10 m "
JOHNSON, Mary 68 f NC

Euf # 313 Laborer
HISMITH, John 18 m Ala
Sarah A. 21 f SC
(See Tarpley Tuequeville).

Euf # 785 Farmer (---15000)
HITCHCOCK, John W. 28 m Ga
Martha A. 28 f "
Mary T. 8 f "
Sarah E. 5 f "
Robert R. 3 m "
HOWARD, Susan A. 17 f "
Laura E. 15 f "
Emma P. 6 f "

Euf # 368
HODGE, Eliza J. 12 f Ala
(See J. R. Hill).

Euf # 941 Hireling
Hodge, Henry H. 18 m Ala
(See Wm. R. Long).

Euf # 354
HODGE, Lee 12 m Ala
(See Geo. W. Patterson).

Euf # 944 (--- 150)
HODGE, Sarah A. 34 f Ga
Henry Harrison 18 m Ala
(Laborer)
Franklin 13 m "
Lawson L. 10 m "
James W. 8 m "
John M. 6 m "
Sarah E. 4 f "
Ada L. 2 f "

Euf # 872 Farmer (17500-22000)
HODGES, E. G. 47 m Ga
Mary C. 23 f "
Sarah V. 2 f Ala
Elias 5/12 m "
BISHOP, Elizabeth 18 f SC
(Teacher)
(Cont.)

(Euf # 872 cont).
HODGES, Sarah 10 f Ala
(---- 18,000)

Euf # 866 Physician (700-7000)
HODGES, H. H. 30 m Fla
E. C. 24 f Ga
LOWMAN, Samuel A. 25 m "
(Farmer, ---4000)
L. Y. " " 21 m "
F. E. " 17 m "

Mt. A. # 898 Farmer (--- 250)
HOLDER, David 24 m Ga
Eliza 20 f "
Thomas 2 m Ala
William 1 m "
Jasper (--- 250) 21 m "
PARKER, Jackson 16 m Ga
(Farm Laborer)
HOLDER, Drucilla 42 f "
($1,000-$250)
JOHNSON, Thomas 5 m Ala

Euf # 181 Seamstress
HOLDER, Drew 19 f Fla
(See Alfred H. Dickerson).

Bkb # 772 Farmer (350-350)
HOLDER, John 45 m Ga
Mary 36 f "
Mary J. 12 f Ala
James A. 6 m "
Susanna C. 1 f "

Mt. A. # 808 Overseer (--- 100)
HOLDER, Thomas 22 m Ala
Mary 18 f "
Georgia A. 8/12 f "

Mdwy # 1006 Clerk (---30,000)
HOLLAND, George W. 36 m Ga
Elizabeth S. 33 f "
George C. 14 m "
Hugh P. 8 m "
William W. 6 m "

Txv # 1184 Farmer (3000-3000)
HOLLAND, J. H. 18 m Ala

Flk # 449 Mechanic (150-50)
HOLLAND, Jesse 25 m Ala
Harriett 22 f "
Sophronia 4 f "
Mary S. 1 f "

Mdwy # 1007
HOLLAND, Joseph A. 12 m Ga
(See J. H. Smith).

Txv # 1222 Farmer (--- 350)
HOLLAND, William 55 m Ga
Lucinda 38 f "
BRYANT, Alice 70 f "

Luvl # 335 Farmer (800-300)
HOLLAND, William H. 32 m SC
Lucy A. 30 f Ala
Mary A. 10 f "
John R. 6 m "
Isaac L. 4 m "
M.D.L. 2 m "

Euf # 251
HOLLEDAY, Catarine 77(?) f NC
Ann E. (Seamstress) 25 f Ga
(See Mariah J. Sneed).

Euf # 1113
HOLLEMAN, Catharine 32 f Ga
Margaret A. 7 f "
John F. 3 m La
(See Catharine Nelson).

Euf # 333 Occp. none (9,000-8,000)
HOLLEMAN, Eli C. 59 m Va
Samantha C. 27 f Ga
Amanda E. 6 f Ala
Marietta 4 f "

Euf # 400
HOLLEMAN, Mary 16 f Ala
Henry 12 m "
(See Thos. E. Morgan).

Txv # 1164 Farmer (---7000)
HOLLOMAN, Wright 58 m NC
Jane E. 47 f SC
M. Jane 20 f Ala
Frances S. 17 f "
John D. 14 m "
Henry S. 12 m "
James L. 10 m "
Trustam H. T. 7 m "

Txv # 1215 Farmer (--- 200)
HOLLEY, Thomas 25 m Ga
Mary 26 f Ala
Lamantha J. 1 f "

Clay # 144 Farmer (1500-300)
HOLLEY, W. B. 30 m Ga
C. 25 f "
E. T. 9 m "
Josephine 6 f "
(Cont.)

(Clay # 144 cont.)
Martha E. 2 f Ga
HOLLEY, H. J. 20 f Ala
COLEMAN, R. B. 22 m "
(Farm Laborer)

Euf 1031 Farmer (500-500)
HOLLY, Bricy 71 m Ga
Elizabeth 50 f SC
Penny 22 f Ga
Jane 20 f Ala
John (Farm hand) 17 m "
Laura 14 f "

Euf # 1044 Overseer (--- 100)
HOLLY, John 30 m Ala
Elizabeth 25 f "
Wesley 8 m "
Jane 6 f "
Mary 4 f "
Elizabeth 1 f "

Euf # 358 Laborer (--- ---)
HOLLY, Welcome 20 m Ga
(See John Vincent)

Mt. A. # 821 Overseer (-- 300)
HOLLINGSWORTH, John K. 34 m Ga
Mary J. 26 f "
Mary J. 9 f Ala
George W. 7 m "
E.O. 5 f "
Fanetta 2 f "
PARKER, Martha 60 f Ga

Clay # 134 Farmer (--- 20)
HOLMAN, Thomas 52 m SC
Sarah 63 f "
James 7 m Ala
HUGHS, William H. 8 m Ga

Euf # 614 Farmer (-- --)
HOLMES, Arthur B. 25 m Ala
Sarah T. 22 f "
Laura A 8/12 f "

Clay # 241 Farmer (--- ---)
HOLMES, Hardy 50 m NC
Mandy 35 f "
Elizabeth 11 f Ala
John E. 9 m "
Stephen H. 5 m "

Luvl # 269 Teacher
HOLMES, J. C. 40 m SC
(See Wm. C. Bostick).

Euf # 611
HOLMES, Jane 10 f Ala
(See John Pipkin).

Nwto # 577
HOLMES, Jane 63 f Ga
Lucy 18 f "
(See Salathiel Bradley).

Luvl # 330
HOLMES, Nathaniel 85 m SC
J. Z. (Farmer) 22 m Ala
Mollie F. 23 f "
(See Wm. Dorman).

Euf # 616 Farmer (200-200)
HOLMES, Owen 65 m NC
Elizabeth 34 f "
Dallas 15 m Ala
Ann 13 f "
Calodonia 8 f "
George 6 m "
Bryant 4 m "
Frances 2 f "

Euf # 581
HOLMES, Sallie 18 f Ala
(See McKinney Wood).

Euf # 613 Farmer (1500-600)
HOLMES, William 52 m NC
Sarah 50 f "
Elizabeth 22 f Ala
Malinda 19 f "
Amanda M. 17 f "
Edney 15 f "
Marion 13 m "
Cintha 8 f "

Nwto # 593 Farmer (1500-1500)
HOLMS, Henry 60 m NC
Martha A. 35 f Ga
Henry R. 20 m "
Benj. F. 17 m "
Josephine 12 f Ala

Euf # 824 Overseer (---13000)
HOLSEY, James H. 39 m Ga
Sarah L. 25 f "
Louisa M. 3 f "
James G. 2 m "
Hopkins 3/12 m Ala

Bkb # 686 Blacksmith
HOLT, Richard 70 m Va
(See James H. Williams).

Euf # 174 Gunsmith
HONIKER, W. H. 28 m Ga

Clay # 21 Coach painter
HOOFMAN, Rudolph 25 m Pru
F. G. 56 m "
(Living in hotel)

Clay # 92 Planter (5000-13800)
HOOLE, Bertram J. 46 m SC
Vealilta W. 38 f "
M. Serena 14 f Ala
Victoria S. 12 f "

Euf # 884 Farmer (2500-7000)
HOOTEN, Henry 45 m Ga
Rachael 40 f NC
Joseph A. (Farmer) 21 m Ga
Henry C. 14 m "
Tryphenia 13 f "
James B. 9 m "
Hannah 7 f Ala
Raymond W. 1 m "
BAYER(?), Eugenia A. 22 f Ga
(Teacher)

Euf # 885 Farmer (--- 500)
HOOTEN, James A. 43 m Ga
Martha 35 f "
Henry J. (Farm hand) 19 m "
Rhemus 12 m "
Romulus 12 m "
John 10 m "
William 8 m "
Robert 6 m Ala

Euf # 670 Farmer (6000-17000)
HORN, Eli 67 m Ga
Sarah 54 f "
Frances M. 17 f Ala
T.E.J. 14 m "
MEARS, E. C. (Farmer) 23 m "

Euf # 919 Farmer (---6000)
HORN, J. F. 35 m SC
Sarah J. 34 f Ga
Sarah J. 16 f Ala
Mary O. 14 f "
Penelope A. 12 f "
James R. 5 m "

Euf 918 Farmer (7500-5500)
HORN, William D. 42 m SC
Louisiana W. 19 f Ga
Susan W. 1 f Ala
Nancy 60 f SC
FLOWERS, Penelope 79 f "
(---$2,500)

Clay # 1236
HORNE, Martha 17 f Ala
(See L. W. Price).

Clay # 1118 Farmer (400-400)
HORNE, Nathan 54 m NC
Margaret 44 f "
Edie 14 f Ala
Henry 11 m "
Catherine 9 f "
Christian 6 f "
Margaret 4 f "

Euf # 1380 Farmer (10,000
21,000)
HORTMAN, John G. 46 m SC
M. A. 41 f "
Margaret 19 f "
James (Farm hand) 17 m "
D. B. 14 m "
William H. 12 m Ga
Sarah 9 f Ala
Mary 7 f "
John 4 m "
Rebecca 1 f "

Bkb # 718 Farmer (--- 250)
HORTON, James C. 53 m Ga
Eliza A. 37 f "
Mary 17 f "
John W. 14 m Ala
James W. 11 m "
Jeremiah 9 m "
Martha W. 6 f "
Samuel 4 m "
Margaret F. 9/12 f "

Euf # 122
HORTON, Martha 66 f Va
Willis (Farmer) 30 m SC
John (Farm hand) 16 m "
Martha J. 16 f "
Elizabeth 11 f "
Benjamin 9 m "
William L. 4 m "
(No. 2: --- $100)

Euf # 1247 Farmer (2800-1000)
HOUSTON, Edward 79 m NC
Sarah 52 f "
Geo. W. (Farmer) 32 m "
Chas. H. " 22 m Ala
G. L. " 21 m "
Samuel 10 m "
Sarah 17 f "
Mary W. 15 f "
(Cont.)

(Euf # 1247 cont.)
Nancy R. 12 f Ala
JOHNSON, Mary 90 f NC
COMMANDER, Peter 21 m SC
(Hireling)

Euf # 99 Sign painter
HOWARD, C. 27 m Vt.
(See David Phelps).

Euf # 457 Farmer (12000-35000)
HOWARD, Robert R. 36 m Ga
Mary L. 27 f "
Sarah V. 9 f Ala
Arabella L. 3 f "
Virginia M. 1 f "
FLOURNOY, Frances 17 f "
(Ward of R. R. Howard).

Euf # 1253 Farmer (200-350)
HOWELL, Joseph 43 m Ga
Martha 26 f "
Samuel J. 14 m Ala
Caroline M. 12 f "
Shack W. 11 m "
Sarah S. 6 f "
Martha 2 f "

Euf # 867
HOWELL, P. A. 35 f SC
Randolph (Overseer) 20 m "
(See William H. Foy).

Euf # 1252 (--- 250)
HOWELL, Sarah 59 f SC
Mary 33 f Ga
Elizabeth 30 f "
John W. 5 m Ala
WRIGHT, Thomas 20 m Ga
(Hireling).

Bkb # 693
HOWELL, Susan 1 f Ala
(See Mary Bell).

Euf # 440 Laborer
HOWELL, T. W. 24 m Fla
(See McNamara's R. R. Gro.)

Euf # 1251 Overseer (1200-400)
HOWELL, Turner 28 m Ga
Mary J. 21 f "
George 4 m "
John 2 m "
Jane 7/12 f "

Luvl # 345 Farmer (--- ---)
HOWERTON, John 31 m Ala
(Cont.)

(Luvl # 345 cont.)
Jane 24 f Ala
Mandy 2 f Ga

Euf # 50 Clerk
HUBNER, Henry 22 m Ger
(Born Hanover, Ger. See Chas. Burrus).

Bkb # 1257 (--- 100)
HUDDLER, Catherine 40 f Ga
Amanda 15 f "
Samuel 10 m Ala

Euf # 952 Farmer (1500-10000)
HUGDINS, Stephen 58 m SC
Mary 50 f "
John 18 m "
Permelia 15 f "
Francis 12 m "

Luvl # 291
HUDSON, Irby 13 m Ala
(See R. G. Jackson).

Clay # 5
HUDSON, Louisanna 4 f Ala
(See Lovard Lee, Jr.).

Euf # 395 Miller (--- 1,000)
HUDSPETH, Columbus 50 m Ga
Jane 35 f "
Amy 13 f Ala
Missouri 11 f "
Martha O. 1 f "
Mary C.(?) 7 f "
George R. 4 m "

Luvl # 389 (-- --)
HUEY, E. J. 66 f NC
William M. 30 m Ga
(Farmer, 1200-8000)

Luvl # 393
HUEY, M. A. K.(?) 10 f Ala
Ellen D. 6 f "
(See B. C. Bennett).

Euf # 940 Farmer (4000-16000)
HUGGINS, Reddin 44 m Ga
Frances 30 f "
David 11 m Ala
Mary 8 f "
Sarah 6 f "
Eliza 5 f "
WINDHAM, L. 17 m "
(Hireling)

Euf # 1319 Hireling (-- 50)
HUGHES, Henry 25 m SC
Charity 24 f Ga
Sarah 6 f Ala
Elizabeth 4 f "
James 3 m "
Andrew 1 m "

Euf # 119 Farmer (--- 200)
HUGHES, Sephen(?) 45 m SC
Ellen 47 f NC
John 10 m Ala
Pallestine 5 f "

Euf # 606
HUGHES, Thomas A. 15 m Ala
(See Thomas Bonner).

Euf # 492 Engineer (--- 200)
HUGHES, William A. 36 m Ga
Mary A. E. 33 f "
William 14 m "
George 12 m "
John 10 m "
Sarah 8 f "
Hiram 5 m Ala
Susan 3 f "
Mary E. 2 f "
SMITH, T. H. 24 m "
(Steam mill supt. --- $200)

Clay 134
HUGHS, William H. 8 m Ga
(See Thomas Holman).

Bkb # 755 Farmer (900-300)
HULIN, Thomas 45 m SC
Elizabeth 45 f "
Caroline 22 f Ala
William (Farmer) 21 m "
Adaline 17 f "
John Thomas 15 m "
Elizabeth 12 f "
Wiley 11 m "
Thomas 10 m "

Euf # 3-3 Butcher (--- 200)
HUNT, Henry W. 45 m Ga
Caroline E. 28 f NC
Lewis W. (Carpenter) 18 m Ga
David J. 16 m "
Henry W. 13 m "
Epsey L. 11 f Ala
Amanda C. 8 f "
Camilla 2 f "

Nwto # 584 Farmer (240-300)
(Cont.)

(Nwto # 584 cont.)
HUNT, Jackson 47 m SC
Mary 36 f "
H.V. 15 f "
Frances 13 f "
Lorenzo 9 m "

Euf # 962 Overseer (--- 200)
HUNT, L. J. 27 m Ga
Susan E. 26 f "
William B. 5 m Ala
Georgiann 2 f "

Euf # 453 Farmer (400-300)
HUNT, Willis G. 33 m Ga
Frances 22 f "
Louisa C. 6 f Ala
Lewis A. 4 m "
Charles C. 3 m "
WARD, Willis 66 m Ga

Euf # 127 Cabinet maker (3,000-2,000)
HUNTER, E. H. 38 m Me
F. H. 39 f "
George A. 6 m Ala
Hariet L. 4 f "
MALLER, H. 28 m Ger
(Cabt. maker, born Allsford).

Euf # 1370
HUNTER, Elizabeth 87 f Ga
(See James Bright).

Euf # 1367 Physician (--3000)
HUNTER, H. M. 47 m Ga
(See Joseph M. Cary)

Luvl # 372 Mechanic
HUNTER, James 26 m SC
(See Daniel G. Beasley)

Euf # 930 Overseer (-- --)
HUNTER, James 22 m SC

Luvl # 386 Farmer (500-500)?
HUNTER, Marshall 60 m SC
Sarah 49 f "
Daniel 21 m Ala
Caroline 13 f "
William 11 m "

Euf # 444 ($8,000-40,000)
HUNTER, Sarah E. 40 f Ga
Mary 14 f "

Euf # 422
HURLEY, John 12 m Md
(See James Rutledge)

Clay # 227 Farmer (--- ---)
HURST, Richard 36 m SC
Luren 36 f "
L.M. 13 f "
S.W. 9 f Ala
John S. 6 m "
Mary J. 5 f "
Thomas 2 m "
K.L. 4/12 f "

Luvl # 307
HURST, Tempe 41 f Ga
John (Farmer) 21 m Ala
Jefferson " 19 m "
James 17 m "
Joseph 14 m "
Susan 12 f "
Jackson 9 m "
RAILEY, Mary 16 f "

Euf # 1009 Overseer
HUTCHINSON, Mark 22 m Ga
(See Joel G. Bark or Baark?)

Mdwy # 1005 Overseer (--- 200)
HUTCHINSON, Thomas 25 m Ala
(See Green B. Turner)

Txv # 1147
HUTSON, Irvin 13 m Ala
Robert 9 m "
(See John Bass).

Nwto # 619
HUTSON, M. 14 f Ala
(See Silas Helms).

Euf # 67 Merchant (8000-20000)
HYATT, N. M. 48 m NY
Elizabeth (---4000) 32 f "
Mary 10 f Ala

Euf # 131 Carriage maker (300-100)
HYDE, Alex 24 m Md
Elizabeth 20 f Ga
HARRISON, John C. 3 m "

Euf # 229
INGLET, Georgia A. 13 f Ala
(See Thos. Steidham).

Euf # 176 Laborer
IRA(?), T. 11 m Ga
(See Edward Williams).

Euf # 862 Shoemaker (3500-12000)
IRBY, H. J. 44 m NC
(Cont.)

(Euf # 862 cont.)

F. M.	35	f	Ga
W. H. C.	15	m	"
Leonidas E.	13	m	"
Mary C.	10	f	"
Louisa J.	7	f	Ala
Charles L.	4	m	"
Fanny	1	f	"
CARY, G. B. (Boat maker)	45	m	NC
MCDOW, G. W. (Tin mfgr.)	47	m	Ga

Mdwy # 1082 Farmer (500-500)

IRVING, James A.	24	m	Ala
Virginia	20	f	Ga
Thomas L.	4/12	m	Ala
STOVALL, L. S. (--- 3200)	43	f	Ga
Mary	18	f	Ga

Flk # 411 Farmer (-- --)

IVEY, John B.	20	m	Ga
Mary	25	f	"
FAULK, Lucretia	11	f	Ala
William	9	m	"
Henry	7	m	"
IVEY, Thomas M.	6/12	m	"

Mdwy # 1029 Farmer (-- --)

IVEY, John T.	32	m	Ga
Elizabeth	30	f	"
Frances	2	f	Ala
Charles W.	1	m	"

Euf # 1093

IVEY, William (See Jane E. Curry).	7	m	SC

Euf # 1057 Farmer (3000-62000)

IVEY, William	36	m	Ga
Amanda A.	26	f	"
Davis McW(?)	13	m	Ala
William L.	10	m	"
Tempe J.	5	f	"
Malachi D.	2	m	"
Anna J.	1/12	f	"

Nwto # 561 Farmer

IVEY, William M. (See Burrell Phillips)	15	m	Ala

Euf # 433 Carriage painter (-- 50)

JACKSON, B. C. (Born Boston).	58	m	Mass
Martha E. (Cont.)	27	f	Ga

(Euf # 433 cont.)

Mary A.	3	f	Ga
Johnson J.	6/12	m	"

Mt. A # 916 Overseer (--- 500)

JACKSON, B. H.	35	m	SC
Amelia H.	25	f	Ga
Martha	25	f	SC

Luvl # 548 Farmer (820-800)

JACKSON, C. J.	26	m	SC
Mary	50	f	"
Erastus D.	22	m	"
Doneilla	16	f	"
John	13	m	"
Ann E.	10	f	"
Rebecca	7	f	"

Flk # 474 Farmer (--- ---)

JACKSON, E. D.	23	m	SC
Mary	47	f	"
Lucilla	16	f	"
John	12	m	"
Ann E.	9	f	"
Rebecca	7	f	"
Charles	27	m	"

Flk # 398 Overseer (--- ---)

JACKSON, Irwin	34	m	SC
Rhoda	32	f	"
Girley	14	m	"
James R.	11	m	"

Luvl # 291 Farmer (2800-3200)

JACKSON, R. G.	29	m	Ga
SCROGGINS, Thos. G. (Farmer)	17	m	Ala
HUDSON, Irby	13	m	"

Clay # 194

JACKSON, Rhoda	43	f	Tenn
Stanley (Brick mason)	21	m	Ala
Wm. H. H. (Farmer)	19	m	"
Rowena E.	17	f	"
Posie	15	f	"
Virginia N.	14	f	"
Glancus C.	12	m	"
Mary F.	7	f	"

Euf 436 Carpenter (500-75)

JACKSON, Thomas	60	m	Ga
Marsha	30	f	"
Thomas	9	m	Ala
Mary C. (?)	5	f	"
Sarah A.	4/12	f	"

Euf # 750 Farmer (500-200)

JACKSON, Thomas J. (Cont.)	48	m	Ga

(Euf # 750 cont.)
Mariah 45 f Ga
William 13 m "
James 13 m "
George 11 m "
Mary 8 f "

Clay # 240 Blacksmith (-- --)
JACKSON, Warren 24 m Ala
Nancy 23 f NC
No name 2 f Ala

Mt. A. # 817 Overseer
JACKSON, William 23 m Ala
(See Henry Farrior)

Euf # 1400 Brick mason (--500)
JACKSON, William 24 m NJ
BARNES, John 26 m Ire
(Laborer)

Euf # 173 Brick mason
JACKSON, William 27 m Ire
(See John Bailey).

Mdwy # 924 Farmer (2500-7500)
JAMES, A. G. Sr., 56 m Ga
L.A. 49 f "
D.M. 24 m "
Rebecca L. 21 f "
Fannie 18 f "
Sallie 15 f "
A.G., Jr. 10 m "

Bkb # 707
JAMES, Enos 20 m Ala
Antoniette 21 f Ga
(Married within the year)

Euf # 1313 (1000-3400)
JAMES, Mary F. 53 f SC
Caroline 21 f Ala
Thomas 17 m "
Green 14 m "
Moselle 12 f "

Euf # 559 R.R. Overseer (---3500)
JAMES, R. T. K. 29 m SC
Sophronia 21 f Ala
Edwin 1 m "
PERRYMAN, Jeremiah 45 m Ga
(R.R. Overseer)

Euf # 1279 Hireling (-- --)
JAMES, Warren 22 m Ga
Amanda 23 f Ala
(Married within the year).

Euf # 435 Farmer (--- 200)
JAMES, W. H. 30 m SC
Mary A. 32 f Ga
Georgia A. O. 11 f Ala
Harriet E. 7 f "
Thomas M. 4 m "
John E. 2 m "

Bkb # 708 Farmer (1000-12000)
JAMES, William M. 47 m SC
Ann 51 f "
Eliza 27 f "
Sophronia 22 f Ga
Westley (Farmer) 18 m "
Lucinda 16 f "
Jane 14 f "
Caroline 12 f Ala
BUNTIN, Seaborn 7 m "

Euf # 1063
JARRETT, Joseph T. 58 m Ga
WOOD, John W. 20 m "
(Student)
JARRETT, Maria 50 f "
Geo. W. (Clerk) 29 m "
Alexr. (Student) 21 m "
Henry F. " 18 m "
Sophia 16 f "
James 13 m "

Mt. A. # 816
JEFFCOAT, A. D. 3 f Ala
(See James Peacock).

Luvl # 266 Student
JEFFRIES, Joseph 15 m Ark.
(See Daniel McKenzie).

Bkb # 702 Farmer (650-10,000)
JENKINS, Daniel 70 m NC
Nancy 65 f "
Daniel (Farmer,--800) 22 m "
Rachael 17 f "
John 15 m "
Annette 13 f "
Joseph 11 m "

Mdwy # 960 Merchant (---3500)
JENKINS, E. L. 28 m NC
T. C. 21 f Ga
C. J. 2 m Ala
infant 2/12 m "

Bkb # 703 Farmer (150-800)
JENKINS, Isham 24 m NC
Martha 23 f Ala

Bkb # 705 Farmer (1200-1600)
(Cont.)

(Bkb # 705 cont.)

JENKINS, Riley	40	m	NC
Lucretia	35	f	"
William H.	16	m	Ala
George A.	13	m	"
Samuel	12	m	"
Nancy R.	10	f	"
Mary A.	7	f	"
Cader	5	m	"

Mt. A. # 810

JENNINGS, L. A.	15	f	Ala
Elizabeth	7	f	"
John W.	4	m	"

(See James Stewart)

Euf 362 Farmer (3000-2700)

JERNIGAN, William	37	m	Ala
Martha	32	f	Ga
Jason J.	13	m	Ala
Stephen D.	12	m	"
Mary J.	10	f	"
Lucinda	9	f	"
Savannah	7	f	"
Emaline	5	f	"
Malinda	3	f	"
William C.	1	m	"
Emily	65	f	NC

(--- $1,800)

Clay # 223 Mechanic (700---)

JERNIGAN, Willis	34	m	NC
Sarah	34	f	Ga
Susan	11	f	"
Jane	10	f	"
Joseph	8	m	"
Willis	7	m	"
James	3	m	"
Martha	1	f	Ala

Euf # 1244

JESTER, Thomas	16	m	Ga

(See Martha Clements).

Euf # 1165 Farmer (600-400)

JEMISON, Job	35	m	Ga
Lucy	36	f	"
Charles A.	14	m	"
James M.	13	m	"
S.A.	11	f	"
Margia	8	f	"
Martha M.	6	f	"
Nancy A	4	f	"
William McD.	1	m	"
WADKINS, Richard	23	m	"

(School teacher).

Euf # 728 Farmer (1100-175)

JIMERSON, William	47	m	Ky
Margaret	35	f	SC
Martha	16	f	Ga
Mary	13	f	"
Sarah	13	f	"
Allice	10	f	"
Robert	6	m	"
Henry	3	m	"
Virginia	5/12	f	Ala

Flk # 412 Planter (8000- 50000)

JOHNS, Francis	53	m	SC
Nancy	54	f	Ga
FAULK, Lafayette	22	m	Ala

(Overseer)

Bkb # 710 Farmer (--- 250)

JOHNS, Jonas P.	24	m	Ga
Martha	22	f	SC
F. A.	2	m	Ga

Euf # 449

JOHNS, Pharos	2	m	Ala

(See Isaac Allbright)

Euf 1373 Hireling (250 ---)

JOHNS, Wallace A.	30	m	Ga
Mary	25	f	"
Mary	4	f	Ala
John	1	m	"

Euf # 905 Farmer (1700-2000)

JOHNSON, A. P.	32	m	Ala
Melvina	26	f	NC
SHIVER, Harrison	18	m	Ala

(Hireling)

Bkb # 689 Farmer (--- 200)

JOHNSON, Abner	40	m	SC
Amanda	36	f	"
HERMIER(?), Eveline	21	f	"
Harriett	16	f	"
JOHNSON, William	14	m	SC
Drote	12	m	"
Thomas	10	m	"
Frances	8	f	"
Mary	6	f	"
Caroline	4	f	"

Euf # 1119 Overseer (--- 300)

JOHNSON, Alex	22	m	Ga
Nancy	21	f	"

Luvl # 304 Farmer (1400-1400)

JOHNSON, Alex	47	m	SC
Catherine F.	20	f	Ala

(Cont.)

(Luvl # 304 cont.)
Wilson (Farmer) 17 m Ala
Martha C. 14 f "
Alex T. (Farmer) 24 m "
Martha 22 f "
Sarah 1 f "

Euf # 881 Laborer
JOHNSON, Alex 24 m SC
(See John W. Hall).

Euf 1307 Overseer (--- 50)
JOHNSON, Almarine 28 m Ga
Seymore 24 f "
William 8 m Ala
Reubin 2 m "
Mary E. 1 f "

Luvl # 356 Farmer
JOHNSON, C. W. 27 m NC
(See Elizabeth McRae).

Clay # 15 (500 ---)
JOHNSON, Catherine 35 f NC
Felix 15 m Ala
Julia 13 f "

Euf # 812
JOHNSON, David 23 m Ga
(See Rufus Jordan).

Euf # 1100 Physician (---- 20,000)
JOHNSON, David 26 m Ga
Martha A. 20 f Ala
William A. 8/12 m "
DOZIER(?), Sarah 20 f Ga

Mt. A. # 914 Grocery Co. (800-600)
JOHNSON, David 38 m SC
Hamy A. 24 f Ala
Cornelia 10 f "
Elizabeth 9 f "
James 7 m "
Mary F. 6 f "
Thomas 5 m "
Nancy J. 1 f "
CREECH, John T. 7 m "

Euf # 529
JOHNSON, F. M. 23 m SC
Mary 22 f Ga

Euf # 519 Farmer (375 ---)
JOHNSON, F. M. 23 m SC
Mary 22 f Ga

Euf 162 Laborer (--- ---)
JOHNSON, Jacob 24 m Ga
Ann 20 f "
John 2 m Ala
Sarah 1 f "

Euf 175 Stable keeper (-- 300)
JOHNSON, James 44 m Va
Susan S. 30 f NC
Fanny 3 f Ala
James T. 6/12 m "

Mt. A. # 859 Farmer (---2,000)
JOHNSON, Jesse 36 m Ala
Sarah 34 f NC
Hartwell T. 11 m Ala
L.A.(?) 9 f "
Timothy B. 7 m "
John H. 5 m "
Mary O. 2 f "
infant 4/12 m "

Euf # 163 Laborer (-- --)
JOHNSON, John 63 m SC
Martha 18 f Ga
James 3 m Ala
Sarah 1 f "
LEE, Callie 8 f "

Mt. A. # 848 Farmer
JOHNSON, John 33 m Ga
William (Farmer) 17 m "
Loronzo " 16 m "
(See A. P. Padget).

Euf # 653 Farmer (800-250)
JOHNSON, John A. 40 m SC
Christina 28 f "
Sallie 15 f "
John P. 13 m Ala
Daniel 9 m "
Vicey 7 f "
Martha 6 f "
Edney 4 f "
Christina 1 f "

Euf # 661
JOHNSON, Joseph 11 m Ala
(See Isaac Dykes).

Mt. A. # 883 Farmer (450-250)
JOHNSON, Joseph C. 25 m Ala
Mary A. L. 18 f Ga
Isiah 1 m Ala
Columbus 2/12 m "

Clay # 188 Farmer (--- 500)
JOHNSON, Judge S. 24 m Ala
Mary A. 19 f "
Alexander 2 m "

Euf # 651
JOHNSON, Julia A. 18 f SC
Thomas J. 4/12 m Ala
(See John A. Oliver)

Euf # 880 Farmer (1400-4000)
JOHNSON, Lewis A. T. 43 m SC
Elizabeth P. 41 f "
Felder 19 m Ala
Elizabeth 15 f "
Roseanna 13 f "
Thomas 10 m "
William 7 m "
Mary 4 f "
Emma 1 f "

Bkb # 774 Farm Laborer
JOHNSON, Lorenzo 17 m Ga
(See Arasmus R. Spergers)

Euf # 783
JOHNSON, Marcian A. 10 m Ala
Isham D. 9 m "
John P. 7 m "
Richard M. 5 m "
(See L. Q. C. Gaston)

Euf # 1247
JOHNSON, Mary 90 f NC
(See Edward Houston).

Clay # 69
JOHNSON, Mary 68 f NC
(See William Hinson).

Clay # 225 Farmer
JOHNSON, Milledge 18 m SC
(See John T. Martin).

Clay # 229
JOHNSON, Penny 20 f SC
(See Thomas Warren).

Txv # 1187 Farmer (100-300)
JOHNSON, Phillip 59 m NC
Mary J. 22 f Ga
Elmyra 17 f Ala

Clay # 41 Physician (-- --)
JOHNSON, R. C. 22 m Ga
Carrie 18 f Ala
(Married within the year).

Luvl # 293 Farmer
JOHNSON, Robert 28 m Ga
Martha C. 18 f "
Robert G. 1 m Ala
(See William H. Jones).

Clay # 191 (--- 1500)
JOHNSON, Sarah 53 f SC
W. W. (Tax collector) 32 m Ala
(8000-10000)
Rachael A. 27 f "
Julia 21 f "
J.H. 20 m "
Lydia E. 16 f "
Frances S. 14 f "
Laura J. 12 f "
Jesse R. 10 m "
Virginia P. 8 f "

Eur # 475
JOHNSON, Susan 14 f Ala
(See Wm. Warlick)

Mt. A. # 898
JOHNSON, Thomas 5 m Ala
(See David Holder).

Mt. A. # 912 Work at mill
(--- 200)
JOHNSON, Timothy 22 m Ala
Elizabeth 28 f Ga
E. S. 2 f Ala
Elias 1 m "

Mt. A. # 858 Farmer (800-400)
JOHNSON, Timothy, Sr. 60 m NC
Elizabeth 61 f SC
Mary M. (Idiotic) 16 f Ala

Mt. A. # 849 Farmer (--- 200)
JOHNSON, Turner 28 m Ga
Margaret 25 f "
John 5 m Ala
Catherine 4 f "
Georgia A. 1 f "

Mdwy # 992 engineer at mill
(--- 1000)
JOHNSON, Wiley 43 m Ga
Mahala 42 f NC
Martha 16 f Ala

Nwto # 638 Farmer (--- 150)
JOHNSON, William 20 m Ala
E.J. 23 f "
John W. 6 m "
L.M. 2 f "
infant 1/12 f "

Mt. A. # 869 Farmer
JOHNSON, William 20 m Ga
(See Sampson D. Helms).

Euf # 476 Laborer (-- --)
JOHNSON, William 29 m Ga
Susan 23 f "
Martha 8 f Ala
Edward 4 m "
Elijah 2 m "

Euf # 476 Farmer (80-50)
JOHNSON, William E. 48 m SC
Mary 45 f "
Sarah J. 25 f Ga
Mary 18 f "
Elizabeth 15 f "
Catharine 13 f "
John S. 10 m "
Polly 3 f "

Clay # 733 Farmer (500-1300)
JOHNSON, William S. 28 m Ala
Elizabeth 21 f "
Amy A. 5 f "
Lydia E. 3 f "
Charity J. 2 f "
Laura I. 7/12 f "

Luvl # 646 Farmer (--- 200)
JOHNSON, Zachariah 30 m Ala
Louisa 24 f "
John J. 1 m "

Nwto # 579
JOHNSTON, Elizabeth 12 f Ala
(See William Trent).

Euf # 279 Public Officer
(3,000-14,000)
JOHNSTON, John W. 38 m Ga
Louisa 30 f SC
John W. 9 m Ala
Edward B. 6 m "
David A. 4 m "
BRYAN, Marriah 22 f SC

Euf # 207 Warehouse (14000-30000)
JOHNSTON, L. F. 40 m Ala
Martha F. 30 f Ga
Claude 15 m Ala
Young 10 m Ala
Sarah 9 f "
Ida 7 f "
Ralph 6 m "
(Cont.)

(Euf # 207 cont.)
Elizabeth 3 f Ala
infant 1/12 f "
WELLBORN, Pat 18 f "
(Student)

Euf # 1241 (1,000-5,000)
JOHNSTON, Mary 64 f SC
JOHNSTON, John W. 28 m "
(Farmer, --- 450)
Georgian 17 f Ala
GRANTHAM, Mary T. 16 f SC

Euf # 1390 Clerk
JOHNSTON, Young M. 18 m Ga
(See Elizabeth S. Bethune).

Euf # 14-14 Merchant (5,500-1,000)
JOICE, E. C. 44 m Ga
Elizabeth 30 f "
Edward 9 m Ala
Martin 7 m "
George 5 m "
William Henry 2 m "
RICHARDS, Wm. (Clerk) 17 m "

Clay # 240 Farmer (800-3300)
JONES, A. D. 39 m NC
Elizabeth E 30 f Ga
Charles W. 8 m "
Joseph W. 6 m "
Thomas R. 4 m Ala
Elizabeth E. 1 f "

Mdwy # 998 Physician (---10000)
JONES, A. T. 27 m Ga
Sarah 24 f "
W. P. 23 m "
(Teacher, 8000-000)

Euf # 1246 Farmer (1200-1000)
JONES, Aerial 38 m NC
Martha 38 f SC
James (Farm hand) 18 m Ala
Mary 16 f "
Ledocia 15 f "
Sephus 14 m "
Newton 12 m "
Amanda 10 f Fla
Calvin 9 m Ala
Missouri 6 f "
Dixon 3 m "
Hilliard 1 m "

Flk # 400 Farmer (-- --)
(Cont.)

(Flk # 400 cont.)
JONES, Alex 24 m Ala
Georgia A. 19 f "
James A. 3/12 m "

Luvl # 271 Clerk (--- 4,000)
JONES, Benjamin 19 m Ala
(See John M. Lampley)

Clay # 83 Farmer (3000-75000)
JONES, C. W., Sr. 34 m Ga
R.E. 24 f "
Roxie 6 f Ala
C.W. 4 m "
P.H. 3 m "
Moselle 1 f "
VINSON, N. W. 17 m Ga
(Clerk)

Flk # 496 Farmer (400-150)
JONES, David 27 m NC
Mary J. 23 f Ala
Eleanor 5 f "
Flora 2 f "

Flk # 443 (2000-7000)
JONES, Ellender 50 f Ga
Joseph 22 m Ala
(Farmer, --- 350)

Euf # 1052
JONES, H. E. 44 f NC
($3,000-$8000)
ROUNDTREE, B. F. 23 m Ga
(Silversmith)
BROWN, C. H. 30 m NY
(Grocer, 250-1700)
BARNETT, P. E. 24 m Ga
(Merchant, 2000-10000)
HALL, E. A. 53 f SC
BARNETT, Ellen G. 18 f "

Euf # 452 Carpenter
JONES, J. W. 25 m NC
(See Thos. G. Jordan).

Euf # 756 Farmer (400-200)
JONES, Jackson 25 m Ala
Cordelia 18 f Ga
Levi 1 m Ala

Euf # 440 Stone Cutter
JONES, James 25 m NY
(See McNamara's R.R. Gro.)

Luvl # 336 Overseer (-- --)
JONES, James H. 26 m Ga
(Cont.)

(Luvl # 336 cont.)
Elizabeth 36 f SC
Jacob 9 m Ga
Lucinda 8 f "
Lucy A. 5 f "
Elizabeth 3 f "
James 2/12 m Ala

Euf # 1245 Farmer (3000-800)
JONES, James W. 50 m NC
Susannah 42 f SC
Thomas S. (Farmer) 21 m Ala
May J. 20 f "
Eliza A. 17 f "
Sarah 16 f "
Clayton R. 14 m "
Cynthia E. 13 f "
James W. 10 m "
John C. 9 m "
Frances C. 8 f "
George C. 7 m "
Susannah A. 5 f "
Georgian 2 f "
Lucinda 5/12 f "

Euf 932 Overseer (--- 150)
JONES, John 30 m Ga
Martha 21 f "
Sarah 1 f Ala

Mt. A. # 823 Farmer (--- 500)
JONES, John 41 m SC
Elizabeth 36 f Ga
Mary M. 16 f Ala
William A. 14 m "
Thomas L. 11 m "
Rebecca 9 f "
Elvina 7 f "
John D. 5 m "
Jeremiah 1 m "

Euf # 569
JONES, John 20 m SC
(See David Shehan).

Flk # 462 Farmer (2000-8000)
JONES, John B. 41 m SC
Mary E. 30 f Ala
Carlton A. 14 m "
Roxa A. E. 12 f "
Cladia A. B. 10 f "
Edwin B. 9 m "
Bascom B. 7 m "
Mary A. 6 f "
Stella A. 4 f "
Charlotte J. 2 f "
Ada A. F. 1 f "

Euf # 998 Farmer (--- 500)
JONES, Joseph (?)56 m NC
Sarah 58 f "
Cornelia H. 24 f "
Mary M. 22 f Ga
Elijah A. (Farmer) 17 m "
James L. " 15 m "
Sarah 14 f "
SINGLETON, Louisa 30 f NC
Henrietta 4 f Ala

Euf # 808 Farmer (--- 5,500)
JONES, Joseph 23 m Ga

Euf # 1336 Physician (3000-14000)
JONES, Joseph 45 m SC
Cornelia C. 35 f Ga
Matty 6 f Ala
Laura 3 f "
JONES, Thomas E. 14 m SC
Samuel H. 12 m "
Densill H. 10 m "

Clay # 239 Farmer (--- 250)
JONES, Lewis A. 30 m Ga
Martha 26 f "
James 8 m Ala
Lewis 5 m "
Jesse 2 m "
infant 2/12 f "

Luvl # 355 farmer (2150-2100)
JONES, Mathew 35 m NC
Isabella 25 f Ala
Victoria 6 f "
Amanda 4 f "
John D. 1 m "

Clay # 175 (250-250)
JONES, Penelope 39 f Ga
James (Farmer) 21 m "
Henry 16 m Ala
Jasper 13 m "
Matilda 7 f "
BISHOP, Brantley 19 m NC
(Farm laborer)

Luvl # 540 Farmer (1000-350)
JONES, Russell 44 m NC
Betsy 43 f "
Alex 13 m Ala
M.A. 10 f "
Mary A. 6 f "
Sarah A. 4 f "
Charles 2 m "

Euf # 280 Cabinet maker (450-450)
JONES, S. P. 32 m Me
Fontain 9 m "

Euf # 806 Farmer (35000-76000)
JONES, Samuel 53 m Ga
Selina 49 f "
Samuel(Student) 20 m Ala
Henry " 18 m "
Elizabeth 10 f "
Louisa R. 2 f "

Euf # 849 Merchant (2000-3000)
JONES, Seaborn 46 m SC
CAWTHORN, Sarah E. 12 f Ala
JONES, John 15 m SC
Wiley 13 m "
Frank 11 m Ala
Mary J. 8 f "
Levi 6 m "
Elizabeth 4 f "
MATHIS, A. W. 25 m SC
(Clerk, ---800).

Euf # 371 Overseer (2800-10000)
JONES, Silas 43 m Ga
Margaret 31 f "
William H. 9 m Ala
Joseph 6 m "
James 4 m "
Thomas 3 m "
HAWES, Emily 18 f Ga

Euf # 61 Farmer (--- ---)
JONES, Thomas 29 m Ga
Lucy 80 f Va

Clay # 101
JONES, Thomas 12 m Ga
(See A. S. Kennedy)

Euf # 807 Farmer (--- 20,000)
JONES, Thomas 27 m Ga

Luvl # 261 Carriage & smith trade (500-8000)
JONES, Thomas H. 35 m Ga
Jane H. 33 f "
Michael B. 10 m Ala
Emma E. 8 f "
Catherine 6 f "
Isabell 3 f "

Euf # 439 Farmer (--- 600)
JONES, William 47 m Va
Nancy 35 f Ga
(Cont.)

(Euf # 439 cont.)
Daniel 16 m Ga
Nancy 12 f "
FUTCH, Mary 12 f "
Catherine 8 f "
Stephen 6 m "

Euf # 500 Farmer (350-300)
JONES, William 45 m Va
Nancy 32 f NC
Nancy 16 f Ga
Daniel 17 m "
FUTCH, Mary 14 f Ala
Catherine 12 f "
Stephen 10 m "

Euf # 258 Carpenter (----)
JONES, William 46 m Ga
Julia F. 45 f "
Peyton W.(Laborer) 18 m "
Catherine 16 f "
Harrington 13 m "
James 12 m "
Martha J. 9 f "
Sarah F. 6 f "

Luvl # 293 Farmer (600-300)
JONES, William H. 40 m Ga
Rebecca 32 f NC
John 13 m Ala
Louisa 12 f "
Hollinger 11 m "
Henry 9 m "
Adaline 7 f "
Mary 5 f "
Lucy 3 f "
Thomas 1 m "
JOHNSON, Robert 28 m Ga
(Farmer)
Martha C 18 f "
Robert G. 1 m Ala
MILES, John 23 m "

Euf # 1064 Clerk (--- ---)
JORDAN, Henry L. 39 m Va
Ann E. 26 f Ga
George M. 13 m Ala
Junius H. 7 m Ga

Euf # 682 Farmer (4000-3500)
JORDAN, John 45 m SC
Catharine 23 f Ga
James David 15 m "
Sampson 12 m "
Mary C. 10 f "
Rufus F. 8 m "
(Cont.)

(Euf # 682 cont.)
John 6 m Ga
Abner 4 m "
Martha 1 f "

Euf # 91 M.E.Minister (400-550)
JORDAN, Joshua W. 45 m NC
Amelia B. 50 f SC

Euf # 96 Merchant (12000-20000)
JORDAN, Junius 47 m Va
Frances H. 40 f Ga
Clarence 18 m "
St. John J. 16 m "
Junius 14 m Ala
Rosalie 12 f "
Adrian 10 m "
Bascomb 6 m "
Eliza 4 f "
Weyman, Rebecca 44 f Ga

Euf # 812 Farmer (3700-13700)
JORDAN, Rufus 30 m Ga
Eugenia 15 f "
Andrew T. M. 4 m "
JOHNSON, David 23 m "
(Farmer)

Euf # 240 Steamboat Pilot
(2,500-1,000)
JORDAN, Thomas 47 m Ga
Levinia C. 27 f "
Thomas C. 13 m "
William H. 11 m "
John R. 3 m Ala
Emma 1 f "

Euf # 452 Farmer (12,000-30,000)
JORDAN, Thomas G. 71 m NC
Mary (--- 100) 54 f Ga
JONES, J. W. 25 m NC
(House carpenter).

Mdwy # 973 Farmer (10,000-12,000)
JORDAN, W. E. 36 m Ga
Frances A. 21 f "
Mary T. 4 f Ala
M.A.M. 2 f "

Mdwy # 956 Farmer (70,000-
25,000)
JORDAN, W. J. 29 m Ga
E. T. 25 f "
Calvin 6 m Ala
Julia 4 f "
Mary 3 f "
infant 8/12 f "
GRIFFIN, Thos. 24 m Ga
(Merchant, ---2700)

Euf # 1278 Farmer (--- 400)
JORDAN, William 32 m Ga
Elmire 23 f "
Sarah 11 f "
John 6 m "
LIGHTFOOT, Benjamin 26 m "

Euf # 327 Laborer (--- ---)
JORDAN, William 19 m Ala
(See Aura Nolin)

Txv # 1204 Farmer (--- 800)
JOWERS, William 64 m SC
Nancy 56 f Ga
Hilliard 34 m Ala
(Farmer, 1500-100)
Maria 21 f "
Martha A. 20 f "
Lurensa 18 f "
Barbara A. 16 f "
Lennard 14 m "
Greenberry 11 m "
Thomas J. 9 m "

Euf 425 Occp. none (2000-65000)
JOYCE, Martin H. 52 m Ga
Sarah A. 34 f "

Clay # 659
JUDIE, Mary 70 f NC
(See Gilbert McEachern).

Euf # 997 Merchant (--- 12000)
KAIGLER, John J. 32 m SC
Julia 26 f Ga
HENSON(?), Elijah 28 m Ala
(Hireling)

Clay # 160 Farmer 6000-25000)
KAIGLER, Reuben 55 m SC
Catherine 54 f "
M. E. 24 f "
E. C. 21 f Ga
E. E. 14 f "

Euf # 151 Baker (--- 500)
KALBFLEISCH, Herman 31 m Ger
(Born Hesse, Germany).
(See Clark W. Foster)

Euf # 215 Farmer (1400-3000)
KAY, Hiram 56 m SC
Newton 20 m Ala
Ann 15 f "
Joseph 13 m "
(Cont.)

(Euf # 215 cont).
Rebecca 11 f Ala
William 9 m "
Dicy 7 f "
Lucinda 5 f "
Nancy 42 f SC
Jesse 8 m Ala

Euf # 440 Quarryman
Kearnes, William 33 m Ire
(See McNamara's R.R. Gro.)

Euf # 440 Quarryman
KEEFE, William 28 m Ire
(See McNamara's R.R. Gro.)

Mt. A. # 797 Overseer (--- 100)
KELLY, George W. 34 m Ala
Jane 33 f SC
George W. 12 m Ala
Fannie 10 f "
Alice 7 f "
Alonzo 2 m "

Nwto # 604 Farmer (400-400)
KELLY, M. K. 46 m Ga
Mary 36 f SC
Jefferson 16 m Ga
Orrin 15 m Ala
Mary J. 14 f "
Sarah A. 11 f "
L.E. 10 f "
James W. 8 m "
Simon 6 m "
John M. 4 m "
Stephen T. 5/12 m "
BELL, Louisa 31 f SC
William J. 1/12 m Ala

Euf # 440 Laborer
KELLY, Patrick 22 m Ire
(See McNamara's R.R. Gro.)

Mt. A. # 886 Laborer (--- 100)
KEMP, John 22 m Ga
Isabella 23 f "
Sarah E. 6/12 f Ala

Mt. A. # 887 Farmer (200-200)
KEMP, Thomas 26 m Ga
Nancy A. 32 f Ala
Roxie A. 2 f "
Sarah J. 1 f "
James M. 15 m "

Euf # 114 Merchant (7000-20000)
KENDALL, James T. 31 m NC
(Cont.)

(Euf # 114 cont.)
Mary J. 25 f NC
Winney J. 6 f "

Euf # 992 Farmer (15000-25000)
KENDRICK, Aaron T. 52 m Ga
Ellener L. 44 f "
William B. (Farmer) 22 m "
John A. " 19 m "
James E. 14 m "
A. T. 12 m "
George P. 5 m "
Edward 1 m Ala
PROCTOR, Mary A. 26 f Ga
(--- 3,500)
Colin 5 m Ala

Euf # 1018 Farmer (--- 700)
KENDRICK, B. E. 23 m Ga
Mary R. 16 f Ala
(Married within the year).

Euf # 969 Physician (4300-15000)
KENDRICK, J. C. 27 m Ga
Ann E. 24 f "
William T. 4 m "
Westley F. 3 m Ala
TERRY, Robert 37 m Ga.
(Overseer)
CODY, Philvea 17 f "

Euf # 994 Farmer (2400-400)
KENDRICK, Robert S. 45 m Ga
Elizabeth 41 f "
Henry T.(?)(Farmer) 24 m "
Daniel " 20 m "
Samuel " 18 m "
Mary A. 16 f "
Rebecca 14 f "
Columbus 7 m "
William H. 3 m Ala
Texana 10/12 f "

Euf # 1097 Occp. none (---4,000)
KENNEDAY, William L. 35 m NC
Sarah 30 f "
Fastletine 13 f "
Arnolphus 12 m "
McDuffie 9 m "
Jane 6 f Ala
Annis 2 f "
KEKLER, Mary M. 86 f NC

Clay # 101 Farmer (800-200)
KENNEDY, A. S. 28 m NC
Nancy A. 26 f "
Louisa 2 f Ala
Henry A. B. 5 m "
William 4/12 m "
BOWDEN, Louisa 30 f NC
JAMES, Thomas 12 m Ga

Euf # 625 Farmer (4000-1700)
KENNEDY, Daniel 50 m Scot
Nancy 40 f NC
Libby A. 14 f Ala
Hugh 12 m "
Hector 10 m "
MCLEAN, Isabella 21 f NC
KENNEDY, Margaret 4 f Ala

Mdwy # 1102 Farmer (--- 300)
KENNEDY, David J. 36 m NC
Harriet 30 f "
D. F. 9 m Ala
Calvin I. 7 m "
Palestine 5 f "
Nancy 3 f "
Moses 4/12 m "

Mdwy # 1053 Occp. none (-- --)
KENNEDY, James 26 m Ga
Fannie 60 f NC
Alsey 21 f Ga
Sarah E. 17 f Ala

Clay # 174 farmer (400-100)
KENNEDY, James 21 m SC
Nancy 19 f Ga
Sarah J. 1 f Ala

Mdwy # 1100 Farmer (2100-8000)
KENNEDY, John 74 m NC

Clay # 173 Farmer (1200-400)
KENNEDY, John 47 m NC
Anna 37 f SC
Spencer (Farmer) 18 m "
Lawrence " 16 m Ala
Sandford 14 m "
Sarah 11 f "
Daniel 3 m "
Thomas C. 8/12 m "
infant 8/12 f "

Mdwy # 1101 Farmer (---300)
KENNEDY, Joseph T. 32 m NC
Mary M. 21 f SC
Naomi E 3 f Ala
Dosia 8/12 f "

Clay # 168 Farmer (-- --)
KENNEDY, Owen 40 m NC
Julia A. 40 f "
James T. 3 m "
Ottaway 2 m "
D. 1/12 m Ala

Clay # 170 Farmer (2000-600)
KENNEDY, Thomas 50 m NC
Martha A. 25 f Ala
Thos. M. (Farmer) 22 m "
Mary R. 20 f "
D. C. 15 m "
William W. 13 m "
PADRICK, J. S. 26 m NC

Euf # 1000 Shoemaker (2000-8500)
KENNEDY, William 70 m NC
Sarah 70 f "
HATCHER, Thos. (Apprentice) 19 m Ga
BARHAM, Rebecca (1,200-10,000) 38 f NC
Romulus 8 m Ala
David 2 m "

Mdwy # 1103 Farmer (600-1500)
KENNEDY, William R. 39 m NC
Sarah 34 f Ala
Joseph 11 m "
Brithy 9 m "
Mary J. 5 f "
Nancy E. 3 f "
Thomas D. 1 m "

Clay # 148 Farm Laborer
KENNINGTON, James 18 m Ga
(See T. C. Millsap, Sr.)

Clay # 181
KENNINGTON, Martha 48 f SC
(See J. W. Newman).

Euf # 908
KENNON, Jane 74 f Ga
(See Green Beauchamp).

Nwto # 615 Farmer (550-200
KENT, Aaron, 43 m Ga
Harriett 40 f "
Nancy 18 f Ala
James 12 m "
Aaron 9 m "
Rebecca 5 f "

Euf # 1097
KEKLER, Mary M. 86 f NC
(See William L. Kenneday).

Nwto # 558 Farmer (960-1000)
KETCHUM, B. W. 34 m Ala
Sarah 37 f NC
W. W. (Farmer) 16 m Ala
James K. P. 14 m "
Lafayette 12 m "
John W. 10 m "
Mary A. 8 f "
Francis M. 6 m "

Nwto # 557 Farmer (400-300)
KETCHUM, Lafayette 23 m Ala
Margaret (800-300) 55 f Ga
CASEY, Annie 37 f Ala
Matilda 20 f "
Benjamin F. (Farmer) 18 m "
Huey 4 m "

Luvl # 343
KEY, Edgar 4 m Ala
(See Elizabeth Morris).

Euf # 173 Brick mason
KEYHOE, John 24 m Ire
(See John Baliey).

Euf # 189 Stone mason
KEYHOE, John 25 m Ire
(See Owen Rials).

Euf # 440 Stone cutter
KEYHOE, John 27 m Ire
(See McNamara's R.R. Gro.)

Euf # 553
KIDD, Eliza 45 f SC
(See David Lore).

Euf 6-6 Clerk (1000-500)
KIELS, Eli M. 38 m Ala
Martha E. 29 f Ga
Alice M. 9 f Ala
Laura F. 5 f "
William C. 2 m "
Nicey 69 f SC

Euf # 38
KIELS, Susan 55 f SC
Georgiann 11 f Ala
(See F. M. Pittman).

Txv # 1174 Overseer on farm (--- 500)
KILPATRICK, Almerine 23 m Ala

Clay # 198 Farmer (--- ---)
KILPATRICK, Andrew 40 m SC
Mary A. 37 f Ga
Earley 16 m Ala
Isaac 11 m "
Rebecca 10 f "
John G. 8 m "
Jepther 4 m "
Mary 3 f "

Clay # 222 Farmer (--- ---)
KILPATRICK, Easley 27 m Ala
Mary W. 29 f SC
William T. 4 m Ala
James S. 3 m "
Martha C. 2 f "
Robert A. 4/12 m "

Clay # 204 Farmer (600-100)
KILPATRICK, Jesse 41 m SC
Harriett 27 f "
M.V. 11 m Ala
S.E. 3 m "

Euf # 1364 Laborer (--- 100)
KILPATRICK, Samuel 21 m Ala
Nancy 24 f NC
Harrison 1/12 m Ala

Clay # 153 Seamstress
KILPATRICK, Sarah 22 f Ala
(See William Blair)

Bkb # 780 Farmer (300-250)
KILPATRICK, Simeon 30 m Ala
Sarah 28 f "
Catherine E. 1 f "

Clay # 19 Stable Clerk
KILPATRICK, T. A. 26 m Ala
(Living in hotel).

Clay # 140 Farmer (2500-1000)
KILPATRICK, W. H. 52 m SC
E.R. 51 f "
M.C. 24 f Ala
Mary E. 22 f "
Martha A. 18 f "
E.(orC.) R. 15 f "
A.H. 13 m "
Frances 11 f "

Mt. A. # 747 Farmer (480-400)
KILPATRICK, Warrie 64 m SC
L. J. 43 f "

Euf # 615
KING, Caroline 17 f Ala
(See David Blackshear).

Luvl # 346 Farmer (5000-25000)
KING, E. M. 40 m Ga
Amanda 40 f "
RUSSELL, William J. 21 m "
(Farmer).

Mdwy # 1014 (3,800-10,500)
KING, Elizabeth 40 f NC
Sarah E. 14 f Ala
Henry L. 12 m "
John T. 10 m "
Elvy P. 5 m "
Harrison L. 3 m "
PUGH, Whitson 22 m "
(Overseer on farm).

Euf # 458 Overseer (--- 200)
KING, G. N. 30 m Ala
Mary 23 f Ga
Thomas F. 4 m Ala
Charles C. 2 m "
Edda 4/12 m "

Euf # 923 Occp. none (-- --)
KING, J. L.(or T.S.) 64 m SC
Susan 25 f Ala
Martha A. 9 f "
Rebecca 4 f "

Euf # 1397 Student (---8,000)
KING, Marshal 19 m Ga

Luvl # 373 Waggoner (-- --)
KING, Reuben 34 m Ga
Georgia A. 33 f Ala
James 11 m "
Benjamin F. 9 m "
Seaborn 7 m "
Robert 4 m "
DANIEL, Martha C. 36 f Ga
Howard 9 m "
Seaborn F. 7 m Fla

Mt. A. # 836 Farmer (4400-13000)
KING, Robert H. 36 m Ga
Mary A. 27 f "
Henry G. 11 m Ala
Ida A. 9 f "
Annie E. 7 f "
Robert P. 5 m "
Otho 4 m "
Ada A. 2 f "

Euf # 1032 Farmer (5000-4000)
KING, T. C. 32 m Ga
Elizabeth C. 33 f Fla
(Cont.)

(Euf # 1032 cont.)
Catharine 11 f Ala
Elizabeth 9 f "
John W. 6 m "
Nancy J. 4 f "
Isabella 2 f "
KING, Laurany 56 f Ga.

Mt. A. # 833 Farmer (4000-15000)
KING, T. W. 30 m Ga
Louisa 25 f Ala
Thomas 5 m "
CATENHEAD, Elizabeth 11 f "

Mdwy # 1069 Farmer (3600-12000)
KING, Thomas 47 m NC
Nancy 54 f "
Levi 15 m Ga
Robert 8 m Ala
PAUL, John 34 m SC
(Overseer on farm, --- 100)
Emma 18 f Ga.

Luvl # 282 farmer (3500-12000)
KING, William 49 m NC
Mary 44 f SC
James (Farmer) 16 m Ala
Susan 12 f "
Elizabeth 8 f "
Daniel 6 m "
William 3 m "
BAKER, Sarah 80 f SC
HERRING, Chloe A. 22 f Ala

Euf # 372 Farmer (800-500)
KING, William H. 28 m Ga
Sarah 32 f "
Hariet 7 f Ala
Adelaide 5 f "
William 3 m "
Drury 4/12 m "

Txv. # 1183 Grocery keeper (1200-300)
KINNAMAN, Andrew 30 m NC

Mt. A. 832 Overseer (-- 200)
KINNARD, Daniel 30 m Ga
Clementine 27 f "
George C. 6 m Ala
James P. 4 m "
Ann H. 1 f "
ALEXANDER, Sarah 63 f SC

Txv # 1173
KIRKLAND, Aaron 11 m Ala
(See Daniel Bass)

Euf # 705 Laborer
KIRKLAND, James 18 m Ala
(See Wm. N. Atkinson).

Euf # 648
KIRKLAND, Martha 10 f Ala
(See John Whidden).

Clay # 178 Pauper in poorhouse
KIRKLAND, Matilda 42 f NC
KIRKLAND, Lucretia 6 f Ala

Euf # 170 Prof. of Music
KLEFFMILLER, Chas. 35 m Ger
Matilda (Fr. Teacher) 27 f "
(Both born Hesse, Ger.)
(See Wm. D. Hailey).

Euf # 726 Farmer (12000-4000)
KNIGHT, Harbit(?) 37 m Ala
Mary 37 f Ga
Charles A. 14 m "
Andrew J. 12 m "
Ann E. T. 10 f "
Mary S. 8 f "
Harmon S. 6 m "
Sophrona 4 f "
Milbry 2 f "
Clayton W. 9/12 m "

Euf # 786 Farmer (1300-500)
KNIGHT, W. B. 37 m Ga
Julia 27 f "
William H. 10 m Ala
FINCH, Charles 8 m "

Euf # 440 Stone Cutter
KYLE, Patrick 28 m Ire
(See McNamara's R.R. Gro.)

Euf # 266 Baker (--- 100)
LaGRANGE, Eugene 31 m Fr
Mary 31 f Ga
Caladonia 9 f "
Henry 2 m "

Clay # 655
LAMPLEY, Catherine 43 f NC
L.J. 14 m Ala
Laura 12 f "
Caleb 8 m "
Edward 4 m "
(See Elizabeth Shipman).

Mdwy # 985 Merchant
LAMPLEY, James M. 25 m Ala
(See Elizabeth A. Owen).

Luvl # 271 Merchant & farmer
(108000-160000)
LAMPLEY, John M. 40 m NC
M.P. 28 f Ala
Harmon 10 m "
Belle 9 f "
Ira 3 m "
LAMPLEY, H. D. 27 m NC
(Merchant, 3000-
75000)
ALLEN, Asa (Clerk) 24 m Ala
JONES, Benj. " 19 m "
(--- 4000)

Euf # 358
LAND, Madison 12 m Ga
(See John Vincent).

Euf # 581
LANDRUM, George 88 m NC
(See McKinney Wood).

Euf 1141 (--- 125)
LANDRUM, Lotty 61 f Ala
FUQUAY, Mary A. 17 f SC

Mt. A. # 750 (200-225)
LANDRUM, Missouri A. 38 f Ga
John R. 20 m "
Nancy J. 17 f "
Mary 15 f Ala
William 10 m "
Franklin 8 m "
Benjamin 5 m "
Sarah F. 2 f "

Clay # 674 Farmer (-- 100)
LANE, Andrew 21 m SC
Margaret 17 f Ala
John B. 1/12 m "

Bkb # 704 Farmer (1300-3500)
LANE, Bryant 49 m SC
Winnie 52 f "
William (Farmer) 19 m "
Osborne " 18 m Ala
Stephen 14 m "
James 12 m "

Euf # 1106 Clerk
LANE, Thomas W. 31 m Ga
(See John F. Treutlen)

Euf. 310 Merchant (12,000-
50,000)
LANEY, Charles D. 49 m NC
Eliza 35 f Miss
Charley H. 11 m Ala
Alberta 7 f "
Andrew B. 8/12 m "

Euf # 37 Minister M.E. (2500-
8000)
Laney, John W. 39 m NC
Harriet A. 33 f Vt
Ella V. 11 f Ala
Cora C. 9 f "
James W. 4 m "

Luvl # 275 Physician (1000-
4000)
LANG, John 56 m Scot
Mary A. 54 f "
James 23 m "

Euf # 528 Farmer (1600-8000)
LANGSTON, R. Y. 37 m Ga
Mary 27 f "
Zach. 8 m Ala
Samuel 6 m "
Julia 4 f "
Sarah 2 f "
MURPHY, Ambrose 17 m Ga
(Farm hand).

Euf # 249 Laborer (300-50)
LANIER, A. F. 24 m Ala
Emma E. 20 f SC

Euf # 248 (1,000-100)
LANIER, Lucy 50 f NC
Mary 22 f Ala
Benjamin T. 11 m "
William W. 3 m "

Mt. A. # 874 Carpenter (-- 200)
LAREY, John R. 38 m Ga
Emeline 29 f Ala
William A. 8 m "
Adaline E. 6 f "
Julius F. 4 m "
Mary E. 3 f "
Narcissia 9/12 f "

Clay # 129 Farmer (2000-12000)
LASSETTER, E. M. 39 m Ga
E.M. 38 f SC
Munroe (Farmer) 18 m Ga
M.T. 16 m "
H.R. 14 f "
(Cont.)

(Clay # 129 cont.)
Nancy E. 12 f Ga
Mary S. 9 f "
John D. 5 m Ala
Frances 5 f "
Elisha 2 m "
Elizabeth 2 f "
PETERSON, Alexander 22 m Ga
(Farm laborer).

Clay # 54
LASSETTER, Henrietta 14 f Ga
(See Ridley Barron).

Clay # 43 Farmer (8000-42000)
LASSETTER, M. M. 33 m Ga
Jane 29 f Ala
Mary 12 f "
Nancy E. 10 f "
Ann 7 f "
Virginia 5 f "
Emma 3 f "

Euf # 1283 Farmer (5000-33000)
LASSETER, Mathew 72 m NC
Mary 57 f Ga

Clay # 119 Farm laborer
LATIMORE, George 69 m Ire
(See Daniel McCraney).

Clay # 178 Pauper in poorhouse
LATON, Lusinda 40 f Ga

Luvl # 647 Farmer (--- 250)
LATON, William 50 m SC
Elizabeth 34 f NC
Robert (Farmer) 23 m Ala
Nancy J. 19 f "
William " 15 m "
Marshall 11 m "
Henry 5 m "

Euf # 454 Overseer (1000-3200)
LAWHORN, Webb H. 30 m NC

Euf # 288 (--- 5,000)
LAWSON, Jane 66 f Ga

Euf # 21-21
LEAIRD, Andrew J. 12 m Ala
(See John W. Clark)

Euf # 1301 Farmer (1000-6500)
LEE, Andrew 50 m SC
Nancy 47 f "
(Cont.)

(Euf # 1301 cont.)
Martha J. 21 f Ala
Mary A. 18 f "
Lucinda E. 16 f "
Nancy A. 12 f "
William A. S. 9 m "
Thomas M. 3 m "

Txv # 1197
LEE, Ann 15 f Ala
(See John Carroll).

Euf # 163
LEE, Callie 8 f Ala
(See John Johnson).

Euf # 639
LEE, James 31 m Ala
(See Jackson Owens).

Clay # 660
LEE, Jane L. 18 f Ala
(See Daniel McEachern).

Euf # 504 Farmer (1800-10000)
LEE, Jesse 54 m Ga
Sarah A. 29 f "
Sarah A. E. 9 f Ala
Mary 7 f "
John 5 m "
Newell 2 f "
Eugenia 5/12 f "
THOMAS, Mary J. 16 f "
John 57 m Ga

Txv # 1125 Farmer (3500-5500)
LEE, Lovard, Sr. 68 m SC
Sarah J. 17 f Ala
Lovard W. 14 m "
(Lovard, Sr., & Sarah J. married within the year).

Clay # 5 Merchant (1800-1500)
LEE, Lovard, Jr. 42 m Ga
Susan E. 36 f "
A.V. 16 m Ala
Julia A. 14 f "
LOVELACE, Elvira 12 f "
HUDSON, Louisianna 4 f "
McEACHERN, John C. 23 m "
(Clerk)

Luvl # 363 Farmer (4000-20000)
LEE, Needham, Jr. 47 m Ga
Emiline 44 f NC
Jefferson 22 m Ala
Nancy 19 f "
(Cont.)

(Luvl # 363 cont).
Licurgus 17 m Ala
Sarah 15 f "
Robert 14 m "
George W. 12 m "
Virginia 10 f "
Needham 7 m "
Joseph 2 m "
WASHBURN, Martin 22 m Ga
(Farmer)

Euf # 633 Farmer (1500-6000)
LEE, Robert 37 m SC
Mary 37 f Ga
Needham T. 16 m Ala
(Farm hand).
Elmira P. 14 f "
Matilda A. 12 f "
Mary A. E. 10 f "

Luvl # 506 (6000-6000)
LEE, S. A. 40 f Ga
Columbus C. 16 m Ala
(Farmer, ---6000)
Winneford (---6000) 14 f "

Euf # 627 Farmer (1400-1000)
LEE, Timothy 33 m SC
Nancy 31 f Ala
Narcissa V. 12 f "
Leman D. 10 m "
Martha A.M. 9 f "
Lipsay 8 f "
William A. 6 m "
Jacob T. 1 m "
PARMER, William W. 22 m "
(Farmer, 300-200)

Luvl # 533 Miss. Bapt. Min.
(4000-400)
LEE, William 41 m Ala
Mary 29 f NC
R.S. 8 f Ala
William M. 5 m "
Acy A. 4 m "
James B. 2 m "
Ann E. 1/12 f "

Clay # 1124 Farmer (180-250)
LEE, Wm. B. W. 21 m Ala
Jane 17 f Ga
Godfrey 1 m Ala
John P. 20 m "
(Farm laborer)

Euf # 1255 Blacksmith (-- --)
LEONARD, James 59 m SC
(Cont.)

(Euf # 1255 cont).
William D. 33 m SC
(Blacksmith)
Lucinda 24 f SC
Jonah 23 m "
(Blacksmith, --- 800)

Euf # 394 Ornamental painter
(500-150)
LEROY, Benj. M. 45 m NY
Frances A. 31 f Ga
Benjamin 12 m Ala
Georgia A 13 f "
Frances 8 f "
Thomas 5 m "

Euf # 176 Carpenter
LESTER, D. 22 m Ga
(See Edward Williams).

Mdwy # 986 Carriage maker
(--- 100)
LESTER, John 30 m Va
(See Sarah Owens)

Luvl # 376 Farmer (2000-15000)
LESTER, Joshua 56 m SC
Ann 45 f NC
Cleopatra 21 f Ala
Elizabeth F. 20 f "
David (Farmer) 18 m "
Sarah A. 16 f "
George W. 14 m "
Francis M. 13 m "
Celia A. 12 f "
Penelope J. 11 f "
John W. 7 m "
Hester A. 5 f "

Mdwy # 1084 Farmer (1600-4500)
LEVERETTE, H. R.(?) 44 m Ga
Beulah A. 46 f SC

Euf # 924
LEVERETT, Lively 65 f Ga
(See John L. Williams).

Euf # 39 Saddler (--- 5,000)
LEWIS, Artemus 45 m NY
Jane E. 35 f Ga
James A. 14 m "
Susan F. 12 f "
Thomas 9 m "

Clay # 89 Mechanic (600-400)
LEWIS, Benjamin 49 m SC
A. J. 46 f Ga
William (Mechanic) 26 m Ala
L. V. 18 f "
(Cont.)

(Clay # 89 cont.)
B. S. 15 m Ala
A. J. 13 m "
N. A. 10 f "
George W. 8 m "
S. C. 6 m "

Mt. A. # 852 (600-550)
LEWIS, C. C. 36 f Ala
Sarah 16 f "
Seymore E. 15 f "
James J. 13 m Miss
Robert R. 11 m Ala
STAFFORD, Judith D. 30 f "
(Blind).

Luvl # 644 (640-500)
LEWIS, Catherine 53 f NC
Robert (Farmer) 28 m "
(--- 125)
Polly 24 f "
William A. (Farmer) 22 m Ga
(600-200)
GRUBBS, Frank 19 m Ala
(Farmer, 200 ---)

Flk # 485 (400-200)
LEWIS, Catherine 55 f NC
Harriett 35 f "
R.D. (Farmer) 26 m "
Mary A. 24 f "
William A.(Farmer) 22 m Ga

Clay # 736 Farmer (500-2600)
LEWIS, Daniel G. 39 m Ala
Lucy 36 f "
Mary 15 f "
Victoria 14 f "
John 12 m "
Harrison 10 m "
William 8 m "
Antoinette 6 f "
Martha 4 f "
Giles 2 m "

Clay # 35 Carpenter (---1000)
LEWIS, Elias 49 m NC
Harriett 29 f SC
Ann 17 f Ala
John 15 m "
James M. 12 m "
Mary J. 9 f "
Chester 6 m "
Thomas 1 m "

Mdwy # 1094 Farmer (12000-33000)

(Cont.)

(Mdwy # 1094 cont.)
LEWIS, Elvy 71 m NC
Nancy 68 f "
BOTTOMS, John 33 m SC
(Overseer, --- 1100)

Flk # 484 farmer (1400-1500)
LEWIS, Hansford 23 m NC
Martha A. 40 f "
GRUBBS, W. W. 20 m Ala
(Overseer, 500 ---)

Flk # 489 Farmer (650-250)
LEWIS, J. D. 23 m NC
Lydia F. 21 f Ala
Harman 2 m "
Columbia 6/12 f "
SMITH, James(Farmer) 16 m "

Luvl # 348
LEWIS, Jane L. 4 f Ala
(See Casa Edge).

Euf # 634 Blacksmith (800-300)
LEWIS, John 50 m NC
Apsey S. (?)40 f "
George W. (?)22 m "
William R. 21 m Ala
Lydia A. 19 f "
James A. (Farmer) 17 m "
Nancy T. 15 f "
Rosetta 13 f "
Green 12 m "
Quincy 9 m "
P. E. 7 f "
Josephine 4 f "
infant 1/12 f "

Nwto # 596
LEWIS, John L. 23 m Ala
Harrison 18 m "
Martha 4 f "
(See Jeremiah Craft)

Euf # 629 Farmer
LEWIS, John W. 27 m NC
Allers 20 f Ala
Abigail J. 1 f "

Mdwy # 1095 Farmer (1600-5000
LEWIS, Joseph J. 35 m NC
Elizabeth 24 f Ga
Elvy S. 7 m Ala
Mary 6 f "
Annie 1 f "

Euf # 48
LEWIS, Margaret 65 f Ga
(See Richard Morris).

Mt. A. # 834
LEWIS, Mary 16 f Ala
Antionette 8 f "
(See Mary Efurd).

Flk # 491 Farmer (800-500)
LEWIS, Musgrove 48 m NC
Elizabeth 30 f Ga
Frances M. 13 f Ala
John C. 8 m "
Susan M. 6 f "
James O. 5 m "
Emma 3 f "
Ella 3 f "
Harriett 8/12 f "
BIZZELL, J. C. 23 m "
(Merchant,---1000)

Mdwy # 1105 Farmer(7200-7200)
LEWIS, Neecy 51 m NC
Rebecca E. 40 f "
Joseph B. 22 m Ala
John T. 20 m "
Elias 19 m "
Charles (Farmer) 18 m "
Susan A. 16 f "
Clara V. 15 f "
James M. 13 m "
Sarah 12 f "
Neecy 9 m "
Rebecca 7 f "
David R. 6 m "
Frances 4 f "
Everline 2 f "
Robert H. 1 m ?

Mt.A # 909 Miller (1500-8000)
LEWIS, O. S.(?) 45 m NC
Mary 38 f "
Della 11 f "
Cora M. 9 f "
Cornelia 7 f Ala
Missouri 5 f "
Mary A. 1 f "
PITTMAN, F, M. 25 m SC
(Eng. at mill)
Susan F. 18 f Ala

Euf # 81 Carriage maker
(2,500-1,000)
LEWIS, Samuel W. 34 m Ga
Elizabeth 29 f SC
Charles 5 m Ala
William 1 m "
LILLY, George 27 m NY
(Carriage painter, ---300)

Euf # 142 Stable keeper
(1200-200)
LEWIS, T. J. 40 m Ga
Jefferson 17 m Ala
Sarah A. 24 f Ga

Euf # 1278
LIGHTFOOT, Benjamin 26 m Ga
(See William Jordan).

Euf # 1150 (--- 300)
LIGHTFOOT, William E. 34 m Ga
Mary 33 f "
Ann E. 7 f "
Allicey 6 f "
Mary C. 4 f "
William P. 2 m Ala
John T. 1 m "

Euf 1350
LIGHTNER, Mrs. 60 f Ga
(See H. P. Adams)

Clay # 82 Farmer (5000-20000)
LIGHTNER, Michael 65 m SC
Martha 30 f Ala
Mary 3 f "
James B. 4 m "
infant 2/12 f "
William 11 m "

Clay # 52 Planter (8000-23000)
LIGHTNER, S. F. 32 m Ala
Mary T. 28 f Ga
George M. 2 m Ala
Susan V. 1 f "
Mary S. (--- 2300) 14 f "

Clay # 46 Farmer (7000-18000)
LIGHTNER, Thomas S. 38 m Ga
Nancy 32 f Ala
Sarah 13 f "
Sophia 11 f "
Frances 8 f "
Alabama 6 f "
W. M. 4 m "
M. T. 2 f "
(A duplicate was recorded on this family with the exception of the age of Alabama was given as 5 years old.)

Euf # 81 Carriage painter
LILLY, George 27 m NY
(See Samuel W. Lewis).

Clay # 732 Farmer (925-3500)
(Cont.)

(Clay # 732 cont.)
LINDSEY, Jeptha 50 m NC
Lydia A. 41 f Ga
Charity J. 12 f Ala
William J. 10 m "
Martha 23 f Ga
Calep 4 m Ala
L. H. 1 f "

Euf # 282 Laborer (450-100)
LINDSEY, John 41 m Ire
Eridocill 25 f Ga
STEWART, T. 31 m Ga
(Cabinet maker).

Mt. A. # 908 Farmer (--- 600)
LINDSEY, Lewis 27 m NC
Lydia A. E. 24 f Ga
Mary F. 9 f Ala
L. A. E. 6 f "
Jeptha A. 4 m "
Laura 2 f "

Euf # 1092 Mechanic (700-250)
LINSEY, Hiram F. 35 m Ga
Mary 32 f "
or SC(?)

Euf # 118 Cabinet maker (1000-1000)Born Werting, Ger.
Link, William 39 m Ger
Sophia (Born Bavaria) 39 f "

Flk # 408 Farmer (---15,000)
Liptrot, John 63 m Ga

Luvl # 269
LITTLE, G. W. - --
(See Wm. C. Bostick).

Bkb # 764 Farmer (--- 150)
LITTLE, James P. 24 m Ala
Elender 24 f "
George W. 2 m "
Josephine 3/12 f "
Henrietta 3/12 f "

Bkb # 763 (--- 100)
LITTLE, Jefferson B. 18 m Ala
Florinda 16 f "
(Married within the year).

Mt. A. # 749 Farm Laborer (--- 150)
LITTLE, John 50 m Ga
Martha 45 f "
William H. 20 m "
Martha 14 f Ala
(Cont.)

(Mt. A. # 749 cont.)
Elizabeth 12 f Ala
Missouri 10 f "
Jesse 8 m "
Rachael 3 f "

Bkb # 762 Farmer (3575-600)
LITTLE, Josiah 58 m NC
Kitsey 36 f "
Catherine 16 f Ala
Issabella 12 f "
Georgia A. 5 f "

Flk # 436 Farmer (--- 100)
LITTLEFIELD, John E. 25 m Ga
Jane 32 f SC
Robert H. 6 m Ala
George 4 m "

Euf # 1012
LOCK, Anna 20 f Fla
(See Hester Phillips).

Euf # 54
LOCKE, A. F. 24 m Ala
(Merchant,---7500)
HART, T. B. (Clerk) 30 m RI
CATTEVILLE, E. L. 23 m Fr
(Steam boat)
No. 2: (--- 200)
No. 3: (---1500)

Euf # 1272 Farmer (800-5000)
LOCKE, Thomas S. 35 m Ala
Mary 31 f "
John 12 m "

Euf # 56 (--- ---)
LOCKE, William H. 28 m Ala
Ann J. 20 f Ga
Ella E. 3 f Ala
Lula 1 f "

Euf # 36 Carpenter (--- ---)
LOCKE, William J. 33 m NC

Euf # 506 & 507 Farmer
LOFLIN, Thomas 32 m Ga
Eliza T. 24 f "
James M. 11 m Ala
Sarah T. 1 f "
T. Nelson 11 m "
(See James Rogers)

Euf # 746 Farmer (2000-300)
LOFTIS, George T. 45 m SC
Ellaney 46 f Ga
BOYD, Nathan N. 14 m Ala

Nwto # 594 Student
LOGANS, William 24 m Ga
(See William Cook).

Luvl # 391 (1,000-1,000)
LONG, Ann 50 f NC
Kate 20 f Ala

Euf # 958 Farmer (8000-6000)
LONG, C. P. 40 m SC
Amanda 23 f Ga
Laura 1 f Ala
Elizabeth 5 f "
Benjamin 14 m "
James (At school) 20 m "
William " " 18 m "
James Wilson 21 m Ga

Euf # 713 Farmer (4000-500)
LONG, Charles 49 m NC
Elizabeth 45 f "
Mary M. 17 f Ala
Feriby 15 f "
Pattey 13 f "
Jane 11 f "
Caroline 9 f "
George (Laborer) 18 m "
Lafayette 16 m "
Adam A. 2 m "

Euf # 349 Student
LONG, James 20 m Ala
(See M. H. Streater)

Euf 963 Teacher(?)
LONG, James 20 m Ala
(See C. B. Streatar).

Clay # 104
LONG, M. 45 f NC
Gilbert 14 m Ala
Newton(Farm laborer) 16 m "
(See Wm. T. J. C. Efurd).

Euf # 999 Farmer (210,000 - 160,000)
LONG, Nimrod W. 60 m Ga
Sophia 49 f "
Grigsby T.(In school) 18 m Ala
Laura R. 16 f "
Frederick 14 m "
James W. 9 m "
MORELAND, Sarah 62 f Ga

Luvl # 296 Farmer (-- --)
LONG, Richard 25 m NC
Martha 16 f Ala

Nwto # 620 Miller (-- 150)
LONG, Thomas 23 m SC
Eliza E. 18 f Ala
(Married within the year).

Euf # 768 Cropper (--- 100)
LONG, Thomas W. 24 m Ala
Eliza A. 18 f "
(Married within the year).

Euf 727
LONG, William 25 m NC
Emily 25 f Ala
Mary E. 6 f "
Malissa 4 f "
William J. 2 m "

Euf 941 Farmer (1500-2000)
LONG, William R. 35 m SC
Frances A. 37 f NC
Susan J. 13 f Ga
Elizabeth S. 14 f Ala
Daniel W. 11 m "
Reuben P. 8 m "
Marietta 2 f "
HODGE, Henry H. 18 m "
(Hireling)

Euf # 553 Farmer (2500-4000)
LORE, David 52 m NJ
Ann 43 f SC
Mary Ella 7 f Ala
KIDD,Eliza 45 f SC

Clay # 1120 Farmer (360-1500)
LOTT, Arthur 32 m Ga
Amanda 30 f "
Mariam M. 10 f La
Mary E. 8 f "
John E. 4 m "
Clement W. 2 m "
William A. 10/12 m Ala

Clay # 1115 (2000-4000)
LOTT, Bidsey 54 f Ga
DRIGGARS, Artemesia 21 f "
Narcissia J. 4 f Ala
Louisianna A. 1 f "
LOTT, Henry W. 17 m "
(Farmer)
Matilda 13 f "

Clay # 1114 Farmer (--- 500)
LOTT, J. T. 27 m Ga
Nancy 24 f Ala
William T. 9 m "
(Cont.)

(Clay # 1114 cont.)
Louisa A. 7 f Ala
Charles 4 m "
Sarah N. 1 f "

Euf # 794 Overseer (--- 100)
LOTT, John D. 30 m Ga
Sarah 20 f "
Leonidas E. 3 m Ala
John T. 6/12 m "

Euf # 834 (500-200)
LOTT, Susan 55 f Ga
Edward 25 m "
Angeline 20 f "
Martha 18 f "
MARSHALL, William 5 m Ala

Txv # 1230
LOTT, William H. 5 m Ala
(See John A. Davis)

Flk # 417 (150-1000)
LOVELACE, E. L. 20 m Ala
(See Nancy Faulk)

Euf # 1199 (400-100)
LOVELACE, Elizabeth 40 f SC
Jordan D. 17 m Ala
Penny 15 f "
William T. 12 m "
Soprona 10 f "
John 8 m "

Clay # 5
LOVELESS, Elvira 12 f Ala
(See Lovard Lee, Jr.)

Euf # 646 Farmer (1200-500)
LOW, John 30 m Ala
Mary E. 21 f "
William F. 4 m "

Euf # 647
LOW, Leonna 65 f SC
WILKERSON, Louisa 16 f Ala
LOW, James M. 1 m "

Bkb # 720 Farmer (3000-1200)
LOWE, Robert N. 53 m NC
Mary H. 51 f Ga
William (Farmer) 21 m NC
Ellen 23 f "
A. B. " 20 m "
Seldon " 18 m Ga
John " 16 m "
Missouri 14 f Ala
Robert 9 m "

Euf # 903 (18,000-78,000)
LOWMAN, Eliza J. 46 f NC
infant 1/12 m Ala
SANDERS, Mary J. 15 f "
WILLIAMS, Mary M. 4 f NC

Luvl # 390 Farmer (-- --)
LOWMAN, G. W. 38 m Ala

Euf # 890 Farmer (3500-20000)
LOWMAN, James L. 37 m SC
Martha E. 21 f "
Mary F. 5 f Ala
Preston 3 m "
Joseph 1 m "

Euf # 893 Farmer (3000-30000)
LOWMAN, John E. 40 m SC
Mary 36 f NC
Robert F. 15 m Ala
Adolphus W. 14 m "
Mariah L. 12 f "
NORTON, William 24 m "
(Overseer)

Euf # 411 (--- ---)
LOWMAN, Julia 38 f SC
George 12 m Ala
Adrian T. 10 m "

Euf # 2-2
LOWMAN, Laura V. 14 f Ala
(See Wm. H. Boswell).

Euf # 441 (---- 4,000)
LOWMAN, Mary H. 54 f SC
Mary S. 18 f "
Sarah A. 16 f "
Benjamin 14 m Ga
Anderson 11 m Ala
Eugene H. 9 m "
SANDERS, Mr.(Tailor) 23 m Ger
WHICHARD, Mr. 23 m Fla
(Telegraph operator)
BEALLE, Mr. (Tailor) 21 m Ger
EVERETT, John 22 m Ga
(Fountry man)
MALONEY, Mr.(Tailor) 27 m Ire

Euf # 866 Farmer (-- --)
LOWMAN, Samuel A. 25 m Ga
L. Y. (Farmer) 21 m "
F. E. " 17 m "
(See H. H. Hodges).

Euf # 891 Farmer (--- 3000)
LOWMAN, William 66 m SC
(Cont.)

(Euf # 891 cont.)
Martha L. 18 f Ga
James O.(?) 15 m "
Catherine 14 f "

Euf # 996 Farmer (6600-36000)
LOWMAN, William H. 45 m SC
John T. 19 m Ga
EIDSON, James J. 25 m "
(Overseer)

Euf # 672
LUDLAM, Elizabeth 18 f Ala
Amanda P. 2 f "
(See Arch'd. McLean).

Euf # 705
LUDLAM, Sarah H. 6 f Ala
Savil 8 f "
(See William N. Atkinson).

Luvl # 370 Farmer
LUDLOW, Wiley 18 m Ala
(See Wm. R. Pool).

Flk # 430 Farmer
LUDLOW, Wiley 20 m Ala
(See Flora A. Shaw).

Euf # 105 Farmer (--- 100)
LUNSFORD, B. F. 30 m Ga
Harriet E. 23 f "
Eliza A. 6 f Ala
Nancy J. 5 f "
Frances E. 4 f "
John W. 2 m "
William M. 4/12 m "

Euf # 221 Farmer (--- 150)
LUNSFORD, Green B. 22 m Ga
Clementine 8 f Ala

Euf # 104 Farmer (500-700)
LUNSFORD, Joseph S. 54 m NC
Serena 53 f Ga
Hardy J. 18 m "
John 16 m "
Henry P. 13 m Ala
Serena E. 9 f "
Sarah L. 7 f "

Euf # 497
LUNSFORD, Thomas P. 22 m Ga
(See Alexr. Robinson, Sr.)

Bkb # 709 Farmer (500-200)
LUNSFORD, William 25 m Ga
Elizabeth 25 f SC
(Cont.)

(Bkb # 709 cont.)
Marcellus 4 m Ala
Mary J. 2 f "
Amanda 3/12 f "

Euf # 44
Mc---------CHIL, Janet 22 f Scot
(See Walter S. McNaughton).

Euf # 1352 Farmer (800-600)
McADAMS, James R. 43 m SC
Levenia 37 f "
William 17 m Ala
Benjamin W. 15 m "
Elizabeth 14 f "
Susan 13 f "
George 12 m "
Goly L. 10 m "
Catharine 7 f "
Margaret 7 f "
Sarah 6 f "
James 4 m "
Cassas 1 m "

Euf # 1053 Carriage maker (2,000-4,000)
McALISTER, John W. 35 m Ga
Endalia 38 f "
James H. 12 m Ala
John T. 8 m "
Leonder C. 6 m "
William A. 1 m "
BURCKLE, John 30 m Conn
(Carriage painter, ---150)
FAULKNER, Peter 27 m Conn
(Carriage trimmer, ---300)

Bkb # 442 Farmer (2000-200)
McALPIN, John S. 52 m NC
Patsey 45 f "
Susan 21 f "
John 16 m "
Jane 14 f "
Mary 8 f Ala
Nancy 4 f "

Clay # 97
McANDREWS, A. 36 f Ga
S. B. 7 m Ala
(See Asa Blakey)

Euf # 176 Mill wright
McANDREWS, J. 25 m --
(See Edw. Williams).

Euf # 518
McANTY(?), Margaret 18 f Ire
(See Jonathan Ford).

Euf # 470 Mill wright (-- --)
McAULY, John W. 27 m Md

Bkb # 758 Teacher (8000-4000)
McBRIDE, James P. 49 m Ga
Sarah E. 49 f SC
Thomas J. 20 m Ga

Clay # 8 Grocer (1200---)
McBRIDE, Samuel 54 m Ga
Stephen (Mechanic) 35 m "
James F. 25 m "
(Shoemaker,150---)
Mary 32 f "
Robert C. (Farmer) 17 m Ala
MORRIS, Elizabeth M. 12 f Ga
McBRIDE, Sarah P. 11 f Ala
Mary A. 8 f "

Luvl # 374
McBRIDE, Sophia J. 20 f Ala
(See Geo. L. Shipman).

Euf # 631 Farmer (--- 150)
McBRIDE, William 24 m Ga
Mary 26 f "
James 2 m Ala
Catharine 8/12 f "
GLOVER, Malissa 8 f "

Clay # 199 Farmer (700-325)
McCALL, A. S. 51 m Ga
Susannah 43 f "
Phebe Ann 25 f "
John B. 18 m "
Mary J. 16 f "
Martha H. 11 f "
Jesse H. 5 m "
Elephair 3 m "
James R. 1/12 m "

Bkb # 761 Blacksmith (--- 150)
McCALL, Daniel 50 m SC
Eliza 47 f "
Mary 21 f Ala
Charles 17 m "
John 15 m "
James 13 m "

Luvl # 334
McCALL, Flora 7 f Ala
Kate (Black) 110 f SC

Luvl # 315 Farmer (8000-4000)
McCALL, Gilbert 39 m NC
(Cont.)

(Luvl # 315 cont.)
Adaline 29 f SC
Daniel S. 13 m Ala

Clay # 154 Farm laborer
McCALL, Nathaniel 21 m Ala
(See Thos. A. Hightower).

Mdwy # 931 Overseer on farm (--- 200)
McCARROLL, Perry 52 m Ga
Hattie 48 f "
Martha 13 f Ala
Victoria 10 f "

Clay # 19 Clerk in Grocery
McCARTY, Elias 28 m Ga
(Living in hotel).

Euf # 1105 M. E. Minister (--- 50,000)
McCARTY, William A. 41 m Tenn
Mary E. 22 f Ga
William E. 17 m Ala
Mary Elizabeth 19 f SC
Sallie E. 15 f Ala
Massilon F. 13 m "
Fanny A. 11 f "
Linda C. 8 f "
GRANT, James 43 m "

Euf # 440
McCAY, Nancy 20 f Ga
(See McNamara's R.R. Gro.)

Euf # 234 Planter (30000-53000)
McCLENDON, John G. 56 m SC
Elizabeth R. 40 f NC
Mary A. 19 f Ala
John C. 12 m "
Angus M. 9 m "
Josephine E. 7 f "
Walter P. 5 m "
BEVERLY, Christian N. 16 f NC
Mary J. 18 f "
McRAE, Mary 95 f "

Euf # 420 Laborer
McCLENDON, Samuel 20 m Ga
(See James Daniels).

Euf # 173 Laborer
McCLOUSKEY, James 24 m Ire
(See John Bailey).

Euf # 420 Laborer
McCLUSKY, James 30 m Ire
(See James Daniels).

Luvl # 320 School Teacher
McCOLLUM, ----- 26 m SC
(See John Bell).

Euf # 1138 Carpenter (--200)
McCORMICK, B. B. 24 m Ala
Belona 19 f Ga
(Married within the year).

Luvl # 253 Merchant (1000-19000)
McCORMICK, William 42 m NC
Ann 41 f Ga
John D. (Bookkeeper) 20 m Ala
George C. (Clerk) 16 m "
William E. 12 m "
Henry L. 5 m "
James A. 3 m "
James E. 25 m NC

Euf # 430 Laborer
McCORMICY(?), Roddy 33 m Ire
P. J. 31 f "
Charles H. 5 m SC
Patrick H. 5/12 m Ga
McNAIR, Patrick 46 m Ire
(Laborer).

Clay # 130 Overseer on farm (--- 3,000)
McCRACKIN, S. Y. 24 m SC

Clay # 119 Farmer (1000-300)
McCRANEY, Daniel 44 m SC
Jane 43 f "
Murdock 13 m "
Issabella 11 f "
Nancy 7 f Ala
John D. 2 m "
LATIMORE, George 69 m Ire
(Farm laborer).

Clay # 115 Farmer (1000-10000)
McCRANEY, Malcom 52 m NC
Arabella 50 f SC
Calvin (Farmer) 24 m "
Murdock " 22 m Ga
John " 20 m "
Neill " 18 m "
Margaret 13 f Ala
James K. 11 m "
Mary 7 f "
BLUE, Sophia 21 f "
(Teacher)

Clay # 123 Farmer 1000-500)
McCRANEY, Norman 33 m SC
(Cont.)

(Clay # 123 Cont.)
Edie 27 f SC
Westley K. 11 m "
Daniel F. 9 m Ala
Murdock J. 7 m "
William H. 5 m "
Sarah J. 2 f "
John R. 1 m "
Christian 77 f Scot
(Born Isle of Sky, Scotland).

Clay # 165 (800-250)
McCRARY, Rebecca 48 f SC
Thomas Mc. (Farmer) 27 m Ala
Warren 20 m "
James 18 m "
Alice 15 f "
Ann 12 f "

Clay # 122 Farmer (760-450)
McCREE, D. W. 71 m NC
M. J. 18 f Ala
L. E. 16 f "
David 14 m "

Clay # 183 School Teacher
McCRIMMON, Daniel 36 m NC
(See L. W. Walker).

Flk # 421 Farmer (3600-5000)
McDANIEL, Frederick 30 m Ga
Easther 26 f "
John F. 5 m "
Mary J. 4 f "
Georgia 2 f "
(See Michael P. Vickars).

Bkb # 716 Farmer (--- 1000)
McDANIEL, Y. H. 40 m Ga
R. C. 27 f "
Anderson (Farmer) 17 m Ala
John H. " 15 m "
Nancy R. 13 f "
Sarah A. 12 f "
Jeremiah 7 m "
James Y. 5 m "
George W. 3 m "
Sidney 4/12 m "
VERDAN, Morgan 24 m SC
(Farm laborer)

Euf # 467 Farmer (--- 500)
McDONALD, Archy 26 m Ga
Catharine 25 f NC
Mary G. 7 f Ala
John T. 5 m "
Carrie 2 f "

Euf # 826 Farmer (300-100)
McDONALD, Colin 75 m NC
Elizabeth 58 f "
James 11 m Ala

Luvl # 382 Farmer (3000---)
McDONALD, Daniel(age torn)Ala
Mary " " Ga

Euf # 180
McDONALD, Eliza 32 f Ala
(See James H. Durham).

Euf # 946
McDONALD, J. 78 m NC
(See M. Patterson).

Euf # 188 Carpenter (120-300)
McDONALD, J. B. 54 m SC
Frances 46 f "
Harriett H. 18 f Ala
Arramettea 16 f "
William 13 m "
Thesalonia 11 f "

Euf # 1111 Carpenter (200-100)
McDONALD, J. B. 54 m SC
Frances 48 f "
Hariet U.(?) 19 f Ala
Arametta 16 f "
William 14 m "
Thessalonia 11 f "

Euf # 865 Occp. none
McDONALD, J.(?) D. 70 m SC
(See L. B. Patterson).

Euf # 304 ($3,000-$20,000)
McDONALD, M. P. 55 f Ga
HARPER, Sally 16 f "

Luvl # 539 Farmer (4000-500)
McDONALD, Malcom 62 m NC
Martha 51 f "
Sarah 26 f "
Robert (Farmer) 24 m Ala
Eliza 22 f "
Catherine 20 f "
Hugh W. 18 m "
Donald 14 m "
Mary 12 f "

Luvl # 341
McDONALD, Mary 55 f NC
John (Farmer, 2500-2000) 36 m "
Sarah 33 f "
(Cont.)

(Luvl # 341 cont.)
Caroline 23 f Ala
William (Farmer) 21 m "
SHEPPARD, G. T. 18 m Ga

Euf # 1206 (1000-4500)
McDONALD, Mary M. 40 f SC
Chas. H. (Farm hand) 20 m Ga
(--- 100)
Sallie 17 f Ala
Polly 14 f "
Celia A. 12 f "
Cornelia 9 f "

Flk # 483 (--- ---)
McDONALD, Nancy 50 f NC
Mary 28 f Ala
John C. (Farmer) 25 m "
Catherine 23 f "
George " 21 m "

Euf # 19-19 Printer
McDOWELL, James 25 m Ga
(See Thos. Robinson).

Euf # 526 Farm hand
McDUFFELL, Augustus 18 m Ga
(See Emanuel McNeice).

Euf # 71 Clerk (1200-1500)
McDUFFIE, John G. 28 m SC

Clay # 660 Farmer (800-1000)
McEACHERN, Daniel 38 m NC
Sarah 28 f Ga
Lovard Lee 6 m Ala
Gilbert L. 4 m "
Issabella 3 f "
LEE, Jane L. 18 f "
BIRD, Jackson (Farmer) 20 m "

Clay # 659 Farmer (2000-3000)
McEACHERN, Gilbert 65 m Scot
Catherine 62 f NC
Catherine 28 f Ala
Gilbert C. 21 m "
JUDIE, Mary 70 f NC
BRYANT, Mary 22 f Ala

Clay # 5 Clerk
McEACHERN, John C. 23 m Ala
(See Lovard Lee, Jr.).

Clay # 1111 Farmer (---400)
McEACHERN, Malcom 28 m Ala
Nancy 21 f "
Mary J. 4 f "
(Cont.)

(Clay # 1111 cont.)
Thomas A. 3 m Ala
Margaret A. 1 f "
Mandy 3/12 f "
CARR, George 20 m "
(Farm laborer).

Euf # 1082 Overseer (--- 1300)
McELROY, C. G. 34 m Ga
Susan 32 f "
M. F. 10/12 f "

Euf # 1393
McENTE, Margaret 18 f Ire
(See Peter Ferrell).

Mdwy # 952 Farmer (5000-25000)
McGEE, Green B. 45 m Ga
O. A. 32 f "
Sarah E. 13 f Ala
Mary A. 11 f "
John T. 6 m "
Georgia A. 5 f "
infant 2 f "
WILLIAMS, William 27 m Ga
(Farm laborer).
Sarah 20 f "
George 3 m "

Luvl # 354 Farmer
McGEE, Jerry 22 m Ga
(See Leonard Card).

Euf # 1058 Overseer (--5000)
McGEE, Samuel 46 m Ga
Elizabeth 38 f "

Euf # 776 Farmer (7000-14200)
McGEHEE, Alfred 49 m Ga
Martha 53 f "
Wm. (In school) 18 m "
Seaborn " " 16 m "
James 14 m Ala

Euf # 617 Farmer (--- 600)
McGEHEE, E. M. 39 m Ga
Mary 35 f "
William (Farmer) 16 m "
Joseph 13 m Ala
Charles 10 m "
Wesley 8 m "
George 6 m "
Anna 2 f "
BURIDINE, Ann 17 f "
James 13 m "

Euf # 1136
McGILL, M. 31 m Ire
(See O. McMurray).

Euf # 456 Ditcher
McGILL, Patrick 40 m Ire
(See Phillip Cunningham).

Txv # 1185 Farmer (--- 200)
McGILVERY, Daniel 39 m NC
Harriett 27 f "
E. J. 8 f Ala
Horatio 5 m "
Columbus 3 m "
Chellie 1 m "
Catherine 5/12 f "
COVINGTON, Emily 15 f Ga

Bfd # 1270 Farmer (3500-13000)
McGILVERY, Duncan 45 m NC
John (Farmer) 43 m "
Daniel " 40 m "
Malcom " 38 m "
Mary 75 f Scot

Clay # 124 Farmer (1000-5000)
McGILVERY, Hugh 28 m Ala
Effie 23 f SC
Daniel 4 m Ala
John 2 m "
Margaret 50 f Scot
Margaret 16 f Ala
GILLIS, Sarah 60 f Scot
McGILVERY, Malcom 23 m Ala
(Farmer, ---1900)
S. E. 20 f "
Mary 1 f "

Bfd # 1264 Farmer (1440-3300)
McGILVERY, James 45 m NC

Euf # 1208 Farmer (3000-22000)
McGILVRAY, James 60 m NC
Anna 38 f "
Mary 10 f Ala
Daniel 8 m "

Clay # 1117 (450-225)
McGILVREY, Sarah 40 f SC
William A. 18 m Ala
John W. 14 m "
Flora A. 15 f "
Neill 11 m "
M. Luther 9 m "
James F. 5 m "

Bfd # 1246 (--- 3000)
McGILVARY, Zilpha A. 10 f Ga
Mary M. 8 f Ala
Charity 4 f "
Joseph E. 6 m "
Milledge J. 2 m "
(See Jonathan Thomas).

Euf # 28 Druggist (3000-7000)
McGINTY, George W. 39 m Ga
Elizabeth C. 39 f "
Fanny 7 f Ala
Willie 5 m "
Harry 10/12 m "
GRIFFITH, Moses 20 m "
(Clerk)

Euf # 663 Farmer (600-2300)
McGLAUN, John T. 40 m Ga
Angeline 34 f "
M. A.(?) 12 f "
James 9 m "
Susan E. 7 f Ala
John W. 5 m "
William R. 3 m "
TYCE, Elizabeth 65 f NC

Euf # 440 Laborer
McGOWEN, Michael 52 m Ire
(See McNamara's R.R. Gro.)

Euf # 978 (--- 5,000)
McGUIRE, Ann 28 f Ga
William 5 m Ala
Laura 3 f "
(See Thos. Rivers).

Euf # 440 Quarryman
McGUINESS, James 42 m Ire
(See McNamara's R.R. Gro.)

Luvl # 292 (2000-3000)
McGUIRE, Temperance 45 f NC
HARRISON, G. W. 28 m "
(Merchant, 6000-10000)
M. A. 19 f Ga
McGUIRE, Ann 15 f Ala
Kate 12 f "

Euf # 440 Laborer
McHENSLE, Andrew 21 m Ga
(See McNamara's R.R. Gro.)

Flk # 423 (2000-200)
McINNIS, Jinny 60 f NC
Peter 34 m "
(Cont.)

(Flk # 423 cont.)
Catherine 25 f Ala
Jane 21 f "
Margaret 19 f "

Luvl # 643 Farmer (3000-500)
McINNIS, John 62 m NC
Christian 52 f "
Daniel (Farmer) 24 m Ala
John M. 22 m "
Catherine 20 f "
Jane 18 f "
Elizabeth 10 f "

Flk # 426 Farmer (2000-12000)
McINNIS, John 70 m NC
CURRIE, Matilda 33 f "

Flk # 424 Lawyer (--- ---)
McINNIS, Malcom 31 m Ala
Marion 21 f "
John L. 10/12 m "

Luvl # 339 Farmer (4000-10000)
McINNIS, Miles 60 m NC
Sally 65 f "

Euf # 1034 Overseer (--- 300)
McINTOSH, Angus A. 25 m SC

Euf # 991 Farmer (2500-2000)
McINTOSH, Daniel 68 m Scot
Mary 30 f SC
Christian 26 f "
Nancy 23 f Ala
Randal (Farm hand) 18 m "
Angus " " 16 m "

Euf # 297 Pres. of Union Female College
McINTOSH, John R. 53 m NC
Caroline M.(Teacher) 36 f Mass
Lizzie T. 14 f NC
John M. 12 m "
TULEY(?). Carrie M. 24 f Mass
(Tutoress).

Euf # 961 (--- 1000)
McINTOSH, Margaret 60 f Scot
John G. 37 m SC
(Farmer, 1000-1000)
Mary (---- 1000) 22 f "
Norman " " 39 m "

Euf # 1137 Occupation none (--- 400)
McIVER, D. 53 m NC
John (School teacher) 16 m "
S. W. 14 m Ga

Luvl # 379
McK----, W. (torn) 65 f SC
Tisher 15 f Ga
(See Sophronia Hatcher)

Euf # 692 Carpenter (--- 200)
McKAY, Alex 48 m NC
Martha 25 f Ga
John 11 m "
James 9 m "
Edwin 7 m "
Sarah 5 f "
Jane 2 f "
McKAY, Angus 56 m NC
(House painter)
Mary 41 f "

Luvl # 371 (2500-7000)
McKAY, Winney 44 f NC
Philip (Farmer) 17 m Ala
Christian 14 f "
Alex 11 m "
Farquar 9 m "
McRAE, Ann 41 f NC

Euf # 273 Occupation, none
McKEE, John 84 m Ire
Martha 65 f Ga

Nwto # 551 Farmer (720-500)
McKELLER, Neill 64 m NC
Sarah 65 f "
John A. 21 m Ala
(Farmer, 160 ---)
Jinsey 17 f "
SEGARS, Martha A. 23 f NC

Euf # 392 Tailor (6000---)
McKENNA, Thomas 38 m Ire
Martha R. A. 40 f Ga
(6,000-30,000)
BOOTH, James 13 m Ala

Euf # 63 Merchant (5000-12000)
McKENZIE, Andrew 46 m Eng
Adalaide J. 43 f Tenn
A. W. (Clerk) 20 m Ala
W. J. " 18 m "
Ada M. 16 f "

Luvl # 270 Merchant & Farmer (3,500-20,000)
McKENZIE, B. B. 22 m Ala
C. C. 20 f "
Edgar F. 1/12 m "

Luvl # 266 Farmer (20,000-65,000)
McKENZIE, Daniel 55 m NC
Amanda 40 f "
Ann 18 f "
Louisa 15 f "
Elizabeth 11 f "
Emma 5 f "
JEFFRIES, Joseph 15 m Ark
(Student)
WARD, Polly 65 f SC

Clay # 10
McKENZIE, Elizabeth 12 f Ala
(See Judge S. Williams).

Euf # 926 Miller (--- 300)
McKENZIE, John H. 35 m SC
Nancy 36 f "
John A. 5 m Ala
Andrew G. 3 m "
Daniel 1 m "
MORRISON, Nancy 36 f Ga

Euf # 1361 Merchant (6000-12700)
McKENZIE, William A. 49 m Eng
Martha 35 f Tenn
William G. 12 m Fla
Edgar C. 5 m Ala
WELLBORN, Virginia 12 f "

Euf # 542 Grocer (--- $1,000)
McKEY, John A. 49 m Ga
L. A. 16 f "
Daniel 17 m "
John 7 m Ala
Phoeby A. 5 f "
Madison 3 m "

Luvl # 299 Farmer (--- ---)
McKINNEY, Andrew 27 m Ga
Mandy J. 23 f Ala
Joseph 5 m "
John F. 3 m "
William B. 1/12 m "

Luvl # 364
McKINNEY, Caroline 17 f SC
(See John G. Beasley)

Euf # 782
McKINNEY, Henry 14 m Ala
(See Thos. A. Roquemore).

Luvl # 303
McKINNEY, James 11 m Ala
(See Theophilus Floyd).

Clay # 244 Overseer on farm
McKINNEY, L. V. 22 m SC
Amanda 19 f Ala
Mary E. 8/12 f "
H. S. 6 m "
Mary H. 4 f "

Clay # 656 (--- 50)
McKINNEY, Sinthia 50 f NC
HATCHER, Sophronia 21 f Ga
Lutitiae 18 f "
ANGLIN, Iomae 16 f "
Lucinda S. 4 f Ala
Pat 2 m "
Columbus 8/12 m "

Euf # 938 (150-100)
McKINNY, Drucilla 48 f NC
William (idiotic) 23 m Ga
Mary J. 15 f Ala

Clay # 65 Clerk
McKINNON, Alex M. 33 m NC
(See Charles Petty).

Nwto # 631 (--- ---)
McKINNON, Barbara 80 f Scot
(Born Isle of Sky).
Isabella 45 f NC
Nancy 25 f "
Daniel (Farmer) 24 m "

Nwto # 630 (1100-500)
McKINNON, Catherine 46 f NC
Nancy 20 f Ala
Dan'l. M. (Farmer) 18 m "
Alex 16 m "
John T. 13 m "

Euf # 804
McKLEROY, James F. 35 m Ga
(See W. I. Cox).

Euf # 11-11 Shoemaker
McKLEVAIN, A. J. 26 m Ala
Malissa 23 f "
Mary A. 2 f "

Euf # 423 Laborer
McKLEVAIN, James 27 m Ala
Adaline 26 f Ga
Tillman 10 m "
Susan E. 1 f "

Euf # 229
McKLEVAIN, Nancy 50 f NC
(See Thomas Steidham).

Euf # 343 Farmer (---150)
McKLEVAIN, Thomas 60 m SC
Elizabeth 40 f "
Elizabeth 19 f Ala
Burrell 16 m "

Euf # 445
McKLROY, Sarah 10 f Ala
(See Junius K. Battle).

Euf # 636 Farmer (1000-100)
McLAIN, Colin 60 m NC
Christian 55 f SC
Angus (Farmer,---100) 23 m Ala
Catharine 21 f "
Elizabeth J. 17 f "

Euf # 1099 Overseer
McLAUGHLIN, A. E. 25 m NC

Euf # 672 Farmer (200-3000)
McLEAN, Archd. 32 m Ga
Mary 27 f "
James W. 9 m Ala
Elizabeth T.(?) 7 f "
John T. M. L. 5 m "
William J. 2 m "
LUDLAM, Elizabeth 18 f "
Amanda P. 2 f "

Bfd # 1260
McLEAN, Cebie 80 f Scot
Margaret 23 f "

Euf # 73
McLEAN, Elizabeth 40 f Ga
Mary C. 19 f Ala
Ursula T. 17 f "
Oregon T. 15 f "
Valney 13 m "
Lorenzo D. 10 m "
Burnett S. 4 m "
Roberta 1 f "

Bfd # 1259 Farmer (1500-5000)
McLEAN, Hugh, Sr. 73 m Scot
Margaret 60 f "
Hugh, Jr. (Farmer) 30 m "
Sarah 27 f "
Amanda 20 f "
Mary A. 18 f NY

Euf # 625
McLEAN, Isabella 21 f NC
(See Daniel Kennedy)

Euf # 1211 Farmer (--- ---)
McLEAN, Jeremiah 60 m SC
(Cont.)

(Euf # 1211 cont.)
Lucy 55 f SC
Sarah A. 30 f Ala
Eliza A. 25 f "
Roxana 15 f "

Mt. A. # 796 Farmer (11,000-40,000)
McLEAN, John 65 m Scot
Catherine 55 f "
Hector 16 m Ala
Annie 14 f "

Flk # 445 Farmer (25,000-12,000)
McLEAN, John 65 m NC
Margaret 61 f "
Daniel 33 m "
(Farmer, 200-4000)
Catherine 25 f Ala
Eliza J. 23 f "
John (Farmer) 20 m "
Angus " 17 m "

Euf # 191 Blacksmith (1500-1500)
McLEAN, Laughlin 50 m NC
Mary W. 43 f Ga
Margaret E. 10 f Ala
Mary L. 3 f "
Eugenia 18 f "

Euf # 693 Student
McLEMORE, John H. 19 m SC
(See Levi Wilkerson)

Euf # 478 Farmer (3000-13000)
McLENDON, John 62 m Ga
Richard (Farmer) 15 m Ala
Jackson " 13 m "
(--- 4,000)

Luvl # 350 Farmer (1800-13,000)
McLENNON, Alexander 68 m NC
Nancy 60 f "
Mary 21 f "
James (Farmer) 20 m "
Annabella 15 f "

Luvl # 269
McLENNON, J. D. -- - --
(See Wm. C. Bostick).

Luvl # 257 Clerk (1200-3000)
McLENNON, Phillip 30 m NC
(See Henry Freeman)

Euf # 928 Farmer (1000-2900)
McLEOD, Alex 45 m NC
Mary A. 17 f Ala
Neil 15 m "
William 13 m "
John 6 m "

Euf # 308 Drayman (5000-1000)
McLEOD, Angus 37 m NC
Josephine 30 f Ga
Susan 4 f "
Pauline 2 f Ala
Elizabeth 1 f "
BEVERLY, William 12 m "

Euf # 888 Farmer (1200-3000)
McLEOD, Archy P. 27 m SC
Louisa 25 f Ala
Daniel J. 1 m "

Euf # 759
McLEOD, Christian 72 f NC
(See John Gillis)

Euf # 1399 Overseer (800-1000)
McLEOD, D. 28 m Ala
Mary C. 5 f "
John A. 3 m "

Clay # 139 Farmer (800-300)
McLEOD, Daniel 36 m SC
Wm. Pleasant (McLeod?) 15 m Ga
(Farm laborer)
McLEOD, Fannie L. 14 f "
Henry 12 m "
WATERS, Delanie 40 f NC
Susan 16 f Ala

Euf # 1304 Shoemaker (---100)
McLEOD, Daniel 32 m SC
Mary 27 f Ga
Andrew T. 2 m Ala
Mary P. 5/12 f "

Euf # 345 Carpenter (2500-400)
McLEOD, Daniel 45 m Ga
Nancy 41 f "
Margaret E. 17 f Ala
Sophronia C. 15 f "
Laura 13 f "
John W. 11 m "
Mary 9 f "
Daniel 7 m "
William 5 m "
James 7/12 m "

Euf # 1296 Farmer (2000-1800)
McLEOD, John 40 m SC
Jane 33 f Ala
Catharine A. 16 f "

Clay # 141
McLEOD, Milly 45 f SC

Txv # 1126 School teacher (-- 200)
McLEOD, Roderick 68 m NC
Catherine 64 f "
Margaret 21 f Ala
RICHARDSON, Sarah F. 7 f "

Euf # 810 (1,500-2,800)
McLEOD, Sally 38 f Ga
Mary 14 f Ala
George 11 m "
Martha 5 f "

Euf # 889 Farmer (3500 ----)
McLEOD, William 30 m SC
Ann 24 f Ala
Mary L. 3 f "
Douglas 1 m "

Euf # 330 Wagon maker (4500-1500)
McLEOD, William 50 m NC
Frances E. 31 f Ga
William F. 8 m Ala
Effy E. 5 f "
Sarah A. 3/12 f "
BIRDSONG, Josephine C. 14 f "

Euf # 252 Painter
McLEOD, William 24 m Ala
(See Joshua Tyler).

Mdwy # 1066 (2,000 ----)
McMILLAN, Catherine 46 f NC
GILLIS, Mary 50 f "
McMILLAN, Elizabeth 18 f Ala
Mary 16 f "
Sarah 14 f "

Clay # 48 Teacher
McMILLAN, Laura 19 f Ga
McMILLIAN, A. 45 m NC
A S P Clergyman & teacher
Eliza 38 f Ga
Teacher in female college.
(See Mary Fenn).

Mdwy # 1063 (---3,000)
McMILLAN, Mary 63 f NC
Farley (Farmer) 28 m "
(5,000-3,500)
(Cont.)

(Mdwy # 1063 cont.)
Edward (Farmer) 22 m Ala
(----3,000)
Charles (Farmer) 19 m "
(----3,000)

Mt. A. # 876 (--- 150)
McMILLAN, Tempe A. 30 f Ga
Mary S. 11 f "
Sarah 8 f "
James 6 m "
John 3 m Ala
(See Green Solomon).

Clay # 237 Lawyer
McMURRAY, G. J. 26 m Ala
(See James W. Mabry).

Euf # 1235 Blacksmith (100-300)
McMURRY, Laird F. 28 m Ga
Minerva 27 f Ala
Joel F. 2 m "
James F. 5/12 m "

Euf # 1136 Laborer (300---)
McMURRY, O. 40 m Ire
Catharine 40 f "
Gerald 7/12 m Ala
McGILL, M. 31 m Ire
CUNNINGHAM, Phillip 24 m "
O'BRIAN, George 19 m "

Clay # 103 Blacksmith (400---)
McMURRAY, Samuel 57 m Ga
Mary 59 f Tenn
Mary W. 20 f Ala
Margaret A. 16 f "
Sarah J.(?) 22 f "

Flk # 440 Farmer (800-500)
McNAB, A. C. 46 m Scot
Piercy 54 m NC
James 10 m Ala
ANDERSON, Stephen 20 m "
(Farmer)
Zachurs (Farmer) 17 m "

Luvl # 285 (1,500-10,000)
McNAB, Isabella 50 f NC
Donald L.(Constable) 22 m SC
Ellen 18 f "
Elizabeth 15 f "
HAMMOND, T. L. 36 m NC
(Farmer, 700-1000)

Euf # 1332 Farmer & merchant (80,000-116,000)
McNAB, John 53 m Scot
Jane 42 f "
(Cont.)

(Eufaula # 1332 cont.)
James G. 25 m NC
(Merchant, ---1000)
John M. (Student) 20 m Ala
Flora 16 f "
Martha 10 f "
Lizzy 6 f "

Clay # 1284 Farmer (500-500)
McNAB, John C. 33 m SC
Lucy A. (---12,000) 28 f "
Mary A. 11 f "
Kate 9 f Ala
Laura 7 f "
Ida 5 f "
Stella 2 f "

Txv # 1140 (1,200-12,000)
McNAIR, Ann C. 37 f Ala
John D. 17 m "
David J. 15 m "
Elizabeth E. 14 f "
Mary J. 8 f "
William N.(Neal) 5 m "
Ann A. (E.) 5 f "
Charles 4 m "
(First 3 children were Jay children by a first marriage and they took the McNair name. Last 4 were children of a second marriage to a McNair).

Clay # 19 Teaching
McNAIR, D. P. 26 m NC
C. A. 21 f "
(Living in hotel).

Euf # 85 Minister O.P.(?) (---7,000)
McNAIR, Evander 47 m NC

Euf # 740 Farmer (350-300)
McNAIR, Janette 47 f NC
Isabella 18 f Ala
Sarah 16 f "
Julia 14 f "
Mary E. 12 f "
David W. 7 m "

Bkb # 781 Laborer (--- 100)
McNAIR, John 30 m Ga
P.A.E. 12 f Ala
Mary A. 10 f "
M.A. 7 f "
(See Annie Sims).

Bkb # 687 Farm laborer
McNAIR, John 32 m NC
Elizabeth 13 f Ala
Susan 10 f "
Malinda 6 f "
(See Geo. R. Scroggins).

Euf # 430 Laborer
McNAIR, Patrick 46 m Ire
(See Roddy McCormicy).

Txv # 1176 Farmer (1600-800)
McNAIR, Randall 48 m NC
Susanna M. 36 f Ala
Nancy 16 f "
Daniel W. 15 m "
Charles T. 13 m "
Sinthia J. 10 f "
Benjamin G. 9 m "
Margaret 7 f "
Elizabeth D. 4 f "
Diana 4/12 f "

Txv # 1142 (--- 250)
McNAIR, Sarah 60 f SC
John (Farmer) 22 m Ga
Amanda 24 f "
Godfrey " 28 m "

Euf # 440 McNamara's R.R. Gro.
PRIMMONS, Jery 35 m Ire
(Laborer)
BROCK, Jacob (Laborer) 28 m Ala
McGOWEN, Michael 52 m Ire
(Laborer)
KELLY, Patrick 22 m "
(Laborer)
HALORAN, Martin 22 m "
(Laborer)
MURPHY, Tim (laborer) 21 m "
McHENSLE, Andrew 21 m Ga
(Laborer)
OWENS, Jno. W. 18 m Ala
(Laborer)
HOWELL, T.W.(Laborer) 24 m Fla
GARY, Thos. 46 m Ire
McPARTLIN, Jas. 24 m "
(Last 2 Quarrymen)
KEEFE, Wm. " 21 m "
McGUINESS, Jas." 42 m "
WHALON, Francis 47 m "
(Quarryman).
McVIELLE, Thos. 35 m "
(Stone mason)
JONES, Jas. 35 m NY
READDY, Andrew 49 m Ire
(Last 2 stone cutters - cont.)

O'HARE, Patrick 31 m Ire
(Stone cutter).
HALOHAND, Michael C. 31 m D.C.
(Born Wash., D. C., stone cutter).
BUTLER, Thos. 21 m Ire
(Stone cutter).
KYLE, Patrick 28 m "
(Stone cutter)
O'KEEFE, John 24 m "
(Stone cutter)
CORLEY, Owen 48 m "
(Stone cutter)
EATON, Chas. 26 m NY
(Stone cutter)
KEYHOE, John 27 m Ire
(Stone cutter)
ROONEY, Nicholas 34 m "
Amelia 29 f Ga.
(Rooney, a quarryman)
McCAY, Nancy 20 f "
HAVERTY, Stephen 34 m Ire
(Quarryman)
WARD, Patrick 32 m Ire
(Quarryman)
KEARNES, William 33 m "
(Quarryman)
Ford, Patrick 26 m "
(Laborer).

Euf # 108 Merchant (1500-6000)
McNAUGHTON, John 44 m Scot
Cecilia J. 30 f NC

Euf # 44 Drayman (--- 1000)
McNAUGHTON, Walter S. 28 m Scot
Janet 76 f "
Mc-----chil, Janet 22 f "
McNAUGHTON, George 32 m "
(Clerk)

Euf # 526 Farmer (---25,000)
McNEICE, Emanual 36 m Ga
Mary 24 f "
Margaret 11 f "
Martha 9 f "
Penny J. 7 f Ala
Martha F. 4 f "
Henrietta 3 f "
Oceanica 1 f "
DUFFELL, Augustus 18 m Ga
(Farm hand).

Euf # 1299 Farmer (---100)
McNEILL, Angus 42 m NC
(Cont.)

(Euf # 1299 cont.)
Elizabeth 20 f Ga
Jane 2 f Ala
Daniel 8/12 m "

McNEILL, Abagail 85 f NC
($250-$500)

Clay # 42 Physician (---40000)
McNEILL, J. C. 45 m NC
Mary A. 36 f SC
S. H. 16 m Ala
Jane 14 f "
Effie 13 f "
John C., Jr. 11 m "
Mary A. 9 f "
Willie 6 m "
Minnie E. 4 f "
Edmund B. 2 m "

Euf # 1298 Blacksmith (---300)
McNEILL, Roderick 39 m NC
Flora A. 36 f Ala

Euf # 440 Quarryman
McPARTLIN, James 24 m Ire
(See McNamara's R.R. Gro.)

Luvl # 332 Farmer (4000-1000)
McRAE, A. K. 35 m NC
Winney 24 f Ala
J. H. 9 m "
Victoria 6 f "
Mary A. 4 f "
Helen A. 2 f "

Luvl # 371
McRAE, Ann 41 f NC
(See Winney McKay).

Luvl # 323 Farmer (1000-1500)
McRAE, C. C. 36 m NC
Ann 30 f "
Thomas W. 8 m Ala
James 5 m "
Mary A. 3 f "
John J. (Farmer) 32 m NC

Luvl # 312 Farmer (1500-4000)
McRAE, C. M. 40 m NC
Abigal 39 f "
Nancy 17 f "
Catherine 15 f Ala
Columbus 12 m "
Henrietta 10 f "
Mary 8 f "
Washington 5 m "
Christian 4/12 f "

Clay # 237 Clerk
McRAE, C. M. 19 m NC
(See James W. Mabry)

Euf # 402 Farmer(5000-1000)
McRAE, C. W. 50 m NC
Harriet 47 f "
Martha 21 f "
Elizabeth 17 f Ga
John 15 m "
Colon 12 m "
Margaret 11 f "
Sarah 9 f "
Stephen 7 m "
Lotty 5 f "

Luvl # 269
McRAE, Christian 23 f Ala
John L. 28 m NC
(Gentlemen, 1000-10,000)
(See Wm. C. Bostick).

Luvl # 255 Farmer (----1500)
McRAE, Daniel 35 m NC
(See Worthy J. Grubbs).

Luvl # 356 Farmer (4000-8000)
McRAE, Elizabeth 30 f NC
William W. 4 m Ala
Margaret 6 f "
John 2 m "
JOHNSON, C. W. 27 m NC
(Farmer)
SMITH, Hardy 37 m Ga
(Clerk).

Clay # 247 Farmer (4350-17000)
McRAE, George W. 49 m NC
Christian 45 f "
William N. 13 m Ala
Mary C. 13 f "
Duncan 10 m "
Peggy J. 7 f "

Luvl # 272 Farmer(700-7000)
McRAE, Harvey A. 36 m NC
Lucy 30 f Ala
James 10 m "
Philip 6 m "
Preston B. 4 m "
Mary J. 2 f "

Euf # 1358 Farmer (---20,000)
McRAE, John 44 m SC
C. G. 21 f Ga
Mary C. 13 f Ala
(Cont.)

(Euf # 1358 cont.)
Amanda A. 12 f Ala
Sarah J. 11 f "
Malcom A. 9 m "
Reubin S. 8 m "
John J. 7 m "

Euf # 208 Farmer (12,000-38,000)
McRAE, John C. 53 m NC
Janet 53 f "
Jabez (Farmer) 32 m "
John L. (Student) 21 m SC
Mariah M. 18 f "
Julia V. 15 f "
GIBSON, James 19 m Ga
(Laborer)

Flk # 431 Farmer (500-200)
McRAE, John N. 33 m NC
Catherine 30 f Ala
Jane C. 6 f "
Phillip 5 m "
Duncan 3 m "
GARRIS, George W. 14 m "
McRAE, Daniel 36 m NC
(Farmer, ---1000)

Luvl # 333 (-- --)
McRAE, John R. 84 m NC
ARRINGTON, Sarah 30 f "
Mary 14 f Ala
James M. 11 m "
Mary J. 10 f "
Margaret 20 f NC

Luvl # 318
McRAE, Margaret 14 f NC
Philip D. 18 m "
(See Daniel Currie).

Euf # 234
McRAE, Mary 95 f NC
(See John G. McClendon).

Luvl # 649 Farmer (800-1500)
McRae, William 62 m NC
Mazie 70 f Scot
Daniel C. 34 m Ala
(Merchant, 500-2000)
Washington 23 m "
(Merchant, 300-2000)
GARRIS, S. A. 12 f "

Nwto # 564 Physician & farmer (10,000-15,500)
McSWAIN, Colen 28 m Ala
(Cont.)

(Nwto # 564 cont.)
Josephine 23 f Ala

Mdwy # 1024 Farmer (-- --)
McSWEAN, Daniel 40 m NC
McSWEAN, Christian 50 f "
Catherine 45 f "
Nancy 38 f "

Mdwy # 1024 Farmer (3600-3000)
McSWEAN, Daniel 40 m NC
Christian (---1200) 50 f "
Catherine (---2500) 45 f "
Nancy (---1500) 38 f "

Euf # 671 Farmer (1500-5500)
McSWEAN, Malcom 28 m NC
Sarah E. 22 f "
Eli 2 m Ala
Sarah J. 1 f "
McSWEAN, Mary 70 f NC
($1,000-$1,400)

Bfd # 1243 Planter (6600-65000)
McSWEAN, R. C. 62 m Scot
Mary 60 f NC
PUGH, Nancy 27 f "
McSWEAN, Angus 25 m "
Sarah J. 23 f Ala

Mdwy # 926 Farmer
McSWEAN, William D. 32 m Fla
Martha A. 26 f Ala
Sarah E. 3 f "
Mary L. 3/12 f "
Finley (Farmer) 22 m NC

Euf # 927 Farmer (12000-28000)
McSWEIN, John C. 33 m NC

Euf # 389 Farmer 20000-100,000)
McTYRE, Robert A. 57 m SC
Caroline 38 f NC
Mary 19 f SC
Thos. (Student) 16 m "
Margaret 14 f "
Sarah 12 f "
John 10 m "
Joseph 8 m "
Frank 6 m Ala
Robert 1 m "

Euf # 17-17 Atty. (5000-2200)
McTYRE, William A. 22 m SC
Theresa W. 20 f Ala
Elizabeth A. 8/12 f "
FULMORE, Joseph R. 52 m "
(---45,000)
Caroline S. 47 f "
Mary 13 f "

Euf # 440 Stone cutter
McVIELLE, Thomas 35 m Ire
(See McNamara's R.R. Gro.)

Clay # 237 (4000-1000)
MABRY, James W. 35 m Ga
Mary 28 f Ala
Seth 4 m "
Daniel 2 m "
infant 1/12 f "
McMURRAY, G. J. 26 m "
(Lawyer, ---300)
McRAE, C. M. 19 m NC
(Clerk, ---3000)
GOLSON, James E. 22 m Ala
(Printer, 600-600)

Clay # 64 Gentlemen (15,000-50,000)
MABRY, Seth 39 m Ga
Nancy 67 f "
HAILEY, J. C. 25 m Ala
(Clerk, 3000-3000).

Euf # 206 Teacher (50-1000)
MACON, J. M. 21 m Ga

Euf # 1022 Farmer (4500-2900)
MADUX, Joseph 58 m Ga
Nancy 52 f "
James R. (Farmer) 21 m "
Louisa 16 f "
Joseph S. 8 m "

Clay # 664
MADDOCK, Matilda 50 f Ga
(See William Anglin).

Euf # 127 Cabinet maker
MALLER, H. 28 m Ger
(Born Allsford, Germany).
(See E. H. Hunter).

Euf # 374 Engineer (--- 250)
MALLORY, C. A. 26 m Ga
Frances J. 22 f "
William T. J. A. 1 m Ala

Mdwy # 997 Farmer (5400-22000)
MALLOY, Duncan 62 m SC
Mary 50 f Ga
William 15 m Ala
John 12 m "
Jannett 10 f "

Euf # 530 M.E. Minister
(15,000-12000)
MALONE, Green 64 m Va
Julia T. 30 f Fla
Mary 6 f Ala
Caroline L. 4 f "
William G. 2 m "
Thomas W. 2/12 m "

Euf # 441 Tailor
MALONEY, Mr. 27 m Ire
(See Mary H. Lowman)

Luvl # 347 Ditching (300-50)
MALONEY, James 28 m Ire
Lucinda 20 f Ala
John 1 m "

Txv # 1186 Farmer (425-300)
MARLEY, James 34 m NC
Margaret 40 f "
Chellie A. 11 f Ala
John 8 m "
Margaret 7 f "
Florentia 5 f "
Virginia 1 f "

Txv # 1181 Farmer (300-200)
MARLEY, S. C. 30 m NC
Sarah M. 23 f Ga
Lovard E. 5 m Ala
Needham J. 3 m "
Sarah J. 1 f "

Euf 509 Overseer (25000-
(Daniel?)55000?)
MARSHALL, David(?) 25 m Ga
Adalaide 23 f "
William 4 m Ala
Mary 2 f "

Euf # 858 Wheelwright (---
500)
MARSHALL, James B. 40 m SC
Mary 34 f Ga
Daniel E. 14 m "
Louisa J. 12 f "
Mary A. 8 f "
John A. 6 m "

Euf # 852 Mechanic
MARSHALL, Thomas 61 m SC
Catherine O. 17 f Ga
(See Reuben E. Brown).

Euf # 834
MARSHALL, William 5 m Ala
(See Susan Lott).

Mt. A. # 866 Farm Laborer
(---150)
MARTIN, A. J. 30 m Ala
Ann 22 f SC
John T. 7 m Ala
Julia 5 f "
Fate 3 m "
William 1 m "

Euf # 276 Trader (---7,000)
MARTIN, James C. 36 m Ga

Euf # 150 Merchant (19000-
20,000)
MARTIN, James G. L. 49 m Fr
Eliza 31 f "
Jas. H. G.(Student) 15 m Ala
Selina V. 13 f "
Charles A. 12 m "
Willie S. 9 m "
Edward T. 4 m "
Eugene C. 2 m "
James 30 m NC
AUSTIN, Eliza J. 26 f NY
(Seamstress - ---300)

Euf # 95 Laborer (-- --)
MARTIN, James R. 47 m SC
Priscilla 43 f "
Nancy H. 18 f Ga
Sarah C. 14 f Ala
Mary A. 11 f "
Eliza T. 9 f "
William A. 3 m "

Euf # 357 Farmer (200-100)
MARTIN, Jere 25 m Ga
Mary 21 f "
William J. W. 4/12 m Ala

Euf # 1170 Farmer (--- 150)
MARTIN, Jere 25 m Ga
Mary 20 f "
William J. W. 6/12 m Ala

Euf # 107 Clerk (6000-600)
MARTIN, John C. 43 m NC
(Cont.)

(Euf # 107 cont.)

Eliza M.	32	f	SC
Mary C.	10	f	Ala
Alex S.	9	m	"
Laura W.	5	f	"
Ada E.	4	f	"
Benjamin F.	3	m	"
Caroline E.	3/12	f	"

Euf # 391 Painter
MARTIN(?), John G. 25 m Ga
MORTON(?)

Bfd 1271 Farmer (480-4000)

MARTIN, John G.	30	m	Ala
Sarah	70	f	Scot

Euf # 412 Bookkeeper (-- --)

MARTIN, John O.(?)	28	m	Ga
Queen E.	19	f	"

Clay # 225 Farmer (1300-6000)

MARTIN, John T.	45	m	SC
Epsy	35	f	NC
Mary C.	14	f	Ala
John T., Jr.	12	m	"
C. O. (Farmer, 2300-3200)	40	m	SC
JOHNSON, Milledge (Farmer)	18	m	SC

Flk # 415 (10,000-18,000)

MARTIN, Margaret	45	f	NC
Murdock	16	m	Ala
Alexander	13	m	"
Phillip	7	m	"
Daniel (---1000)	33	m	NC

Bkb # 713 Farmer (1000-1200)

MARTIN, Ransom	75	m	NC
Susan	65	f	Ga
Caroline	35	f	"
Kendal	12	m	Ala
Floyd (Farmer)	27	m	"
Elizabeth	20	f	Ga
John P.	1	m	Ala

Euf # 1212 (350-2,600)

MARTIN, Sarah	65	f	Scot
John	30	m	NC

Euf # 1288 (3,000-7,000)

MARTIN, Sarah C.	55	f	Ga
Andrew J. (Farmer, ---200)	37	m	"
George W. (Farmer, ---150)	28	m	"

(Cont.)

(Euf # 1288 cont.)

Madison (Student)	16	m	Ala
Caroline	14	f	"
James L.	11	m	"

Euf # 960 Farmer (2000-1000)

MARTIN, Sylvester	42	m	NC
Susan	34	f	"
Sylvester, Jr.(--100)	22	m	Ga
Sarah	18	f	"
Peyton	17	m	"
Thomas	15	m	"
Benjamin	11	m	Ala
Hilliard G.	9	m	"
Josephine	5	f	"
Henry	3	m	"
Martha A.	2/12	f	"
Martha	19	f	Ga

Euf # 1194 Farmer (300-500)

MARTIN, William J.	34	m	Ga
Christian M.A.	30	f	Ala
BELL, Elizabeth	10	f	Ga

Luvl # 322 Farmer (-- --)

MASSEY, Joseph R.	26	m	Ga
Frances E.	21	f	"
Sarah J.	1/12	f	Ala

Euf # 1372
MASSEY, Mary J. 21 f Ga
(See Mariah L. Engram).

Mt. A. # 880 Farmer (400-500)

MASSEY, Nathaniel D.	37	m	Ga
Ruthy	32	f	"
Sidney B.	15	m	"
Giford M.	11	m	"
Simeon N.	9	m	"
Martha A.S.	7	f	Ala
James L.	5	m	"
Ruthy J.	3	f	"
B. L. U.	1	f	"

Euf # 829 (3,500-12,000)

MASSEY Sarah	58	f	NC
Charles F. (Farmer)	24	m	Ga
GARLAND, Jeff (Hireling).	22	m	"

Mt. A. # 790 Farmer (150-350)

MASSEY, Simeon	51	m	NC
Jane	54	f	SC
Lydia W.	17	f	Ga
Artemesia T.	15	f	"
Lucy L.	11	f	"

Clay # 185 Laborer
MATHEWS, Harrison 20 m Ga
(See Elisha Davis).

Euf # 849 Clerk
MATHIS, A. W. 25 m SC
(See Seaborn Jones).

Txv # 1143 Farmer (1000-300)
MATHIS, Abel 50 m NC
Martha 25 f Ala
Amanda 23 f "
Frank 20 m "
Susan 18 f "
William 14 m "
Liddie 10 f "
James 8 m "
Julia 5 f "
Hortman 2 m "

Euf # 1398 Farmer (--- 300)
MAY, S. B. 42 m Ga
Elizabeth 35 f "
Benjamin 11 m Ala
Mary E. 9 f "
Nancy 6 f "
Julia 3 f "
John 1 m "

Euf # 1008 Physician (200-3,000)
MAYES, W. A. 39 m Ga
Martha H. 30 f "

Euf # 1176 Farmer (800-400)
MAYNARD, Green C. 38 m Ga
Caroline 31 f "
Elizabeth 12 f "
Sallie 10 f "
Emily 8 f "
Medelia 6 f "
Amanda 5 f "
John 2 m Ala

Euf # 471 Governess
MAYNARD, Florence P. 21 f Va
(See Gazaway D. Williams).

Txv # 1169 Farmer (2500-3000)
MAYO, John 60 m SC
Olive 39 f Ga
T. A. 22 f "
Charity E. 20 f Ala
John L. 17 m "
Marcus W. 14 m "
Jane N. 5 f "

Euf # 670 Farmer
MEARS, E. C. 23 m Ala
(See Eli Horn).

Euf # 842 Shoemaker (--- 300)
MEDOWS, N. B. 33 m Ga
Lucretia 34 f "

Euf # 689 Farmer (8000-12000)
MEDLEY, Eldridge 60 m NC
Mary 50 f "
William 23 m Ala
Joseph (Farmer) 21 m "
Sarah 19 f "
Laurence " 17 m "
Eldridge 12 m "
Newton 10 m "
John 8 m "
George 6 m "
Monroe 4 m "
infant 5/12 m "
THOMAS, J. W. 19 m "
(Laborer)

Euf # 576 Tailor (b. Charleston)
MENTON(?), Sante 38 m SC

Luvl # 258 Mechanic (---1300)
MERRITT, G. W. 36 m Ga
Mary L. 33 f "
Nancy 14 f "
Georgia A. 12 f "
Emily J. 10 f "
William 7 m Ala
John W. 5 m "
Frank G. 2 m "

Euf # 1024 Farmer (4000-8000)
MERIT, J. H. 35 m Ga
Catharine 34 f "
Sarah P. 9 f "
Amanda 7 f "
William H. 5 m "
MERIT, W. P. 25 m "
(Farmer, ---6000).

Euf # 1021 Farmer
MERIT, M. C. 27 m Ga
(See Joseph Goode).

Ruf # 263 (2000-25000)
MERRILL, Elizabeth A. 41 f SC
Eliza A. 16 f Ala
Allen H. 14 m "

Euf # 983 Engineer (--- 200)
MERSHON, E. B. 25 m Ga
(Cont.)

(Euf # 983 cont.)
Rebecca 23 f Ala
EADEY, Josephine 16 f "

Nwto # 585 Farmer (300-200)
MESSICK, George 65 m Ga
Sally 55 f "
Betsy 28 f "
C. J. 23 f "
Isaac G. 19 m "
Henry C. 15 m "
Medford 3 m Ala

Euf # 351 Laborer (-- --)
MIDDLETON, Hansell 26 m Ga
Sarah 20 f "
William 4 m "
Laura 6/12 f Ala
VINCENT, William H. 34 m Ga
Matilda 30 f "
Sanford F. 13 m "
John F. 11 m "
Mary E. 10 f "
James E. 6 m "
Fidelia M. 2 f Ala
(W.H. Vincent, ---500)

Euf 285 Laborer (--- ---)
MIDDLETON, Hugh 66 m NC
Leah 57 f Ga

Euf # 284 Laborer (--- ---)
MIDDLETON, John 27 m Ga
(See John Bedsole).

Flk # 410 Farmer (1200-300)
MILES, Frank 26 m SC
Jane 21 f Ala
Andy C. 4 m "
Ann 1 f "

Luvl # 274 Waggoning (250-650)
MILES, J. A. 27 m Ga
Mary 26 f Ala
Warren 1 m "

Luvl # 293
MILES, John 23 m Ala
(See William H. Jones)

Clay # 86 Shoemaker (150 ---)
MILES, W. W. 25 m Ga
C. M. 21 f "
Mary 12 f "

Flk # 413 Farmer (200-100)
MILLER, A. J. 43 m NC
(Cont.)

(Flk # 413 cont.)
E. A. 32 f Ala
Nancy V. 15 f "
John W. 13 m "
Lucretia 11 f "
William P. 7 m "
Julia A. 5 f "
C. E. 3 m "

Mt. A. # 897 Work at steam mill (--- 250)
MILLER, Anderson 19 m Ga
Sarah 20 f "
Annie 2 f Ala

Euf # 1179 (-- 75)
MILLER, Arty 40 f SC
William 18 m Ala
Thomas 16 m "
Rhiney 14 f "
Epsey 11 f "

Euf # 937 Farmer (4000-11000)
MILLER, Asa T. 55 m NC
Elizabeth 32 f Ala
Martha M. 12 f "
Priscilla N. 10 f "
Mary A. 8 f "
Sarah 6 f "
Nancy 4 f "
Benne V. 1 f "

Mt. A. # 895 Farmer (3000-3000)
MILLER, George W. S. 50 m Ga
Martha A. 37 f "
L. M. 16 f "
Alie E. 14 f "
Nancy L. 12 f "
John W. 9 m "
Francis M. 7 m Ala
George W. 5 m "
Levi H. 3 m "
Tempe A. E. 1 f "

Mdwy # 1074 Farmer (5500-2400)
MILLER, J. M. 20 m Ga
Rebecca M. 19 f Ala
Mary F. 1 f "

Euf # 708 Farmer (100-100)
MILLER, John 22 m Ga
Emily 19 f Ala

Clay # 12 Planter (50000-70000)
MILLER, John H. 48 m SC
Ann C. 41 f "
(Cont.)

(Clay # 12 cont.)
Zenobia C. 19 f SC
Thomas T. 17 m "
Albert A. 15 m "
Ann E. 13 f "
Leona T. 11 f "
Cornelia 7 f "
W. S. 5 m "
E. C. 3 f Ala
Edwin F. 1 m "

Mt. A. # 896 Farmer (3000-8000)
MILLER, Levi 40 m Ga
Roxie A. 16 f "
Frances M. 14 f "
Peyton 12 m "
Nancy 10 f "
John 9 m "
Mary J. 7 f Ala
Lucinda 5 f "
Missouri 5/12 f "

Euf # 1181 Farmer (--- 200)
MILLER, Lewis 26 m Ala
Elizabeth 24 f Ga
Nancy J. 5 f Ala
William 2 m "
Elizabeth 6/12 f "

Euf # 419
MILLER, M. L. 30 f Ga
(See T. C. Wright).

Euf # 878
MILLER, Martha 28 f Ga

Euf # 1178 Farmer (1200-400)
MILLER, Martin 49 m NC
Jane 48 f Ga
Jane 22 f Ala
William (Farmer) 17 m "
Joseph B. 15 m "
Lucinda 13 f "
John 11 m "
Zachariah 8 m "

Clay # 661 Physician & planter
MILLER, W. John 25 m Ala
Cornelia J. 20 f Ga

Euf # 1039 Overseer (---1500)
MILLS, E. 47 m Ga
Jane A. 42 f "
David O. 12 m Ala
Jane A. 7 f "

Clay # 21
MILLS, U. W. 27 m Ky
(Living in hotel)

Clay # 148 Farmer (3000-15000)
MILLSAP, T. C., Sr. 42 m Ga
Emma E. 33 f "
Thomas S. 12 m Ala
William L. 10 m "
Sallie 6 f "
T. C., Jr. 3 m "
Reuben 1 m "
KENNINGTON, James 18 m Ga
(Farm laborer).

Euf # 70 Watch maker (1300-5000)
MILTON, James 28 m Eng

Nwto # 599 Farmer (3000-2500)
MINSHEW, Elizabeth 44 f NC
Bryant (insane) 27 m Ga
M.A.S. 24 f "
M.S.A. 22 f Ala
Mary 20 f "
V.I.(orJ.) (Farmer) 17 m "
Clary 16 f "
Charlotte 14 f "
Caroline 13 f "
James A. 12 m "
Huldy 11 f "
Nancy 10 f "
Benjamin A. 7 m "
Alfred B. 7 m "
N. M. (Farmer) 65 m NC
H.B.E. 2 f Ala

Flk # 472 Farmer (1200-500)
MINSHEW, M. N. 32 m Ala
Elizabeth 23 f "
Sarah J. 5 f "
Harriett E. 3 f "
John 4/12 m "

Euf # 848
MINTER, M. S. 55 f Ga
(See S. C. Echols).

Euf # 25
MINTON, Mary A. 23 f Ala
William A. 3 m "
(See Jason Pleghorn).

Euf # 1070 Farmer (80,000-266,000)
MITCHELL, A. C. 40 m Ga
Mary E. 36 f "
J. C. (In school) 18 m Ala
J. B. " " 16 m "
W. A. 13 m "
A. C., Jr. 10 m "

Euf # 1071
MITCHELL, Catharine 60 f Ga

Euf # 363
MITCHELL, Elizabeth 20 f Ga
(See H. W. Barrow).

Txv # 1132
MITCHELL, Hiram 13 m Ala
(See James Baxley).

Clay # 50
MITCHELL, Mary 16 f Ga
(See B. A. Thorn).

Euf # 1101 Occupation, none
MITCHELL, N. B. 31 m Ga

Euf # 1072 (15,000-78,000)
MITCHELL, Martha 35 f NC
Randolph (Student) 19 m Ala
Uriah " 18 m Ga
Elizabeth 12 f Ala
Claudia 10 f "

Mt. A. # 855
MOODY, J. H. 16 m Ga
(See D. G. Watson).

Clay # 61 Painter (210-100)
MOODY, Thomas H. 33 m Ga
M.A. 26 f "
Benjamin F. 4 m Ala
M.H. 2 f "
R.A. 1/12 m "

Euf # 226 Farmer (300-100)
MOONEYHAM, William 49 m Ga
Martha 49 f "
Martha 18 f "
John A. 15 m "
Frances 12 f Ala
Sarah 10 f "
Jefferson 6 m "

Clay # 3 Clerk
MOORE, Edwin 18 m Ala
(See Anon Willis)

Euf # 841 Shoemaker (--- 100)
MOORE, C. R. 30 m NC
Sarah A. 32 f Fla
Mary 9 f Ga
Louisa T. 6 f "
Nancy A. 4 f "
Laura 9/12 f "
BOGGS, Harriett E. 14 f "
Sarah A. E. 13 f "

Mdwy # 1075 Farmer (--- 6500)
MOORE, George W. 37 m Ga
Sarah E. 25 f Ala
Joseph 5 m "
Mary A. R. 3 f "
Elizabeth 1 f "

Euf 560 Farmer (6000-22500)
MOORE, John C. 27 m Ga
Caroline E. 3 f Ala
Martha V. 21 f "
James G. 1 m "

Euf # 838 Farmer (3000-12,000)
MOORE, W. A. 29 m Ga
Mary 12 f "
Sarah 6 f "
John E. 4 m "
George 2 m Ala
Louisa 2/12 f "
Martha 26 f "

Mdwy # 1076 Both men overseers
(Both men ---- 100)
MOORE, W. J. 24 m Ga
DUKE, W. W. 40 m Ga

Mdwy # 965 Farmer (500-20000)
MOORE, W. M. 42 m NC
Martha 37 f "
Martha J. 16 f "
Nancy S. 15 f "
Sarah A. 14 f "
Rachael L. 10 f Ala
Andrew 8 m "
Julia A. 1 f "
John T. 8/12 m "

Flk # 451 Farmer (1000-400)
MORELAND, H. H. 33 m Ga
Mary 34 f "
Louisa J. 11 f Ala
Bithia A. 9 f "
Eldonido E. 5 f "
Pochatuntas 3 f "
Susanna 1 f "

Euf # 999
MORELAND, Sarah 62 f Ga
(See Nimrod W. Long.)

Luvl # 257 Physician (---1000)
MORETON(?), W. W. 25 m Ga
(See Henry Freeman)

Euf # 400 Carpenter (1000-1500)
MORGAN, Thomas E. 33 m Ga
Amanda 39 f "
(Cont.)

(Euf # 400 cont.)
HOLLEMAN, Mary 16 f Ala
Henry 12 m "

Luvl # 344 Farmer (5000-13000)
MORRIS, A. J. 28 m Ga
Mary F. 25 f "
Fannie 5 f "
Willis 3 m "

Txv # 1217 Laborer (--- 100)
MORRIS, Abram 26 m Ala
Mary 22 f "
George 1 m "
(See Molsey Farmer).

Euf # 40
MORRIS, Anna C. 27 f NY
(See Rollin A. Wellborn).

Clay # 6 Merchant (1500-8000)
MORRIS, Benjamin 30 m Va
Roxana 21 f Ala
M.W. 2 m "
Edwin B. 1 m "
BLAIR, William L. 18 m "
(Clerk)

Luvl # 543 (400-6,600)
MORRIS, Elizabeth 58 f SC
S.M. 21 f Tenn
KEY, Edgar 4 m Ala

Clay # 8
MORRIS, Elizabeth M. 12 f Ga
(See Samuel McBride).

Luvl #342 Farmer (4000-10,000)
MORRIS, John A. 38 m SC
Georgia A. 27 f Ga
William W. 8 m "
Henry W. 5 m Ala
Mary C. 3 f "
Isabella 1 f "
DAWSON, William C. 20 m Ga

Clay # 142
MORRIS, Mary 21 f SC
(See M. Quick).

Euf # 770 Carpenter (---500)
MORRIS, N. E. 48 m NC
Elizabeth 39 f "
Henry N. (Laborer) 21 m Ga
Norfleet W. " 18 m "
Miles T. " 17 m "
Martha E. C. 13 f "
(Cont.)

(Euf # 770 cont.)
Pinckney S. 9 m Ga
Ceciro F. 5 m "
Susam W. M. 7 f "
Iola W. 3 f "
Shade J. B. 2 m "

Euf # 48 Clerk (--- ---)
MORRIS, Richard 40 m Va
LEWIS, Margaret 65 f Ga
MORRIS, Sarah S. 5 f Ala

Clay # 128 Farm laborer (-- --)
MORRIS, Riley 19 m Ga
(See James A. Bowden).

Euf # 57 Merchant (---7000)
MORRISON, A. W. 21 m Ala

Euf # 579 Laborer (-- --)
MORRISON, Benjamin 30 m SC
Theresa 28 f Ga
Mary J. 10 f Ala
Ira P. 7 m "

Euf # 1293 Blacksmith (300-400)
MORRISON, Daniel 39 m SC
Amey 35 f Ga
Andrew M. 15 m "
Daniel A. 13 m "
John W. 11 m Ala
George W. 9 m "
Margaret 4 f "

Euf # 995 (895) Farmer (2500-12000)
MORRISON, M. B. 33 m SC
Sarah C. 24 f Ga
Eugene E. 1 m Ala
Flora 36 f SC

Euf # 926
MORRISON, Nancy 36 f Ga
(See John H. McKenzie)

Euf 524 Farmer (400-200)
MORRISON, Neil 27 m Ga
Mary N. 33 f Ala
BUSH, William M. 9 m "
MORRISON, Catherine 63 f NC

Mdwy # 958 Farmer (12,000-35,000)
MORTON, William 56 m Ga
E. B. 45 f "
J. T. 24 m "
Elizabeth V. 18 f Ala
Thomas 16 m "
(Cont.)

(Mdwy # 958 cont.)
Retensa 14 f Ala
Sarah 12 f "
Charles 10 m "
Alpheus 5 m "

Euf # 753
MOSLEY, Elizabeth 26 f Ala
James W. 7 m "
Luctia 5 f "
John 5/12 m "
(See Leonard Wright).

Mdwy # 1083 Farmer (--- 200)
MOSELEY, F. M., Sr. 44 m Ga
Mary A. 45 f "
William D. 19 m Ala
Elizabeth 16 f "
F. M., Jr. 14 m "
Mary A. R. 12 f "
Martha V. 10 f "
Sophrona C. 7 f "
Thomas J. 5 m "
Henry L. 3 m "

Euf # 1347 Farmer (3000-8000)
MOSELEY, James 24 m Ga
Sarah 19 f Ala
Joseph 27 m Ga
(Lawyer, ---- 500).

Euf #. 844
MOSIER, Mariah 25 f SC
Anna 7 f Ala
William 3 m "
(See G. G. Hill).

Mdwy # 953 (--- 4,000)
MOSS, Mary B. 68 f Conn
(See J. E. Henderson).

Flk # 401 Farmer (--- ---)
MOTES, William 40 m Ala
Sarah 35 f "
Madison (Farmer) 16 m Miss
Elizabeth 14 f "
Taylor 12 m Ala
Harrison 10 m "
Jackson 8 m "
James 2 m "

Euf # 986 M.E. Minister (3000-10,000)
MULKEY, H. V. 52 m Ga
Sarah 58 f SC
Virginia 18 f Ga
Zood(?) 13 f "

Euf # 989
MULKEY, Indiana 16 f Ga.
(See Mary Swinney).

Clay # 19 Bookkeeper
MULLEN, W. T. 26 m Ga
(Living in hotel)

Euf # 603 (--- 1,600)
MUNCUS, Cintha 59 f SC
Richard (laborer) 23 m Ga

Euf # 1280 Hireling
MURDOCK, James H. 21 m SC
(See Robert Sandifer).

Euf # 1222
MURFIT, Thomas 25 m Ga
Jane 24 f "
William 7/12 m Ala

Euf # 528 Farm hand
MURPHY, Ambrose 17 m Ga
(See R. Y. Langston).

Euf # 440 Laborer
MURPHY, Tim 21 m Ire
(See McNamara's R.R. Gro.)

Euf # 292 Laborer
MURRAY, A. J. 32 m Ga
Margaret A. 22 f NC
William 2/12 m Ala

Euf # 1130
MYERS, Ellen 18 f Ala
(See Jane Forehand).

Clay # 166 Farmer
MYERS, William 47 m SC
(See Elizabeth Britt).

Flk # 494 Farmer (300 ---)
NANCE, Sylvester 42 m SC
Sarah C. 32 f "
David 11 m Ala
Mary A. 7 f "
Martha A. 5 f "
James W. 3 m "

Euf # 535 Blind
NASH, Margaret 92 f NC
(See Elizabeth Hardy).

Clay # 70 Tanner Born Gultembery, Germany
NEATHAMER, Louis 68 m Ger.
Caroline 42 f SC
Mary J. 17 f Ala
Wm. A. (Shoemaker) 15 m "
(Cont.)

(Clay # 70 cont.)

James T.	12	m	Ala
L. A.	13	f	"

Euf # 873 Farmer (12,500-40,000)

NEELY, A. G.	49	m	Tenn
Louisa W.	31	f	"
George	14	m	Fla
Jesse	12	m	Tenn
John	9	m	Ala
Ruth	7	f	"
infant	1/12	m	"

Euf # 1113 (400-8,900)

NELSON, Catharine	40	f	Ga
James S.	13	m	Ala
John G.	11	m	"
Jacob B.	9	m	"
HOLLEMAN, Catharine	32	f	Ga
Margaret A.	7	f	"
John F.	3	m	La

Euf # 197 Watch maker

NEVILLE, E. H.	36	m	Fla
Matilda F.	24	f	Va
Libley	9	f	NY
Ada	5	f	Ala
Marion	1	f	"

(1. ---- ----)
(2. 9,000-15000)

Euf # 219 Occp. - none

NEWBERRY, James	65	m	Ga
Hannah	62	f	"
James (Laborer)	25	m	"
Joseph "	21	m	"
Thomas "	17	m	"
Ginn Jas.	12	m	"
Levina	10	f	"

(1. --- 250)
(2. --- 300)

Euf # 731 Laborer (--- 100)

NEWMAN, Charles H.	23	m	Ala
Susan	25	f	Fla

Mdwy # 972 Clerk (--- 2500)

NEWMAN, Frank	21	m	Ga
S. C.	17	f	"

Clay # 181 Overseer (--- 1200)

NEWMAN, J. W.	33	m	Ga
Patience M.	23	f	"
Samuel E.	6	m	Ala
William Henry	4	m	"
Martha A.	2	f	"

(Cont.)

Clay # 181 cont.)

John D.	1/12	m	Ala
KENNINGTON, Martha	48	f	SC

Euf # 217

NEWMAN, Joseph	12	m	Ga

(See Elijah Nolin).

Euf # 132 Carpenter (--- ---)

NEWMAN, Reddin	25	m	Ga
Martha J.	39	f	"
Joseph	14	m	Ala
William	10	m	"
WILLIAMS, Eliza	14	f	Ga
William (Laborer)	16	m	"
Mary	13	f	"
Zack	10	m	"

Euf # 31 Carpenter

NEWMAN, William	46	m	Ga
Nancy	35	f	Ala
Lurania	17	f	"
Charity	15	f	"
Ann	13	f	"
Canzada	12	f	"
Milly	10	f	"
Kitty	8	f	"
infant	1	m	"

Clay # 1238 Farmer (--- 600)

NEWTON, Crawford	39	m	Ga
Eliza	41	f	"
Martha	12	f	"
William	9	m	"
Frances	7	f	"
Luke	5	m	"
Mary	2	f	"
BRIDGES, John (Laborer)	15	m	"

Bfd # 1241 Farmer (500-300)

NEWTON, Frederick	78	m	NC
Sarah	73	f	"
BRIDGER, Martha	10	f	Ga
William	8	m	"
George	4	m	"

Euf # 1359 Laborer

NICHOLS, Dougald	26	m	Ala

(See David S. Reaves).

Flk # 405 Farmer (--- ---)

NICHOLS, Elijah	18	m	Ala
Nicey	16	f	"

(Married within the year).

Bfd # 1276 Farmer (1200-800)

NIX, David	39	m	Ga

(Cont.)

(Bfd # 1276 cont.)
Elizabeth 41 f Ga
Wm. S. (In school) 16 m "
Gideon Y. 14 m "
Martha T. 11 f "
John E. 9 m "
Joseph M. 7 m "
Sarah E. 4 f "
David 1 m Ala

Euf # 286 Farmer (1500-3000)
NIX, John N. 35 m SC
Frances 23 f "
John H.(?) 1 m Ala

Clay # 111 Farmer (800-500)
NIX, John S. 26 m Ga
Wm. S. (Farmer) 60 m "
Mary 60 f "
Martha 23 f "
Amanda 6 f "
Mary 4 f "
Eugenia 2 f "
FUTCH, Elijah 13 m "

Euf # 550 Overseer (2000-500)
NIX, Thomas E. 29 m SC
Virginia 21 f "
Paul D. L. 5 m Ala
William H. 2 m "

Clay # 178 Pauper in poorhouse
NIXON, Elijah 23 m Ala

Euf # 187 Carpenter (500 ---)
NIXON, Hugh A. 34 m SC
Sarah J. 28 f "
Sabra A. P. 4 f Ala
William H. 1 m "

Mt. A. # 804 Farmer (600-650)
NOBLES, L. N. 32 m Ga
Mary 26 f "
Lucy J. 6 f Ala
Joseph H. 3 m "
John W. 2 m "

Clay # 158 Overseer
NOBLES, S. F. 22 m Ala
(See William Bishop).

Euf # 327 Farmer (10,000-6,000)
NOLIN, Avra 55 m SC
Milly 54 f "
(Cont.)

(Euf # 327 cont.)
Catharine 26 f Ala
Nancy 24 f "
JORDAN, William 19 m "
(Laborer).

Euf # 1325 Farmer (5000-2500)
NOLIN, Daniel 53 m SC
Elizabeth 45 f Ga
Eliza 23 f Ala
John W. 21 m "
Elizabeth 18 f "
Nancy 15 f "
Daniel B. 13 m "
Amanda 12 f "
William 10 m "
Dennis 7 m "
James 5 m "
Sarah 2 f "
Jackson 1 m "

Euf # 217 Farmer (1000-800)
NOLIN, Elijah 28 m Ala
Ann 22 f Ga
NEWMAN, Joseph 12 m "
ROGERS, Sidney 15 m Ala
(Laborer).

Euf # 1290 Laborer (--- ---)
NOLIN, F. D. 20 m Ala
Mariah H. 19 f "
James 5 m "
Mary A. 2 f "

Euf # 386 Farmer (200-100)
NOLIN, Fair D. 27 m Ala
Mariah 26 f Ga
Emaline 11 f Ala
John 7 m "
James 4 m "
Mary A. 2 f "

Euf # 385 Farmer (1440-500)
NOLIN, James B. 60 m SC
Polly A. 50 f "
Daniel H. 11 m Ala
Marion 9 m "
James B. 7 m "
Rosetta 4 f "

Euf # 1289 Farmer (1600-400)
NOLIN, James B. 60 m SC
Polly A. 50 f "
Daniel H. 12 m Ala
(Cont.)

(Euf # 1289 cont.)
Francis D. 10 m Ala
James A. 8 m "
Rosetta 6 f "

Euf # 1263 (--- 50)
NOLIN, Mary 77 f SC
Amanda 6 f Ala
Wesley P. 4 m "

Euf # 1285 Farmer (800-250)
NOLIN, Simpson W. 35 m Ga
Ruth J. 30 f Ala
Emily M. 9 f "
Mary E. 7 f "
John A. 5 m "
Caroline 4 f "
James M. 11/12 m "

Euf # 875 Overseer (--- 100)
NOLIN, Thomas W. 28 m Ga
Hellen M. 20 f Ala
John 7 m Ga
James J. 6/12 m Ala

Euf # 828 Laborer (--- ---)
NOLIN, W. A. 30 m Ala
Rebecca A. 36 f "
John T. 8 m "

Euf # 550 Laborer (--- ---)
NOLIN, W.(N.?) A. 28 m Ala
Rebecca 36 f "
John 9 m "
SMITH, Bennett 30 m "

Euf # 1284 Farmer (--- 150)
NOLIN, Wheaton G. 30 m Ga
Permelia 30 f "
Frances 14 f "
William D. 13 m "
Mary E. 11 f Ala
John W. 10 m "
Henrietta 8 f "
Daniel N. 5 m "
James J. 2 m "

Euf # 523 Overseer (--- ---)
NORTON, Andrew J. 23 m Ala

Euf # 883 Farmer (4000-35000)
NORTON, Daniel 46 m SC
Lucinda 48 f "
James (Laborer) 23 m Ala
Julia A. 20 f "
Lewis F.(Laborer) 16 m "
(Cont.)

(Euf # 883 cont.)
Ann E. 14 f Ala
Josephine 12 f "
Frances C. 10 f "

Euf # 868 Medical Student
NORTON, Ed A. 23 m Ala
(See Chas. Pickett).

Clay # 65 Farmer (1300 ---)
NORTON, Isabella 50 f NC
Franklin (Farmer) 16 m Ala
Thomas 14 m "
Talbot M. 12 m "
Irvin W. 10 m "

Euf # 950 Overseer (--- ---)
NORTON, J. D. 23 m Ala

Clay # 99 Farmer (2500-22000)
NORTON, James R. 54 m SC
Margaret 50 f "
Catherine 25 f Ala
Martha A. 23 f "
James 21 m "
Westley 19 m "
Fletcher J. 18 m "
P. C. 16 f "
Harriett 14 f "
Cornelia 8 f "

Clay # 1109 Farmer(3500-1000)
NORTON, John (J.) 33 m NC
Nancy 35 f "
Elbert T. 18 m Ala
Laura 16 f "
Mary A. 14 f "
Erasmus H. 12 m "
Henry T. 10 m "
Emeline 8 f "
Martha J. 7 f "
James R. 5 m "
John 3/12 m "

Euf # 876 Farmer (4000-16000)
NORTON, John K. 44 m SC
Christian 45 f "
Nancy A. 19 f Ala
William C.(In school) 19 m "
Sarah J. 17 f "
Mary E. 15 f "
Viney M. 13 f "
Laura 6 f "
Franklin P. 3 m "

Euf # 892 M.E. Minister
(2500-12500)

(Cont.)

(Euf # 892 cont.)
NORTON, John W. 66 m SC
Jane 30 f Ala
Lucy C.(?) 28 f "
Wilber F. (Student) 20 m "
Georgianna 18 f "
Thomas C. 15 m "
Cornelia A. C. 11 f "

Clay # 243 Farmer (100-500)
NORTON, Lewis V. 27 m Ala
Roxana 25 f "
James 7 m "
Aurena 1 f "

Clay # 100 Farmer (--- 1500)
NORTON, Russell 24 m Ala
Julia A. 18 f "
John A. 2 m "
Emma 9/12 f "

Euf # 893 Overseer (--- ---)
NORTON, William 24 m Ala
(See John E. Lowman).

Euf # 935 Laborer (--- ---)
NORTON, William A. 43 m SC
Eliza A. 37 f "
James (Laborer) 17 m Ga
Thomas " 15 m "
Nathan 12 m "
Lucy 10 f Ala
Daniel 3 m "

Euf # 1136 (--- ---)
O'BRIAN, George 19 m Ire
(See O. McMurray)

Euf # 52
ODOM, Gabella 12 f SC
(See Wm. N. Hamilton)

Euf # 420 Laborer (--- ---)
ODOM, Jack 29 m Ala
(See James Daniels).

Euf # 387 Laborer (--- ---)
ODOM, W. J. 29 m Ala

Euf # 334 Farmer (2500-16500)
O'HARA, Allen M. 60 m SC
Charity 47 f "
Waddy T. (Farmer) 22 m Ala
Louisiana 17 f "
BURTON, William A. 10 m "

Clay # 19 Blacksmith
(Born Lemerick, Ireland).
O'HARA, Edward 23 m Ire
(Living in hotel)

Euf # 413 Farmer (4500-35000)
O'HARA, James 71 m SC
Cintha 61 f "
Elizabeth 35 f "
E. E.(C.?)(Laborer) 32 m "
Augustus (Farmer) 30 m "
Virginia 18 f Ala

Euf # 440 Stone cutter
O'HARE, Patrick 31 m Ire
(See McNamara's R.R. Gro).

Euf # 440 Stone cutter
O'KEEFE, John 24 m Ire
(See McNamara's R.R. Gro.)

Clay # 18 Planter (4000-14000)
OLIVER, A. L. 34 m Ga
Ann M. 27 f Ala
C. M. 9 m "
C. W. 7 m "
L. S. 5 f "
John L. 2 m "
WALKER, William J. 25 m Ga
(Overseer)

Luvl # 269
OLIVER, A. W. D. -- -- --
(See Wm. C. Bostick).

Mdwy # 1060 Overseer (--- 200)
OLIVER, James H. 30 m Ga
Sarah M. 9 f Ala
John McD. 7 m "
Milbry 57 f NC

Clay # 154 M.E. Minister
OLIVER, John 62 m NC
(See Thomas A. Hightower)

Euf # 651 Farmer (300-50)
OLIVER, John A. 21 m SC
Rebecca 26 f Ala
JOHNSON, Julia A. 18 f SC
Thomas J. 4/12 m Ala

Euf # 668 Wheelright (--- 100)
OLIVER, Joseph 54 m Ga
John 7 m Ala

Clay # 51 Planter (13000-34000)
OLIVER, M. D. Sr. 34 m Ga
(Cont.)

(Clay # 51 cont.)
Nancy 27 f Ga
Sarah 11 f Ala
Amanda 9 f "
Wiley 7 m "
Cherry 6 f "
Jasper 4 m "
Henrietta 1 f "

Euf # 694 (600 ---)
OLIVER, Mahala 50 f SC
(See J. W. Shipes).

Luvl # 370
OLIVER, Sarah 30 f NC
(See Wm. R. Pool.).

Mdwy # 970 Farmer (3200-18000)
OLIVER, W. A. 28 m Ga
John L.(Farmer,--200)60 m NC
C. L. 30 f Ga
Lucy A. 23 f "

Euf # 4-4 Clerk (2500-10000)
OLIVER, W.(or M.) D. 30 m Ga
Parelle 17 f "

Euf # 649 Laborer
OLIVER, William 23 m SC
Malinda 21 f Ala
Everett A. 3 m "

Euf # 702 Merchant (800-3000)
(Born Hamburg, Germany)
OPPERT, Henry 43 m Ger
Nancy 17 f Ala
Ulian A. 5 f "

Euf # 1240 (---2,000)
ORR, Jane 27 f Ala
William 12 m "
James 10 m "
Elizabeth 8 f "

Euf # 522 Farmer (28,000-58,000)
OTT, Edward S. 45 m SC
Amanda 30 f Ga
Anna M. 13 f "
Eugenia 12 f "
William 11 m "
Mary 7 f Ala

Mdwy # 985 Hotel keeper
(--- 25,000)
OWEN, Elizabeth A. 51 f Ga
FASON, Elizabeth 30 f "
(---4,000)
(Cont).

(Mdwy # 985 cont.)
Rebecca (--- 3000) 22 f Ga
OWEN, John H. 13 m Ala
DRURY, William O. 6 m "
John W. 4 m "
FASON, Rosaline A. 6 f "
LAMPLEY, James M. 25 m "
(Merchant)
WALDROP, Larkin 20 m "
(Clerk)

Clay # 729 (--- ---)
OWENS, Harriett 35 f Ga
James 11 m Ala
Charles 1 m "

Euf # 536 Laborer (-- --)
OWENS, Henry M. 19 m Mass
(See Elizabeth Gibhart).

Txv # 1163 Farmer (240-240)
OWENS, J. H. 26 m Ala
E. A. 21 f "
Walter 2 m "

Euf # 639 Farmer (----350)
OWENS, Jackson 20 m Ala
Martha 20 f "
Henry T. 1 m "
LEE, James 31 m "
(Occupation - none).

Euf # 440 Laborer
OWENS, John W. 18 m Ala
(See McNamara's R.R. Gro.)

Euf # 246 Seamstress (1000 ---)
OWENS, Martha E. 39 f Ga
Henrietta A. 17 f "
(Seamstress)
Charles E. 13 m "

Euf # 555 Miller (--- 2500)
OWENS, Nathaniel 53 m Mass
Martha 30 f Me
George F. 22 m Ala
Clarence 2 m "

Mdwy # 986 Hotel keeper
(--- 2,000)
OWENS, Sarah 46 f SC
Isaac (Carpenter) 21 m Ga
George J. 19 m "
WALDROP, Thos. 24 m "
(Painter)
LESTER, John 30 m Va
(Carriage maker, --- $100)
(Cont.)

(Mdwy # 986 cont.)
ELDER, John -- -- --
(Tanner)
HALL, J. M. 26 m Ga
(Physician, ---800)
HAWKINS, John 45 m NC
(Shoemaker, ---100)
GRIFFIN, Robert -- m --
BLAKY, Columbus 30 m Ga
(Painter, ---200)

Mdwy # 1079 Farmer (8800-25,000)
OWENS, Whitman H. 66 m NC
Nancy A. 50 f Ga

Euf # 1000 Overseer (---1200)
OWENS, William H. 41 m Ga
Jane 25 f "
Elizabeth 14 f Ala
John 8 m Ga
Oliver 6 m "
Antonett 4 f Ala

Mt. A. # 848 Farmer (550-300)
PADGET, A. P. 51 f Ga
JOHNSON, John 33 m "
(Farmer)
William (Farmer) 17 m "
Lorenzo " 16 m "
ARPE, Martha 19 f "
PADGET, Elizabeth 13 f "
Fannie 10 f "
ARPE, M. D. 4 f Ala

Clay # 940 Farmer (1600-7000)
PADGET, Henry 48 m SC
Maria 36 f Ga

Clay # 170
PADRICK, J. S. 26 m NC
(See Thos. Kennedy)

Flk # 459 Farmer
PAGE, Allen 40 m NC
(See Joseph Powell)

Nwto # 561 Farmer
PAGE, Samuel 70 m NC
(See Burell Phillips).

Luvl # 381 Farmer
PAINE, Thomas (torn) Ala.
(See Allen Teal)

Mdwy # 1093 Farmer (5100-10,500)
PARHAM, James A. 40 m SC
(Cont.)

(Mdwy # 1093 cont.)
Narcissa A. 36 f SC
Elisha 10 m "
Mary 6 f "
Clarissa A. 4 f "
E. E. 2 f "
THOMPSON, Mary 42 f "
PARHAM, William 10 m "
(Farm laborer)

Euf # 714 Blacksmith (---125)
PARISH, James P. 47 m SC
Christian 35 f NC
Thomas J. 15 m Ala
Sarah A. 9 f "
Nancy 8 f "

Euf # 754
PARISH, M. 43 f Ala
(See C. Bruton).

Euf # 580 Farmer (--- 100)
PARISH, Thomas 27 m Ga
Margaret 30 f "
William 4 m Ala
John 2 m "
James 1 m "

Clay # 224 Miller (--- ---)
PARK, A. L. 48 m SC
Ruthy A. 37 f "
W. T. (Farmer) 18 m Ala
Mary A. 12 f "
Martha J. 10 f "
John 8 m "
George 6 m "
Margaret C. 4 f "
Isabella 4/12 f "

Mt. A. 837 Prim. Bap. Minister (7450-11,500)
PARKER, Cater A., Sr. 51 m NC
Louisa C. 54 f Ga
Cater A., Jr. 18 m Ga
(At school).
Stephen P. (at school) 16 m "
Daniel H. " " 15 m "
Wm. A. " " 12 m "
SHELBY, Uzial 27 m "
(Overseer)

Clay # 938 Farmer (--- 300)
PARKER, Hiram 39 m Ga
Flora 38 f NC
PETERSON, Lucinda 20 f Ga
Josephine S. 16 f "
William N. 13 m "
(Cont.)

(Clay # 938 cont.)
Elizabeth 11 f Ala
Rosalie 9 f "
Sarah L. 7 f "
Margaret A. 5 f "
Peter 18 m Ga

Euf # 1084 Farmer (23000-60000)
PARKER, J. D. 28 m Ga
Catharine R.69 (or) 19 f Ga
Pinckney J.(Student) 20 m "
Joseph M. " 18 m "
Josephine A. 17 f Ala

Mt. A. # 898 Farm laborer
PARKER, Jackson 16 m Ga
(See David Holder).

Mdwy # 979 Farmer (---5,500)
PARKER, Jesse 26 m SC
Sarah J. 18 f Ga

Mt. A. # 815 Farmer (---3,500)
PARKER, Joel J. 33 m NC
SHEPPARD, R. A. 37 f "
Nancy 7 f Ala
Martha B. 34 f NC
Easther P. 27 f "

Mt. A. # 821
PARKER, Martha 60 f Ga
(See John K. Hollingsworth).

Euf # 1217 School teacher (1150-1500)
PARKER, Thomas C. 27 m NC
Martha 22 f Ala
Mary E. 8/12 f "

Mt. A. # 915 Laborer
PARKER, West 22 m Ga

Clay # 21 Brick mason
PARKER, William F. 34 m Ga
(Living in hotel)

Euf # 1175 (--- ---)
PARMER, Adaline 33 f SC
James B. 10 m Ala
Lydia 8 f "
William 6 m "
Enos 4 m "
Margaret 3 f "
infant 2 m "

Bkb # 694 Farmer (600-4000)
PARMER, B. E. G. 29 m Ala
Mary A. 36 f Ga
(Cont.)

(Bkb 694 cont.)
Aaron 9 m Ala
Moses 6 m "
Martha J. 4 f "

Euf # 1166 Farmer (1000-200)
PARMER, George 63 m Ga
Nancy 40 f SC
Wm. W.(Farmer,--100) 22 m Ala

Euf # 1262 Student
PARMER, George W. 21 m Ala
(See John P. DuBose)

Euf 1201 Farmer (1500-12000)
PARMER, Jacob Sr. 65 m Ga
Martha 64 f NC
Rebecca 25 f Ala
Jefferson 55 m Ga
(Occp. none - 300-800)

Euf 1271 Occp. none (--- 100)
PARMER, Jacob H. 36 m Ala
Lydia F. 30 f "
Mary P. 11 f "
Sarah E. 4 f "
Ann R. 3 f "
infant 1/12 m "

Euf # 1232 Farmer (800-400)
PARMER, James L. 31 m Ala
Mary 27 f "
Jane 5 f "
John W. 3 m "
George W. 9/12 m "

Euf # 1200 Farmer (--- 150)
PARMER, John W. 19 m Ala
Alelany 18 f "
(Married within the year)

Euf # 1270 (--- 200)
PARMER, Joseph (L.) 24 m Ala
Roxy 22 f "
Gouldin M. 5 m "

Euf # 627
PARMER, William W. 22 m Ala
(See Timothy Lee).

Mdwy # 1051 Overseer (2000-2000)
PARR, L. L. 41 m Ga
Sarah 31 f "
James 12 m "
Sarah 10 f "
Ida 7 f Ala
infant 3 m "

Euf # 9-9
PARSONS, Elizabeth 10 f Ala
(See James Bigham).

Euf # 1371 Farmer (200-300)
PARSONS, John L. 54 m NC
Linsey A. 37 f Ga
Susan 14 f Ala
Sally A. 12 f "
Marietta 9 f "
Elisha O. C. 6 m "
John C. 2 m "
Elizabeth 5/12 f "

Euf # 1037 Farmer (1000-6000)
PASCHAL, Dennis 44 m Ga
Jane L. 40 f "
Thomas S. 15 m "
George D. 12 m "
Albert E. 10 m "
Frances J. 8 f "
Mary 6 f Ala
John F. 3 m "
Ellen M. 7/12 f "

Euf # 860 Blacksmith (--- 150)
PASSMORE, G. W. 48 m SC
Eliza A. 43 f "
Henrietta 20 f Ga
Sylvanus(At school). 16 m "
Legrand 14 m "

Luvl # 337 Farmer (2400-15000)
PASSMORE, J. R. A. 31 m Ga
Mary 74 f "
B. M. (insane) 29 m Ala

Luvl # 654 Farmer (4000-2000)
PASSMORE, Lemuel 58 m Ga
Sarah 60 f SC
George W.(Idiotic) 26 m Ala
William (Farmer) 24 m "
Martha 24 f "
Polly 22 f "
Icabod (Farmer) 21 m "
Caroline 20 f "
Elizabeth 18 f "
Mary F. 4 f "

Txv # 1150 Farmer (800-500)
PASSMORE, Stephen 43 m Ga
Elizabeth 35 f "
Jesse (Farmer) 17 m "
Samuel " 16 m "
Edwin 13 m "
Stephen 11 m Ala
Elizabeth J. 9 f "
(Cont.)

(Txv # 1150 cont).
Mary J. 8 f Ala
Epsy J. 5 f "
Alex 2 m "

Euf # 828 Overseer (--- 200)
PATE, Thomas 28 m Ga
Mary A. 23 f "
Mary E. 4 f "
Benjamin 1 m "
HIGDON, Mary 45 f SC

Mdwy # 1015 Teacher (--- 1000)
PATTERSON, Dougald 30 m NC
(See Lorenzo Faulk).

Euf # 354 Farmer (500-500)
PATTERSON, George W. 22 m Fla
Margaret 22 f Ala
HODGE, Lee 12 m "

Bfd # 1248 School teacher (--- 8000)
PATTERSON, L. 35 m NC
Martha 28 f Ga
Edward 2 m Ala
James D. 28 m NC

Euf # 865 Overseer (--- 400)
PATTERSON, L. B. 35 m SC
Sarah 48 f "
Pleasant 12 m Ala
Sarah 8 f "
McDONALD, J. D. 70 m SC

Euf # 946 Overseer (--- 200)
PATTERSON, M. 35 m Ala
Mary C. 50 f Ga
Pleasant P. 15 m Ala
Sarah 8 f "
McDONALD, J.(Tailor) 78 m NC

Euf # 355 (2200 ---)
PATTERSON, Rebecca 50 f Ga
Daniel N. (Farmer) 25 m "
Ann 18 f Fla
Franklin 14 m "
Solomon 12 m "

Txv # 1152 Farm laborer
PATTERSON, Seth 19 m Ala
(See Augustus Glover)

Euf # 190 Wheelwright (--- 600)
PATTERSON, T. D. 49 m NC
Missouri 18 f "
Cornelia 15 f "
William 13 m "
(Cont.)

(Euf # 190 cont.)
LeRoy 8 m NC
Octavia 11 f "
Elvira 9 f "

Euf # 546 Occp. none
PATTERSON, Thos. 24 m NC
Caroline 25 f SC
RACHAELS, Fereby 87 f Ga

Mdwy # 1070 Farmer (---- 500)
PAUL, H. K. 36 m SC
R. J. 32 f Ala
D. G. 8 m "
Sarah E. 6 f "
Mary S. 5 f "
A.J. 3 f "
Josephine R. 1 f "

Mdwy # 1069 Overseer (--- 100)
PAUL, John 34 m SC
Emma 18 f Ga
(See Thomas King).

Nwto # 603
PAUL, Lucinda 11 f Ala
(See Charlotte Cox).

Clay # 1 M. Bapt. Minister
PAULLIN, J. S. 23 m Ala
(See H. D. Clayton).

Euf # 309 Clerk (4500-1200)
Paulin, William S. 48 m NJ
Eliza S. 58 f SC

Euf # 674 Farmer (--- 200)
PAYNE, Absalom 18 m Ga
Mary A. 20 f "

Euf # 676 (--- 250)
PAYNE, Elizabeth 65 f SC
Frankey 30 f Ala
Wm. (Farmer) 21 m "
Jno. (Farm hand) 18 m "

Euf 673 Farmer (6400-8200)
PAYNE, Joseph 50 m Ga
Lydia 45 f "
Nancy 17 f "
Judge 15 m "
Elizabeth 12 f Ala
Joseph 6 m "
Lydia 5/12 f "

Euf # 677 Farmer (--- 50)
PAYNE, William C. 45 m SC
Isabella 40 f Ga
Jno. (Laborer) 17 m Ala
(Cont.).

(Euf # 677 cont.)
Crawford 15 m Ala
Mary 12 f "
Jackson 9 m "
AMOS, William 5 m "

Mt. A. 816 Farmer (150-200)
PEACOCK, James 49 m SC
Rebecca 46 f "
Nancy A. 22 f Ga
W. H. 18 m Ala
Sarah A. F. 13 f "
Charles H. 11 m "
Bethena 7 f "
JEFFCOAT, A. D. 3 f "

Mt. A. # 818
PEACOCK, John J. 16 m Ala
(See Frank Baker).

Euf # 503 Farmer (--- 400)
PEAKE, John 29 m Ga
Rebecca 29 f "
Frances J. 7 f Ala
Mary M. 5 f "
John 3 m "
Sarah E. 1 f "
THOMAS, Allen 13 m "

Clay # 1285 Farmer (3600-38000)
PEARSON, Benjamin F. 50 m NC
H. M. (---30,000) 39 f "
Herbert (In school) 18 m Ala
James A. 14 m "
Robert H. 12 m "
Rosa T. 9 f "
Sarah E. 7 f "
Hattie 4 f "
JONES, G. D. (Clerk) 18 m "

Euf # 772 Laborer (--- 100)
PEARSON, William T. 33 m Ga.
Sarah A. 28 f "
Joseph W. 6 m "
Henry R. 4 m "
William J. 2 m "
James A. 4/12 m Ala
BROWN, Nancy E. 18 f Ga

Euf # 49 Tinner
PEAVY, John J. 28 m Ga
STEVENS, Henry R. 18 m Ala
(Tinner)

Mdwy # 1068 Farmer (14000-35000)
PENICK, Lazarus 35 m Ga
Martha C. 27 f SC
M.A. 8 f Ala
(Cont.)

(Mdwy # 10 68 cont).
Joseph P. 5 m Ala
C.C. 3 f "
Martha (---14500) 57 f Ga

Clay # 19 Tailor
PENNEGER, F. 40 m. Ger
(living in hotel - Born Breman).

Euf # 173 Carpenter (--- ---)
PENTECASTER, D. H. 60 m Pa.
(Living in Hotel - See John Bailey - Planter's Hotel).

Euf # 871 Farmer (125 ---)
PERDUE, Colley 55 m SC
John 24 m Ala
Martha 14 f "
Wilson 10 m "
PERDUE, Marshall 17 m "
(Hireling)
PERDUE, Edward 49 m SC
(Hireling)
Hall, Mary 20 f "

Euf # 902 Farmer (800-250)
PERKINS, James M. 42 m Ga
Frances 42 f "
Frances 14 f Ala
Elizabeth 12 f "
Josephine 10 f "
Eliza A. 6 f "

Euf # 501 Laborer (---150)
PERKINS, John 28 m Tenn
Mary 28 f Ga
Louisa 7 f Ala
George 5 m "
James 1 m "

Euf # 901 Farmer (1000-1200)
PERKINS, John 37 m Ga
Sarah A. 34 f "
John 4 m Ala
Martha 2 f "
infant 1 f "

Euf # 559 Overseer (--- ---)
PERRYMAN, Jeremiah 45 m Ga
(Overseer of R.R. See R. T. K. James).

Mdwy # 1039 Farmer (3800-15000)
PERSONS, John W. 22 m Ga
Paulline 18 f "
(Married within the year).

Clay # 129 Laborer
PETERSON, Alexander 22 m Ga
(See E. M. Lasetter).

Clay # 149 Farmer (600-250)
PETERSON, D. C. 33 m NC
Adaline 30 f Ga
Amanda 11 f Ala
Marion 8 m "
Mary 6 f "
Malcom 4 m "
John 6/12 m "

Clay # 938
Peterson, Lucinda 20 f Ga
Josephine S. 16 f "
William N. 13 m "
Elizabeth 11 f Ala
Roselie 9 f "
Sarah L. 7 f "
Margaret A. 5 f "
Peter 18 m Ga
(See Hiram Parker).

Clay # 102 Farmer (--- ---)
Peterson, M. J. 26 m Ga
A. W. (Farmer) 24 m "
Catherine E. 20 f "
Archibald Farmer 18 m "
John R. " 17 m "
Ann 15 f "

Clay # 151
PETERSON, Munroe 13 m Ga
(See Thos. Vanadore).

Euf # 416
PETERSON, Permelia 16 f Ga
John (Student) 18 m Ga
(See Isham Carroll).

Nwto # 597 Farmer (300-350)
PETERSON, William 35 m NC
Sarah 24 f "
POWELL, A. M. 15 f Ga

Clay # 27 Carriage mfgr. (12,00-8000)
PETTY, B. F. Sr. 53 m NY
Mary E. 25 f Ala
B.F., Jr.(apprentice) 18 m "
Mary C. 13 f "
Julia S. 11 f "
Elizabeth 9 f "
Ella 8 f "
P. L. 2 f "
(Cont.)

(Clay # 27 cont.)
Leila 8/12 f Ala
PLACE, Jonah W. 30 m NY
(Foreman of shop).

Clay # 65 Merchant (7000-30,000)
Petty, Charles 35 m NY
Narcissa 32 f SC
Edward O. 15 m Ala
Anna 11 f "
Dick 5 m "
PETTY, Jas. P. 1 m "
MCKINNON, Alex M. 33 m NC
(Clerk, --- $500).

Clay # 193 Farmer (2400-700)
PETTY, Charles L. 20 m Ala
Adelia (---,3415) 16 f "

Clay # 11 Clerk (--- ---)
PETTY, N. A. 33 m NY
N.A. 23 f Ala
W. B. 3 m "
J. V. 1 m "

Euf # 99 Bookkeeper (-- --)
PHELPS, David 37 m Ga
Laura 22 f "
Francis 6 m "
Lucy 4 f "
Charles 1 m Ala
Johnston 1/12 m "
HOWARD, C. 27 m Vt
(Sign painter).

Nwto # 560 Farmer (3500-3500)
PHILLIPS, A. H. H. 31 m Ga
Jesse H. 12 m Ala
Thomas C. 10 m "
Needham B. 8 m "
Annie E. 5 f "
James A. 3 m "

Nwto # 561 Farmer (1600-1800)
PHILLIPS, Burrell 35 m Ga
Caroline M. 17 f Ala
PAGE, Sam'l.(Farmer) 70 m NC
IVEY, Wm. M. " 15 m Ala

Nwto # 563 (800-400)
PHILLIPS, C. S. 37 f Ga
N. E. 15 f Ala
Milly (black) 110 f Va
(See Elizabeth Sutton).

Euf # 638 (150-50)
PHILLIPS, Emanuel 30 m Ga
Elizabeth 21 f Ala
J.W. 8/12 m "
(See Allen Hardy)

Euf # 1012 (1,000-200)
PHILLIPS, Hester 79 f NC
Margaret 27 f SC
SPAIGHT, Esther 7 f Fla
Louis P. 5 m "
LOCK, Anna 20 f "
PHILLIPS, Robert 18 m Ala
(Laborer)
James (Laborer) 22 m "

Nwto # 625 (1200-1000) M.E.C. Minister.
PHILLIPS, J. J. 42 m Ga
L. A. 34 f "
S. J. (Farmer) 17 m "
J. M. 14 m "
G. M. 12 m "
L. A. F. 9 f "
C. C. 2 f Ala

Euf # 238 Blacksmith
PHILLIPS, John 37 m Ire
(See John W. Cameron)

Euf # 265 Confectioner (-- 200)
PHILLIPE, Lewis 36 m NY
Mary 28 f Ire
STEWART, M. 51 f Eng
(--- 1000, Dress maker).

Euf # 116 Peddler
PHILLIPE, Louis 25 m Pol
(Russian Poland - see H.Bernstien)

Nwto # 559 Farmer (2200-7000)
PHILLIPS, T. P. C. 29 m Ga
Huldy 28 f Ala
M. A. E. 7 f "

Bkb # 769
PICKETT, G. F. 22 m Ga
Lucas 16 m "
Lucinda 24 f "
(See Wm. H. Spergers).

Euf # 868 Physician (600-3500)
PICKETT, Charles 37 m SC
Charity 33 f "
James 7 m Ala
Mary 4 f "
(Cont.)

(Euf # 868 cont.)

Sally	2	f	Ala
NORTON, Ed A. (Med. student).	23	m	"

Mt. A. # 860

PICKETT, Mary A.	21	f	Ga
George H.	3	m	Ala

(See Peter Draper)

Mdwy # 1077 (1250-3000)

PICKETT, Sarah	65	f	Ga

Mt. A. # 851 Farmer (150-100)

PICKETT, Thomas	26	m	Ga
Samantha	19	f	Ala
W. D.	7/12	m	"

Clay # 44 In jail.

PICKETT, William S.	43	m	Ga

Txv # 1182 Confectioner (--- 500)

PIERCE, Jesse	67	m	NC
Winneford	62	f	SC
Susanna	21	f	Ga

Mt. A. # 903 Blacksmith (300-1000)

PIERCE, John L.	27	m	Ga
Effie	25	f	"
Louisa	6	f	"
Daniel	4	m	"
Milly	3	f	"
Mary	1	f	Ala
SILAS, Rebecca (300-150)	60	f	Ga

Txv # 1138 Farmer (800-525)

PIERCE, Lovard L.	34	m	Ga.
Annie J.	30	f	"
Mary E.	14	f	"
Thomas J.	12	m	Ala
Missouri	8	f	"
Martha J.	6	f	"
Susan F.	3	f	"
Jesse T.	1	m	"

Euf # 597

PINKSTON, Catherine	78	f	Ga

(See John F. Searcy).

Euf # 1362 Mail Contractor (8000-11000)

PIPER, Samuel	27	m	Ga
Rachael	17	f	Fla
Richard	1	m	Ala

Mdwy # 975 Farmer (6000-25000)

PIPKIN, Haywood	48	m	NC
Eliza	39	f	"
Frances	16	f	Ala
Caroline	10	f	"
Isaac	8	m	"
John	6	m	"
Elizabeth	4	f	"
Hettie	4	f	"
Sarah J.	3	f	"
HANCOCK, Isam (Clerk in store,--3800)	20	m	"

Euf # 611 Farmer (160-200)

PIPKIN, John	32	m	NC
Priscilla	28	f	"
Henry	5	m	Ala
William	1	m	"
HOLMES, Jane	10	f	"

Euf # 594 Laborer (--- 100)

PIPPIN, Benjamin	51	m	SC
Kitty Ann	30	f	"
Frances	19	f	"
John R.	15	m	"
Joseph	9	m	"
Debora	8	f	"
Levi	7	m	"
Neeks N.	6	m	Ala
Micajah	4	m	"
Franklin	3	m	"

Euf # 1323 Farmer (1200-800)

PIPPIN, Calvin	45	m	NC
Sarah	45	f	Ga
Lewis (Laborer)	23	m	"
Stow "	21	m	"
Jackson "	17	m	"
Berian	14	m	"
Taylor	11	m	"
Franklin	8	m	Ala
Belcher	5	m	"
Isabella	2	f	"

Euf # 171 Bar & Restaurant keeper (7,000-10,000)

PIPPIN, Watts (?)	45	m	SC
Mary	40	f	Ga
William B.	15	m	Ala
A. P.	13	m	"
G. M.	11	m	"

Mt. A. # 909 Engineer at mill

PITTMAN, F. M.	25	m	SC
Susan F.	18	f	Ala

(See O. S. Lewis).

Euf # 38 Clerk (illegible)
PITTMAN, F. M. 26 m SC
Susan 15 f Ga
KIELS, Susan 55 f SC
Georgiann 11 f Ala

Euf # 716 Occp. none (---200)
PITTS, Allen A. 21 m Ga
Martha 20 f Ala
(Married within the year).

Euf # 703 Student (--- 800)
PITTS, John W. 16 m Ala
(See William Helms).

Clay # 27 Foreman of Shop
PLACE, Jonah W. 30 NY
(See B. F. Petty, Sr.)

Euf # 296 Sur. Dentist (--500)
PLANT, Ebenezer 50 m Conn

Euf # 25 Laborer (--- ---)
PLEGHORN, Jason 37 m Ga
Mary A. 26 f "
Lucinda M. 10 f Ala
William J. 5 m "
MINTON, Mary A. 23 f "
William A. 3 m "

Bkb # 717 Miller (--- 250)
POOL, F. A. 54 m SC
Mary 41 f "
Ellen 19 f "
Federick (Farmer) 17 m "
Madison " 15 m "
Charlotte 12 f "
Verity 8 m Ala
Aaron 2 m "

Luvl # 370 Farmer (1000-150)
POOL, William R. 35 m SC
Jane 40 f NC
Alfred (Farmer) 15 m Ga
George A. 13 m "
William D. 11 m "
Thomas J. 9 m "
Norman M. 6 m "
OLIVER, Sarah 30 f NC
LUDLOW, Wiley 18 m Ala
(Farmer)
CHAMBERS, Joseph 26 m "

Euf # 202 Physician (7000-7000)
POPE, C. J. 45 m Ga
Jane R. 39 f "
Sarah E. 17 f Ala
(Cont.)

(Euf # 101 cont.)
Ella M. 14 f Ala
Mary S. 13 f "
John G. 10 m "
Susan 7 f "
Matilda T. 5 f "
Leila C. 3 f "
CARUTHERS, Louisa M. 14 f Ga

Euf # 361 Occp. none (--- ---)
POPE, Jacob 80 m NC
Mary 70 f "

Euf 1066 Teamster (--- 100)
POPE, Jonathan 31 m NC
Mary E. 32 f Ga
Elizabeth 6 f Ala
Roxana 5 f "
Mary T. 3 f "
Anzenetta 1 f "

Mt. A. # 915 Laborer in brick yard
POPE, Manson (?) 23 m Ga
(See Moses Shelby)

Euf # 106 Clerk (--- ---)
POPE, R. C. 19 m Ga

Clay # 25 Clerk (--- ---)
POPE, William S. 27 m Va
Martha F. 20 f Ala
SEABROOK, M. J. 16 f "
POPE, M. A. 2 f "
H. J. 2/12 f "

Euf # 10-10 Merchant (--5000)
PORTER, George W. 26 m Ga
RONEY, Wm. N. (Clerk) 22 m Ala
(--- 5000)
CARTER, John J. 28 m "
(Merchant, 1200-8000)

Clay # 20 Printer (500-1000)
POST, John 27 m Ga
Mary 17 f "

Euf # 201 Mill wright (2000-4000)
POSTON, Emanuel 56 m SC
Elizabeth 54 f Ga
James R. 16 m Ala
John H. 14 m "
Manfredonia 11 f "
Arabella H. 7 f "
BLACK, Polly 18 f "

Euf # 797 Farmer (1300-600)
POTTER, Augustus 43 m Ga
Hannah 41 f Ala
Jackson(Farm hand) 20 m "
Mary 20 f "
Susan 17 f "
Wesley 15 m "
Frank 14 m "
Julia A. 10 f Ga

Euf # 679 Farmer (700-8000)
POTTS, John 51 m Ga
Jane 48 f "
CHILDERS, Elijah 26 m Ala
(Farmer, 600-200)

Euf # 680 Farmer (1800-220)
POTTS, John B. 24 m Ga
Sarah 23 f Ala
Rhody A. 4 f Ga
Judge S. M. 2 m Ala
Lydia A. S. 1 f "

Euf # 262 (500-100)
POURNELL, Elmire 42 f Ga
George P. 16 m Ala
(Bridge keeper)
Alexander (Clerk) 15 m "

Nwto # 597
POWELL, A. M. 15 f Ga
(See Wm. Peterson)

Nwto # 552 Laborer (--- 100)
POWELL, Benj. L. 22 m Ala
Margaret 23 f "

Nwto # 596
POWELL, Caroline 12 f Ala
R. A. 10 f "
(See Jeremiah Craft).

Clay # 85 Mechanic (1000-2500)
POWELL, George W. 48 m Ga

Euf # 257 Carpenter (--- 100)
POWELL, John 33 m Ga
Edy 33 f NC
Mary A. 10 f Ga
John R. 5 m "
Winny C. 1 f Ala

Bkb # 723 Farmer (500-2000)
POWELL, John 46 m Ga

Flk # 459 Farmer (500-300)
POWELL, Joseph 30 m SC
Matilda 25 f "
PAGE, Allen(Farmer) 40 m NC

Clay # 32 Clerk (--- 600)
POWELL, L. W. 26 m Ala
M. J. 20 f "
B. A. 57 m SC
H. C. M. 23 f Ala

Flk # 458
POWELL, Matilda 17 f Ala
(See William Stokes)

Euf # 173
POWELL, Nancy 52 f Ga
(See John Bailey, Planter's Hotel).

Mt. A. 806 Farmer (150-150
POWELL, William 32 m Ala
Sarah A. 26 f Ga
Thomas 7 m Ala
Georgia A. 4 f "
Mary A. 2 f "
Winneford 2/12 m "

Euf # 1205 Grocer (--- 200)
POWELL, William B. 33 m SC
Elizabeth 31 f Ga
Samuel 10 m Ala
George W. 8 m "
Caroline M. 6 f "
John A. 4 m "
Mary J. (or I.) 2 f "

Euf # 87 Clerk (--- ---)
POWER, Paterick 27 m Ire

Mdwy # 1042 Planter (18,750-60,000)
POU, Joseph 52 m Ga
Mary 35 f "
BEALL, Alice 16 f "
Thomas 14 m "
Mittie 13 f "

Clay 1283 School teacher (--50)
POYNER, John W. 55 m NC
(See Robert Hightower).

Euf # 90 Bank clerk (--- ---)
PRATT, H.(?) P. 35 m Conn
CHERRY, Robert 25 m Ga
(Clerk, 3000 - 2500).

Euf # 205 Merchant (--- ---)
PREER, Charles D. 20 m Ga

Txv # 1146 Farmer (5920-500)
PRICE, Burrell 50 m NC
Rebecca 49 f "
(Cont.)

(Txv # 1146 cont.)
David E. (Farmer) 21 m Ala
John P. " 16 m "
Lear A. 15 f "
Lavina P. 11 f "
Effie A. 9 f "
GODWIN, Right H. 24 m Ga
(Farmer)

Euf # 1129 Laborer (--- 100)
PRICE, H. D. 65 m SC

Euf # 823 Overseer (--- 150)
PRICE, John M. 30 m Ga
Marticia 29 f "
Joseph W. 8 m "
John M. 6 m "
William O. 2 m "
Mary E. 8/12 f "

Clay # 1236 Farmer (1200-500)
Price, L. W. 26 m NC
E. J. 23 f Ala
Sarah A. 5 f "
Aaron W. 4 m "
Mary J. 2 f "
infant 1/12 f "
HORNE, Martha 17 f "

Clay # 72 Farmer (--- ---)
PRICE, Levin 64 m NC
Smitha (300 ---) 47 f --
(Married within the year).

Clay # 109 Farmer (--- 150)
PRICE, Louis 27 m NC
Mary E. 23 f Ala
SPEARS, Lucinda 9 f "

Euf # 338
PRICE, Mary T. 9 f Ala
(See James R. Hill).

Euf # 738 Farmer (1000-250)
PRICE, Riley A. 30 m NC
Zylphia L. 25 f "
Burwell A. 5 m Ala
John W. 3 m "
Milbry P. 11/12 f "

Luvl # 368 Farmer (---5000)
PRICE, Robert E. 47 m SC
Celie 42 f "
William (Farmer) 27 m "
Mary A. 25 f "
Martha J. 23 f "
Patience 21 f "
(Cont.)

(Luvl # 368 cont.)
Margaret 19 f SC
James P. 17 m "
Caroline 15 f Ala
Celie A. 13 f "
Robert J. 11 m "

Euf # 1080 Farmer (3500-30000)
PRICE, William E. 41 m SC
Emma M. 37 f Ga
Willie J. 9 m Ala
Eliza 7 f Ga
Samuel L. 6 m Ala
Edward B. 5 m "
Caroline L. 2 f "
Eugene H. 4/12 m "
PRICE, Jesse Wood 20 m Ga
(M.E. Minister (---10,000).

Euf # 536 Cabinet maker (-- --)
PRIEST, Ebenezer 21 m Ga
(See Eliza Gibhart).

Clay # 233 Farmer (8000-4000)
PRIM, Abraham 60 m NC
Eliza A. 58 f Ga
Jas.(Stage driver) 22 m "
B. F. (Farmer) 20 m "
CARMICHAEL, Nancy J. 10 f Ala

Euf # 440 Laborer
PRIMMONS, Jery 35 m Ire
(See McNamara's R.R. Gro.)

Euf # 992 (---3,500)
PROCTOR, Mary A. 26 f Ga
Colin 5 m Ala
(See Aaron T. Kendrick)

Mdwy # 1011 Farmer (5000-25000)
PRUETT, A. H. 37 m Ga
Frances 37 f "
M.A.E. 16 f "
Jacob 14 m "
Meling 12 m "
John K. 10 m "
Mary 9 f "
Alvyn 7 m "
James 5 m Ala
Frances 3 f "
infant 1/12 m "

Mdwy # 961 Planter (16000-75000)
PRUETT, J. M. 44 m Ga
Louisa 42 f "
William H. 19 m Ala
John 17 m "
(Cont.)

(Mdwy # 961 cont.).
Samuel T. 14 m Ala
James 12 m "
Seth G. 10 m "
George 8 m "
Louisa 5 f "

Mdwy # 984
PRUETT, Virginia 12 f Ala
(See W. T. Coleman).

Nwto # 637 Work at mill (--- 200)
PUGH, J. T. 36 m Ala
S.J. 24 f "
James T. 8 m "
S.C. 6 f "
B. 4 m "
C.S. 2 m "

Euf # 574 Lawyer (35000-60000)
PUGH, James L. 40 m Ga
Sarah S. 31 f SC
Laura T. 10 f Ala
Edward L. 4 m "
Sarah S. 8/12 f "
GREEN, Isabella 25 f "
(---3000)
Violetta(---3000) 19 f "
Marion " " 16 f "
Ann " " 14 f "

Bfd # 1243
PUGH, Nancy 27 f NC
(See R. C. McSwean).

Mdwy # 1014 Overseer
PUGH, Whitson 22 m Ala
(See Elizabeth King).

Euf # 762 Farmer (4000-2000)
PURSWELL, Gabriel 51 m SC
Elizabeth 48 f "
Mary E. 8 f Ala
SPROWL, Eliza I. 20 f Fla

Euf # 764 Farmer (--- 100)
PURSWELL, H. D. 24 m Ala
Amanda 21 f Ga
Henry W. 1 m Ala

Euf # 1320 Occp. none (300-100)
PURSWELL, Henry 79 m SC
Catherine 70 f "

Euf # 763 Farmer (1000-400)
PURSWELL, William S. 30 m SC
Elizabeth 27 f Ala
(Cont.)

(Euf # 763 cont.)
John 7 m Ala
Henry 5 m "
Sarah J. 3 f "
Amanda O. 2 f "
CONDRY, Penelope 12 f "

Euf # 424 School teacher
PYNN, John 63 m NC

Clay # 141 Laborer
QUICK (?), Jefferson 19 m Ga
(See Frank Deshazo).

Clay # 167 Farmer (--- ---)
QUICK, John 57 m SC
Sarah 52 f Ga
Martha 22 f "
W.J. 16 f "

Clay # 143 Farmer (250-400)
Quick, M. 30 m Ga
Louisa 22 f Ala
J. T. 6 m "
James W. 4 m "
John 6/12 m "
MORRIS, Mary 21 f SC

Euf # 1123 Farmer (400-150)
QUICK, Sanders 30 m Ga
Malinda 37 f "
Henry H. 15 m "
Elizabeth 13 f "
William J. 1 m Ala

Clay # 665 Farmer (--- 250)
Quinton, H. W. 38 m SC
Mary A. 32 f Ga
John H. 15 m "
Hugh A. 13 m "
Martha L. 12 f "
Jane 11 f "
Margaret 9 f "
David 7 m "
Clarisi 6 f "
Thomas 1 m "

Euf # 546
RACHAELS, Fereby 87 f Ga
(See Thomas Patterson).

Euf # 336 Farmer (1,000-2,500)
RACHAELS, Hamp 51 m Ga
Sarah 37 f SC
Elizabeth 16 f Ala
Mary J. 15 f Ala
George D. 14 m "
(Cont.)

(Euf # 336 cont.)
James 13 m Ala
Effy A. 12 f "
Barwell 11 m "
Nancy 10 f "
Catharine 9 f "
Hamblin 8 m "
Daniel 7 m "
HARRELL, Henry 23 m Ga
(Laborer)

Euf # 1068 Farmer (21000-120,000)
RAIFORD, John M. 55 m SC

Luvl # 309
RAILEY, Hulda 17 f Ala
(See Wilson Collins).

Luvl # 249 Farmer (--- ---_
RAILEY, John W. 40 m Ga
Priscilla 37 f SC
(1500-3000)
HERRING, H. J. 15 f Ala
G. W. 13 m "
RAILEY, Ann C. 11 f "
John 8 m "
Tempe 6 f "
Walter 6/12 m "

Luvl # 307
RAILEY, Mary 16 f Ala
(See Tempe Hurst).

Clay # 39
RAILEY, Nancy 15 f Ala
Josephine 12 f "
(See M. Collins).

Clay # 91
RAINES, Elizabeth 24 f Ga
(See Thos. C. Schley).

Euf # 120 Tinner (500-2500)
RALEIGH, A. A. 35 m Ala
Harriet 26 f Ga
Arad L. 8 m Ala

Euf # 121 (1200-200)
RALEIGH, Elizabeth 61 f Va
Sarah (dress maker) 45 f Ga
Eliza " " 40 f Ala
John (Tinner) 25 m "

Euf # 264
RALEIGH, Thomas 4 m Ala
(See Phillip A. Sapp).

Euf # 450 Cabt. Maker (7000-8000)
RAMSER, Jacob 47 m Switz
Mary (Born Wertg.,) 36 f Ger
William T. 13 m Ga
Mary J. 11 f "
Paulina 10 f "
Frances B. 5 f Ala
Jacob S. 4 m "
Thomas T. 1 m "

Euf # 451 Daguerreotype artist (5;00-10,000)
RAMSER, Ursus 51 m Switz

Euf # 1401 Brickmason (--- 1200)
RAMSAY, A. J. 28 m Can
COLLINS, Thomas 29 m Ire
(Laborer)

Luvl # 384 Occp. none (--- ---)
RAMSEY, Joseph 60 m NC
Mary (?)19 f Ala
James (Farmer) 23 m "
Robert " 16 m "

Euf # 1388 Carpenter (--- 200)
RANDOLPH, John 25 m NC

Clay # 19
RAULS, Sallie A. 17 f NC
(Living in hotel).

Euf # 1163 Farmer (600-500)
RAY, Elijah 40 m Ala
Denita 35 f "
Thos. L. (In school) 16 m "
Susan E. 15 f "
Felix P. 14 m "
Joseph M. 12 m "
William W. 11 m "
Sullivan N. 9 m "
Japhet J. 7 m "
Willis H. 6 m "
Mary E. 4 f "
Moses 3 m "
Henry E. 1 m "

Mdwy # 1012 Physician (---7000)
RAY, J. C. 33 m Ga
Ann E. 29 f "
HENDERSON, W. I. 11 m Ala
(--- 3,500)
John C. (---3,500) 7 m "

Euf # 589 Farmer (1000-2500)
RAY, Manning 49 m Ky(?)
Hannah 45 f SC
(Cont.)

(Euf # 589 cont.)
Minerva 21 f Ala
James 16 m "
Cintha 14 f "
Joseph 9 m "
Mary 7 f "
John E. 6 m "
Lee A. 3 m "

Euf # 590 Farmer (200-400)
RAY, Stephen B. 25 m Ala
Miriam 26 f Ga
Robert 4 m "
William E. 3 m "
James M. 4/12 m "

Euf # 440 Stone cutter
READDY, Andrew 49 m Ire
(See McNamara's R.R. Gro.)

Euf # 697 Farmer (--- ---)
READER, Abijah 38 m SC
Mary E. 33 f "
Nancy 15 f "
William 13 m "
Daniel 11 m "
Sarah A. 8 f "
Clarky S. 6 f Ala
Marshall F. 3 m "
Matilda 1 f "

Euf # 1355 Farmer (4500-30,000)
REAVES, Asbur 61 m NC
Ellener C. 45 f Ga
Nancy 13 f Ala
Martha C. 11 f "
Narcissa E. 7 f "
Margaret 5 f "

Euf # 1359 Farmer (2000-1000)
REAVES, David S.(or L.) 38 m Ga
Mahala 36 f Ala
Thomas 15 m "
Cintha 12 f "
John 7 m "
Sally 4 f "
Wellborn 2 m "
Mary 8/12 f "
NICKOLS, Dougald 26 m "
(Laborer).

Euf # 1239 Farmer (8000-7000)
REAVES, H. F. 38 m Ga
Martha 36 f "
Columbus C.(Laborer) 18 m Ala
Walter M. " 17 m Ga
(Cont.)

(Euf # 1239 cont.)
Moses S. (Laborer) 16 m Ala
Julia 14 f "
Jane 12 f "
Minerva 11 f "
Frances 9 f "
Ada 8 f "
Emily 5 f "
John H. 2 m "

Nwto # 640 Farmer (12000-15000)
REDDING, R. C. 54 m Ga
Martha 40 f "
Charles 19 m "
(Merchant, 2,500)
Arthur 16 m "
Timothy 12 m "
Florella 9 f "
Elizabeth 7 f "
Lula 5 f "
Anna 3 f "
BIVIN(?), James F. 21 m "
(Planter, 3,000-12,000)
RICE, Sallie E. 29 f "
(Teacher, ---500)

Luvl # 641 Farmer (---6000)
REDDING, W. A. 22 m Ga
Rebecca 19 f "
Robert L. 2/12 m Ala

Euf # 213 Farmer (300-300)
REDMON, Charles 29 m SC
Elizabeth 23 f Ala
Emma C. 2 f "
Missilla 60 f SC

Euf # 417 Laborer (---200)
REDMON, Peter 36 m SC
Cintha 35 f "
Frances 12 f Ala
Mary A. 10 f "
Sarah 4 f "
Martha 6 f "
Caroline 10/12 f "

Euf # 564 (700-600)
REED, Jane 52 f SC
James H.(Farmer,1500-)26 m "
Caroline 16 f Ala
J. W. 14 m "
Margaret 90 f Ire

Mt. A. # 867 Farmer (1700-350)
REED, John N. 37 m Ga
Ellen 36 f "
Charlton 16 m "
Fredk. S. 15 m "
Robt. N. 12 m "
Mary F. 7 f "

Mt. A. # 868 Farmer(640-100).
REED, Walter 35 m Ga
Caroline 35 f "
Margaret A. 16 f "
John C. 14 m "
Elizabeth J. 12 f "
Mary C. 10 f "
Turner V. 8 m Ala
Jefferson 6 m "
Sarah 3 f "
James G. 4/12 m "

Euf # 532 Laborer
REEDY, James 19 m SC
(See John J. T. Hatfield)

Bkb # 743 Farm laborer
RENFROE, John 18 m Ala
(See Isaac H. Greathouse)

Flk # 480 Farmer (1000-200)
RENFROE, Peter 30 m Ala
Martha 28 f "
John 5 m "
Sarah E. 2 f "

Flk # 453 Farmer
RENFROE, Sampson 24 m Ala
(See William Sasser).

Flk # 481
RENFROE, Sarah 50 f Ga
Phillip 18 m Ala
Nathan 14 m "

Flk # 396 Physician & farmer (15,000-25,000)
REYNOLDS, John A. 41 m NC
Sarah E. 36 f "
Robert D. 15 m Ala
Mary J. 13 f "
John B. 9 m "
Amanda 3 f "
James 11/12 m "
(See G. W. Harrell).

Mdwy # 995 Shoemaker (---500)
REYNOLDS, O. S. 36 m SC
Antoinette 28 f Ga
Martha A. 11 f Ala
Sarah 6 f "
Jannett 7 f "
Mary 5 f "
R.I. 3 m "
John W. 1 m "
HENLEY, Mourning 60 f Ga

Euf # 854 Farmer (1000-100)
REYNOLDS, W. M 38 m Ga
Ellen 15 f Ala
Rebecca 11 f "
Laura 8 f "
Marietta 5 f "
John D. 1 m "

Euf # 307 Bank teller (3000-7000)
RHODES, C. 36 m Conn
Elizabeth 24 f Ga
C. L. 10/12 m Ala

Clay # 178
RHODES, Frances 6 f Ala
Thomas 8 m "
(In poorhouse).

Euf # 189 Wheel wright (---500)
RIALS, Owen 44 m Ga
Emily 43 f Fla
James (Laborer) 19 m Ala
Mary 16 f Ga
Emily 14 f "
William 8 m Ala
Richard W. 4 m "
KEYHOE, John 25 m Ire
(Stone mason ---500)

Euf # 587
RICCO, Jane 49 f SC
(See Johnathan Smith).

Euf # 1159
RICO, Nancy 14 f Ala
Malissa 20 f "
(See Elizabeth Smith)

Nwto # 640 School teacher (---500)
RICE, SALLIE E. 29 f Ga
(See R. C. Redding).

Euf # 42 Carpenter (--- ---)
RICHARDS, Edward 35 m Tenn
Elizabeth 30 f NC
John 6 m Tenn
William 3 m Ala
Julius 1 m "
TOWLER, W. W.(Laborer) 25 m Ga

Euf # 1153 Farmer (4000-5000)
RICHARDS, George W. 32 m Ala
Mary A. 27 f "
William 11 m "
Jane 9 f "
Sarah 7 f "
Robert 5 m "
John 1 m "

Euf # 601 Farmer (1200
3500)
RICHARDS, Giles W. 25 m Ala
Sarah A. 24 f Ga
Ava A. 4 f "
Lucy T.(?) 2/12 f "
PUNNELLS, Henry 18 m Ga
(Laborer).

Euf 607 Farmer (7000-
11,500)
RICHARDS, James 49 m SC
Louisa 52 f Ga
Nancy E. 20 f Ala
Matilda 18 f "
Wm. A. (Clerk) 17 m "
James L. 15 m "
Robert D. 13 m "
Andrew P. 11 m "

Euf # 815
RICHARDS, Mary 26 f NC
Jacob 10 m Ala

Euf # 608 Farmer (2000-7000)
RICHARDS, Matilda 54 f SC
James M. (Farmer) 21 m Ala
Louisa 19 f "
Thomas D. 15 m "
Robert 13 m "
Elizabeth C. 10 f "
(No. 2: ---100)

Euf # 223 (--- ---)
RICHARDS, Robert E. 26 m Ala
Thomas H. 2 m "

Euf # 222 Farmer (4000-22000)
RICHARDS, Thomas 61 m SC
Lucy 54 f Ga
Thos. (Med. student) 22 m Ala
Wm. W. (Farmer) 18 m "
Lucy A. 16 f "
Alonzo L. 12 m "

Luvl # 316 Farmer (3000-1900)
RICHARDS, Thomas W. 39 m Ala
Temperance 35 f SC
James M. 14 m Ala
William H. 12 m "
Thomas J. 9 m "
John Q. 7 m "
Mary J. 5 f "
Sarah 3 f "
Robert 2/12 m "
Robert J. 2 or 32 m "

Euf # 14-14 Clerk
RICHARDS, William 17 m Ala
(See E. C. Joice).

Euf # 1338 Farmer (12000-40000)
RICHARDSON, James W. 28 m Ga
Mary 19 f Fla
Ida 3 f Ala
James 1 m "
WILLIAMS, Ab 22 m "
(Overseer, ---800)

Euf # 1043
RICHARDSON, Jane 59 f Ga
(See LeRoy Upshaw).

Txv # 1126
RICHARDSON, Sarah F. 7 f Ala
(See Roderick McLeod)

Euf # 1086 Farmer (26,000-
55,000)
RICHARDSON, Walker 34 m Ga
Martha E. 21 f "
Sanford 1 m Ala

Clay # 121 Farmer (---150)
RICHARDSON, William 35 m Ga
Effie 32 f Ala
Frances 6 f "
Nancy 3 f "
Margaret 1 f "

Clay # 673 (600-800)
RIGDEN, Eliza 49 f Ga
William (Farmer) 21 m "
Benjamin " 16 m "
Elizabeth 15 f "
George 13 m Ala

Luvl # 366
RIGDON, John 18 m Ala
(See F. W. Eidson).

Euf # 1162 School teacher
RILEY, F. W. 45 m NY
Harriet 36 f SC

Euf # 173 Brick mason
RILEY, John 32 m Ire
(See John Bailey's Planters
Hotel)

Bkb 767 Farmer (300-200)
RILEY, Joseph 53 m Ga
Temperance 47 f "
M. F. 23 f "
Leonora 20 f "
(Cont.)

(Bkb # 767 cont.)
Caroline 19 f Ga
L.E. 17 f Ala
Alafair 15 f "
Lucy A. 11 f "
Ansoline 9 f "
Josephine 6 f "

Euf # 979 Farmer (---7,000)
RIVERS, A. A. 25 m Ga

Clay # 19 Gentlemen
RIVERS, Ervin 34 m Ga
(Living in hotel).

Euf # 1045 Farmer (20,000-45,000)
RIVERS, John F. 42 m Ga
Sarah F. 35 f "
Edward W. H. 7 m Ala
Charles E. 2 m "

Euf # 907 Occp. none (-- --)
RIVERS, Robert 60 m Ga
Susan 60 f SC

Euf # 1341 Farmer (23,000-12,000)
RIVERS, T. H. B. 49 m Ga
Anna D. 44 f "
Thos. T. (Student) 20 m "
Sarah T. 17 f "
Caroline V. 15 f "
Fannie D. 11 f "
Eugene R. 6 m "
Acey M. 4 f Ala
GLENN, D. V. 27 m SC
Rebecca C. 23 f "

Euf # 978 Occp. none (6000-17,000)
RIVERS, Thomas 83 m Va
Mary 68 f "
William 39 m Ga
(Occp. none, ---11,000)
McGUIRE, Ann 28 f "
(---5,000)
William 5 m Ala
Laura 3 f "

Euf # 513 Overseer
ROACH, Nathaniel, Jr. 22 m NC
(See Edmund Dillard).

Euf 15-15 Sur. Dentist 700-4,000)
ROBERSON, James T. 24 m Ga
(Cont.)

(Euf # 15-15 cont.)
Susan 25 f Ga
Homer 1 m "
Sylvanius 28 m "
(Sur. Dentist, --- $2,000)

Euf # 795 Overseer
ROBERSON, William 22 m Ga
(See Wilson H. Sterns.)

Euf # 1389 Apprentice Printer
ROBERTS, Andrew J. 19 m Ga
(See John Black)

Euf # 725 Farmer (3000-300)
ROBERTS, Bryant 40 m Ga
Martha 41 f "
Lydia A. 14 f "
William J. 12 m "
Susan F. 9 f "
Bytha A. 8/12 f Ala
JONES, Sarah C. 15 f "
Solomon D. 14 m "
Mary S. 11 f "
Henry H. 9 m "
Newton J. 8 m "
George W. 5 m "

Euf 235 Trader (8000-13000)
ROBERTS, G. A. 34 m Va
Ann A. 34 f Ga
Anna 12 f Ala
Noah W. 9 m "
M. Stow 2 m "
William W. 2/12 m "
Eliza J. (--- 8000) 55 f Va

Euf # 664 Farmer (3300-850)
ROBERTS, Henry 40 m Ga
Margaret 37 f SC
James N. 15 m Ga
Nancy 13 f "
Thomas 11 m "
William U.(?),(W.?) 9 m "
Green 6 m "
Perry 4 m "
Elizabeth 1 f Ala

Luvl # 361
ROBERTS, Lavinia 9 f Ala
(See William R. Cowan)

Clay # 215
ROBERTS, Sarah 16 f Ala
(See John Runnels)

Euf # 914
ROBERTS, Sarah L. 35 f Ga
(Cont.)

(Euf # 914 Cont.)
CARR, James 16 m Ala
(Hireling)
ROBERTS, Catharine 12 f "

Bkb # 690 Mechanic (1500-500)
ROBERTS, Snowden B. 32 m Ga
Elizabeth 28 f "
James L. 8 m Ala
Mary L. 6 f "
A. M. 4 m "
SCROGGINS, Americus 18 f Ga

Flk # 501 Farmer (1200-500)
ROBERTS, Thos. H. 28 m Va
Ann E. (--- 2,000) 25 f Fla
Mary E. 6 f Ala
Robert A. 4 m "

Euf # 274 Cabt. maker (---100)
ROBERTS, Wiley 48 m Fla
Sarah 30 f Ga
Margarite 10 f Ala
Mary 8 f "
Harriett 3 f "

Luvl # 365
ROBERTS, William 14 m Ala
(See John Flournoy)

Euf # 1061 Merchant (800-500)
ROBERTSON, W. W. 37 m Ga

Euf # 497 Farmer (---125)
ROBINSON, Alexr., Sr. 68 m NC
Eliza 43 f Ga
Eady 39 f "
Nancy 32 f "
Erasmus (Farm hand) 19 m "
John T. " " 17 m "
Britton M. 14 m Ala
Serena 12 f "
Roxana M. 4 f "
Sophia 3 f "
Queen V. 3 f "
LUNSFORD, Thos. P. 22 m Ga
(Occp. - none).
ROBINSON, Narcissa 16 f "
James O. 11 m Ala

Nwto # 614 Farmer (500-150)
ROBINSON, John J. 25 m Ga
Emeline 19 f "

Euf # 1360 Negro Trader (---10,000)
ROBINSON, John R. 56 m NC
(Cont.)

(Euf # 1360 cont.)
Frances C. 40 f Ga
Sarah E. 19 f "

Euf # 704
ROBINSON, Mary 3 f Ala
(See Jacob Haigler).

Euf # 19-19 Sheriff Barbour Co. (10,000-17,000)
ROBINSON, Thomas 47 m NC
Cornelia 20 f Ala
Chas. C. (Student) 18 m "
William F. 16 m "
(Student U.S. Naval Academy)
Antonette 15 f "
Margarette 13 f "
Sarah 11 f "
McDOWELL, James 25 m Ga
(Printer)

Euf # 173 Carriage painter
RODREGUS, George 43 m Va
(See Jno. Bailey, Planters Hotel)

Euf # 505 Farmer (---11,000)
ROGERS, James 40 m Ga
Susan 26 f "
LOFLIN, Thomas 32 m "
Farmer, ---150)
Eliza 24 f "
James M. 11 m Ala
Sarah T. 1 f "
T. Nelson 11 m "

Euf # 217 Laborer
ROGERS, Sidney 15 m Ala
(See Elijah Nolin)

Euf # 696 (---100)
ROLAND, Sarah 27 f Ga
Susan 61 f SC
(See Nathan Walker)

Nwto # 553
ROLLIN, George 55 m NC
Betsy 55 f "
Cater 35 m Ala
(See A. C. Thompson).

Euf 818 Farmer (2,000-500)
ROLLINS, G. W. 39 m SC
Elizabeth 31 f "
Joanna 13 f "
Hixon 11 m "
Franklin 9 m Ala
Josephine 7 f "
(Cont.)

(Euf # 818 cont.)
Judge 6 m Ala
George 4 m "
Jane 2 f "

Luvl # 361
ROLLINS, John R. 16 m Ga
(See William R. Cowan).

Euf # 10-10 Clerk (--5000)
RONEY, William N. 22 m Ala
(See Geo. W. Porter).

Euf # 440 Quarryman
ROONEY, Nicholas 34 m Ire
Amelia 29 f Ga
(See McNamara's R.R. Gro.)

Euf # 510 Farmer (----8,500)
ROQUEMORE, James A. 24 m Ga
HARPER, H. H. 22 m "
(Overseer)
Vicey 18 f "

Euf 1122 Farmer (4200-18000)
ROQUEMORE, John P. 40 m Ga
Martha C. 43 f "
ARNOLD, Sallie 17 f "

Euf # 782 Farmer (37,500-82,000)
ROQUEMORE, Thos. A. 44 m Ga
Eliza W. 42 f SC
Watsonia C. 16 f Ala
Eliza J. 14 f "
Leonora R. 12 f "
John W. 9 m "
STOVALL, Mary 19 f "
McKINNEY, Henry 14 m "
WILSON, A. J. 27 m Va
(Physician, ---2500)
Mary 32 f "
GLENN, John S. 46 m SC
(Farmer)

Euf # 508 Farmer (25,000-55,000)
ROQUEMORE, Zach 50 m Ga
Julia A. 42 f "
Charles (Occp. none) 20 m Ala
John 13 m "

Euf # 988
ROSE, Mary 9 f Ga
(See H. G. Spears)

Clay # 19 Clerk Born Hessen, Ger.
ROSENBERRY, M. 16 m Ger
(Living in hotel).

Mdwy # 987 Carriage maker (---- 7,800)
ROSS, James 34 m Fr
(Born Isle of France)
Sarah 26 f Ga
Alice M. 6 f Ala
Ida W. 4 f "
Charles R. 2 m "

Euf # 170 Clerk
ROSS, John 20 m Ga
(See Wm. D. Hailey)

Euf # 1134 P.B. Minister (700-200)
ROSS, William 50 m Ga
Isabella 39 f "
D.A.P.J. 17 f "
F.K.M. 12 m "
F.J.T. 10 f Ala
M.L.B. 8 f "
C.C.E. 5 f "
C.M.J.L. 1 m "

Euf # 1052 Silversmith
ROUNDTREE, B. F. 23 m Ga
(See H. E. Jones).

Mt. A. # 827 Farmer (---2600)
ROUSE, Allen J. 22 m Ala
Julia A. 26 f SC

Flk # 432 Farmer (400-150)
ROUSE, John 30 m NC
Frances 28 f Ga
Sarah E. 12 f "
Amena 8 f "
James 7 m "
John 7 m "
Nathan 5 m "
Catherine 4 f "
Marion 3 m Ala
Martin 5/12 m "

Mt. A. # 829 Farmer (---250)
ROUSE, Louis, Jr. 39 m NC
Mary A. 23 f SC
Henry L. 14 m Ala
M.A. 13 f "
John 10 m "
Joseph 8 m "
William 3 m "

Mt. A. # 828 Farmer (4400-16,000)
ROUSE, Louis J., Sr. 70 m NC
Irvin 20 m Ala
(Farmer, ---6,000)
(Cont.)

(Mt. A. # 828 cont.)
Matilda 21 f Ga
Elizabeth 2 f Ala
Josephine 6/12 f "
(----2,000)

Mt. A. 830 Farmer (2000-2000)
ROUSE, Thomas 29 m NC
D.O. 31 f Ga
Robert J. 6 m Ala
Louis I. (or J.) 4 m "
C.B. 2 f "
William H. 2/12 m "

Mt. A. # 809 Planter (29,000-52,000)
RUMPH, J. D. Sr. 48 m SC
Christian W. 16 f "
L. L. 14 m "
M. M. 13 f "
James D., Jr. 12 m "
John M. 10 m "
C. E. 7 f "
A. E. 5 f Ala
L. D. (--- 700) 24 m SC

Euf. # 601 Laborer
RUNNELLS, Henry 18 m Ga
(See Giles W. Richards)

Clay # 215 Carpenter (--- ---)
RUNNELLS, John 36 m Ga
Sarah 26 f "
George A. 11 m "
James 8 m "
William 5 m "
Susan 2 f Ala
ROBERTS, Sarah 16 f "

Flk # 493 Farmer
RUNNELS, John A. 23 m Ga
(See A. W. Faulk).

Flk # 434 Farmer (1200-1800)
RUSH, Benj. G. 27 m NC
Catherine 28 f "
Harrison K. (Farmer) 19 m "
John R. " 17 m "

Mdwy # 1064 Overseer (---450)
RUSHING, George W. 25 m Ga

Euf # 245 Carpenter
RUSSEAU, William 20 m Ga
(See Jasper J. Sawyers).

Euf 178 Trader
RUSSELL, George W. 28 m NC
(Cont.)

(Euf # 178 cont.)
H. C. (Marble dealer) 33 m NC
(See James Tansey)

Clay # 19 Clerk
RUSSELL, J. R. 17 m Ala
(Living in hotel).

Euf # 8-8 Clerk
RUSSELL, James H. H. 19 m Ala
(See James M. Espy)

Mt. A. # 919 Planter (13835-45000)
RUSSELL, Joseph C. 47 m NC
Mary A. 46 f "
George W. 23 m Ala
Helen 16 f "
Emma A. 13 f "
Joanna 11 f "
BEVERLY, Ann E. 18 f NC
(School teacher).

Clay # 154
RUSSELL, Mary A. 70 f NC
(See Thos. A. Hightower).

Clay # 234 Farmer (1000-1000)
RUSSELL, W. K. O. 25 m NC
Fanny L. 19 f Ga
Sally 1 f Ala

Mt. A. 923 Overseer (---500)
RUSSELL, William H. 23 m Ga
M.F. 21 f NC
Ellen 3 f Ala
infant 4/12 m "
Usanley 45 f NC
Lucius A. 14 m Ala

Luvl # 346 Farmer
RUSSELL, William J. 21 m Ga
(See E. M. King)

Mt. A. # 922 Overseer (---12,000)
RUSSELL, William M. 43 m NC
Mary J. 23 f Ga
Emeline 9 f Ala
William T. 7 m "
Catherine 6 f "
Georgia A. 4 f "
Mary J. 2 f "
Morgan S. 5/12 m "

Euf # 422 Laborer (--- ---)
RUTLEDGE, James 30 m Ire
Ellen 24 f Md
Hurley, John 12 m "

Clay # 147 Farmer (1200-500)
RUTLIN, Reddin 61 m SC
C.H. 39 f Ga
Emanuel (Farmer) 22 m Ala
William W. " 18 m "
James R. " 16 m "
Moses H. " 15 m "
G.(L.?) T. 13 m "
Sarah M. 11 f "
Thomas E. 3 m "

Euf # 1206 Farmer (2500-28000)
RYAN, Hampton 63 m Ga
Susan 35 f SC
John M. 5 m Ala
Emily C. 4 f "
SEALBOTTOMS, Jno. W. 22 m SC
(Hireling).

Euf # 429 Laborer (--- ---)
RYAN, Michael (?) 22 m Ire
Bridget 66 f "
Michael (Laborer) 22 m "
Agnes 14 f Scot
Mary 9 f Ohio

Euf # 427 Laborer (--- ---)
Ryan, Patrick 43 m Ire
Rose 37 f "
Mary 7 f SC
Bridget 5 f "

Euf # 184 Machinist
RYAN, Patrick I. 26 m Ire
(See Chas. P. Smith)

Euf # 428 Laborer (--- ---)
RYAN, Peter 33 m Ire
Jane (20 or) 26 f "
Thomas 3 m SC
Mary R. 8/12 f Ga

Euf # 907 Overseer (---7000)
RYAN, R. B. 38 m Ala
Malinda 27 f SC
John 6 m Ala
James 5 m "
Mary 3 f "
William 2 m "

Euf # 295 Blacksmith (--- ---)
RYAN, Roderick 49 m NC

Mt. A. # 876 Farmer (960-400)
SALMAN, Green 33 m Ga
Jno. (Farmer,--100) 23 m "
Julia 25 f "
(Cont.)

(Mt. A. # 876 cont).
Jane 20 f Ga
McMILLAN, Tempe A. 30 f "
(---150)
Mary 11 f "
Sarah 8 f "
James 6 m "
John 3 m Ala

Euf #582 Farmer (400-150)
SAMPLER, Samuel J. 23 m Ga
Anna 18 f "

Euf # 441 Tailor
SANDERS, Mr. 23 m Ger
(See Mary H. Lowman)

Euf # 315 Overseer (--- ---)
SANDERS, C. M. 29 m Ga

Euf # 272 Overseer (---2,000)
SANDERS, James R. 33 m Ga
Susannah A. 20 f "
Emma K. 2 f "
Nancy 1 f Ala

Mdwy # 1043 Overseer (---1000)
SANDERS, John A. 30 m Ga
Jane 22 f Ala

Euf # 729 Laborer
SANDERS, John L. 18 m SC
(See Julia Watty).

Euf # 903
SANDERS, Mary J. 15 f Ala
(See Eliza J. Lowman).

Euf # 123 Laborer (--- 45)
SANDERS, Moses 29 m SC
Debora 25 f "
Elizabeth 7 f "
Mary J. 5 f "
Joannah 3 f Ala
Thomas 7/12 m "

Euf # 984 Wheel wright (---200)
SANDERS, Phillip 51 m Va
Eliza 35 f Ga
Frances 16 f Ala
Virginia 12 f "
William 10 m "
Cornelius G. 8 m "
Charles H. 6 m "
John H. 6/12 m "

Euf # 985 Wheel wright (---2150)
SANDERS, Reubin 46 m Va
Rebecca 15 f Ala

Euf # 1280 Hireling
SANDIFER, Robert 56 m SC
Elizabeth 34 f "
MURDOCK, James H. 21 m "
(Hireling)

Euf # 250 Master carpenter (3,000-1,000)
SANDIFORD, Sanuel 45 m (Washington, D. C.)
Martha 39 f Ga
Emma 14 f Ala
ANDERSON, Charles 10 m
(Born Washington, D. C.)

Euf # 1085 (44,000-176,000)
SANFORD, Sophia M. 39 f Ga

Euf # 264 Farmer (3000-54000)
SAPP, Phillip A. 27 m Ga
Julia 26 f SC
RALEIGH, Thomas 4 m Ala

Euf # 563
SAPP, William 19 m Ga
(See Thos. S. Smart)

Luvl # 547 Farmer (600-350)
SASSER, John 74 m Ga
Rebecca 68 f "
GARRIS, Elizabeth 35 f Ala
Brittain 17 m "
Elizabeth 11 f "
DANIEL, Jane 18 f "
Jane E 4/12 f "
Martha 15 f "

Flk # 450 Farmer (1500-1000)
SASSER, S. D. 45 m Ga
Elizabeth J. 37 f NC
Jacob F. 13 m Ala
Sarah A. 9 f "
Julia F. 8 f "
Mary J. 6 f "

Flk # 453 Farmer (1200-500)
SASSER, William 36 m Ala
Martha M. 36 f "
Joseph G. 12 m "
Epsey D. 8 f "
Martha E. 2/12 f "
RENFROE, Sampson 24 m "
(Farmer)

Nwto #
SAUCER, Joseph 22 m Ala
Louisiana 17 f "
(Married in April).

Nwto
SAUCER, Martha 60 f NC
Della 25 f Ala

Bkb # 789 Farmer (600-200)
SAULS, John 20 m Ala
S.A. 14 f "
(Married within the year).

Euf # 931 Farmer (24000-10000)
SAULSBERY, Joseph A. 48 m Ga
Sarah M. 43 f SC
Francis A. 15 m Ala
Laura E. 14 f "
Rosana 12 f "
Sarah A. 9 f "
Henrietta S. 6 f "
Levi R. 4 m "

Clay # 157 Farmer (3000-6000)
SAUNDERS, Andrew 59 m SC
Nancy J. 28 f Ga
F.C. 6 m Ala
G. V. 5 f "
S.P. 3 f "
A.W.J. 8/12 m "

Txv # 1196 (---100)
SAUNDERS, Catherine 34 f SC
Martha 12 f Ala
John 10 m "
William C. 9 m "
Rachael M. 7 f "
Mary V. 6 f "
James 3/12 m "

Clay # 60 Mechanic (--- ---)
SAUNDERS, James 32 m Ga
Mary 32 f "

Clay # 156 Farmer (2000-4000)
SAUNDERS, S. P. 35 m SC
Margaret 30 f NC
Elizabeth 6 f Ala
SPENCE, James 20 m "
(Laborer on farm).

Luvl # 327 Farmer (300-100)
SAUNDERS, Thomas 50 m SC
Sarah 52 f "
Patsy 21 f "
John S. (Farmer) 19 m "
Samuel 14 m "
Sarah R. 12 f Ga

Euf # 245 Carpenter (--- ---)
SAWYERS, Jasper J. 32 m Ga
(Cont.)

(Euf # 245 cont.)
Emily R. 23 f Ala
Mary A. 7 f "
Joseph E. 6 m "
Walker W. 2 m "
James M. M. 4/12 m "
RUSSEAU, William 20 m Ga
(Carpenter)

Euf # 527 Carpenter (400-100)
SAWYERS, Joshua 25 m Ga
Letty 25 f "
Mary A. 4 f Ala
BECK, Samuel 7 m "

Euf # 438 Occp. none (--- ---)
SAWYER, Kindred 42 m SC
Susan 40 f Ga
William 15 m "
Greenbery 14 m "
Maxey 11 m "
Josiah 5 m "
Mary E. 1 f "

Mt. A. # 813 Farmer (---300)
SCARBROUGH, Hardy F. 28 m Ga
Melvina 25 f "
George 6 m Ala
Charles 4 m "
Mary L. 2 f "

Mt. A. # 842 Farmer (2000-16,000)
SCARBOROUGH, James A. 50 m SC
Mary A. 48 f NC
John F. 20 m Ga
Louisa 17 f "
Susan 16 f Ala
Sarah 15 f "
Mary 10 f "
DASHER, Thomas 18 m Ga
(Farmer).

Clay # 91 Overseer (--- ---)
SCHLEY, Thomas C. 34 m SC
Emeline 26 f Ga
RAINES, Elizabeth 24 f "
SCHLEY, Hiram M. 6 m Ala
Susan 2 f "

Euf # 113 Merchant (---20000)
SCHWARZ, Lewis 39 m Ger
(Born Wertemburg, Germany).

Euf # 237 (--- 300)
SCOTT, Frances 38 f Ga
(Cont.)

(Euf # 237 cont.)
William 13 m Ga
Sarry (?) 10 f "
Missouri 7 f Ala

Euf # 339 Farmer (750-600)
SCOTT, James N. 53 m NC
Martha 56 f Va
Mary E. 21 f Tenn

Euf # 325 Laborer (---100)
SCOTT, James P. 30 m SC
Matilda 23 f Ga
Ann E. 5 f Ala
George F. 4 m "
James L. 3 m "
EVERETT, R. E. 10 m "
Jane 6 f Ala

Euf # 1087 Overseer (---600)
SCOTT, John P. 26 m SC
Mary E. 20 f Ga
Corine A. 5/12 f Ala

Mdwy # 1013
SCOTT, Rosa 12 f Ala
Susan 9 f "
(See Sarah Abbet).

Euf # 784 Overseer (---100)
SCOTT, Simon S. 25 m Ga
Mary 20 f "
Emma 7/12 f "

Euf # 1076 Occp. none (1,200-25,000)
SCREWS, Clarisa H. 45 f NC
Melanshthon (Student) 19 m Miss
William 16 m "
Edward H. 14 m "
James 12 m Mass?
Porter J. 8 m "
John R. 6 m "

Euf # 1345 Farmer (-- ---)
SCREWS, Henry O. 38 m NC
Angeline 30 f SC
Jesse 6 m Ala
Henry 1 m "
(See Elizabeth Glenn).

Clay # 19 Proprietress of hotel (6,000-4,000)
SCREWS, M. J. 41 f NC
M.E.(Music teacher) 18 f Ala
B.H. (Appt. clerk) 17 m "
McNAIR, D. P. 26 m NC
(Teacher)
(Cont.)

(Clay # 19 cont.)
C.A. 21 f NC
RAULS, Sallie A. 17 f "
TARVER, J. F. M. 22 m Ala
(Law student)
FLERSHIEM, S. 26 m Ger
(Merchant, ---4000, Born Hessen, Germany)
ROSENBURG, M. 16 m Ger
(Clerk, Born Hessen, Ger.)
RIVES, Irvin 34 m Ga
(Gentlemen, ---11500)
McCARTY, Elias 28 m Ga
(Clerk in grocery,---600).
BARTLETT, D. D. 24 m SC
(Harness maker)
COLEMAN, John L. 25 m Ga
(Druggist, ---15000)
MULLEN, W. T. 26 m "
(Bookkeeper).
WARREN, Monroe 22 m Ala
(Doctor, 1000-5000)
WILLIAMS, Stephen L. 28 m "
(Bookeeper)
RUSSELL, J. R. 17 m "
(Clerk)
BARKSDALE, H. M. 21 m "
(Law student)
PENNEGER, F. 40 m Ger
(Born Breman, Germany)
VAN HOUTEN, E. 32 m NY
(Tinsmith, ---500)
HAMILTON, J. S. 31 m Md
(Painter, ---300)

O'HARA, Edward 23 m Ire
(Blacksmith, born Lemerech).
WELSH, John B. 30 m Ire
(Carriage maker)
ELGEA, James A. 24 m NJ
(Carriage maker)
KILPATRICK, T. A. 26 m Ala
(Stable clerk,----800)

Bkb # 690
SCROGGINS, Americus 18 f Ga
(See Snowden B. Roberts)

Bkb # 687 Farmer (1500-2500)
SCROGGINS, Geo. R. 37 m Ga
Elizabeth 39 f "
HERON, Richard 20 m Ala
(Farmer)
McNAIR, John 32 m NC
(Farm laborer)
(Cont.)

(Bkb # 687 cont.)
Elizabeth 13 f Ala
Susan 10 f "
Malinda 6 f "
SIMMS, Amy 50 f SC

Txv # 1168 Farmer (200-150)
SCOGGINS, Griffin 50 m Ga
Martha 45 f SC
Martha 18 f Ala
Jerry 16 m "
Nancy 14 f "
Humphrey 13 m "
Jasper 6 m "
Mary 6 f "

Luvl # 509 Farmer (400---)
SCROGGINS, Grissom 48 m Ga
Elizabeth 35 f "
Sarah A. 14 f Ala
Susan C. 12 f "
George L. 13 m "
John G. 8 m Ga
William H. 6 m Ala
Andrew J. 1/12 m "

Nwto # 550 Farm laborer (2500-200)
SCROGGINS, H. L. 24 m SC
E.J. 24 f "
John C. 2 m Ala
Easther P. 1 f "

Flk # 498 Farmer (1200---)
SCROGGINS, Henry L. 25 m SC
Elizabeth J. 24 f "
John C. 3 m Ala
Easther P. 1 f "

Luvl # 520 (300-75)
SCROGGINS, James 70 m Ga
Judy 67 f "

Flk # 414 Farmer (--- ---)
SCROGGINS, James A. 34 m SC
Elizabeth 28 f Ga
Blanton 8 m "
John 6 m "
Joseph J. 3 m Ala
James R. 1 m "
SHEPPARD, Elizabeth 50 f Ga
Mary A. 30 f "
Julia N. 20 f "

Luvl # 519 Farmer (200-100)
SCROGGINS, James E. 29 m Ga
Ann E. 21 f Ala
John M. 3 m "
James I. 1 m "

Flk # 452 Mechanic 54 m SC
Julia A. 29 f Ga
Melvina 19 f "
Narcissa 16 f "
Westley 14 m "
Georgia A. 6 f "
Mary 3 "

Luvl # 521 Blacksmith (-- --)
SCROGGINS, Snowden 24 m Ga
M.F. 21 f Ala
C.A. 4/12 m "

Luvl # 291 Farmer
SCROGGINS, Thos, G. 17 m Ala
(See R. G. Jackson)

Luvl # 518 Farmer (400-80)
SCROGGINS, W. C. 46 m Ga
Harriett 55 f "
THOMAS, Elizabeth 20 f "
SCROGGINS, Americus 16 f "
William H. 14 m "
Antoniette 9 f "
THOMAS, Gerogia A. 1 f Ala

Clay # 25
SEABROOK, M. J. 16 f Ala
(See William S. Pope).

Euf # 1206 Hireling
SEALBOTTOMS, John W. 22 m SC
(See Hampton Ryan).

Clay # 24 Lawyer & Planter
(20,000-50,000)
SEALS, D. M. 40 m Ga
E.A. 30 f "
W.A. 14 m Ala
Henry B. 10 m "
Martha J. 6 f "
C.B. 5 m "

Luvl # 273 Farmer (1200-1500)
SEALS, John D. 43 m Ga
Eveline 18 f Ala
Warren D. 18 m "
Laura J. 15 f "
Mary A. 13 f "
Martha A. 11 f "
Amanda L. 9 f "
Endora 7 f "
Emma S. 5 f "
William H. 3/12 m "
DAY, Henry 23 m Ala
(Farmer, ---400)
(Cont.)

(Luvl # 273 cont.)
Ann F. 20 f Ala
infant 3/12 m "

Euf # 959 Farmer (---12,000)
SEAY, C. 35 m Ga
SEAY, Vann (Farmer) 25 m "

Euf # 597 Farmer (800-400)
SEARCY, John G. 25 m NC
Catherine 22 f Ala
Green A. 7 m "
PINKSTON, Catharine 78 f Ga
(--- 5,000)
SEARCY, James W. 28 m NC
(Farmer, 650-295)
Mahala 19 f Ala
Louisa 3 f "
Young L. 5/12 m "
BECK, Millard 10 m "

Euf # 609 Laborer (-- --)
SEARCY, King 20 m Ga
(See Wright Flowers)

Euf # 598 Laborer (--- 100)
SEARCY, Westley 24 m Ga
Calista 22 f Ala

Mt. A. # 792 Farmer (600-300)
SEAY, H. M. 56 m SC
Ann W. 53 f "
Maria 17 f Ala
Henry C. 16 m "
Zach 14 m "
William T. 8 m "

Mdwy # 1021 (--- 50,000)
SEAY, Harriett M. 15 f Ala
Caroline G.(---50,000) 13 f "
(See R. D. Thornton).

Mdwy # 1050 Overseer (--- ---)
SEAY, John 22 or 27 m Ala
(See A. E. Bass)

Mdwy # 925 Planter (20,000-
41,000)
SEAY, John W. 27 m Ga
James McCormick(?) 31 m Ire
A.R. 23 f Ga
Ann E. 4 f Ala
Sarah A. 2 f "
John W. 1 m "
Benjamin F. 19 m "
(15,000-41000).

Mdwy # 1023 Farmer (1600-15000)
SEAY, Monroe 37 m SC
Emily 30 f Ga
Sarah E. 9 f Ala
Henry 5 m "
William 3 m "
Harley 6/12 m "

Nwto # 551
SEGARS, Martha A. 23 f NC
(See Neill McKeller).

Luvl # 544 Farmer 500-220)
SEGARS, S. B. 26 m Ga
M.A. 14 f "
James W. 8 m Ala
Sarah 29 f "

Clay # 90 Carpenter
SEGLER, E. C. 36 m SC
Mary J. 23 f Ala
(Married within the year).

Euf # 111 Physician (600-400)
SEGLER, T. F. 29 m Ga
Rebecca 60 f SC
Silas (farm hand) 21 m Ga
Matilda A. 12 f "
GARDENER, John 10 m --
Benjamin 7 m --

Bkb # 759 (---150)
SELF, Mary 41 f Ga
George (Farmer) 22 m Ala
William 17 m "
Chapel 14 m "

Euf # 566
SELLERS, Jane 60 f SC
(See James Stanton).

Euf # 1248 Farmer (800-200)
SENN, Lemuel 56 m SC
Mary 54 f "
Henry (Farm hand) 23 m "
David " " 18 m "
Frances 16 f "
Mary 14 f Ala
Rachael 12 f "
James 5 m "
Margaret 4 f Ga

Nwto # 562
SHANKS, James T. 4 m Ala
(See James Davis)

Nwto # 598
SHANKS, James T. 4 m Ala
(See James K. Turner).

Flk # 430 Farmer (--- ---)
SHAW, Flora A. 38 f Ala
John 19 m "
Alexander 14 m "
Catherine 11 f "
Margery A. 9 f "
Peyton 7 m "
Frances 1 f "
LUDLOW, Wiley 20 m "
(Farmer)

Euf # 569 Ditcher (--- 400)
SHEHAN, Daniel 46 m Ire
Martha (2000-200) 46 f Ga
Catherine 17 f Ala
Merill 15 m "
William 14 m "
Daniel 12 m Ga
Robert 10 m "
Eugene 7 m Ala
CREYON, James(Laborer) 20 m "
JONES, John " 20 m SC

Nwto # 582 Farmer (1200-1000)
SHEHANE, Daniel 43 m SC
Mary 52 f Scot
(Born Isle of Skye, Scotland).
Donald (Farmer) 19 m Ga

Nwto # 583
SHEHANE, William M.C. 21 m Ga
(See R. P. Andrews)

Mt. A. # 877 Farmer (1000-800)
SHELBY, Calvin 38 m NC
Emeline 31 f Ala
John W. 12 m "
James W. 7 m "
Jesse Fox 4 m "
Lawson 1 m "

Mt. A. # 846 Farmer (2000-300)
SHELBY, James W. 30 m Ga
Nancy 23 f "
Louisa 5 f Ala
Moses F. 3 m "
Harriett 9/12 f "

Mt. A. # 902 Farmer (---250)
SHELBY, Kelly 28 m Ga
Adeline 15 f Ala
William J. 5/12 m "

Mt. A. 915 Farmer (1000-2000)
SHELBY, Moses 65 m NC
Harriett 60 f "
William T. 20 m Ga
HAIGLER, Washington 33 m NC
PARKER, West 22 m Ga
(Laborer in brick yard).
POPE, Manson 23 m "
(Laborer in brick yard).

Mt. A. # 837 Overseer
SHELBY, Uzial 27 m Ga
(See Cater A. Parker, Sr.)

Euf # 196 Physician (2500-10,000)
SHEPHERD, Edmund 69 m NJ
William P. 38 m "

Euf # 683 (400-150)
SHEPHERD, Jane 60 f Ga
Henry (Farm hand) 18 m "
Josephine 16 f Ala

Euf # 701 Farmer (1000-400)
SHEPHERD, Thomas 39 m Ala
Margaret 34 f SC
Nancy 14 f Ala
Matthew A. 12 m "
Thomas M. 10 m "
James W. (idiot) 7 m "
Mary 5 f "
David 2 m "
Amanda 2/12 f "
COX, John (Laborer) 16 m "

Euf # 684 Farmer (---250)
SHEPHERD, William 30 m Ga
Rachael 17 f "

Euf # 706 Laborer (150-125)
SHEPPERD, Charles 45 m Ga
Sarah J. 36 f "
Thos. J. (Laborer) 18 m Ala
Rebecca J. 12 f "
Jackson 14 m "
Henry T. 10 m "
Charles 8 m "
Susan C. 6 f "
William H. 3 m "

Flk # 414
SHEPPARD, Elizabeth 50 f Ga
Mary A. 30 f "
Julia N. 20 f "
(See James A. Scroggins).

Luvl # 341 Farmer
SHEPPARD, G. T. 18 m Ga
(See Mary McDonald).

Euf # 777 Farmer (800-300)
SHEPPERD, Oliver 24 m Ga
Georgia 21 f "
Jennett 3 f Ala
Green 1 m "

Mt. A. 815
SHEPPARD, R. A. 37 f NC
Nancy A. 7 f Ala
Martha B. 34 f NC
Easther P. 27 f "
(See Joel J. Parker).

Euf # 707 Farmer (1000-400)
SHEPPHERD, Thos., Sr. 59 m Ga
Emily 45 f "
Elizabeth 25 f Ala
Benj. P. (Farm hand) 18 m "
Sarah 13 f "
Arvena 12 f "

Clay # 666
SHEPPARD, Wm. Harriett 4 f Ala
(See G. W. Cooper)

Euf 516 Farmer (---5500)
SHERMAN, E. T. 48 m Va
Louisa M. 44 f Ga
Rebecca 18 f "
Martha A. 9 f Ala
George 8 m "
Sarah 7 f "
Julia 5 f "
CONNER, William 19 m "
(Laborer)
Louisa 17 f "
Sophronia 14 f "
George 10 m "

Mdwy # 990 Carriage trimmer (---1000)
SHEILDS, M. C. 48 m Ga
Rebecca A. 40 f "
Susan E. 19 f "
Julia 14 f "
Catherine E. 10 f "
Mary J. 8 f Ala

Euf # 655 Farmer (3000-7300)
SHIPES, Andrew 48 m SC
Christina 48 f "
Nathan 24 m "
(Farmer, ---1,000)
(Cont.)

(Euf # 655 cont.)
Josephine 16 f Ala
William 16 m "
(Farm Hand)

Euf # 694 Farmer (--- 300)
SHIPES, J. W. 21 m Ala
Sarah 19 f "
Martha E. 1/12 f "
OLIVER, Mahala 50 f SC
(600----)

Luvl # 541 Farmer (2500-500)
SHIPMAN, Alexander 40 m NC
Mary M. 44 f "
Sarah E. 18 f Ala
Ann E. 16 f "
John 14 m "
James 13 m "
Alexander 11 m "
Louis 9 m "
Mary 7 f "
Mandy 6 f "
Lucy 4 f "

Clay # 655 (3,000-3,000)
SHIPMAN, Elizabeth 63 f NC
James L. 40 m Ala
Eluiza 32 f "
F. B. 22 m "
LAMPLEY, Catherine 43 f NC
L. J. 14 m Ala
Laura 12 f "
Caleb 8 m "
Edward 4 m "

Luvl # 374 Farmer (2,000-, 3,500)
SHIPMAN, George L. 30 m Ala
Eliza T,(?)(F.?) 26 f "
William F. 1 m "
VINING, Mary A. 46 f Ga
(600-1800)
McBRIDE, Sophia J. 20 f Ala

Euf # 723 Wagoner
SHIRAH, Charles 33 m SC

Euf # 700 Farmer (1500-500)
SHIRAH, Silas K. 41 m SC
Rhody 36 f Ga
Mary 15 f Ala
John N. 13 m "
Daniel D. 10 m "
Piety M. 8 f "
Joseph P. 3 m "
Lydia F. 2 f "

Euf # 622 Farm hand
SHIRAH, Solomon B. 31 m Ga
Temperance 20 f "
Elizabeth 10 f Ala
John 6 m "
William 1 m "

Euf # 1291 Farmer (---300)
SHIRLEY, John 29 m Ala
Natala P. 28 f "
Marion 3 m "
James 1 m "

Euf # 905
SHIVER, Harrison 18 m Ala
(See A. P. Johnson).

Euf # 572 Lawyer (80,000-75,000)
SHORTER, Eli S. 37 m Ga
Marietta 27 f "
William 9 m Ala
Anna 11 f "
Clement 4 m "
Eli 2 m "

Euf # 536
SHORTER, Harriet 52 f SC
Caroline 20 f "
(See Eliza Gibhart).

Euf # 164 Lawyer (15000-35000)
SHORTER, Henry R. 28 m Ga
Adriana 24 f SC

Euf # 571 Judge (45000-125,000)
SHORTER, John B. 42 m Ga
Mary J. 34 f "
Mary 16 f Ala

Euf # 238
SHORTER, Mary B. 63 f Ga
(See John W. Cameron).

Euf # 195 Brick mason (800-200)
SIBLEY, S. S. 37 m SC
Nancy A. 34 f Ga
Caroline E. 15 f Ala
Emily L. 14 f "
Mary J. 12 f "
Nancy A. 10 f "
Jane 9 f "
Laura 5 f "
Sidney 3 f "
William H. 7 m "
infant 3/12 f "

Euf # 822 Farmer (---100)
SIKES, John 19 m Ala
Mary J. 22 f Ga
(Married within the year).

Euf # 821 Farmer (1500-1000)
SIKES, Richard 55 m NC
Seleta 55 f Ga
Martha C. 16 f Ala
Hetty E. 15 f "
Nancy J. 13 f "
STEWART. Mary A. 22 f "
Eliza J. 2 f "

Euf # 773 Farmer (---400)
SILAS, L. C. 28 m Ga
Emaline 23 f Ala
Patrick 1 m "
John S. 2/12 m "

Mt. A. # 903 (300-150)
SILAS, Rebecca 60 f Ga
(See John L. Pierce).

Euf # 830 Farmer (2300-11000)
SILAS T. J. 32 m Ga
Matilda H. 32 f "
John 9 m Ala
Sanders 7 m "
Mary A. 5 f "
Jane 3 f "
Natilla 9/12 f "

Clay # 44 In jail
SIMMONS, Allen 42 m SC

Clay # 182 Farmer (500-250)
SIMMONS, David 44 m Ga
Rachael 39 f "
Mary A. 17 f Ala
James M. 14 m "
Virginia 12 f "
Nancy A. 6 f "
John F. 3 m "

Euf # 998 Farmer (2300-500)
SIMPSON, James B. 54 m Ga
Caroline 45 f "
Victoria 21 f "
Valeria 17 f "
Ella 14 f "
Eugenia 12 f Ala
James 10 m "
John 8 m "

Euf # 939 (500-7,000)
SIMPSON, Sarah A. 36 f Ga
Virginia 9 f "
David J.T. 7 m Ala

Euf # 160 Merchant(6000-10,000)
SIMPSON, W. T. 33 m Ga
Mary 24 f "
Callie 8 f Ala
Eva 5 f "
Lula 10/12 f "

Bkb # 687
Simms, Amy 50 f SC
(See Geo. R. Scroggins)

Flk # 394 Farmer (3000-6000)
SIMMS, Anderson 50 m Ga
Elizabeth 40 f "
M. A. 14 f "
Icifena 12 f "
James A. 10 m "
William 8 m "
Amanda 6 f "
Fletar 4 f "
BLACK, H. W. 38 m SC
(Teacher)

Bkb # 781 (--- ---)
SIMS, Annie 69 f NC
McNAIR, John 30 m Ga
(Laborer, ---100)
P.A.E. 12 f Ala
Mary A. 10 f "
M.A. 7 f "

Clay # 231 Farmer (--- ---)
SIMS, Henry 32 m Ga
Jane 27 f SC
Mary E. 6 f Ala
Henry T. 4 m "
G. W. 1 m "

Luvl # 280 Farmer (500-800)
SIMS, James 26 m Fla
Caroline 23 f Ga
Anna 6 f Ala
Susan 5 f "
Christian 3 f "
Sophronia 1 f "

Euf # 489 M.B. Minister (1,500-600)
SIMS, Joel 61 m Ga
Jane 59 f "
Mary A. 30 f "
Daniel (Farmer) 19 m Ala
Harriet T. 16 f "
Andrew J. 13 m "

Euf # 1382 Farmer (---200)
SIMS, Samuel A. 25 m Ala
Mary E. 20 f "

Euf # 1028 Hireling (--- ---)
SINGLETARY, Isaac 21 m Ga

Clay # 727 Farmer (---100)
SINGLETON, Joseph 41 m Ala
Mary 42 f Ga
Joseph (Farmer) 16 m Ala
Mary A. 20 f "
Mary M. 14 f "
Mary 12 f "
Martha 9 f "
William J. 8 m "
S.M. 4 m "
John W. 1 m "
WILLIAMS, Abner 22 m "
(Laborer)

Euf # 998 (898)
SINGLETON, Louisa 30 f NC
Henrietta 4 f Ala

Clay # 939 (---200)
SINGLETON, Mary 30 f SC
Andrew 14 m Ala

Clay # 205 Overseer (--- ---)
SINGLETON, Ranson 29 m Ala
Caroline 32 f SC
Taylor 9 m Ala
Martha 8 f "
William B. 5 m "

Clay # 230 Farmer (600-300)
SINGLETON, Solomon S. 35 m Ala
Angeline 40 f Ga
Polly Ann 16 f Ala
William 14 m "
Martha A. 12 f "
Elizabeth 9 f "
Angeline 6 f "
Susan 3 f "

Txv # 1191 Farmer (---200)
SINGLETON, William 25 m Ala
Dilly 22 f "
Mary 2 f "
Betsy 6/12 f "

Euf # 159
SINQUEFIELD, Linney 57 f Ga
Thenie W. 20 f "
(See A. L. Gaston)

Nwto # 633 (---25)
SIZEMORE, Lenny (?) 40 f Ga
Puss 20 f Ala

Clay # 146 Mechanic (300-100)
SKINNER, James 48 m Ga
M. 40 f SC
Jasper (Farmer) 18 m Ga
McD. " 16 m "
Elmyra 14 f "
Eliza 12 f "
S. 9 f "
Johnson 5 m "

Euf # 771 Miller
SLACK, Jesse (Insane) 35 m Ga
(See C. J. M. Andrews)

Clay # 941 Farmer (3500-10,000)
SLAUGHTER, George 28 m Ala
Mary J. 17 f Ga
James P. 2 m Ala
Elizabeth F. 1 f "
Elias 25 m "
TAYLOR, Westley 18 m "
SLAUGHTER, Issabella 73 f Ga

Euf # 572 (---- ----)
SLAUGHTER, Samuel 50 m Ga
Jane 27 f "

Euf # 318 (1,200---)
SLAUGHTER, Saul 50 m Ga
Martha T. 30 f "

Luvl # 278 Farmer (3,000-3,000)
SLOAN, John 38 m Ga
Nancy 39 f "
FAULK, Sarah 16 f Ala
(1,000---)
Mary (---1,500) 15 f "
James " 10 m "
Martha " 8 f "

Flk # 504
SMART, George W. 10 m Ala
(See Lucinda Warren).

Euf # 239 (2,000-10,000)
SMART, P. N. 56 m NC
TARVER, Jacob A. 28 m Ala
(---1,700)

Euf # 563 Farmer (4000-16000)
SMART, Thomas S. 37 m NC
Cleopatra 24 f Ga
George 10 m Ala
Albert D. 8 m "
Lee 6 m "
Kate 4 f "
(Cont.)

(Euf # 563 cont.)
Joann 2 f Ala
Emma 4/12 f "
Martin(?) W. 71 m Va
SAPP, Wm. (Laborer) 19 m Ga

Euf # 565 (---12,000)
SMART, W. S.(?) 32 m SC
Georgiana 20 f Ala
Benjamin F. 3 m "

Euf # 1243 Farmer (---500)
SMART, William 30 m NC
Mary 28 f "
BOWDEN, John C. 25 m "
(Hireling).
Mary J. 8 f Ala

Nwto # 573 Farmer (800-1000)
SMILEY, Austin 45 m Ga
Adaline 33 f "
Henry 14 m Ala
Daniel 12 m "
James 10 m "
Mary 8 f "
John 6 m "
Issabella 3 f "

Mt. A. # 921 Farmer (6000-2200)
SMITH, A. G. 45 m Va
Annie 23 f Ga
Jesse 5 m Ala
Fannie 7/12 f "
Louisiana 14 f "
Henrietta 11 f "
Mary J. 9 f "
Alexander 7 m "
Richard 5 m "
DAVIS, Mason 21 m "
(Overseer on farm).

Euf # 1126 Farmer (---5000)
SMITH, Allen 47 m Ga
Martha J. 38 f "
Andrew J. 18 m Ala
(Farm hand).
Nathan J. 16 m "
Jicey C. 13 f "
Susan 9 f "
Sidney 7 m "
Martha 5 f "
Victoria 3 f "
Alonzo 1 m "

Euf # 558
SMITH, Bennett 30 m Ala
(See W. A. Nolin).

Euf # 184 Machinist (-- --_
SMITH, Charles P. 23 m NC
BLAIR, Wm. (---500) 29 m Ga
(Foundry mgr.)
Ryan, Patrick I. 26 m Ire
(Machinist).

Euf # 1159 (600-300)
SMITH, Elizabeth 68 f NC
Joshua L. (Farmer) 18 m Ala
Isaiah 16 m "
RICO, Nancy 14 f "
Malissa 20 f "

Mdwy # 929
SMITH, Francis K. 6 m Ga
(See Francis M. Spencer).

Luvl # 309
SMITH, Firtha 13 m Ala
Rebecca 9 f "
Louisiana 4 f "
(See Wilson Collins).

Mt. A. 904 Overseer (---225)
SMITH, G. W. 36 m Ga
Sarah 30 f Ala
E.A.E. 11 f "
George M. 9 m "
George F. 8 m "
James A. 6 m "
Sophrona 3 f "

Euf # 368
SMITH, Green 18 m Ga
(See J. R. Hill).

Luvl # 356 Clerk
SMITH, Hardy 37 m Ga
(See Elizabeth McRae).

Clay # 658 Farmer (---200)
SMITH, Henry 30 m Ga
Annie 32 f Ala
Sarah J. 5 f "
Mary 2 f "

Euf # 1156 Farmer (---200)
SMITH, Henry 27 m Ga
Mary 26 f Ala
Elizabeth 7 f "
William 5 m "
Isaiah 3 m "
Sarah 6/12 f "

Mdwy # 1099 Farmer (200-200)
SMITH, Hezekiah 34 m Ga
(Cont.)

(Mdwy # 1099 cont.)
Harriett 34 f NC
Emeline 12 f Ala
John W. 11 m "

Euf # 88 Accountant
SMITH, Horace M. 22 NY

Euf # 610 Farm hand (-- --)
SMITH, J.(T?) B. 25 m Ga
Susan R. 23 f NC

Mdwy # 1007 Farmer (5000-30,000)
SMITH, J. H. 33 m SC
Elizabeth A. 28 f Ga
Oceona 1 f Ala
ELY, Wm. B. 27 m Ga
(Farmer, ---500)
HOLLAND, Joseph A. 12 m "

Euf # 1155 Farmer (---300)
SMITH, J. T. 30 m Ala
Cintha E. 25 f "
Amanda 7 f "
James W. 5 m "
Lewis J. 3 m "
William H. 1 m "

Euf # 29 Druggist (---17000)
SMITH, Jacob 55 m NY

Flk # 489 Farmer
SMITH, James 16 m Ala
(See J. D. Lewis)

Euf # 600 Overseer (-- --)
SMITH, James 21 m Ala
Martha E. 23 f "
Elizabeth 2 f Ala

Mt. A. # 745 Farmer (400-200)
SMITH, James M. 37 m Ga
Sarah A. 35 f "
W.W.D. 9 m "
Joseph 8 m Ala
Sarah J. 6 f "
Mary L. 3 f "
James T. 1 m "

Mt. A. # 901 Farmer (1200-1000)
SMITH, Jeremiah 43 m Ga
Lucinda 38 f "
Frances 12 f "
Roxie 8 f "
(Cont.)

(Mt. A. # 901 cont.)
Calphernia 6 f Ga
Laura 5 f Ala

Euf # 774 Farmer (---300)
SMITH, John 25 m Ga
Sarah 20 f "
Thomas L. 3 m "
Malissa 2 f "

Euf # 365 Farmer (600-1400)
SMITH, John M. 30 m Ga
Mary 24 f SC
John 3 m Ala
Jemima 1 f "

Euf # 721 Farmer (--100)
SMITH, John N. 67 m SC
Rachael 58 f "
Jincy 19 f Ala
Timmey 15 f "
George 11 m "

Luvl # 514 Farmer (1600-1000)
SMITH, John W. 45 m Ga
Melvina 44 f "
Walter W. (Farmer) 21 m "

Luvl # 316 Farmer (1000-2000)
SMITH, John W. 45 m Ga
Melvina 43 f "
Walter W. (Farmer) 31 m "

Euf # 587 Laborer (-- 50)
Smith, Johnathan 22 m Ala
Lucinda 21 f "
Tabitha 2 f "
RICCO, Jane 49 f SC

Mt. A. # 905 Clerk (---2000)
SMITH, Joseph W. 31 m Ga
Delila 84 f NC
L.E. 36 f Ga
SWANSON, W. S. 24 m "
(Physician, 216-5000)

Mdwy # 993 Tending at mill. (---500)
SMITH, Josiah 48 m Ga
Sarah 42 f SC
Catherine 11 f Ga

Euf # 244
SMITH, Mary 58 f NC
(See Elizabeth Williams).

Clay # 26 (---1200)
SMITH, Mary 55 f Va
Wm. (Mechanic) 27 m Ala
Susan 23 f "
Mary A. 20 f "
Henry 3 m "

Euf 1180 Farmer (---250)
SMITH, Moses 24 m Ga
Nancy 20 f Ala
Frances 8/12 f "

Mdwy # 1009 Marchant & farmer 7,000-31,000)
SMITH, N. C.? Wm. 40 m NC
Sarah E. 25 f Ga
Andy J. 15 m NC
M. W. 13 m "
Ellen 10 f "
Joseph W. 4 m Ala
C. W. 1 m "
COLEMAN, Mary E. 8 f "

Euf # 568 Miller (---150)
SMITH, Nathan E. 26 m Ala
Louisa 22 f "
infant 3/12 f "

Mt. A. 814 carpenter (---200)
SMITH, Nicholas 40 m Ala
Nancy G. 37 f NC
John P. 12 m Ala
Elizabeth D. 11 f "
Joel W. 9 m "

Euf # 515
SMITH, Quincy 23 f Ala
Mary 1 f "
(See John Gibbons)

Luvl # 523 Farmer (---300)
SMITH, Samuel F. 25 m Ga
Mary J. 22 f "
John W. 1 m Ala

Euf # 1035 (10,000-40,000)
SMITH, Sarah 30 f Ala
Nathan A. 10 m "
Isadore F. 8 f "
Eliza M. 4 f "

Euf # 117 Machinist (---400)
SMITH, Seaborn 29 m Ga
Elizabeth A. 28 f "
Charles L. 5 m "
Tallula J. 9/12 f Ala

Mt. A. # 906 Farmer (---500)
SMITH, Sidney A. 60 m SC
Rebecca 55 f Ga

Euf # 289 Farmer (3000-15000)
SMITH, Siman R. 30 m Ala
L.A. 31 f Ga
Caladonia 2 f Ala

Euf # 356 Farmer (2000-6000)
SMITH, Sion W. 28 m Ala
Henrietta M. 27 f SC
Georgianna 7 f Ala
SMITH, Mary J. 49 f SC
Thomas 2 m Ark

Euf # 364 Farmer (1500-5000)
SMITH, T. B. R. 52 m Ga
Barbara 50 f "
Sarah 24 f "
Martha 22 f "
Mary 21 f "
Prudence 20 f "
Susan 18 f Ala
Nancy 16 f "
William 14 m "
Acton 12 m "
James 10 m "
Elizabeth 6 f "
Robert 4 m "

Euf # 492
SMITH, T. H. 24 m Ala
(See Wm. A. Hughes).

Euf # 1303 Farmer (1200-2500)
SMITH, T. J. 25 m Ala
Margaret V. 18 f "
Thomas S. 2 m Ark

Euf # 72 Clerk (8000-7000)
SMITH, T. N. 29 m Ga
Mary F. 21 f Ala
Ida C. 2 f "

Euf # 845 Overseer (---300)
SMITH, Thomas A. 27 m Ga
Georgian 25 f "
Laura 5 f "
Mary 3 f Ala
Sarah 6/12 f "

Euf # 1311
SMITH, Turner 20 m Ga
Mary 18 f "
(See Sampson Worsley).

Flk # 490 Student
SMITH, William 20 m Ala
Ann 17 f "
Mary 14 f "
(See Mary B. Whitehurst)

Txv # 1167 Farmer (---250)
SMITH, William 35 m Ga
Elizabeth 35 f Ala
Calip J. 2 m "
Mary 1 f "

Euf # 1157 Farmer (600-200)
SMITH, William 32 m SC
Eliza 28 f Ala
George W. 10 m "
Elizabeth 8 f "
Isaiah 5 m "
John 4 m "
Jefferson 2 m "
Lydia A. 1 f "

Euf # 270 Laborer
SMITH, William 22 m Ala
(See James A. Bell)

Mdwy # 957 Farmer (3800-5000)
SMITH, Wm. E.(or C.) 42 m SC
Jannett 36 f "
William C. 14 m Ga
CARMICHAEL, John 27 m SC
(Physician)

Euf # 463
SMITH, William J. 8 m Ga
(See W. G. Spence)

Euf # 306 (--- ---)
SMITHA, Mary 34 f Md
Anna S. 12 f D.C.

Euf # 75 Livery stable
(500-10,000)
SMITHA, William 47 m Ky
Sophia 12 f D.C.
(Sophia born Washington, D.C.)

Euf # 373 Sawyer (3000-300)
SMOOT, George 54 m Va
Theresa 43 f Ga
Nancy M. 17 f "
Marcellus 13 m Ala
James 11 m "
Josephine 9 f "

Txv # 1231 Farmer (1000-350)
SNEAD, Daniel B. 31 m NC
Elizabeth 26 f Ala
(Cont.)

(Txv # 1231 cont).
Marcus 5 m Ala
John T. 3 m "
Edward A. 1/12 m "

Euf # 1190 Farmer (600-500)
SNEAD, Daniel B. 52 m Ga
Elizabeth 41 f "
Sarah 21 f "
William H. 19 m "
John M. 16 m "
Nancy E. 14 f "
Martha E. 12 f "
Samuel J. 10 m "
Benjamin F. 9 m "
Margaritta 6 f "
Lecy M. 4 f "
May L. 2 f Ala

Euf # 1192 Farmer (600-500)
SNEAD, Joseph 24 m Ga
Mary 25 f Miss
Mary S. 3 f Ala
BELL, James 9 m Ga

Euf # 1193 Farmer (300-2,500)
SNEAD, Wm. M. 50 m NC
Nancy 58 f Ga
John 18 m "
William 13 m "

Euf # 251 Seamstress (1200 ---)
SNEED, Mariah J. 57 f NC
HOLLEDAY, Catarine (?) 77 f "
Ann E.(Seamstress) 25 f Ga

Bfd # 1256 Farmer (--- 500)
SNELL, Nathaniel 50 m SC
Mary 31 f Ala
John F. 4 m "
Georgianna 6/12 f "

Euf # 688 Farmer (--- 4,000)
SNELLINGS, Joel 23 m Ga
Ellen 21 f Ala
infant 6/12 m "

Euf # 277 Physician (---8,000)
SNIPES, Charles D. * 30 m SC
M. E. * 28 f SC
Charles * 6 m "
Dora (?) * 3 f Ala

* (From Family History & Probate
Records:)
Martha (wife of Chas. D. Snipes)
Charles (son of " " "
Medora (dau." " " "

Euf # 1329 Farmer (20,000-27,000)
SNIPES, John D. * 21 m SC
CUNNINGHAM, Archy 23 m Ala
(Overseer)

Euf # 1308 (9,000-18,000)
SNIPES, M. R. ** 25 f Ala
William H. 6 m "
Sarah (Jane) 4 f "

Euf # 381 (---18,000)
SNIPES, Marion *** 17 f Ala
(See Edw. C. Bullock)

Euf # 198 Dentist (--- ---)
SNOW, C.(?) W. 44 m Me
Emily C. 34 f Ga
Charles H. 12 m Ala
Jane M. 11 f "
Emily H. 8 f "
Ellenor W. 6 f "
Mary E. 4 f "
Ella A. 1 f Kans
(See 1850 Barbour Census).

Clay # 196 Farmer (300 ---)
SOMMERSETT, George 63 m NC
Elizabeth 78 f "

Clay # 197 Farmer
SOMMERSETT, Joseph J. 37 m Ga
Lucinda 21 f "
Elizabeth 5 f Ala
Joseph T. 8/12 m "

Euf # 27 Drug clerk (-- --)
SOUTHWICK, D. L. 26 m NY

Euf # 1012
SPAIGHT, Esther 7 f Fla
Louis P. 5 m "
(See Hester Phillips)

Euf # 1321 Farmer (3,200-6,000)
SPARKS, Samuel 46 m Ga
Mary 39 f NC
Mary 22 f Ga
(Cont.)

(Euf # 1321 cont.)
Sarah 19 f Ga
Martha 17 f "
Julia 16 f "
Fredonia 12 f "
George 11 m Ala
Susan 9 f "
Samuel 8 m "
Harrison 6 m "
Thomas J. 4 m "

Euf # 562 Farmer (3000-6000)
SPARKS, Thos. P. 42 m Ga
Janett 39 f "
Mary E. 18 f "
Samuel 17 m "
William D. 16 m "
Charles E. 12 m "
Joseph 11 m "
Thomas P. 4 m Ala
Janett 2 f "
WELLS, William H. 67 m Va
Martha A. 24 f Ga

Euf # 988 Farmer (2000-5000)
SPEARS, H. G. 34 m Fla
Emily C. 26 f Ga
ROSE, Mary 9 f "

Clay # 109
SPEARS, Lucinda 9 f Ala
(See Louis Price).

Clay # 117
SPEARS, Luvinca 34 f NC
BOWDEN, Sarah E. 17 f Ala
SPEARS, Betsy A. 11 f "
Narsissa 4 f "
BERRYHILL, Henry 20 m Ga
(Laborer on farm).

Clay # 663 (--- ---)
SPEARS, Mary 26 f Ala
James 12 m Miss
Richard 10 m "
Newton 8 m "
Jasper 6 m "

* Married Flora Ann Hooks 25 Dec. 1866, dau of Dan'l. & Flora Rankin Hooks, Bullock Co., Ala.

** Margaret R. Cunningham Snipes, dau. of Duncan Cunningham, wife of Henry C. Snipes.

*** Dau. of Mariah & Wm. H. Snipes. Married Dr. Samuel Wesley Anthony, lived Milam County, Tex. E. C. Bullock was a brother-in-law.

Luvl # 329 Farmer (500-1500)
SPENCE, A. T. 50 m Ga
Pharaba 40 f NC
S.L. (Student) 23 m Ga
Nancy C. 20 f Ala
(School teacher)
Riley T. (Farmer) 21 m "
James W. " 19 m "
Julien P. 14 m "

Euf # 775 Farmer (1500-6000)
SPENCE, Calvin 40 m SC
Ellen H. 31 f Ga
John W. (Student) 16 m SC

Mdwy # 929 Overseer (--- 500)
SPENCE, Francis M. 26 m Ga
Martha A. 19 f "
Howard J. 1 m "
SMITH, Francis K. 6 m "

Clay # 156 Laborer on farm
SPENCE, James 20 m Ala
(See S. P. Saunders).

Clay # 1108 Farm laborer (---100)
SPENCE, K.(?) T. 22 m Ala
(See James M. Vickars).

Mdwy # 1015
SPENCE, Lewis 22 m Ala
(See Lorenzo Faulk)

Mdwy # 932 Overseer (---200)
SPENCE, William B. 51 m SC
Mary 45 f Ga
Susan A.J. 17 f Ala
Mary C. 14 f "
John W. 11 m "
Henry McT. 7 m "
Margaret L. 3 f "

Euf # 463 Overseer (---1500)
SPENCE, W. G. 28 m Ga
Frances 24 f "
Fitz James 4 m Ala
Florence 1 f "
SMITH, William J. 8 m Ga

Bkb # 774 Farmer (2000-2000)
SPERGERS, Arasmus R. 58 m SC
Florinda 48 f Ga
John M. 8 m Ala
SPERGERS, E. T. 15 m Ga
(Cont.)

(Bkb # 774 cont.)
Mary J. 20 f Ala
(E.T. & Mary married within year)
JOHNSON, Lorenzo 17 m Ga
(Farm laborer)

Bkb # 775
SPERGERS, Lorenzo 24 m Ga
L.A. 18 f Ala

Bkb # 769 Farmer (1400-1500)
SPERGERS, Wm. H. 34 m Ga
Ann 36 f "
Amanda 12 f "
Iverson 9 m "
Elizabeth 5 f Ala
Lucinda 3 f "
William 1 m "
PICKETT, B. F. 22 m Ga
Lucas 16 m "
Lucinda 24 f "

Clay # 228 (100-75)
SPIRES, Martha 38 f SC
Jas. W. (Farmer) 18 m "
Martha A. 16 f "
Eliza C. 14 f "
Joel H. 11 m Ga
Mary J. 9 f Ala
W. T. 5 m "

Euf # 660 Farmer (---100)
SPIVEY, Curtis 30 m Ga
Mary J. 25 f "
Sarah 2 f Ala
C. J. 4/12 m "

Euf # 744 Farmer (1000-350)
SPIVEY, Josiah S. 49 m Ga
Sithe 40 f SC
Josiah P. 18 m Ga
Sarah A. 16 f "
Benjamin J. 18 m "
David P. 14 m Ala
Josiah(?), A 12 m "
John E. 11 m Ga
Edward A. 10 m "
Martha C. 9 f Ala
Samuel T. 7 m "
Margaret 6 f Ga
Doctor P. 4 m "
E. E. 1/12 f "

Euf # 762
SPROWL, Eliza I. 20 f Fla
(See Gabriel Purswell).

Clay # 208 Farmer (100-50)
SPROUL, J. J. 52 m NC
Catherine 36 f Ga
James M. 14 m Ala
William J. 12 m "
David M. 9 m "
Jackson 7 m "
Mary 4 f "
Henry C. 1 m "

Euf # 604 Farmer (---100)
SPURLOCK, Green 27 m Ala
Martha 22 f "
Jefferson 6/12 m "
Rasbury (Laborer) 19 m "

Euf # 154
SPURLOCK, Sarah 24 f Ga
John 8 m Ala
Nancy 4 f "
Columbus 2 m "
(See Jeremiah Bird).

Euf # 204 Overseer (---2000)
SPURLOCK, Solomon 65 m Ga
Mariah 47 f SC
John (Revy Soldier) 104 m NC
Calvin 15 m Ala

Mt. A. # 852 Blind
STAFFORD, Judith D. 30 f Ala
(See C. C. Lewis)

Luvl # 268 (600---)
STAFFORD, Leroy E. 25 m Ala
Elizabeth 21 f "
Sarah J. 6/12 f "
FAULK, Sarah 18 f "

Euf # 138 Grocer (---1000)
STAMMERS, William E. 26 m NY
Mary E. 21 f "

Euf # 1257 Farmer (---100)
STANDIFER, William R. 26 m Ala
Eliza 25 f SC
Charlotte M. 6 f Ala
John J. 2/12 m "

Euf # 534 Farmer (3000-6000)
STANFORD, Monroe 30 m NC
Ellenor 30 f Ala
Thomas 9 m "
William 7 m "
James 5 m "
Mary D. 2 f "
DYER, Thos. A 23 m Ga
(Laborer)

Clay # 73 (---300)
STANLEY, E. T. 56 f Ga
John 20 m Ala
P. B. 18 m "
Sallie 16 f "

Euf # 566 Farmer (500-300)
STANTON, James 44 m SC
Sarah A. 38 f "
Jacob 15 m "
William 13 m "
Wiley 11 m "
Thomas 9 m "
Benjamin 7 m Ala
Joseph 6 m "
Martha 4 f "
Elizabeth 3 f "
Susan 4/12 f "
SELLERS, Jane 60 f SC

Euf # 1038 Farmer (5000-45000)
STARKE, A. B. 45 m Ala
M. A. 26 f "
B. A. 14 m "
O. H. 11 m "
J. S. 2 m "

Euf # 401 P.E. Minister (20,000-6,000)
STEEL, William M. 42 m Va
Sarah 30 f Tenn
William W. 9 m Ala
Mary F. 2 f Tenn

Euf # 229 Shoe maker (500-150)
STEIDHAM, Thomas 48 m NC
Rose Ann 35 f Ga
INGLET, Georgia A. 13 f Ala
McKLEVAIN, Nancy 50 f NC

Mdwy # 1010 Carpenter (150-200)
STEPHENS, C. 36 m Ga
Susan F. 32 f "
Sarah J. 14 f "
Mary F. 12 f "
A. M. 10 f "
F. N. 8 m "

Luvl # 388 Farmer (3000-8000)
STEPHENS, David D. 46 m SC
Nancy 45 f NC
Nelson (Farmer) 19 m SC
William " 17 m "
Franklin 14 m NC
Robert 12 m "
Thomas 12 m "
(Cont.)

(Luvl # 388 cont.)
Mary A. 9 f Ala
John 6 m "
Philip 4 m "

Euf # 1004 Farmer (3000-17,000)
STEPHENS, Green 56 m Ga
Georgia 17 f "
Elizabeth 8 f Ala
Isabella 6 f "

Bfd # 1249 Farmer (---300)
STEPHENS, James 47 m SC
Nancy 47 f "
William 18 m Ala
Martha 16 f "
Newton 14 m "
Nancy 11 f "
James 8 m "
infant 5 m "

Bkb # 756 Farmer (1400-3500)
STEPHENS, W. W. 45 m Ga
Mahala 36 f "
Lewis 12 m "
Sarah 11 f "
Eliza 9 f "
Julytha 4 f Ala
Caroline 2 f "

Euf # 795 Farmer (7000-15000)
STERNS(?), Wilson H. 47 m Ga
Jane 44 f NC
Martha A. 16 f Ga
William C. 14 m "
Louisa 12 f "
Julia 10 f "
Eugenia 8 f Ala
ROBERSON, William 22 m Ga
(Overseer)

Euf # 420 Laborer
STERRIT, Clark 24 m Tenn
(See James Daniels).

Euf # 176 Mill wright
STEVENS, Mr. 40 m --
Alex (Laborer) 15 m Ga
(See Edward Williams).

Euf # 49 Tinner
STEVENS, Henry R. 18 m Ala
(See John J. Peavy).

Euf. # 194 Joiner (1200-2500)
STEVENS, Lewis 51 m Conn
(Cont.)

(Euf # 194 cont).
Aaron (joiner) 29 m Conn
Joel C. " 42 m "
(2. ---- 1000)
(3. 500-1000))

Luvl # 283
STEVENS, Mary 17 f Ala
(See E. W. Harrison).

Euf # 540 Laborer (--- ---)
STEVENS, Micajah 48 m NC
Elizabeth 27 f Ala
James 9 m Fla
Cullen 4 m Ala
infant 1 f "

Euf # 130 Blk. smith (--- ---)
STEVENS, William 23 m Ga
Nancy A. 22 f Ala
Rose Ann 2 f "
Elijah 4/12 m "

Txv # 1171 Farmer (---1350)
STEVENS, Williams 34 m SC
Elizabeth 35 f "
James D. (Farmer) 15 m Ala
John C. 13 m "
Adeline 11 f "
F. Marion 4 m "
Lamanda C. 2 f "
C. C. 3/12 m "

Euf # 1128 Farmer (3500-16000)
STEVENSON, Count 33 or 54 m Ga
Susan 27 f "
Elizabeth 22 f "
Dicy 16 f "
Frances 14 f "
Queen 13 f "
Peter 12 m Ala
George 10 m "
James 8 m "
Louisa 6 f "
Henrietta 4 f "
Emma 1 f "

Clay # 180 Farmer (1200-150)
STEVENSON, John 50 m SC
Civel 42 f Ga
Joseph (Farmer) 20 m "
Sarah E. 22 f "
Duncan (Farmer) 18 m "
Willoughby 15 m Ala
James A. 13 m "
Charles 9 m "
Moses 2 m "

Clay # 133 (---50)
STEVENSON, Sarah 46 f Ga
Elizabeth 16 f "
James M. 9 m "

Euf # 1273
STEWARD, Mary 22 f Ala
Eliza T.(?) 2 f "
(See Richard Sykes).

Euf # 1227 Farmer (500-11000)
STEWART, Alex 63 m NC
Nancy 55 f "
Ann E. 21 f Ala
Alex A. (Farm hand) 19 m "
Catharine 16 f "
Sarah A. 14 f "

Txv # 1179
STEWART, Ann P. 16 f Ala
(See Solomon Butts).

Euf # 247 Stage Driver (-- --)
STEWART, D. W. 27 m Ga
Josephine E. 18 f "
(Seamstress).

Euf # 1226 Farmer (2000-12000)
STEWART, Daniel 45 m NC
Frances 24 f Ga
Sarah J. 4 f Ala
Anna 81 f NC

Mt. A. # 802 Farmer (---200)
STEWART, Eli 21 m Ala
Jane 17 f SC
Mary E. 9/12 f Ala

Mdwy # 1041 Farmer (---100)
STEWART, Eugene G. 21 m Ala
James A. (Farmer) 24 m Ga.
(---100)
Sarah C. 20 f "
Sarah 4/12 f Ala

Euf # 1395 Farmer (10,000-27,000)
STEWART, J. S. 39 m Ga
Martha 31 f "
James 8 m Ala
Susan 6 f "
John 2 m "

Mt. A. # 810 Farmer (---2500)
STEWART, James 25 m Ga
Cornelia 28 f SC
JENNINGS, L. A. 15 f Ala
(Cont.)

(Mt. A. # 810 cont.)
Elizabeth 7 f Ala
John W. 4 m "

Euf # 384 Farmer (1680-8000)
STEWART, James, Sr. 63 m Ga
Sarah 62 f "
Candice 25 f Ala

Euf # 965 Clerk (--- ---)
STEWART, James R. 31 m SC

Euf # 1215 (1500-2800)
STEWART, Jane 46 f SC
James (Farmer) 25 m SC
Celia 24 f "
Chas. F. " 22 m "
Caroline 20 f "
John (Farm hand) 18 m "
Hamilton (Farm hand) 16 m "
Frances 14 f "
Jefferson 12 m "
Dallas 11 m "
Archy 10 m "
Margaret 8 f "

Euf # 1228 Farmer (1200-4000)
STEWART, John L. 60 m NC
Catherine 25 f "
Jas. R. (Farm hand) 23 m Ala
Anna 19 f "
Celia 16 f "
John 14 m "
Mary 11 f "
Daniel 8 m "

Euf # 265 Dressmaker
STEWART, M. 51 f Eng
(See Lewis Phillips)

Euf # 821
STEWART, Mary A. 22 f Ala
Eliza J. 2 f "
(See Richard Sikes)

Euf # 964 (500-300)
STEWART, Pennina 52 f SC
Daniel A. (Farmer) 19 m "
Chas. W. " 16 m "
Janett N. 13 f Ala

Euf # 282 Cabinet maker
STEWART, T. 31 m Ga
(See John Lindsey).

Clay # 667 Farmer (1500-1500)
STEWART, Thomas 60 m SC
(Cont.)

(Clay # 667 cont)
Jane 50 f Ga
Elizabeth 28 f "
Delila 28 f "
Mary 24 f "
Catherine 22 f "
Thos. (Farmer) 18 m Ala

Euf # 1402 Farmer (6000-14000)
STEWART, William N. 36 m Ga
Camilla S. 33 f "
Laura A. 9 f Ala
Lou C. 7 f "
Ida W. 5 f "
Edward N. 3 m "

Euf # 1249 Hireling (-- --)
STINSELL, James 42 m SC
Martha 26 f Ala
Mary 5 f "
GILCHRIST, Lowell 14 m NC

Euf # 517 Master carpenter (1,00-500)
St. LEDGER, Dennis 27 m Ire
Margaret 26 f "
William 3 m Ga
Marion E. 2 f Ala

Euf # 46 Boat maker (1500-1000)
STOCKWELL, Richard 43 m Eng
Harriet W. 29 f Fla
Mary V. 6 f Ala
Susan P. 4 f "
Harriet W. 1 f "

Luvl # 251 Farmer (3000-6000)
STOKES, Henry 49 m SC
Martha A. 45 f Ga
Jane 22 f Ala
Susan 19 f "
Mary 15 f "
Melvina 13 f "
Emma 8 f "
Judge S. 7 m "
G. J. S. 6 m "
Willis 3 m "

Euf # 1259 Farmer (---200)
STOKES, Hubbard 32 m SC
Elizabeth 25 f Ala
James 10 m "
John 7 m "
Sarah J. 11 f "
William 4 m "
Parthena 3/12 f "

Flk # 477 Farmer (1500-800)
STOKES, Irwin J. 57 m SC
Matilda 54 f "
Jefferson (Farmer) 25 m Ala
(150-20)
Henry " 23 m "
Mary A. 21 f "
Jackson " 18 m "
George W. " 15 m "
Joel D. " 29 m "
(600-75)
William T. 2 m "

Euf # 618 Farm hand (--- ---)
STOKES, James K. 16 m Ala
(See Young Wood).

Euf # 294 Farmer (800-300)
STOKES, Joel D. 37 m SC
Elizabeth 33 f Ala
Amanda J. 17 f "
Moses E. 15 m "
Mary E. 12 f "
Julia A. 7 f "
James D. 4 m "
Sarah A. 2 f "

Euf # 1258 Farmer (600-300)
STOKES, John 76 m SC
Mary 68 f "
Asbury 22 m Ala
Sarah A. 17 f "

Luvl # 252 Farmer (--- ---)
STOKES, John S. 19 m Ala
(See Elijah Childs).

Nwto # 592 Farmer (1,000-400)
STOKES, Robert J. 30 m Ala
Martha 30 f Ga
Martha 12 f Ala
Adaline 10 f "
Henry 8 m "
George 1 m "
Queen 1 f "

Flk # 458 Farmer (600-250)
STOKES, William 28 m Ala
Mary 26 f "
Mary A. 3 f "
John W. 5/12 m "
POWELL, Matilda 17 f "

Mdwy # 1062 Brick Mason (---200)
STONE, Henry 20 m Ala
Lucinda 24 f Ga
(Married within the year)
BONDS, Stephen 21 m Ala

Bkb # 765 Farmer (200-150)
STONE, John C. 29 m Ga
Fanny C. 27 f Ala

Clay # 680 Farmer (500-200)
STORY, David 26 m Ga
Margaret 20 f Ala
Franklin 2 m "
infant 1/12 f "

Mdwy # 1082 (---3,200)
STOVALL, L. S. 43 f Ga
Mary 18 f "
(See James A. Irving).

Euf # 782
STOVALL, Mary 19 f Ala
(See Thos. A. Roquemore).

Euf # 209 Merchant (8,000-20,000)
STOW, Anthony 44 m Conn
T. A. 42 f Ga
Edward (Clerk) 20 m Ala
James 11 m "
Kate 8 f "
Maty 2 f "

Euf # 554 Miller (500-25)
STRATTON, T. S. 32 m Mass
Jane F. 25 f "
H. O. 7 m "
T. W. 4 m "
Sallie 55 f "

Clay # 728 (--- ---)
STRAUGHTER, Caroline 26 f Ala
Amelia 2 f "
Mary S. 1 f "

Euf # 353 Farmer (7,500-10,000)
STREATER, Benjamin F. 34 m NC

Euf # 963 Farmer (4000-3500)
STREATAR, C. B. 32 m NC
LONG, James 20 m Ala
(Teacher?).

Euf # 349 Farmer (200-65,000)
STREATER, M. H. 42 m NC
LONG, Jas.(Student) 20 m Ala

Euf # 971 Farmer (12,000-35,000)
STREATAR, S. M. 68 m NC
Mary 55 f "
(Cont.)

(Euf # 971 cont.)
Godwin (Farmer) 26 m NC
(---25000)
Masselon 20 m "
DEAS, Plumer(Student) 18 m SC
HINSON, Nancy 85 f NC

Euf # 974 Farmer (16000-46,500)
STREATAR, W. P. 25 m NC
Richard (Farmer) 27 m "
Mary A. 35 f "
Edny 28 f "
Thos. H. (Farmer) 24 m "
John H. 19 m Ala
Emaline 16 f "

Nwto # 549 Laborer (---200)
STRENGTH, P. J. 29 m Ala
Mary J. 25 f Ga
Lucinderilla 9 f Ala
Catherine 8 f "
James P. 6 m "
Josiah 2 m "
Elizabeth 2/12 f "
DURDEN, Sallie 57 f SC

Euf # 312 Laborer (--- ---)
STRICKLIN, Evan 27 m NC
Sarah 29 f "
William H. 5 m Ala
John 3 m "
Mary 4/12 f "

Euf # 301 Farmer (500-500)
STRICKLIN, Harman 36 m NC
Feriby 33 f "
William 14 m "
Daniel 12 m "
Nancy E. 10 f Ala
Hardy 8 m "
Martha J. 7 f "
Laney A. 3 f "
Harman W. 10/12 m "
Eveline L. 18 f NC
Mary C. 11 f Ala

Euf # 512
STRICKLIN, Martha 5 f Ala
(See William Thomas).

Euf # 300 Farmer (400-600)
STRICKLIN, Mathew 52 m NC
Elizabeth 54 f "
Mary 23 f "
Elizabeth 20 f "
(Cont.)

(Euf # 300 Cont.)
Jesse (Farmer) 17 m NC
Martha 16 f "
John D. 14 m "

Bkb # 691 Store Keeper (---2000)
STRICKLAND, Benj. 32 m NC
L. N. 32 f Ga
I. W. 3 m Ala
J. A. 1 m "

Txv # 1162 Farmer (800-300)
STRICKLAND, David 40 m NC
C. G. 40 f "
Morris C. 18 m "
John W. 16 m "
A. S. 15 f "
William G. 13 m "
George R. 11 m "
Monroe 9 m Ala
Angie 5 f "
Mary A. 2 f "
Daniel 1/12 m "
James H. 25 m NC

Luvl # 526 Farmer(1300-1000)
STRICKLAND, Jesse 65 m NC
Mary 64 f "
Jesse (Farmer) 42 m "
Celie 34 f "
Lucy 30 f Tenn
Mary Jane 26 f NC
Eliza 22 f Ala
Mahala 19 f "
Lot (Farmer) 32 m NC

Mt. A. # 748
STRICKLAND, Louisa 12 f Ala
(See Elizabeth Craptree).

Euf # 491
STRINGER, E. L. 13 f Ala
(See E. Y. Van Hoose).

Clay # 169 Overseer (--- ---)
STRINGER, Thomas H. 29 m Ga
Sophia T. 23 f Ala

Mdwy # 955 Farmer (--- 1600)
STRIPLING, Wiley 29 m Ala
Mary 24 f "
William 5 m "
Warren 3 m "
Westley 2 m "

Flk # 499 Well digger (-- --)
STUBBS, J. B. 33 m NC
Linda 27 f Ga
James W. 10 m "
John P. 7 m "
Uriah M. 5 m "
Frances V. 2 f "
WILLIAMS, Mary 18 f "

Flk # 488 Farmer (300---)
STUBBS, Uriah 47 m NC
Frances E. 36 f "
David (Farmer) 16 m Ala
Elizabeth A. 14 f Ga
Henry C. 10 m "
Francis M. 7 m "
Cavon V. 6 f "
Thomas R. 4 m "

Euf # 767 Farmer (---300)
STUCKEY, C. S. 25 m Ala
Christianson 21 f "

Euf # 657(675?) Farm hand (---100)
STUCKEY, Enos H. 36 m NC
Elizabeth 39 f "
William 14 m Ala
Sarah C. 13 f "
Martha E. 10 f "
Josephine 6 f "
Roxanna 4 f "
Thadeus 1 m "

Mdwy # 1015
STUCKEY, Mary J. 6 f Ala
(See Lorenzo Faulk).

Bkb # 698 Farmer (400-500)
STUCKEY, Owen 52 m NC
E. J. 49 f "
Frank (Farmer) 23 m Tenn
L. H. " 17 m "
Mary 11 f "
Martha A. 7 f Ala

Euf # 494 Farmer (---500)
Summerlin, J. 42 m SC
Rhody 34 f Ga
Angeline 14 f Ala
Eugenia 13 f "
Josephine 10 f "
Collier 9 m "
Quitman 8 m "
Preston 5 m "
Robert 2 m "
Henry W. 10/12 m "

Mdwy # 988 Mechanic (---500)
SURLS, A. W. 25 m Ga
H. E. 17 f "

Nwto # 563 (1,500-4,000)
SUTTON, Elizabeth 64 f Ga
PHILLIPS, C. S. 37 f "
(800-400)
SUTTON, Matilda 21 f Ala
Benj. H. (Farmer) 19 m "
PHILLIPS, N. E. 15 f "
Milly (Black) 110 f Va

Flk # 492 Farmer (---200)
SUTTON, Needham 39 m Ga
Sarah 35 f Ala
Elizabeth 12 f "
William J. 11 m "
Jacob 10 m "
CAMPBELL, Alex 11 m "

Bkb # 692 Farmer (---200)
SWAIN, Joseph 47 m NC
Susan E. 25 f Ga
William R. 11 m Ala
James H. 13 m "
Mary A. 9 f "
George T. 8 m "
John H. 5 m "
Charles A. 1/12 m "

Nwto # 601 Farmer (500-800)
SWANER, Thomas 51 m NC
Lydia 51 f "
Martha 23 f "
James (500---) 22 m "
L. E. A. 18 f "
Ellen F. 16 f "
S. A. 14 f "
Z. T. 13 m "
H. S. 11 m Ala

Euf # 987 (-- --)
SWANSON, Joseph 29 m Ga
Caroline 20 f "
Susan 10/12 f "

Mt. A. # 905 Physician (216-5,000)
SWANSON, W. S. 24 m Ga
(See Joseph W. Smith).

Euf # 981 Overseer (--- ---)
SWINEY, James P. 41 m SC
Dobbs 73 m NC
(Cont.).

(Euf # 981 cont.)
(Ages for last two could be wrong - ink smeared - (41 or 47) (13 or 73).

Euf # 989 (300-2,500)
SWINNEY, Mary 45 f SC
Nancy 9 f Ala
Margaret 7 f "
Hannah 5 f "
Mary 2 f "
MULKEY, Indiana 16 f Ga
(---300)

Euf # 972 Hireling (--- ---)
SWINNY, Ned 20 m SC
(See E. P. Head)

Euf # 1274 Hireling (---150)
SYKES, John R. 20 m Ala
Mary J. 21 f Ga

Euf # 1273 Farmer (1400-1200)
SYKES, Richard 54 m NC
Seleta 55 f Ga
Martha 15 f Ala
Hetty 14 f "
Jane 12 f "
STEWARD, Mary 22 f "
Eliza T.(?) 2 f "

Euf # 570 Farmer (2,500-12,000)
SYLVESTER, D. * 63 m SC
Mary A. * 52 f "
Mary A. 27 f "
Frances A. 19 f Ala
Camilla T.(?) 18 f "

Euf # 227 (County) Clerk (1,600-6,500)
SYLVESTER, Thomas R. 40 m SC
Allethia T. 37 f "
Martha A. ** 17 f "
James E. 15 m Ala
William O. 13 m "
Leonidas T. 11 m "
Thomas R. 5 m "
Emma 7 f "
Joseph 1 m "

* Demarcus Sylvester, Sumter, SC.
* Mary Ann Rembert, wife of Demarcus, Sumter, SC.
** Dau. of D. & Mary A. Sylvester.

Clay # 677 Farmer (1200-800)
TAMPLIN, John 56 m Ga
Elizabeth 60 f "
S. C. 20 f "
William 18 m "
Elizabeth 14 f "
BLACK, John 8 m "
Mary J. 6 f Ala

Euf # 178 Marble Worker (1000-2000)
TANSY, James 31 m Eng
Margaret 29 f NC
RUSSELL, Geo. W. 28 m "
(Trader)
H. C.(Marble dealer) 33 m "
(---5,000)
TOTTON, Christopher 40 m Ire
(Painter)

Euf # 1011 Farmer (14,000-25,000)
TARVER, Anderson L. 48 m Ga
Julia 37 f "
Rebecca 17 f "
Mary L. 15 f "
Leonidas W. 13 m "
Cornelia P. 12 f "
Laura P. 10 f "
Sarah M. 7 f "
Julia F. 5 f "
Green B. 1 m "

Clay # 19 Law Student
TARVER, J. F. M. 22 m Ala
(Living in hotel).

Euf # 239 Farmer (-- --)
TARVER, Jacob A. 28 m Ala
(See P. N. Smart).

Euf # 1231 Hireling (-- --)
TATE, Howard 32 m Ga
Emily 30 f Ala
Julia 10 f "
Mary 8 f "
Amanda 6 f "
Samantha 4 f "
Malissa 1 f "
HALL, Nancy 74 f SC

Euf # 1145 Farmer (---150)
TATE, James 22 m Ala
Sarah 18 f Ga
Linson 2 m Ala
Ezekiel 1 m "

Clay # 138 Farmer (---200)
TATE, R. T. 36 m Ga
Nancy (---100) 25 f "
M. A. E. 13 f Ala
M. A. 8 f "
M. A. M. 5 f "
James P. 7/12 m "
APPLETON, S. E. 21 f "

Euf # 1146
TATE, Sarah 53 f Ga
(See Jackson Clemons).

Euf # 406 (--- ---)
TAYLOR, Caroline 30 f Ala
William G. 3 m "

Mdwy # 951 (4,800-22,000)
TAYLOR, Elizabeth 60 f Ga
John J. 20 m Ala
D. A. 18 m "

Euf # 47 Boat maker (---400)
TAYLOR, H. H. 30 m SC
Alabama R. 18 f Ga

Euf # 593
TAYLOR, Jesse 26 m Ga
(See Benj. Culpepper).

Mdwy # 1087 Blacksmith (--300)
TAYLOR, John M. 48 m SC
Caroline 42 f "

Euf # 929 Farmer (2000-4500)
TAYLOR, Luke 48 m SC
Jane 48 f "
Mary C. 10 f "
WRIGHT, Ira 23 m "
(Hireling).

Clay # 179
TAYLOR, Robert T. 8 m Ala
(See Robert Bradley).

Luvl # 250 (---700)
TAYLOR, Sarah A. 46 f NC
Susan (---1000) 19 f Ala

Bkb # 712 Farmer (600-300)
TAYLOR, Thomas 44 m SC
Elizabeth 34 f Ga
Jas. F. (Farmer) 15 m "
Sarah J. 13 f "
Thos. W. 12 m "
Susan 10 f Ala
George W. 7 m "
Martha F. 5 f "
Edward M. 6/12 m "

Euf # 556 Laborer (-- --)
TAYLOR, Thomas B. 23 m Ala
Martha J. 19 f Ga
Sarah J. 5/12 f Ala
TAYLOR, Reddin 50 m Ga
(Lawyer, 200-200)
Martha 45 f "
William 15 m Ala
HALES, Eliza 20 f Ga

Clay # 941
TAYLOR, Westley 18 m Ala
(See George Slaughter)

Luvl # 543 Farmer (---400)
TEAL, A. C. 22 m NC
Christian 24 f Ala

Luvl # 381 Farmer (---3000)
TEAL, Allen 60 m NC
Mary 25 f Ga
Nancy 38 f NC
Elizabeth 11 f Ala
Wiley 9 m "
Sarah "
Mary "
David "
Louisa "
PAINE, Thomas
(Page torn for last five).

Euf # 730 Farmer (600-200)
TEAL, Christopher C. 25 m NC
Dinah 23 f Ala
James B. 2 m "
Jesse S. 6/12 m "
CAMPBELL, David 7 m "

Flk # 425 Farmer (---1,000)
TEAL, Daniel 35 m NC
Sarah 29 f Ga
Thomas J. 1/12 m Ala

Euf # 1305 Farmer (300-4,000)
TEAL, Daniel N. 34 m NC
Mary 34 f "
Eliza J. 6 f Ala
Mary J. 4 f "
Julia E. 2 f "
Della 1 f "

Euf # 1196 Farmer (---500)
TEAL, Joel T.(or F.) 31 m Ala
Margy 28 f Ga
Henry W. 4 m Ala
(Cont.)

(Euf # 1196 cont.)
Robert P. 3 m Ala
James M. 2 m "
John A. 1/12 m "

Euf # 405 Farmer (---400)
TEAL, Robert 69 m Tenn
Hester 65 f Ga

Euf # 732 Farmer (400-2000)
TEAL, William 61 m NC
Charlotte 31 f SC
Margaret 12 f Ala

Euf # 1210 Overseer (---100)
TEAL, William 38 m Ala
Keziah 30 f Ga
Jane 12 f Ala
John 10 m "
Elizabeth 8 f "
William 6 m "
James 4 m "
Benjamin 1 m "

Clay # 141 Laborer
TENICH (?), Jefferson 19 m Ga
(See Frank Deshazo)

Euf # 24 Physician (3000-5000)
TERRY, Carlisle 36 m Conn
Elizabeth G. 33 f Ga
Edward W. 13 m "
Carlisle 9 m "
Emma 6 f "
Charles 3 m "
Emma G. (---2000) 22 f Conn
BROOKS, Susan 8 f Ga

Euf # 969 Overseer
TERRY, Robert 37 m Ga
(See J. C. Kendrick).

Euf # 324 Farmer (---1,000)
TERRY, William 36 m Ga
Sarah A. 38 f "
John B. 15 m "
George E. 13 m "
Savannah 12 f "
William H.(?) 10 m "
Obediah 8 m "
Mary 6 f Ala
Charles 5 m "
Freeman 3 m "
infant 10/12 m "

Euf # 1002 Physician (---300)
TEMPLE, W. B. 37 m SC

Euf 641 Farmer (750-200)
TEW, Allen 40 m NC
Sarah 36 f Ala
Cintilla 16 f "
Peter F. 14 m "
James A. 13 m "
Isaac J. 11 m "
Levi N. 8 m "
Leroy 6 m "
Sarah Z. 2 f "

Euf # 658
TEW, Hez 23 m Ala
(See John H. Walker)

Euf # 644 Farmer (250-150)
TEW, James 39 m NC
Viney 45 f SC
Martha J. 18 f Ala
Sarah A. 13 f "
Joseph S. 11 m "
Susan E. 8 f "
John W. 6 m "
Allen P.(?) 4 m "
Alexander 21 m "
(Farm hand).

Euf # 650 Farmer (500-200)
TEW, John 30 m Ala
Eliza A. 25 f NC
Thomas J. 7 m "
Elizabeth 6 f "
Elmira 3 f "
Martha A. 1/12 f "
(Last four listed as born in North Carolina).

Txv # 1147 Farm Laborer
TEW, John 20 m Ala
(See John Bass).

Euf # 645
TEW, Patience 72 f NC
Patience 53 f "
TEW, Patience Ann 21 f Ala
Joel (Laborer) 18 m "
Sarah E. -- f "

Euf # 652
TEW, Rebecca 42 f NC
John 19 m Ala
(See John D. Collins).

Euf # 642 Farmer (800-700)
TEW, Wallace 56 m NC
Martha 46 f Ga
Zack (Farm hand) 19 m Ala
Sam'l. " " 16 m "
Mary A. 15 f "
Asbury 13 m "
Martha A. 11 f "
Allen A. 6 m "
Ephriam J. 3 m "
TEW, Nathan 26 m "
(Occp. none)
Eady 21 f Ga

Flk # 495 Farmer (800-000)
THARPE, William A. 56 m Ga
Elvira 37 f NC
John (Farmer) 20 m Ala
Henry " 19 m "
Riddon " 16 m "
Jackson 10 m "

Euf # 43 Clerk (---550)
THOMAS, Aaron 28 m Ala
Almira C. 31 f Ga
Charles 6 m Ala
Augustus C. 1 m "
HEITT(?),(HEIDT) Sarah 61 f NC
(---2000) (See 1850 Census)
BART, Sarah B. 28 f Ga
John W. 10 m Ala

Nwto # 617 Farmer (500-300)
THOMAS, Abram 26 m Ala
Mary A. 21 f "
(Married within the year).

Euf # 719 Farmer (1500-2000)
THOMAS, Adam J. 34 m NC

Clay # 107 Farmer (600-200)
THOMAS, Alfred 53 m Ga
Melinda 37 f "
Jasper (Farmer) 20 m "
Benj. F. (cripple) 18 m "
Sarah L. 15 f "
P.L. 13 m Ala
Mary C. 10 f "
C.L. 7 f "
William 5 m "
Burrell 2 m "

Euf # 503
THOMAS, Allen 13 m Ala
(See John Peake).

Euf # 711 Farmer (200-7000)
THOMAS, Daniel 22 m Ala
(See Joseph Whigham).

Euf # 360 Farmer (1000-300)
THOMAS, David 39 m Ga
Elizabeth 37 f "
James 10 m "
John 8 m "

Euf # 1264
THOMAS, Drucilla A. 26 f SC
Jesse N. 5 m Ala
(See Seaborn DuBose).

Txv # 1156 Farm laborer
THOMAS, Elijah W. 22 m Ga
(See Allen Bass).

Luvl # 518
THOMAS, Elizabeth 20 f Ga
Georgia A. 1 f Ala
(See W. C. Scroggins).

Euf # 253 Laborer (900-000)
THOMAS, Elliot 30 m Ala
Lucinda 20 f Ga
infant 1 f Ala

Euf # 840 Shoemaker (300-150)
THOMAS, Henry 45 m Conn
Susan 16 f NC
Martha A. 14 f Ga
Floyd W. 12 m "
Mary S. 10 f "
John C. 8 m "
James M. 8 m "

Euf # 1316 Laborer (--- 100)
THOMAS, Henry A. 22 m Ala
Feriby 18 f Ga

Mdwy # 1081 Farmer (3500-3000)
THOMAS, J. S. 30 m NY
Aramantha 23 f Ala
Elizabeth 4 f "
W.B. 8/12 m "

Euf # 689 Laborer
THOMAS, J. W. 19 m Ala
(See Eldridge Medley)

Bfd # 1247 Laborer (2000-200)
(Deaf & Dumb)
THOMAS, James E. 41 m Ga
Dorcas 40 f NC
Ann 20 f Ala
(Cont.)

(Bfd # 1247 cont.)
Josephine 13 f Ala
Margaret 10 f "
John 8 m "
Florida P. 3 f "

Nwto # 616 Farmer (1000-1500)
THOMAS, John 64 m NC
Anne 63 f "
Mahala 39 f "
Ada 27 f "
Lecie 22 f Ala
Obediah (Farmer) 20 m "
HELMS, L. E. 6 f "
Mary 5 f "

Euf # 298 Farmer (18000-35000)
THOMAS, John W. 41 m Ga
Lucy A. 33 f "
Harriett 10 f "
Winny M. 10 f "
Emma C. 8 f "
John W. 6 m "
Lucy 4 f "
Milton 1 m "

Bfd # 1246, (1226, 1227, 1228)
Farmer (8000-35,000)
THOMAS, Jonathan 45 m Ga
Maria J. 41 f "
James E. (Farmer) 20 m Ala
Wm. H. " 18 m "
Henry C. " 16 m "
J. C. 14 m "
David K. 12 m "
Aloinia P. 10 f "
Charity C. 8 f "
Ada L. 6 f "
M. L. 2 m "
A. M. (#1227) 24 f "
(--- 400)
George H. (---3000) 15 m "
Z. T. " " 12 m "
#1228
McGILVRAY, Zilpha A. 10 f "
(--- 3000)
Mary M. 8 f Ala
Charity 4 f "
Joseph E. 6 m "
Milledge J. 2 m "
(# 1246)

Bkb # 682 Farmer (100-150)
THOMAS, Leroy Jr. 30 m Ga
Sarah 26 f "
(Cont.)

(Bkb # 682 cont.)
Leroy 10 m Ala
Thomas J. 8 m "
M.A.N. 6 f "
John Gill S. 4 m "
David A. 1 m "

Bfd # 1258
THOMAS, Mahala N. 16 f Ala
(See Dennis Condry).

Luvl # 305 (---700)
THOMAS, Mary 41 f Ala
Martha 14 f "
Joseph D. 11 m "
Narcissa 8 f "
Cornelia J. 5 f "

Euf # 504
THOMAS, Mary J. 16 f Ala
John 57 m Ga
(See Jesse Lee).

Euf 718 Farmer (---1500)
THOMAS, Moses 55 m NC
Catharine 54 f "

Euf # 717 Farmer (1700-600)
THOMAS, Moses W. 31 m NC
Mary 29 f "
William P. 8 m Ala
Lydia J. 6 f "
John W. 4 m "
Mary E. 3 f "
Ann 1 f "

Euf # 1317 (500-100)
THOMAS, Nancy 55 f NC
Nancy J. 13 f Ala
Christiana 12 f "

Euf # 254 (--- ---)
THOMAS, Nancy 52 f Ga
Nancy 14 f Ala
Ann 12 f "

Euf # 512 Farmer (--- 200)
THOMAS, William 57 m Ga
Sarah 54 f "
STRICKLIN, Martha 5 f Ala

Bkb # 683 Farmer (--- 160)
THOMAS, William 40 m Ga
Elizabeth 35 f "
James M. (Farmer) 17 m Ala
William " 15 m "
Francis M. 13 m "
(Cont.)

(Bkb # 683 cont.)
Nicey A. 10 f Ala
Emma 8 f "

Euf # 843 Shoemaker (--- ---)
THOMAS, William H. 24 m Ga
Dolly B. 26 f "
Celia A. S. 6 f "
Ella F. N. 4 f Ala
Martha 10/12 f "

Mdwy # 1028 Farmer (---9000)
THOMASSON, G. Y. 40 m Ga
Lucy 32 f "
W. A. 7 f "
Daniel A. 3 m Ala
Mary E. 3 f "
Lucy W. 2 f "

Euf # 74 Carriage maker (2500-2500)
THOMPKINS, Charles C. 39 m NJ
Elizabeth 27 f Fla
Albert 2 m Ala
BURDINE, David M. 35 m NY
(Carriage painter).
CHAMBERS, James H. 23 m Ohio
(Carriage maker).

Nwto # 553 Farmer (---200)
THOMPSON, A. C. 23 m Ala
Lucinda 25 f "
Florence 2 f "
ROLLIN, George 55 m NC
Betsy 55 f "
Cater 35 m Ala
GRUBBS, Morgin 2 m "

Nwto # 600 Farmer (800-650)
THOMPSON, Alladin 44 m SC
S. N. 37 f Ga
Henry H. 14 m Ala
Jesse D. K. 12 m "
Robert G. 10 m "
Sarah J. 8 f "
C. D. 6 f "
William P. 4 m "
C. 1 m "

Euf # 228 R.R. Contractor (----200,000)
THOMPSON, Asa E. 48 m Ga

Flk # 460 Farmer (1000-500)
THOMPSON, Enoch 35 m Ala
Julia A. 32 f Ga
(Cont.)

(Flk # 460 cont)
James M. 6 m Ala
Martha J. 3 f "

Euf # 1043 Farmer (19,000-80,000)
THOMPSON, George W. 45 m Ga
S. W. 38 f "
Eugene 2 m Ala

Txv # 1212 Farmer (---150)
THOMPSON, James 65 m NC
Nancy 66 f "
David (Farmer) 18 m Ala

Euf # 1281 Farmer (30,000-11,000)
THOMPSON, John 75 m SC
Mary 74 f NC
FLOYD, Mary A. 17 f Ga
Hardy 13 m "

Nwto # 554 Farmer (---300)
THOMPSON, John 30 m Ala
Martha 25 f "
John 4 m "

Euf # 1046 (3,000-45,000)
THOMPSON, Louisa H. 35 f Ga

Mdwy # 1093
THOMPSON, Mary 42 f SC
(See James A. Parham).

Euf # 521
THOMPSON, Mary W. 45 f Ga
(See John A. Wells).

Flk # 461 Farmer
THOMPSON, Robert 25 m Ala
(See Rhoda Graves)

Euf # 377 Farmer (2,800-5,500)
THOMPSON, Shadrach 43 m NC
Martha 33 f Ga
Louisa 8 f Ala
Milton A. 1 m "

Clay # 50 Eating house (---300)
THORN, B. A. 56 m Md
Matilda 19 f Ala
Francis 2 f "
MITCHELL, Mary 16 f Ga

Nwto # 590 Farmer (---250)
THORN, John 35 m SC
Martha A. 26 f Ga
James 10 m Ala
Frances 8 f "
Nancy 6 f "
Mary A. 2 f "

Clay 679 Farmer (600-180)
THORN, Joseph 39 m SC
Martha 24 f Ala
Laura 6 f "
Zachariah 4 m "
F. M. 1 m "

Mdwy # 954 Farmer (2000-4000)
THORNTON, George G. 25 m Ga
Martha 18 f Ala
Charles 1 m "

Mdwy # 1016 Farmer (6000-30,000)
THORNTON, Green H. 64 m Ky
Rhoda 54 f Ga
R. B.(Farmer, ---4500) 26 m "
CARTLEDGE, Green T. 1 m Ala

Euf # 827 Farmer (6,000-22,000)
THORNTON, J. M. 44 m Ga
Rebecca N. 28 f Va
E. D. (Clerk) 21 m Ala
R. J. (Student) 19 m "
Hester A.(At school) 17 f "
Henry " " 15 m "
Dawson R. 13 m "
Nathan N. 12 m "
Jonathan 10 m "
Martha 8 f "
Rebecca T. 3 f "
Frederick 2 m "

Mdwy # 978 (--- ---)
THORNTON, Milly 46 f Ga
W.E. (Farmer, ___5000) 25 m "
Reuben C. " 15 m "
Eliza M. 12 f "

Euf # 16-16 Merchant (---3,300)
THORNTON, R. D.(?) 28 m Ga
Nat. H. (Merchant) 22 m Ga
(---1,400)

Mdwy # 1021 Farmer (10,000-40,000)
THORNTON, R. D. 30 m Ga
Ann E. 25 f "
(Cont.)

(Mdwy # 1021 cont.)
Elizabeth 4 f Ala
John 6/12 m "
SEAY, Harriett M. 15 f "
(------50,000)
Caroline G. 13 f "
(------50,000)

Euf # 283 Physician (40,000-65,000)
THORNTON, William H. 42 m Ga
Mary B. 32 f "
Mary R. 13 f Ala
Laura V. 11 f "
Anna 9 f "
Sallie 5 f "
Willie 2 f "
Joseph B. 22 m Ga
(---5,000, Med. student).

Mdwy # 1038 Farmer (3800-20,000)
THRASH, H. D. 33 m Ga
Anne E. 30 f "
Martha A. 8 f "
Henry D. 6 m Ala
William A. 5 m "
Louisiana 2 f "
infant 6/12 m "

Clay # 108 Farm laborer
THRLINGTON(?), James 23 m Ala
(See Franklin Watkins).

Euf # 748 Laborer (300-100)
THURMAN, Jere 49 m SC
Celia 46 f Ga
William (Laborer) 19 m Ala
Emanuel " 17 m "
Darling 14 f "
Sarah A. 10 f "
Elizabeth 8 f "
James L. 7 m "

Euf # 1315 Farmer (----500)
THWEATT, Daniel 45 m SC
Martha 32 f "
Adam 13 m Ala
Joseph H. 10 m "
Alfred M. 7 m "
Sarah H. 6 f "
Daniel 4 m "
Mary E. 2 f "
James 6/12 m "

Euf # 70 Saddler (400-1500)
THWEAT, John W. 45 m SC
Elizabeth 33 f Ga
Alonzo M. 15 m Ala
Moses Ann 15 f "
Levi M. 13 m "
John 10 m "

Euf # 1033 Farmer (1500-6500)
THWEATT, L. M. 39 m SC
Ann 32 f Ga
Ann E. 9 f Ala
John 8 m "
Oscar 6 m "
Laura 3 f "
Lula 5/23 f "

Mdwy # 982 Supt. of mill (----500)
TIDWELL, H. D. 46 m Ga
Frances 44 f "
Elizabeth 23 f Ala
CARDIN, Phoebe C. 18 f Ga
TIDWELL, Emily 16 f "
Frances 13 f Ala
William 9 m "
Everline 2 f "
CARDIN, Mary 1 f "

Luvl # 524
TILMAN, Nancy 60 f NC
CASEY, Mary 30 f "

Luvl # 538
TILLMAN, Harriett 28 f NC
Mary A. 8 f Ala
John 6 m "
Robert 4 m "
Stephen 2 m "
(See Zilphy Westbrook).

Nwto # 635 Work at saw mill (---150)
TILLMAN, Jonathan 35 m Ga
Zilphy E. 25 f Ala
Elizabeth 6 f "
Daniel 3 m "
Isaac 4/12 m "

Euf # 66 Farmer (800-250)
TINDALL, William D. 30 m SC
Margaret 30 f Ga
James B. 2 m Ala
John 1 m "
Wm. L. Yancy 1/12 m "

Clay # 184 (3,100-6,000)
Tinsley, Alvenia 45 f Ga
Sally 25 f "
Lucy 21 f "
James (Farmer) 15 m "
Charles 12 m Ala
Albert 10 m "

Euf # 1098 Farmer (30,000-87,000)
TISON, James G. 40 m SC
Adriana C. 32 f "
V. E. (Blind). 17 f Ala
A. C. 16 f "
James A. 14 m "
Sarah E. 11 f "
Mary C. 8 f "
Ann E. 6 f "
Margaret H. 3 f "

Luvl # 284 Farmer (4,000-5000)
Tomberlin, Carson 48 m NC
Mary 48 f "
Wilson (Farmer) 25 m "
(1500-350)
David (Farmer) 10 m Ala
Mary 15 f "
Emeline 14 f "
Mela 12 f "
Alexander 10 m "
James 8 m "

Euf # 894 Hireling
TOMLIN, T. J. 20 m Ga
(See Leroy G. Hightower).

Clay # 1288 Retired lawyer (6000-15000)
TOMPKINS, Henry M. 47 m SC
H. M. 36 f Ga
Henry B. 15 m Ala
Mary A. 4 f "
Hamilton M.(Idiotic) 23 m "

Euf # 455 Farmer (20,000-40,000)
TONEY, Washington 47 m SC
Sarah A. 39 f Ga
Mary E. 18 f Ala
William 17 m Ga
Eliza J. 15 f "
Caroline H. 13 f Ala
Sterling B. 11 m "
Tandy W. 9 m "
(Cont.)

(Euf # 455 cont.)
Ida 2 f Ala
Flora(?) 2/12 f "
BASS, Samuel (Blind) 53 m Ga
(----5,400)
E. J. (----11,000) 50 f "

Euf # 178 Painter
TOTTON, Christopher 40 m Ire
(See James Tansey).

Euf # 817 Farmer (---100)
TOWLER, J. R. 32 m Ga
Sarah A. 22 f "
Mary J. 2 f Ala
George W. 9/12 m "
Williams, Rebecca A. 15 f "

Euf # 42 Laborer
TOWLER, W. W. 25 m Ga
(See Edward Richards).

Euf # 322 Farmer (---200)
TOWLER, William H. 60 m Ga
Matilda 60 f "
Frances A. 19 f "
Jud S. 14 m "

Txv # 1192
TRAMMELL, Eliza J. 23 f Ga
John H. 20 m Ala
J.A.P.J. 17 f "
(See P. N. Cannon).

Euf # 656 Farmer (1400-200)
TRAWICK, H. J. 29 m Ala
Matilda 23 f S.C.
Christina J. 4 f "
George 2 m "
Nancy (?)1/12 f "

Euf # 1331 Farmer (17,000-96,000)
TREADWELL, B. F. 51 m SC

Euf # 1369 (30,000-45000)
TREADWELL, Marie M. 43 f SC

Euf 410 Farmer (100-11,000)
TREADWELL, Samuel 81 m NC
Mary 83 f NJ

Nwto # 579 Farmer (----150)
Trent, Willis 24 m Ga
Frances 25 f Ala
William 4 m "
(Cont.)

(Nwto # 579 cont.)
James 3 m Ala
Sarah Jane 1 f "
JOHNSTON, Elizabeth 12 f "

Euf # 1110
TREUTLEN, C. 18 f Ala
Julia G. 16 f "
(See A. W. Barnett)

Euf 1106 Marchant (5000-15000)
TREUTLEN, John F. 29 m SC
Carrie 22 f "
Anna 4 f Ala
Edward 2 m "
Charles 1/12 m "
LANE, Thos. W. 31 m Ga
(Clerk).
CHAPMAN, Henry 17 m "
(Clerk).

Euf # 637 Farmer (350-150)
TRINNEL(?), James 30 m Ala
Ruthy 25 f "
James 5 m "
Elizabeth 2 f "

Txv # 1170
TROY, Elizabeth 18 f Ala
Lurinda 16 f Ga
Zora 14 f "
John 12 m "
Andrew 9 m "
(See John Barberee)

Mt. A. # 894 Farm laborer
TUCKER, Daniel T. 21 m Ga
(See Newton L. C. Bullard).

Euf # 920 Farmer (5000-17,500)
TUCKER, James 60 m Ga
Eliza 50 f "
Daniel (Farmer) 22 m Ala
Sarah 21 f "
Francis (farm hand) 18 m "
James A. " " 16 m "
John E. 14 m "
Mary C. 12 f "

Clay # 21
TUCKER, John W. 22 m Va
(Living in hotel)

Euf # 567
TUCKER, Louisa 24 f Ga
(See Exekiel Alexander).

Euf # 922 Farmer (1800-4500)
TUCKER, William 33 m Ala
Mary 28 f SC
Mary E. 10 f Ala
James B. 8 m "
Harriett 6 f "
William 6 m "
Sallie 1 f "

Euf # 313 Laborer (--- ---)
TUEQUEVILLE, Tarpley 69 m SC
Hariet 52 f "
HISMITH, John 18 m Ala
(Laborer)
Sarah A. 21 f SC
TUEQUEVILLE, Geo. W. 11 m Ala

Euf # 297 Tutoress
TULEY(?), Carrie M. 24 f Mass
(See John R. McIntosh).

Mdwy # 1061 Physician & farmer (20,000-50,000)
TULLIS, Thomas E. 31 m SC
Laura 24 f Ga
Lila 5 f Ala
T. W. 3 m "

Euf # 879 Farmer (800-2000)
TURK, George 29 m Fla
Ella 28 f SC
VAUGHAN, Frank 18 m "

Clay # 1235 Farmer (320-320
TURLINGTON, Wm. T. 27 m Ala
Ruthy A. 29 f NC
James M. 2 m Ala
William W. 1 m "

Mdwy # 981 Farmer (2860-25000)
TURMAN, G. J. 31 m Ga
BARR, Sarah F. 11 f Ala

Euf # 1363 Farmer (1500-2000)
TURNAGE, Carney 53 m NC
Ann 26 f Ga
Phillip 20 m NC
Louisa 11 f Ala
Wiley 10 m "
Moses 7 m "
(Cont.)

(Euf # 1363 cont.)
Julia 5 f Ala
Mary 2 f "
Malissa 6/12 f "

Mt. A. 879 Farmer (435-200)
TURNER, Aerial 54 m NC
Keziah 45 f "
John E. 20 m "
(Farm laborer)
Mary J. 18 f Ala
M.A. 12 f "
Jason J. 8 m "
George H. 3 m "

Euf # 1225 Physician (2,000-8,000)
TURNER, Alex 40 m Scot
Charlott G. 26 f Va
Betty J. 4/12 f Ala

Txv # 1203
Turner, Caroline 22 f Ga
(See Benj. Farmer).

Euf # 472 Overseer (---100)
TURNER, Elam 23 m Ga

Euf # 487 Farmer (---200)
TURNER, George 22 m Ala
Sarah 16 f Ga
Villula 6/12 f Ala

Mdwy # 1005 Farmer (10,000-28,000)
TURNER, Green B. 30 m Ga
Mary A. 24 f "
Frances O. 3 f Ala
Sarah 1 f "
HUTCHINSON, Thos. 25 m "
(Overseer on farm).

Euf # 1120 Farmer (1,000-300)
TURNER, H. F. 31 m Ga
Mary J. 25 f "
Gazaway 5 m Ala
John G. H. 3 m "
Mary J. 1 f "

Mdwy # 1045 Farmer (10,3000-28,000)
TURNER, J. Henry 34 m Ga
Sarah C. 29 f "
Columbus H. 11 m "
N.R.W. 8 f "
H.L. 6 m "
Victoria A. 2 f Ala

Mt. A. # 798
TURNER, James 23 m Ga
(See Henry Bullard).

Nwto # 598 Farmer (1500-4000)
TURNER, James K. 50 m Ga
Sarah 54 f "
James (Farmer) 17 m "
SHANKS, James T. 4 m Ala

Clay # 114 Farmer (1800-5000)
TURNER, Noel W. 56 m SC
Margaret 55 f NC

Clay # 120 Farmer (800-200)
TURNER, Robert W. 32 m Ala
Mary (B.?) (?) 31 f "
John A. 10 m "
Sidney 8 f "
George W. 4 m "
L. E. 1 f "

Flk # 407
Turner, Sarah L. 18 f Ala
John 23 m Ga
(See Monroe Crocker).

Mdwy # 1048 Planter (5000-23000)
TURNER, Warren H. 48 m Ga

Euf # 663
TYCE, Elizabeth 65 f NC
(See John T. McGlaun).

Euf # 669 (---100)
TYCE, Elizabeth A. 28 f Ala
Martha 16 f "
Jane 14 f "
Elizabeth 11 f "
James 9 m "

Clay # 178 Blind.
TYLER, James 48 m SC
(In poorhouse).

Euf # 252 Butcher (3,500-400)
TYLER, Joshua 41 m SC
Ann J. 41 f "
R.A. 20 f "
E.L. 17 f "
M.A. 15 f "
Ann J. 13 f "
Ursula A. 11 f "
Pauline 5 f "
Elizabeth 2 f Ala
McLEOD, Wm.(printer). 24 m "
Wilkins, Jas.(Laborer) 16 m "

Bfd # 1265 (Blind) (100-100)
TYLER, William 53 m SC
Rebecca 30 f "

Euf # 1045 (9000-36,300)
UPSHAW, Eugenia 10 f Ala
(See George D. Conner).

Euf # 1043 Farmer (27,000-90,000)
UPSHAW, LeRoy 37 m Ga
Ann S. 25 f "
RICHARDSON, Jane 59 f "
ALMAN, Thomas 23 m "

Euf # 1040 (15,000-50,000)
UPSHAW, Mary E. 35 f Ga
Jack 18 m Ala
Susan 15 f "
Louisa 13 f "
Fanny 11 f "
Tallula 10 f "
James 8 m "
Mary W. 6 f "

Mt. A. # 872
UPTON, Rebecca 46 f SC
Louisa 14 f Ga
(See James Channell).

Euf # 602 Farmer (1000-650)
URQUHART, B. F. 32 m Ga
Elizabeth 30 f "
Sarah E. 9 f "
Mary N. 3 f Ala
Martha T.(?) C. 10/12 f "

Euf # 857 Overseer (---800)
URQUHART, Henry 38 m Ga
William 13 m Ala
Mary 11 f "

Euf # 1324 Farmer (---250)
USRY, William 34 m Ga
Mary 36 f SC
Sarah J. 7 f "
Elizabeth 5 f "
William M. 3 m "
John 1 m "

Flk # 446 Farmer (2000-3500)
UTSEY, Jacob 68 m SC
Mary 60 f "
Gavon (Farmer) 29 m Ala
Mary 20 f "
R. V. 18 f "

Clay # 178 (Insane)
VAINWRIGHT, Charlotte 40 f Ga
(In poorhouse)

Euf # 491 M.B. Minister (1,500-12,000)
VAN HOOSE, E. Y. 39 m Tenn
S.A. 36 f Ga
A.M. 1 m Ala
STRINGER, E.L. 13 f "
(----35,000).

Clay # 19 Tinsmith
VAN HOUTEN, E. 32 m NY
(Living in hotel).

Euf # 1093
VANN, Francis 7 m Ala
(See Jane E. Curry).

Euf # 1095 Dentist (-- --)
VANN, Horatio 35 m NC

Euf # 1094 (---7,000)
VANN, Penelope 65 f NC

Clay # 151 Overseer (--- ---)
VARNADORE, Thomas 31 m Ga
Nancy 26 f "
PETERSON, Munroe 13 m "
VARNADORE, William 2 m Ala
GREEN, G.A. 33 f Ga
John D. 8 m Ala

Euf # 1003 Farmer (500-500)
VAUGHAN, Asa 44 m SC
Sarah A. 35 f "
Webster (in school) 17 m Ga
Mary J. 15 f "
Delilah 12 f "
Adaline 11 f "
Lafayette 9 m "
Parry 7 f "
Georgia 5 f Ala
Jeremiah 4 m "
infant 6/12 f "

Euf # 1112 Wheelwright (800-200)
VAUGHN, Daniel M. 46 m Ga
Rachael 47 f "
Harriet 18 f "
Susan 13 f "
John J. 12 m "
Joseph 11 m "
Zach T. 9 m "
Lou G. 6 f "

Euf # 879
VAUGHAN, Frank 18 m SC
(See George Turk).

Euf # 275 Laborer (600-100)
VAUGHN, John 46 m Ga
Rebecca 44 f "
Cintha 17 f "
George 14 m "
James 10 m Ala
Henry 8 m "
Eli 5 m "
Elizabeth 3 f "
Sarah 5/12 f "

Euf # 124 Montua maker
VAUGHN, Martha E. 29 f SC
Noel 10 m "
Henry B. 2/12 m Ala
(See Jack Hardman).

Euf # 1036 Hireling
VAUGHN, Webster 17 m Ga
(See Thomas. J. Florence).

Euf # 1006 Cabt. maker (----100)
VAUGHAN, Wm. B. 32 m Ga
Mary A. 33 f "
William C. 13 m "
Willis W. 10 m "
Cornelia M. 5 f Ala
Mary E. 2 f "
James A. 2/12 m "

Euf # 69 Tailor (---200)
VEAL, A. J. 30 m NC
Susan O. 27 f "
Charles E. 6 m "
Julius W. 3 m Ala
infant 1 m "

Euf # 133 Harness maker (600-2000)
VEAL, E. 60 m NC
Elizabeth 59 f "
Louisa 28 f "
Alexander (Clerk) 22 m "
Susan A.(?) 15 f "
Elizabeth J. 14 f "
Sarah A. 13 f "

Luvl # 260 Farmer (---1000)
VEAL, F. D. 25 m Ga
H.A.C. 18 f Ala
Mary E. 1 f "

Euf # 134 Harness maker (--100)
VEAL, John 24 m NC
Lucy 18 f "
John B. 9/12 m Ala

Clay # 195 Farmer (3000-7000)
VENTRESS, James 41 m Ga
Mary J. 32 f Ala
Sarah O. 13 f "
Ella V. 11 f "
John R. 9 m "
Thomas 7 m "
Charles 5 m "
William 3 m "
James 2 m "

Clay # 87
VENTRESS, Mollie E. 23 f Ala
VENTRESS, W. E. 21 m "
(Clerk)
(See Louisa Collins).

Clay # 210 Farmer (2000-12000)
VENTRESS, Thomas 46 m Ga
Mary A. 33 f Ala
Stephen (Farmer) 16 m "
Martha A. 14 f "
Thomas H. 12 m "
Ann E. 5 f "
A. C. 3 f "
James C. 2 m "

Bkb # 716 Farm laborer
VERDON, Morgan 24 m SC
(See Y. H. McDaniel).

Bkb # 776 Farm laborer
VERDON, Morgan 22 m SC

Euf # 231 Carpenter (--- ---)
VESSELLA, John F. 50 m SC
Elizabeth 40 f Ga
Jas. (---200) 20 m Ala
Julius (---300) 18 m "
(Laborer)
Andrew 15 m "
William 12 m "
Charles 9 m "
Sally 7 f "

Clay # 1108 Carpenter (---500)
VICKARS, James M. 30 m Fla
Mary 23 f Ala
John T. 1 m "
SPENCE, K.(?) T. 22 m "
(Farm laborer, ---100)

Flk # 447 Farmer (2000-500)
VICKARS, John R. 57 m Ga
Amanda M. 32 f "
Lucitta V. 7 f Ala
Mary V. 6 f "
Georgia A. 3 f "
Eliza J. 2 f "

Flk # 421 Farmer (2000-2000)
VICKARS, Michael P. 44 m Ga
Sarah A. E. 34 f "
John J. R. 14 m Ala
Jane M. 13 f "
James S. 11 m "
Thomas H. 7 m "
Jerry K. 2 m "
Sarah A. E. 6/12 f "
McDANIEL, Frederick 30 m Ga
(Farmer, 3000-5000)
Easther 26 f "
John F. 5 m "
Mary J. 4 f "
Georgia 2 f "

Clay # 1107 Master carpenter (---800)
VICKARS, Solomon W. 36 m Ala
Rebecca 20 f "
Sidney N. 4 m "
Lilly A. 7/12 f "

Clay # 76 Mechanic (4,500-500).
VICKERS, James(?) W. 40 m Ga
Camelia 30 f NC
John J. 2 m Ala
Joseph 11/12 m "
BUSH, Sarah A. 10 f "

Euf # 51 Electrician (---500)
VILLERET, F. 32 m Fr.

Euf # 358 Farmer (600-1150)
VINCENT, John 60 m Ga
Elizabeth 46 f "
Barbara 16 f "
Margery P. 10 f "
LAND, Madison 12 m "
HOLLY,Welcome 20 m "
(Laborer).

Euf # 461 Farmer (1000-500)
VINING, J.(?) A. 39 m Ga
Elizabeth 28 f "
John S. 10 m Ala
Adaline 9 f "
(Cont.)

(Euf # 461 cont.)
Macon 6 m Ala
Sophrona 4 f "
Amoriva 1 f "

Luvl # 374 (600-1800)
VINING, Mary A. 46 f Ga
(See Geo. L. Shipman).

Euf # 1169 Farmer (500-150)
VINSON, James 23 m Ga
Matilda 25 f "
John 4 m "
Henry 2 m Ala
Mary 3/12 f "

Clay # 83 Clerk
VINSON, N. W. 17 m Ga
(See C. W. Jones, Sr.)

Euf # 761 Farmer (600-400)
VINSON, William 35 m Ga
Matilda 31 f "
Sanford F. 13 m "
John F. 11 m "
Mary E. 10 f "
James E. 5 m "
Fidelia M. 3 f "

Clay # 190 Farmer (--- ---)
VOLENTINE, James 32 m NC
Martha 22 f Ala
John T. 3 m "
Ann E. 3/12 f "

Clay # 238 Farmer (500-500)
VOLENTINE, Mathew 65 m NC
Catherine 55 f "
Rebecca 22 f "
Christian 20 f "
Isaac (Farmer) 21 m Ala
Mary 18 f "
Marion (Farmer) 15 m "
Frances 13 f "

Mt. A. # 838 Farmer (1000-10,000)
VOORHEES, Cornelius 48 m NJ
Elizabeth 35 f Fla
Jemima 16 f "
John 13 m "
Eliza 11 f "
James 7 m Ala
Elbridge 5 m "
Bascombe 2 m "

Euf # 1165 School teacher
WADKINS, Richard 23 m Ga
(See Job Jemison).

Euf # 908 Overseer (---300)
WADSWORTH, Charles 33 m Ga
Malinda 30 f "
William 11 m "
Mary J. 8 f Ala
Charles 6 m "
Robert 5 m "
Frances 4 f "
Lula 6/12 f "

Euf # 1265 Physician (---1000)
WAGREEN(?), John T. 28 m Ga

Euf # 595 Farmer (2000-600)
WALDEN, Albert 44 m Ga
Rebecca 42 f NC
Thomas H. H. 17 m Ga
George W. 15 m Ala
David 13 m "
John W. 11 m "
Ira 8 m "
Caroline 6 f "
William 3 m "

Mdwy # 1091 Farm laborer (---310)
WALDROP, F. M. 22 m Ga
Louisa 22 f "
Sarah J. 1 f "

Mdwy # 1090 Farm laborer (---100)
WALDROP, L. L. 28 m Ga
Sarah B. 26 f "
Mary 8 f "
Sarah 6 f "
Milton 4 m "
Larkin 3 m "
Louisa 1 f "

Mdwy # 985 Clerk
WALDROP, Larkin 20 m Ala
(See Elizabeth A. Owen).

Mdwy # 1089 Farmer (5000-7000)
WALDROP, Milton 48 m SC
Sarah 47 f "
W. H. 20 m Ga
Sarah 15 f "
H. A. 14 f "
Mary M. 12 f "
Milton A. 9 m "
Martha H. 7 f "

Mdwy # 986 Painter
WALDROP, Thomas 24 m Ga
(See Sarah Owens).

Euf 92 Clerk (--- ---)
WALKER, Adison A.(?) 25 m Ga
Frances 22 f Ala
Beverly C. 7/12 m "

Euf # 662 (1000-6500)
WALKER, Barbary 50 f Ala
John F. 22 m SC
James R. (Farmer) 21 m "
Barsilla 19 m Ala
Phillip J. 15 m "
Andrew J. 13 m "
Jason J. 10 m "
Genl. Irvin 6 m "
BENTLEY, Vicey A. 10 f "

Txv # 1200 Farmer (240-250)
WALKER, Daniel 26 m Ga
Sarah J. 21 f Ala
John L. 8/12 m "
Wm. V. (Idiotic) 25 m Ga

Euf # 359 Farmer (500-300)
WALKER, George 38 m SC
Mary 32 f Ga
Lucy 14 f Ala
Sarah A. 11 f "
Daniel 9 m "
Susan 7 f "
Mary A. 5 f "
Lucinda A. 3 f "
Barbara M. 1 f "
Sarah 75 f NC

Euf # 887 Hireling (---100)
WALKER, John 34 m Ga
Sarah 35 f "
John G. 7 m Ala
Ann E. 5 f "
Elizabeth 2 f "
Luther 6/12 m "

Euf # 1337 Merchant (---4,000)
WALKER, John H. 33 m Ga
Mary 34 f "
John T. 9 m "
Robert 3 m Ala
Edgar 8/12 m "

Euf # 658 Farmer (2500-2000)
WALKER, John H. 35 m SC
Elizabeth 34 f "
Robert 4 m Ala
Franklin 2 m "
Jeremiah 6/12 m "
TEW, Hez (Laborer) 23 m "

Clay # 183 Planter (16000-100,000)
WALKER, L. W. 37 m Ga
M. V. 29 f "
M. V. 9 f Ala
T. T. 7 m "
J. L. 6 f "
H. B. 5 m "
E. B. 3 f "
B. L. 2 m "
A. 1 f "
McCRIMMON, Daniel 36 m NC
(School teacher).

Bfd # 1251 Farmer (1800-600)
WALKER, Lewis 66 m NC
Nancy 45 f "
Mazie 27 f Ala
Nancy J. 25 f "
Mary 22 f "
John A. 19 m "
Amanda 16 f "
David 14 m "
James S. 11 m "
Sinthia C. 9 f "

Euf # 696 Farmer (3000-3500)
WALKER, Nathan 50 m SC
Jane 42 f "
Darling 15 m Ala
Mary 13 f "
Arrena 11 f "
Christina 9 f "
Jason 7 m "
Mary J. 4 f "
Rebecca A. 2 f "
ROLAND, Sarah 27 f Ga
Susan (---100) 61 f SC

Clay # 187 Planter (8700-33,800)
WALKER, Virgil H. 34 m Ga
Antoinette 27 f "
Ann L. 6 f Ala
Ida L. 4 f "
Preston 3 m "
child 2 m "
infant 2/12 m "
Jas. L. (Farmer) 22 m Ga

Clay # 18 (--- ---)
WALKER, William J. 25 m Ga
(See A. L. Oliver).

Clay # 110 Farmer (---500)
WALL, James 59 m Ga
(Cont.)

(Clay # 110 cont).
Mary 51 f Ga
Mary M. 16 f Ala
James T. 9 m "
BUSH, Mary 5 f Tex

Nwto # 574 Farmer (4000-3000)
WALL, Josiah 43 m Ga
Lavica 45 f "

Mdwy # 1018 Farmer (800-500)
WALLER, B. H. 42 m NC
Rhoda C. 34 f SC
Ethmore 13 m Ala
Delila E. 10 f "
Martha B. 7 f "
Mary 3 f "
Nellie 2 f "
Benjamin 1 m "
Delila 75 f NC

Clay # 189 Idiotic
WALLER, Elizabeth 50 f NC
(See Amariah Day).

Euf # 182 Gin maker (100-300)
WAMBLE, Andrew 52 m NC
Caroline 35 f SC
Thomas 8 m Ala

Clay # 44 In jail
WARD, C. H. 35 m Ga

Flk # 503 Farmer (550-225)
WARD, H. C. 30 m Ala
Amelia L. 22 f "

Euf # 599
WARD, Lafayette 9 m Fla
(See Robert H. Dawkins).

Clay # 186 Farmer
WARD, Lewis D. 34 m Ala
Julia 22 f "
Henry R. 4 m "
Mary F. 2 f "
COHEN, Jas. (Farmer) 22 m "
HILL, Augustus " 21 m "
GREEN, Thomas " 21 m Ga

Euf # 440 Quarryman
WARD, Patrick 32 m Ire
(See McNamara's R.R. Gro.)

Euf # 420 Laborer
WARD, Patrick 30 m Scot
(See James Daniels).

Luvl # 266
WARD, Polly 65 f SC
(See Daniel McKenzie)

Euf # 453
WARD, Willis 66 m Ga
(See Willis G. Hunt).

Euf # 352 Retired teacher (---9,500)
WARE, (Ward?) James R. 57 m Eng.
(Lived London, Eng.)

Luvl # 545 Farmer (4000-4000)
WARICK, D. G. 35 m Ala
Martha 24 f Ga
John T. 4/12 m Ala
Sarah 72 f NC

Euf # 475 Farmer (----4500)
WARLICK, William 33 m SC
Ann 25 f Ala
Mary 5 f "
Eliza 4 f "
Louisa 1 f "
JOHNSON, Susan 14 f "

Txv # 1190 Farmer (1000-650)
WARR, E. S. 38 m SC
Parasada 34 f Ala
Sarah J. 13 f "
Martha 11 f "
Mary E. 10 f "
Adam S. 7 m "
George W. 5 m "
D.M.C. 2 f "
BLAKEY, Asa 19 m Ga

Txv # 1165 Farmer (---200)
WARR, J. W. 25 m Ga
Margaret L. 24 f Ala
Nancy A. 1 f "

Txv # 1166 Farmer (1500-800)
WARR, James Thomas 48 m SC
Maria 48 f "
Mary J. 18 f Ga
John E. 13 m "
BAKER, James M. 25 m SC
(Farm laborer)
Alexander 21 m Ala
(Farm laborer)

Clay # 1121 Farmer (800-500)
WARR, John 63 m SC
Nancy A. 64 f "
HARTZOG, Margaret 23 f Ga

Txv # 1136 Farmer (500-500)
WARR, John B. 27 m SC
Elizabeth J. 25 f NC
E.M. 5 f Ala
John W. 3 m "
R.J. 2 f "
C.A.M. 4/12 f "

Clay # 1122 Farmer (400-300)
WARR, William F. 25 m SC
Elizabeth 20 f Ala

Mt. A. # 801 Farmer (2000-21000)
WARREN, C. M. 40 m SC
Mary 38 f "
Elizabeth 13 f "
Frank E. 10 m "
Seaborn E. 7 m Ala

Clay # 158
WARREN, James E. 17 m Ala
(See William Bishop)

Flk # 504 (2000-10,000)
WARREN, Lucinda 49 f SC
Jas. B. (Farmer) 21 m Ala
(1000-7000)
Bates (Farmer) 18 m Ala
(1000-3000)
SMART, George W. 10 m "

Clay # 19 Physician
WARREN, Monroe 22 m Ala
(Living in hotel).

Clay # 242 (3,000-10,000)
WARREN, Nancy 75 f SC

Euf # 21-21
WARREN, Sarah E. 18 f Ala
(See John W. Clark).

Clay # 229 Farmer (---250)
WARREN, Thomas 39 m Ala
Frances S. 25 f "
William E. 7 m "
W.S. 5 m "
N.E. 4 f "
Julia 1 f "
JOHNSON, Penny 20 f SC
WARREN, E. P. 13 m Ala
WORTHINGTON, E. E. 24 f Ga

Clay # 245 Farmer (---2000)
WARREN, Thomas M. 19 m Ala
Joel M. (---2000) 14 m "
(See Thomas C. Helms).

Euf # 1001 Overseer (4200-000)
WARREN, Thomas W. 40 m Ga
(See M. R. Hill).

Luvl # 313 Shoemaker (700-60)
WASHBURN, H. M. 62 m Miss
Rachael 47 f Ga
Francis (Shoemaker) 19 m "
Sinthia A. 17 f "
Lavinia 19 f "
Emily 20 f "
Willis 14 m "

Luvl # 363 Farmer
WASHBURN, Martin 22 m Ga
(See Needham Lee, Jr.)

Clay # 139
WATERS, Delanie 40 f NC
Susan 16 f Ala
(See Daniel McLeod).

Clay # 108 Farmer (120-2800)
WATKINS, Franklin 45 m SC
L.E. 35 f Ga
John T. 17 m "
Susan A. E. 15 f "
Laura 12 f "
M.E. 9 f Ala
Isaac L. 8 m "
Franklin 6 m "
Westley 3 m "
THRLINGTON(?), James 23 m "
(Farm Laborer).

Clay # 178 In poorhouse
WATLEY, Eliza 15 f Ala
Emma 11 f "
William 6 m "

Euf # 729
WATLEY, Julia 25 m SC
Reubin 5 m Ala
Mary 3 f "
Sarah 1 f "
SANDERS, John L. 18 m SC
(Laborer).

Luvl # 328 (--- ---)
WATLEY, Julia E. 27 f SC
Reuben 5 m Ala
Mary 3 f "
Sarah 2 f "

Clay # 178 In poorhouse
WATSON, Claiborne 68 m Ga
(Cont.)

(Clay # 178 cont).
Claiborne, Jr. 6 m Ala
Jane 45 f Ga
Elizabeth 11 f Ala
Rachael 4 f "

Mt. A. # 855 Farmer (1200-400)
WATSON, D. G. 37 m Ala
Everlina 26 f "
R.H. 7 m La
J.M. 6 m "
E.L. 4 f Ala
E.G. 3 m "
MOODY, J. H. 16 m Ga

Mdwy # 1071 (---800)
WATSON, Elizabeth 64 f Ga
K.C. (Nathan C.) 30 m Ala
(Farmer, ---50).
J.F. (Jas. Francis) 25 m "
(Farmer, ---50)
P.W. (Peter W.) 23 m "
(Farmer, ---50)
J.J. (John J.) 28 m "
(Farmer, ---100)
A.R. 20 f "
J.T. 1 m "

Euf # 26 Farmer (200-5,000)
WATSON, George 60 m Pa
Sarah 62 f SC

Euf # 293 Farmer (2,500-9,000)
WATSON, George L. 33 m Ga
Elizabeth 22 f "
Josephine 6 f Ala
Lewis 4 m "
James 2 m "
Andrew 2/12 m "

Euf # 1256 Farmer (4500-13,000)
WATSON, John 34 m Ga
Mary R. 25 f Ala
Anas 9 m "
Caroline 8 f "
Mary 7 f "
George 6 m "
Leonora 5 f "
Ward 2 m "
CARTER, Mary 55 f SC

Euf # 1242 Farmer (1800-15000)
WATSON, M. M. 32 m Ga
Patience 34 f SC
Frances V. 6 f Ala
John 4 m "
Leonora 2 f "

Euf # 103 (300-200)
WATSON, Priscilla 53 f Ga
HARRELL, Elijah 12 m Ala
BISHOP, Elizabeth 19 f "
Mary E. 1 f "
HARRELL, Joshua C. 23 m Ga
(Farmer)
Amanda 15 f "

Clay # 212 (500-500)
WATSON, Susan P. 59 f Ga
P. H. (waggoning) 23 m "
Benjamin J. 16 m "
WILDER, Martha S. 8 f Ala

Txv # 1227 Farmer (---200)
WATTS, Thomas 25 m Ga
Jane 26 f "
William 5 m Ala
Martha L. 4/12 f "
Sarah 2 f "

Luvl # 510 Farmer (--- ---)
WATTS, Thomas 24 m Ga
Jane H. 29 f "
William F. 3 m "
M.L. 4/12 f Ala

Luvl # 262 Mechanic (-- --)
WATTS, William 35 m Ga
Matilda 29 f "
Benj. G. 13 m "
Josephine 11 f "
Rebecca 60 f NC

Clay # 226 Overseer (---400)
WEATHERS, Thomas 27 m Ga
Virginia 18 f "

Euf # 790 Farmer (3000-6000)
WEATHERS, William 70 m Ga
Elizabeth 18 f "

Euf # 1019 Farmer (8,000-28,000)
WEAVER, Absolem 55 m Ga
Mary 52 f "
Louisa 20 f "
Minerva 18 f "
Larkin 17 m "
Jacob 15 m "
Ellen 13 f Ala
Zachry 11 m "
Ann S. 9 f "

Euf # 916
WEAVER, Ellen 29 f SC
(See Hansford Dowling).

Flk # 464 Farmer (--- ---)
WEBB, John 33 m Ala
Delitha 30 f NC
Mary A. E. 14 f Ala
John R. A. 11 m "
Amanda M. 7 f "
Benj. F. 5 m "
George W. 4 m "
Louisa 2 f "

Euf # 173 Laborer
WECLOCK(?), Matthew 25 m Ire
(See John Bailey's hotel)

Euf # 583 (---3,500)
WELLBORN, Elizabeth 51 f Ga
Juan F. 27 m "
Victoria 10 f Ala
Missouri 8 f "

Clay # 36 Dentist (1500---)
WELLBORN, J. S. 31 m Ga
A. M. (milliner) 34 f "
BARRON, Helon 16 f "

Euf # 62 Clerk (7,000-3,500)
WELLBORN, L. S. 42 m Ga
Ann S. 39 f SC
WILSON, Margaret 71 f "
(---5,000)

Euf # 207 Student
WELLBORN, Pat 18 m Ala
(See L. F. Johnston).

Euf # 40 Warehouse man (---300)
WELLBORN, Rollin A. 26 m Ga
Hellen 26 f NY
MORRIS, Anna C. 27 f "

Euf # 1334 (5,000-10,000)
WELLBORN, Roxana 53 f Ga
William 20 m Ala
(St. Boat Clerk, ---300).

Euf # 60 Clerk (---9,500)
WELLBORN, Solon 39 m Ga
Constantine (Clerk) 17 m Ala
Randoplh W. 15 m "
Solon N. 13 m "
Ambrose J. 11 m "
William F. 6 m "

Euf # 1361
WELLBORN, Virginia 12 f Ala
(See Wm. A. McKenzie)

Bkb # 754 Farmer (1000-1500)
WELLBORN, William W. 53 m SC
Sarah 56 f Ga
Dorothy 18 f "

Mt. A. # 795 Farmer (250-350)
WELDEN, William H. 43 m Ga
Dennina 57 f SC
Frances E. 20 f Ga

Euf # 521 Farmer (2,250-4,000)
WELLS, John A. 29 m Ga
Laura V. 21 f "
Edward 5 m "
Seta 3 f "
infant 5/12 f Ala
THOMPSON, Mary W. 45 f Ga

Euf # 1221 Farmer (---100)
WELLS, Shade 28 m Ga
Sarah 28 f "
Henry 8 m "
Charles 6 m "
Warren 3 m Ala
Georgia 3/12 f "

Euf # 1125 Farmer (---500)
WELLS, William 68 m Ga
Nancy 68 f Ind
Osborn S. 24 m Ala
(Public officer).

Euf # 562
WELLS, William H. 67 m Va
Martha A. 24 f Ga
(See Thos. P. Sparks).

Euf # 367 Farmer (500-500)
WELSH, James A. 35 m Miss
Harriet 32 f Ga
Frances 14 f Ala
Martha J. 12 f "
Roxana 7 f "
Laura L. 5 f "
ENDFINGER, William 21 m "
(Laborer, ---80)

Clay # 19 Carriage Maker
WELSH, John B. 30 m Ire
(Living in hotel).

Euf # 628 Farmer (2000-1800)
WEST, Alfred 50 m NC
Elizabeth 48 f "
(Cont.)

(Euf # 628 cont.)
Fairnetta 18 f Ala
Mahala 16 f "
Allen 15 m "
Amos 13 m "
William 10 m "
Cornelius 7 m "
Andrew 4 m "

Mdwy # 933 Planter (17,000-36,000).
WEST, Joseph 54 m NC
Angeline 16 f Ala
Hettie 14 f "
John 11 m "
David 9 m "
Ritta 8 f "

Mt. A. # 870 Farm laborer
WEST, William 25 m Ga
(See James Wilkie).

Luvl # 537 Farmer (600-600)
WESTBROOK, John M. 36 m NC
Sarah A. 34 f Ala
William W. 10 m "
Z. A. 9 f "
Lucy A. 8 f "
James B. 6 m "
Clifford L. 4 m "
Mary J. 2 f "
John M. 1/12 m "

Luvl # 538 (800-200)
WESTBROOK, Zilpha 58 f NC
Henry C.(Farmer,400--) 26 m "
James W. " 22 m Ala
TILLMAN, Harriett 28 f NC
Mary A. 8 f Ala
John 6 m "
Robert 4 m "
Stephen 2 m "

Bkb # 699 Miss. Bapt. Minister (1,500-1,500)
WESTERN, W. W. B., Sr. 53 m SC
Martha 46 f "
W. W. B., Jr. 23 m "
Charles W. 20 m "
George M. 17 m Ala
Texana 15 f "
John 13 m "
Daniel M. 9 m "
Sarah R. 7 f "

Euf # 1069 Post Master & Merchant (1200-1000)
WESTON, Daniel M. 51 m SC
Sarah 40 f "
Newton A. (Clerk) 20 m "
Amanda 17 f Ga
Mary E. 15 f Ala
James K. P. 13 m "
Delia 9 f "
Martha 11 f "
Lucy 7 f "
Daniel 4 m "
infant 4/12 f "

Euf # 96
WEYMAN, Rebecca 44 f Ga
(See Junius Jordan).

Euf # 440 Quarryman
WHALON, Francis 47 m Ire
(See McNamara's R.R. Gro.)

Euf # 441 Telehraph operator
WHICHARD, Mr. 23 m Fla
(See Mary H. Lowman).

Euf # 648 Farmer (500-225)
WHIDDEN, John 36 m Ga
Mary J. 26 f "
Josephine 4 f Ala
Allen E. 2 m "
Drucilla 1 f "
Kirkland, Martha 10 f "

Euf # 900 Overseer (-- --)
WHIGHAM, Joseph 31 m Ga

Euf # 711 Farmer (5,500-7,000)
WHIGHAM, Joseph 32 m Ga
Jane E. 29 f "
William L. A. 12 m Ala
John S. 10 m "
Sarah J. 8 f "
Joseph 5 m "
Georgian A. 2 f "
THOMAS, Daniel 22 m "
(Farmer, 200-7,000)

Euf # 287 Farmer (3200-7000)
WHIGHAM, Samuel A. 35 m Ga
Sarah A. 32 f "
Thomas E. 7 m "
Andrew L. 4 m "
James F. 6/12 m Ala

Euf # 899 Farmer (77,000-15,000)
WHIGHAM, William A. 38 m Ga
Sarah J. 31 f "
James 14 m "
Eliza 12 f "
Levinia 10 f Ala
Joseph 8 m "
Isabella 8/12 f "

Euf # 1383 Master Carpenter (7,700-13,000)
WHIPPLE, George W. 43 m RI

Euf # 173
WHITCOME, Mahala 30 f Fla
(See John Bailey's hotel).

Euf 1152 Farmer (---100)
WHITE, Augustus M. 24 m Ga.
Elizabeth 26 f "
Abner P. 9 m "
Mary A. 7 f "
John 5 m "
Martha 3 f Ala
Robert 1 m "

Clay # 178 Insane grief
WHITE, Elizabeth 28 f Ga
(Living in poorhouse).

Mt. A. # 819 Farmer (3450-8000)
WHITE, John C. 40 m Ga
Henry (Farmer,---1500) 36 m "
ELAM, Elizabeth 60 f "

Mdwy # 1054 (---5,000)
WHITE, Mary A. 31 f Ga
Thomas 14 m Ala
Emma 12 f "
George 11 m "
Ella 9 f "
John 8 m "
Eugenia 7 f "
Walter 5 m "
Adolphus 3 m "
(Each of the eight children had ----1,250).

Clay. # 49 Farmer (4000-20,000)
WHITE, Robert T. 54 m Ga
Mary E. 50 f "
Florence 20 f Ala
Ellen 18 f "
William J. 17 m "
(Cont.)

(Clay # 49 cont.)
Walter S. 16 m Ala
Joseph 14 m "
Atlanta 12 f "

Clay # 166
WHITE, Sarah 19 f Ala
(See Elizabeth Britt).

Euf # 143 House painter
WHITE, William H. 25 m Conn
GRAY, J. H. 25 m NY
(Carpenter).
1. -----$500
2. -----$500

Txv # 1134 Laborer (---200)
WHITE, William J. 40 m Ga
E.A.E. 33 f SC
Nancy A. 15 f Ala
Martha A. S. 13 f "
William S. 11 m "
Jane 9 f "
Ellen A. 7 f "
Judie 5 f "
Ezekiel S. 3 m "

Euf # 1083 Overseer (--- ---)
WHITEHEAD, E. D. 27 m Ga
Ann 21 f "
Elizabeth 5/12 f Ala

Euf # 626 Farmer (1000-300)
WHITEHURST, Jesse 34 m NC
Julia A. 24 f Ga
W. M. F. 7 m Ala
Amas 4 m "
Alfred W. 1 m "

Flk # 490 (4,000-15,000)
WHITEHURST, Mary B. 45 f Ga
Mary A. 11 f Ala
SMITH, William 20 m "
Ann 17 f "
Mary 14 f "

Euf # 1327 Mechanic (400-5,000)
WHITMORE, C. J. 43 m NC

Bfd # 1263 (160-125)
WHITSETT, Catherine 36 f SC

Euf # 376 Grocer (1400-2000)
WHITTINGTON, Henry 24 m Ga

Euf # 375 Farmer
WHITTINGTON, John 67 m SC
(Cont.)

(Euf # 375 cont.)
Mary 60 f SC
Aurelia (Farmer) 25 m Ga
Jeremiah " 21 m "
(See Issac Copeland).

Mdwy # 936 (---150)
WHITTLE, Elizabeth 45 f SC
Charity 24 f "
Jinsey 18 f Ala
Emeline 16 f "
Ednie 15 f "
Sarah 13 f "
Sindie (Lucinda) 11 f "
Wade 10 m "
Elizabeth 9 f "

Clay # 211 Farmer (350-200)
WILDER, John 53 m Ga
Sally 45 f "
Archy (Farmer) 17 m Ala
John 13 m "
Mary Jane 10 f "
Philip 6 m "
Adeline 2 f "

Clay # 212
WILDER, Martha S. 8 f Ala
(See Susan P. Watson).

Luvl # 286 Mechanic (700-700)
WILKERSON, J. O. C. 40 m NC
Nancy 47 f SC
Elizabeth 17 f Ala
Mary 13 f "
Sarah 12 f "
Amanda 7 f "

Euf # 693 Farmer (1000-1800)
WILKERSON, Levi 27 m Ala
Mary 23 f Ga
Green B. 4 m Ala
Winfield S. 2 m "
Levi 3/12 m "
McLEMORE, John H. 19 m SC
(Student).

Euf # 647
WILKERSON, Louisa 16 f Ala
(See Leonna Low).

Clay # 735 Farmer (400-300)
WILKERSON, Noah 44 m SC
Emeline 38 f NC
C.S. 18 f Ga
John W. 14 m "
Henry A. 8 m "
Barney L. 3 m Ala

Mt. A. 878 Farmer (400-400)
WILKERSON, Noah 50 m SC
Emily 45 f Ga
John 14 m "
Alfred 8 m "
Barney B. 3 m Ala

Euf # 666 Farmer (3000-10,000)
WILKERSON, Samuel 43 m SC
Elmira 41 or 47 f Ga
Jeremiah B. 20 m Ala
(Farm hand).
Ailsey J. 17 f "
Greenberry 14 m "
Samuel 13 m "
Levi 9 m "

Luvl # 642
WILKES, Caroline 38 f SC
(See Mary Gullege)

Luvl # 530 Farmer (800-300)
WILKES, E. U. 49 m SC
Susan M. 37 f Ga
John W. (Farmer) 17 m Ala
Samuel 15 m "
Elias 13 m "
Isaac 12 m "
Mary J. 9 f "
James 5 m "
Martha A. 3 f "
William J. 5/12 m "

Luvl # 530 Farmer (150---)
WILKES, Jesse U. 33 m SC
Mary 22 f Ga
Sarah E. 2 f Ala
Judge S. 2/12 m "

Mt. A. # 800 Farmer (---225)
WILKES, Marion 30 m Ga
Sarah A. 23 f "
Francis 8 m Ala
Susanna 6 f "
John J. 4 m "
Charles 1 m "
Susan 26 f Ga
Lydia 24 f "

Luvl # 528 Farmer (8000-1000)
WILKES, William U. 42 m SC
Sarah 38 f Ga
William 14 m Ala
Laura A. 10 f "
John 8 m "
Sarah 1 f "

Mt. A. # 870 (---1000)
WILKIE, James 34 m NC
Eliza 37 f SC
Henry F. 8 m Ala
David 76 m NC
Catherine 65 f "
WEST, Wm. (Laborer) 25 m Ga
WILKIE, William D. 18 m NC

Mt. A. # 843 Farmer (1200-450)
WILKIE, Zachariah 25 m NC
Sarah 21 f Ga
Sarah J. 3 f Ala
Mary L. 2 f "
HAIGLER, Henry 21 m "
Phillip 25 m "
(Last two farm laborer)
CHANNELL, Susan 25 f Ga

Luvl # 279 Mechanic (--- ---)
WILKINS, Andrew 48 m NC
Sarah 38 f SC
Caroline 18 f Ala
Sarah J. 15 f "
William 12 m "
Elizabeth 8 f "
James 4 m "
Amarintha 2 f "

Euf # 252 Laborer
WILKINS, James 16 m Ala
(See Joshua Tyler).

Euf # 259 Engineer (---100)
WILKINS, John W. 23 m Ala
Sarah F. 18 f "

Euf # 956 Carpenter (---300)
WILKINS, Robert F. 35 m Va
Caroline 38 f Ga
Frances 18 f Ala
John 16 m "
Napoleon 14 m "
Sarah A. 12 f "
Rosa 5 f "
William H. 3 m "
Annetta 1 f "

Euf # 1338 Overseer
WILLIAMS, Ab 22 m Ala
(See James W. Richardson).

Clay # 727 Laborer
WILLIAMS, Abner 22 m Ala
(See Joseph Singleton).

(Clay # 44 cont.)

Clay # 44 Jailor (4,500-4,000)

WILLIAMS, B.(Buckner)	65	m	Ga
Rhoda	49	f	SC
Ann L.	22	f	Ala
Leona (Leonora)	14	f	"
Mary	20	f	"
William H.	18	m	"
Laura	10	f	"
Thomas J.	7	m	"
(Inmates in jail):			
CARROLL, Edward	44	m	Ire
WARD, C. H.	35	m	Ga
ADCOCK, William	26	m	Ga
PICKETT, William S.	43	m	"
SIMMONS, Allen	42	m	SC
CRAIG, Thos. J.	21	m	Ala

Euf # 1183 Hireling (--- ---)

WILLIAMS, Cornelius	32	m	SC
Martha J.	24	f	Ala
Susan	4	f	"
Mary J.	2	f	"
John A.	1/12	m	"

Euf # 176 (1500-200)

WILLIAMS, Edward	73	m	NC
Cintha	28	f	Ga
STEVENS, Mr. (Mill wright).	40	m	--
McANDREWS, J. (Mill wright)	25	m	--
STEVENS, Alex (Laborer)	15	m	Ga
Ira(?) T. (Laborer)	11	m	"
LESTER, D. (Carpenter)	22	m	"

Euf # 305 (2500-500)

WILLIAMS, Effy	46	f	NC
Elizabeth A.	21	f	"
Mary C.	19	f	"
Effy T.	17	f	"

Euf # 132

WILLIAMS, Eliza	14	f	Ga
William (Laborer)	16	m	"
Mary	13	f	"
Zach	10	m	"

(See Reddin Newman)

Euf # 244 (--- ---)

WILLIAMS, Elizabeth	53	f	SC
Jno. M. (Stage driver).	22	m	Ala

(Cont.)

Euf # 244 cont.)

George N.(Laborer)	17	m	Ala
Thomas D.	12	m	"
SMITH, Mary	58	f	NC

Mt. A. # 888 (--- ---)

WILLIAMS, Elizabeth	38	f	Ga
James M.	14	m	"
Sarah A. H.	12	f	"
Henry T.	10	m	"
Mary E.	9	f	Ala
Candis C.	6	f	"
Harriett A.	4	f	"
William W.	2	m	"
Georgia A.	6/12	f	"

Bkb # 685 Blacksmith (---200)

WILLIAMS, F. M.	24	m	Ga
Frances	21	f	"
Hiriam	2	m	Ala
Hiriam	60	m	Ga

Euf # 464 Planting (45,000-64,000)

WILLIAMS, G. E. (Geraldine E.)	32	f	Ga
Anna M.	6	f	Ala
Zach W.	4	m	"
Gazaway D.	3	m	"
Mary B.	2	f	"

Euf # 925 Farmer (---12,000)

WILLIAMS, G. W.	42	m	Ga
Sarah A.	35	f	"
R. Pitt (In school)	16	m	Ala
John C.	12	m	"
Charles M.	8	m	"
Sarah M.	6	f	"
Rachael	4	f	"
Lula	6/12	f	"

Euf # 471 Farmer (25,000-45,000)

WILLIAMS, Gazaway D.	41	m	Ga
Sarah E.	36	f	Ala
Gazarbee	14	f	"
Mary	12	f	"
Anderson	10	m	"
Eddie	8	f	"
Robert	5	m	"
Mattie	3	f	"
Evaline	1	f	"
MAYNARD, Florence P. (Governess)	21	f	Va

Clay # 31 Jeweller
WILLIAMS, George W. 29 m Ala
Adaline 19 f "
B. W. 3/12 m "

Euf # 243 teamster (--- ---)
WILLIAMS, H. D. 25 m Ga
Sarah W. 21 f "

Mdwy # 1096 Overseer (---150)
WILLIAMS, Henry 40 m Ga
Nancy 30 f "
Berry 8 m "
John 5 m "
Webb 3 m Ala
Elizabeth 1/12 f "

Euf # 220 Farmer (---150)
WILLIAMS, James 40 m NC
Christian 35 f SC
Thos. (Laborer) 18 m Ga
Sarah 13 f "
William G. 12 m "
Philip C. 10 m Ala
Frances 8 f "
James C. 5 m "

Euf # 1282 Farmer (---200)
WILLIAMS, James 45 m NC
Christian 40 f SC
James C. 6 m Ala
Sallie 14 f "
William G. 13 m "
Phil C. 10 m "
Frances 8 f "

Bkb # 686 Blacksmith (---300)
WILLIAMS, James H. 30 m Ga
Maria 30 f "
Hiriam 7 "
Mary F. 3 f Ala
HOLT, Richard 70 m Va
(Blacksmith)

Euf # 591
WILLIAMS, James R. 24 m Ga(?)
(See John S. Espey)

Mdwy # 942 Overseer (1000-500)
WILLIAMS, John 46 m Ga
Mary A. 43 f "
John (Idiotic) 21 m "
Josephine 13 f Ala
Oliver 16 m "
James 11 m "
(Cont.)

(Mdwy # 942 cont.)
Holland 5 m Ala
Maria A. 15 f "

Euf # 924 Farmer (5,700-5,800)
WILLIAMS, John L. 54 m Ga
Sarah 47 f "
Louisianna J. 21 f Ala
John C. (Farmer) 19 m "
Sarah C. 18 f "
Geo. R. (In school) 16 m "
Charles F. 15 m "
Susan V. 13 f "
Mary E. 10 f "
Ann E. 4 f "
LEVERETT, Lively 65 f Ga

Txv # 1199 Farmer (---100)
WILLIAMS, John T. 60 m NC
Nancy 60 f SC
Mary 30 f Ala
Joseph 12 m "
Pleasant 9 m "
Sarah 2 f "

Clay # 10 Probate Judge & M.E. Minister (18,000-325,000)
WILLIAMS, Judge S. 56 m Ga
Euphemia 53 f NC
Jeremiah (Lawyer) 29 m Ala
(600-300)
John (Idiotic) 27 m "
Emily 22 f "
Richard(Probate clerk) 20 m "
Victoria 17 f "
McKENZIE, Elizabeth 12 f "

Euf # 1182 (700-200)
WILLIAMS, Mary 53 f SC
Jno. W. (Farm hand) 23 m "
Caleb " " 16 m Ala
WILSON, Mary 21 f "
Mary 1 f "

Flk # 499
WILLIAMS, Mary 18 f Ga
(See J. B. Stubbs).

Euf # 903
WILLIAMS, Mary M. 4 f NC
(See Eliza J. Lowman)

Flk # 444 (---60)
WILLIAMS, Nancy 35 f Ala
Lafayette 12 m "
John 9 m "
(Cont.)

(Flk # 444 cont.)
Lewis 6 m Ala
Casey 4 m "
Samuel 1 m "

Euf # 1184 Hireling (--- ---)
WILLIAMS, Nathan 30 m SC
Martha 29 f Ala
John 6 m "
Morgan 4 m "
Augustus 1/12 m "

Euf # 817
WILLIAMS, Rebecca A. 15 f Ala
(See J. R. Towler).

Clay # 1286 (1500-4000)
WILLIAMS, Sophia 50 f Ga
Jas. M. (---4000) 15 m Ala

Clay # 19 Bookkeeper
WILLIAMS, Stephen L. 28 m Ala
(Living in hotel).

Mt. A. # 910 Workman (---200)
WILLIAMS, Thomas 25 m Ala
Sarah 20 f "
Joel 3 m "
Mary 1 f "

Clay # 676 Farmer (---100)
WILLIAMS, Thomas 40 m Ga
Sarah 26 f "
Mary 8 f "
Thomas 7 m Ala
Nancy 5 f "
Jimmy 2 m "

Euf # 1197 Hireling
WILLIAMS, Thomas 17 m Ga
(See John Bullock).

Euf # 904 Farmer (---3,000)
WILLIAMS, Turner 75 m NC

Clay # 16 Clerk (--- ---)
WILLIAMS, W. J. 20 m Ala
L. F. 16 f Ga

Euf # 1342 Overseer (--- ---)
WILLIAMS, W. T. 26 m Ala
Amanda 20 f Ga
Charles 8/12 m Ala

Euf # 551 Laborer (--- ---)
WILLIAMS, Washington 34 m Ga
Martha 19 f "
Taylor 12 m "
(Cont).

(Euf # 551 cont.)
Allen 7 m Ga
Benjamin 14 m Ala
John W. 10 m Ga
Lilly 3 f "

Mt. A. # 831 Farmer (1000-2000)
WILLIAMS, Westley P. 40 m NC
Mary 38 f Ga
Clara B. 8 f Ala
Alice 2 f "
Eugenia V. 3/12 f "

Euf # 1266 Farmer (5000-4000)
WILLIAMS, William 43 m Ga
Jane 17 f "
Columbia 14 f "
Sarah 12 f "
Lucy 9 f "

Mdwy # 952 Laborer
WILLIAMS, William 27 m Ga
Sarah 20 f "
George 3 m "
(See Green B. McGee).

Luvl # 536 Farmer (--- ---)
WILLIAMS, William W. 45 m NC
Ann Eliza 44 f "
Elizabeth 18 f Ga
Mary A. V. 16 f "
Nancy L. 14 f Ala
Benjamin F. 10 m "
William S. 7 m "

Euf # 1374 Overseer (1500-1000)
WILLIAMS, Willis 49 m Ga
Margaret 51 f SC
Saletha 20 f Ga
Joseph 13 m "
Jesse 11 m "
Cornelia 9 f Ala
Paul G. 7 m "

Euf # 1254 Farmer (---100)
WILLIAMSON, Chas. 26 m Ga
Sarah A. 22 f Ala
Martha 6 f "
Rebecca J. 4 f "
Ezekiel 1 m "

Bkb # 788 Farmer (500-250)
WILLIAMSON, Green 32 m Ga
Susan 35 f "
Leonna 11 f Ala
(Cont.)

(Bkb # 788 cont.)
Mary J. 9 f Ala
Elizabeth 7 f "
Susanna 5 f "
George 3 m "
Benjamin F. 1 m "

Euf # 955 Overseer (---200)
WILLIAMSON, Henry 23 m NC

Nwto # 591 Farmer (1500-300)
WILLIAMSON, John W. 28 m NC
Elizabeth 18 f Ga
William H. 1/12 m Ala

Clay # 662 (4,000-1,500)
WILLIAMSON, Mary 59 f SC
Thomas (Farmer) 23 m Ala
(---200)
Mary 16 f "
Eli 19 m "
Simeon (Farmer) 21 m "

Euf # 1250
WILLIAMSON, Narcissa E. 6 f Ala
(See Ezekiel Wise)

Mt. A. 835 Farmer (4,200-16,000)
WILLIAMSON, William 67 m SC
Naomi 50 f "
Josiah (Farmer) 23 m "
Minerva A. 19 f "
Sidney " 18 m "
Thomas " 16 m "
Susanna 14 f "
Jane 12 f "

Euf # 1027 Hireling (--- ---)
WILLIAMSON, William 31 m Ala
Faithy 30 f "
Zach 8 m "
James 6 m "
Wallace 5 m "
Susan 3 f "
John 1 m "

Euf # 945 (---3,500)
WILLIFORD, G. W. 20 m Ga
Marthena C. 18 f "
(Married within the year).

Euf # 855 Farmer (7000-25,500)
WILLIFORD, M. E. 44 m Ga
Lesina 29 f "
(Cont.)

(Euf # 855 cont.)
Harrison (Clerk) 19 m Ga
Franklin 14 m "
John T. 12 m "
Benjamin 10 m "
George B. 8 m "
Leroy 6 m Ala
Marianna 5 f "
Frances 3 f "
infant 1/12 m "

Clay # 3 Bailiff (--- ---)
WILLIS, Anon 36 m Ala
Ann Eliza 30 f "
J. T. 13 m "
Epsy Ann 11 f "
A. A. 7 m "
Zenabia 5 f "
E. W. 8/12 m "
MOORE, Edwin (Clerk) 18 m "

Mt. A. # 840 Farmer(2000-2500)
WILLIS, Edmund 40 m Ala
Missouri 32 f Ga
Cary 12 m Ala
Baker 10 m "
Monroe 8 m "
Mary 6 f "
Oats 4 m "
Elizabeth 2 f "
Martha 11/12 f "
HERRINGTON, Mary 19 f "

Mt. A. # 913 Farmer (650-400)
WILLIS, Joel G. 28 m Ga
Martha E. 23 f "
William T. 2 m Ala

Mt. A. # 853
WILLIS, Joel 75 m NC
Elizabeth 66 f Ga
(See Richard E. Head).

Euf # 782 Physician
WILSON, A. J. 27 m Va
Mary J. 32 f "
(See Thos. A. Roquemore).

Euf # 949
WILSON, Caroline 18 f Ala
(See Joel Hameter).

Euf # 109 Farmer (2000-9000)
WILSON, Coridin 58 m NC
Eliza 48 f "
Augustine E. 21 m "
(Med. student).
(Cont.)

(Euf # 109 cont.)
Jesse 17 m NC
Rufus 11 m Ala
America 4 f "

Euf # 1173 Farmer (1,200-6,000)
WILSON, David 55 m NC
Nancy 45 f SC
Chas. (Farmer) 23 m Ga
Elizabeth 19 f Ala
John 17 m "
Emaline 18 f "
David 12 m "
Nancy 14 f "
William 10 m "

Bkb # 715 Farmer (---200)
WILSON, John W. 35 m Ga
Elizabeth 30 f "
Frances 12 f "
Elizabeth 10 f "
Susan 8 f "
John W. 3 m Ala

Euf # 861 Farmer (10,000-42,000)
WILSON, Levi R. 49 m SC
Margaret P. 49 f "
Martha R. 13 f "
HEAD, Neal 22 m Ala
(Overseer).

Euf # 62
WILSON, Margaret 71 f SC
(See L. S. Wellborn)

Euf # 1182
WILSON, Mary 21 f Ala
Mary 1 f "
(See Mary Williams).

Flk # 476 Mechanic (---65)
WINCHESTER, S. A. 35 m NC
Emily J. 23 f "
William R. 4 m Ga
Sarah T. D. 10/12 f Ala

Clay # 1119 Farm laborer (---200)
WINDBURN, Josiah 35 m Ga
A.E.M. 21 f "
P.J. 4 f Ala
Nancy A.M. 2 f "
Mary A.M. 4/12 f "

Euf # 1234 Farmer (1,6000-2,000)

(Cont.

(Euf # 1234 cont.)
WINDHAM, Anthony 51 m SC
Martha 24 f Ala
Abner 19 m "
Rebeca 17 f "
Wright 15 m "
Julia A. 13 f "
Mary 11 f "
Sophronia 9 f "
Martha 8 f "
John 6 m "
Shorter 4 m "
BUSH, Francis M. 11 m "

Euf # 323 Farmer (---500)
WINDHAM, J. D. 43 m SC
Nancy R. 38 f Ga
Jesse (Farmer) 17 m Fla
Augustus L. 15 m Ala
Frances E. 13 f "
James M. 11 m "
Warren S. 9 m "
Florida F. 7 f "
Virginia 3 f "
infant 3/12 f "

Clay # 726 Farmer (---100)
WINDHAM, Kenian 28 m Ga
Irena 30 f SC
A.L. 10 f Tex
N.C. 6 f Ala
G.F. 5 f "
Abigail 3 f "

Euf # 940 Hireling
WINDHAM, L. 17 m Ala
(See Reddin Huggins).

Euf # 787 Overseer (--- ---)
WINN, John 24 m Ga

Clay # 143 Owner of farm (800-100)
WINSLETT, Nancy 55 f Ga
T. C. (Farmer) 20 m Ala
Minerva 13 f "

Clay # 38 Druggest (1800-6000)
WISE, A. C. 51 m SC
E. D. 40 f Ga
BARNETT, S. V. 12 f Ala

Euf # 1189 Farmer (500-400)
WISE, Ephriam 61 m NC
Martha A. 40 f "
Ezekiel (Farmer---100) 22 m Ala
(Cont.)

(Euf # 1189 cont.)
John 14 m Ala
Sarah M. 12 f "
Leroy 9 m "
Francis A. 8 m "
Margy A. 6 f "

Euf # 1250 Farmer (4000-1100)
WISE, Ezekiel 63 m Ga
Winneyford 52 f Ala
Lemuel (Farmer) 23 m "
Thomas " 18 m "
John 14 m "
Amanda 12 f "
WILLIAMSON, Narcissa E. 6 f "

Txv # 1210 Farmer (640-225)
WISE, William 30 m Ala
Jane 30 f "
Greenberry 7 m "
Frederick 5 m "
Henry 3 m "
Mary 1 f "

Euf # 836 Farmer
WITHERINGTON, Chas. M. 21 m Ga
Ann A. 20 f "
Susan 1 f Ala
(See James J. Cade).

Euf # 816 Farmer (1600-500)
WITHERINGTON, Obediah 33 m Ga
Mary A. 31 f "
William J. 8 m "
Napoleon 6 m Ala
Thomas 5 m "
Georgeann 2 f "
Savannah 1 f "

Euf # 943 Farmer (3000-7000)
WITHERINGTON, R. T. 32 m NC
Mary E. 23 f "
Mary F. 7 f Ala
Susan V. 6 f "
Montgomery A. 4 m "
Robert H. 1 m "

Bfd # 1261 Farmer (480-250)
WOOD, Clinton 49 m NC
Sarah 44 f "
T. M. 18 f "
Adaline 16 f "
Sir William 14 m "
James C. 10 m "
Susan C. 8 f "
(Cont.)

(Bfd # 1261 cont.)
Samuel W. 4 m NC
Sarah G. D. 9/12 f Ala

Txv # 1223 Farmer (240-300)
WOOD, F. F. 43 m NC
Mary 42 f "
Elizabeth 20 f Ala
C. G. 18 f "
Annie E. 12 f "
Arthur C. 15 m "
Marion 12 m "
Sarah C. 10 f "
William McD. 8 m "
Mary J. 5 f "
Lindsay 2 f "
infant 1/12 m "

Clay # 45 Lawyer (2000-2500)
WOOD, F. M. 26 m NC
S. R. 22 f Ala

Euf # 619 Farmer (---550)
WOOD, Green 30 m NC
Mary E. 24 f Ga

Euf # 533 Farmer (175-200)
WOOD, Green W. 47 m NC
Elizabeth 26 f "
E. A. 16 f Ala
John A. 15 m "
Minerva A. 13 f "
George F. 11 m "
Lemuel 6 m "
Abagail 9/12 f "

Euf # 1294
WOOD, James 18 m Ala
(See N. H. Goodson).

Euf # 1294 Student
WOOD, James 18 m Ala
(See N. H. Goodson).

Euf # 1063 Student
WOOD, John W. 20 m Ga
(See Joseph T. Jarrett).

Bfd # 1254 Teacher
WOOD, Josephine 19 f Ala
(See D. G. Campbell)

Euf # 581 Miller & Farmer
WOOD, McKinney 47 m NC
Frances 39 f Ga
Pauline 21 f Ala
(Cont.)

(Euf # 581 cont.)
Hellen 19 f Ala
Sophia 17 f "
James 14 m "
Marion 12 m "
Abagail 10 f "
William 8 m "
Samuel 3 m "
LANDRUM, George 88 m NC
WOOD, Wm. (Laborer) 59 m "
HOLMES, Sallie 18 f Ala
(Estate of McK. Wood: 7,000-1,000)

Clay # 4 (3,000-510)
WOOD, Nancy 43 f NC
Olin P. (Farmer) 50 m "
Amanda 18 f Ala
Josephine 17 f "
James P. 16 m "
Leonora 15 f "

Clay # 1 Lawyer & Surveyor
WOOD, Wm. D. 23 m Ala
(See H. D. Clayton).

Euf # 618 Farmer (1600-1600)
WOOD, Young 65 m NC
Rosa A. 58 f "
John R. (Farmer) 32 m "
(125-300)
BIRD, Benjamin F. 21 m Ala
(Idiot, ----2000)
STOKES, James K. 16 m "
(Farm hand).

Euf # 68 Broker (7000-35,000)
WOODS, C. R. 50 m SC
Harriet E. 49 f "
(----3,000)
William H.(?) 19 m Ala
(Boat clerk, ---2,000)
Robert J. 17 m "
Clayton R. 15 m "
Mary C. 12 f "
Martha J. 11 f "
Samuel W. 9 m "

Flk # 402 Farmer (1340-5000)
WOODS, E. P. 30 m Ga
Sarah 25 f "
Mary 6 f Ala
Ella 4 f "
William 2 m "
Laura 4/12 f "

Bfd # 1266 Farmer (240-300)
WOODS, William 46 m SC
Nancy 35 f "
Tabitha 16 f Ga
John 7 m Ala
Nancy 5 f "
Sarah 75 f SC

Txv # 1221 Farmer (---250)
WOODARD, John 47 m SC
S. E. 44 f "
Thomas 26 m Ala
Stephen 22 m "
Mahala A. 17 f "
Elizabeth 15 f "
Jame 13 f "
Nancy 12 f "

Euf # 1075 Overseer (--- ---)
WOODWARD, O. P. 32 m Ga

Luvl # 364 Farmer (--- ---)
WOODWARD, Thomas 23 m Ga

Euf # 261 Planter (--- ---)
WOOTEN, Charles 24 m NY
Jane 19 f "

Euf # 1311 Farmer (100-300)
WORSLEY, Sampson 77 m NC
Albena (---35) 50 f "
Mary (1200-400) 35 f Ga
SMITH, Turner 20 m "
Mary 18 f "

Clay # 229
WORTHINGTON, E. E. 24 f Ga
(See Thos. Warren).

Euf # 839 Physician (---800)
WORTHINGTON(?) Moses 57 m Ga
(WITHERINGTON,(?)

Clay # 21 Carriage trimmer
WOUTERS, John 35 m Hol
(Living in hotel).

Mt. A. # 891 Farmer (---300)
WRIGHT 54 m Ga
Elizabeth 40 f "
Isaac H. (Farmer) 18 m "
W. M. " 16 m "
Charles J. 14 m "
E. L. 8 m "
Mary F. 5 f "
Eleazer 2 m Ala

Clay # 668 (---250)
WRIGHT, Elizabeth 40 f Ga
Wm. E. (Farmer) 16 m "
Eugenia 8 f "

Nwto # 629 Farmer (950-200)
WRIGHT, Henry 25 m Ga
Mary 22 f SC
Ezekiel 4/12 m Ala
Westley (Farmer) 23 m "
William " 22 m "

Euf # 929 Hireling
WRIGHT, Ira 23 m SC
(See Luke Taylor).

Euf # 1348 M.E. Minister (---300)
WRIGHT, J. M. 35 m Tenn
Mary 25 f "

Euf # 781 Overseer (---6,500)
WRIGHT, James A. 45 m Ga

Euf # 1014 (--- ---)
WRIGHT, James T. 28 m Ga
Sarah 26 f SC
John 3/12 m Ala

Euf # 1013 Farmer (10,000-30,000)
WRIGHT, John 57 m Ga
Sarah 51 f "
William 32 m "
John L. 24 m "
Richard E. 21 m "
Nancy 19 f "
Henry C. 17 m "
Thomas D. 15 m "
George 12 m "

Euf # 753 Farmer (500---)
WRIGHT, Leonard 34 m Ga
Lucretia 40 f "
Sarah A. 10 f "
John W. 6 m Ala
Nancy 3 f "
MOSLEY, Elizabeth 26 f "
James W. 7 m "
Luctia 5 f "
John 5/12 m "

Euf # 419 Farmer (1000-300)
WRIGHT, T. C. 28 m SC
Mary 26 f "
John B. 5 m "
Preston S.(?) B. 3 m Ala
(Cont.)

(Euf # 419 cont.)
Robert 2 m Ala
MILLER, M. L. 30 f Ga

Euf # 1252 Hireling
WRIGHT, Thomas 20 m Ga
(See Sarah Howell)

Euf # 877 Farmer (800-200)
WRIGHT, Thomas C. 28 m SC
Mary 25 f "
Belton(?) 5 m "
Brooks 3 m Ala
Robert 1 m "

Mt. A. # 889 Farmer (---150)
WRIGHT, William M. 21 m Ga
Amanda 18 f "

Euf # 835
WYLIE, Catherine 60 f SC
Wm. A. (Farmer) 35 m "
(1200-11,000)

Luvl # 527 Farmer (---150)
WYNN, William J. 26 m Ala
Catherine 25 f "
Indianna 5 f "
Laura 2 f "
Manuel J. 1 m "

Bfd # 1262 (--- ---)
YAWN, John 75 m NC
Sallie 73 f "
Amanda 25 f Ala
Mary A. 8 f "
Thomas 4/12 m "

Mt. A. # 826 Farm Laborer (---150)
YOUNG, Augustus 22 m Ga
Mary 22 f Ala
(See Joseph E. Hardy).

Euf # 86 Merchant (35,500-30,000)
YOUNG, Edward B. 57 m NY
Ann F. 49 f Ga
Henry A.(Merchant) 24 m "
Anna B. 18 f Ala
Mary E. C. 17 f "
Ada L. 14 f "
Hellen A. 12 f "
Edward B. 9 m "
Caroline 5 f "
(Henry's estate: 1,000-6000)

Bkb # 760 Farmer (---200)
YOUNG, Garrett 51 or 57 m SC
Nancy 51 or 57 f Ga
James 24 m Ala
Garrett 15 m "

Euf # 97 Merchant (5,000-12,000)
YOUNG, Isaac 24 m Ger
(Born Wertemburg, Ger.)
DESSON, A. (Clerk) 25 m Ger
(Born Bavaria, Ger.)

Luvl 532 Farmer (2500-6500)
YOUNG, J. B. 45 m NC
Emily 27 f Ga
Sarah 15 f Ala
Frances 14 f "
Daniel 13 m "
Rebecca 12 f "
James 10 m "
William 8 m "
Washington 6 m "
Alice 1/12 f "

Euf # 183 Machinist (15,000-6,000)
YOUNG, James W. 25 m NY
Anna A. 22 f NJ
Charlie 4 m Ala

Mt. A. # 899 Farmer (1000-1000)
YOUNG, Reuben 48 m Ga
Dicey 40 f "
Matilda 25 f "
Calvin B. 23 m "
P. H. 21 f Ala
William F. 17 m "
Louisa 15 f "
Harriett 13 f "
James 10 m "
Yancey 8 m "
Mary A. 6 f "
Reuben 2 m "

Txv # 1214 Farmer (2400-6000)
ZORN, David 42 m SC
Sarah A. 38 f "
Nancy C. 18 f Ala
William 16 m "
(In school)
Mary 14 f "
Nicholas 12 m "
Esther 11 f "
(Cont.)

(Euf # 766 cont).
Abagail 4 f Ala
Anderson C. 2 m "

Txv # 1213 Farmer (600-1800)
ZORN, James D. 24 m Ala
Josephine R. 20 f "
Mary C. 1/12 f "
(Married within the year).

Txv # 1214 Farmer (2400-6000)
ZORN, Nicholas 52 m SC
Sarah 51 f "
Dennis (Farmer) 16 m Ala
George W. 13 m "
Taylor 11 m "

www.ingramcontent.com/pod-product-compliance
Lightning Source LLC
Chambersburg PA
CBHW031121020426
42333CB00012B/184
* 9 7 8 1 6 3 9 1 4 3 1 0 8 *